D1236662

LUCKNOW: THE LAST PHASE OF AN
ORIENTAL CULTURE

Lucknow: The Last Phase of an Oriental Culture

ABDUL HALIM SHARAR

Translated and edited by
E. S. Harcourt and Fakhir Hussain

PAUL ELEK LONDON

To the late Muhammad Amir Ahmad Khan,
Raja of Mahmudabad,
one of the last from old Lucknow

Published in Great Britain 1975 by
Elek Books Limited
54–58 Caledonian Road, London N1 9RN

ISBN 0 236 30932 3

Sahitya Akademi
English Translation: UNESCO 1974

UNESCO Collection of Representative Works
Indian Series

This book belongs to the Indian Series of the
Translations Collection of the United Nations
Educational, Scientific and Cultural Organization
(UNESCO)

Set in Monotype Times

Printed in Great Britain by The Anchor Press Ltd
and bound by Wm Brendon & Son Ltd
both of Tiptree, Essex

Contents

Contents

Illustrations

PLATES

List of Illustrations

MAPS

Acknowledgements: Illustrations Nos. 1, 2, 3, 4, 5, 6, 7, 9, 10, 11, 12, 13, 14, 15, 16, 17, 18, 19, 20, 21, 22, 27, and 28 are reproduced by permission of the India Office Library and Records, London; Nos. 8, 25, 30, 31, and 32 by permission of the Victoria and Albert Museum (Crown Copyright); No. 22 by permission of the family of Abdul Halim Sharar; No. 23 by permission of Dr Syed J. Iqbal and P. Hussain; and Nos. 24 and 26 by permission of Syed Najmul Hasan.

Introduction

Like all civilizations, the Indo-Mughal was grounded in a powerful set of ideas related to a specific social context. These ideas, expressed in institutions, ceremonies, ritual and language, underlined a markedly class-based society that, however unrepresentative and élitist, was in itself cohesive and harmonious. But inevitably, such a civilization could not remain static. New forces emerged, old ideas were challenged and the framework of the established order was disturbed. It is on this period of Indo-Muslim civilization, at its zenith which was also its last phase, when its centre was transferred from Delhi to Lucknow, that the present work concentrates. In *Lucknow: The Last Phase of an Oriental Culture*, the essayist, historian and novelist Abdul Halim Sharar (1860–1926), himself a native of Lucknow, describes in detail many aspects of this civilization and particularly its more tangible manifestations in everyday life. In effect, he also deals with the religious, political and socio-economic patterns on which it was based, and the power of those ideas which provided its vitality. Whatever aspects he is dealing with, he makes the importance of the underlying ideas very clear. When they were powerful, so was the society embodying them; when they declined, so also did the society, though of course there were many other contributory factors.

The Indo-Mughal civilization developed during the long reign of the Mughal[17]* Emperors. These Mongol-Turks, who originally came from Central Asia, established themselves in 1526/7 in parts of north India and later expanded their empire in the sub-continent. Their rule effectively lasted until the middle of the eighteenth century, though it nominally continued until 1857. It is generally agreed that it reached its peak during the reign of Akbar (1556–1605),[73] and started to show signs of decay during the rule of Aurangzeb (1658–1707).[76] Thereafter, military and political strife became rampant in the capital as well as in other parts of the empire. The ensuing turmoil was brought about by the rapid rise and fall of many rulers in Delhi and those parts of the empire that had become independent. The chaos was quickly exploited by invaders from the north-east and political unrest did not end until the British gradually began to intervene. They became de facto rulers of Bengal in 1764. It took them another century, however, to establish themselves throughout the sub-continent.

The Mughals were the last group of invading Muslims who brought with them to India their own distinctive religious ideas, Islamic customs and social institutions. The contact of Islam with India had begun long before the Mughals'

---

* Index superior numbers throughout this book refer to the Notes which begin on page 233.

arrival, and Muslims had even established themselves as kings in parts of north India before 1526/7: consequently the Mughals' impact was far more profound than that of their predecessors. In part this was due to the longevity of their dynasty. But more particularly it was due to the new social style, religious spirit and system of administration which they introduced. However, the new home of the Mughals also had a civilization of its own, which was later to have important repercussions.

The Indus Valley civilization, as it is known today, existed in parts of the north-west of India in the third millennium before Christ. These people were invaded by the Aryans, who are presumed to have come from southern Russia. They conquered the non-Aryans, fought among themselves, looked after their cattle and organized pastoral life in villages. 'It was they who gave us the gift of the Sanskrit language, the horse and a religion' (Gokhale, p. 21).*

Indeed, the all-embracing influence of the Aryans still survives, since the *Rig Veda*, the book of their religious beliefs concerning the thirty-three Gods and ritual practices, remains the most holy scripture in India up to the present day. This survived from one generation to the next through oral tradition, and there later developed from it the texts known as *Brahmanas*,[34] which concern the correct performance of rituals. By 1500 BC the Aryans had extended their rule to the present region of Delhi. Their civilization seems to have reached its high-point with the legends of their wars and high-minded warriors which became the subject of the national epics *Ramayana* and *Mahabharata*.[5] From the Aryan sense of values evolved a pattern of social organization having a strict code of behaviour, with ideas of moral and physical courage at its centre.

Aryan values dominated India almost totally until the twelfth and early thirteenth centuries when the Muslims became dominant in the north of India. Even after their arrival, however, these values remained supreme for the non-Muslims and are still important today.

The source of this value system was the religious spirit formalized in the *Rig Veda*: polytheism and incipient monotheism with leanings towards pantheism, and a constant concern for correct ritual. This gave rise to the study and development of the books of revelation, the four *Vedas*,[362] the *Upanishads*, explaining the doctrines of Brahman, Karma and Atman—creation and re-birth in the process of life and death—as well as a body of literature which elucidated these doctrines, such as the *Sāstras* and the law codes of *Manu*. In addition, there was the *Bhagavad-Gita* dealing with the manifold aspects of religion in relation to the complexities of everyday life, and also the literature propounding the Buddhist and Jain view-points. From these major sources Hindu philosophy developed over the course of centuries. Since most of this literature was in Sanskrit, the language flourished, both as the vehicle of intellectual discourse and because of its rich literary merit. In society at large, therefore, a respect for education and learning developed which culminated in the rise of universities such as Nalanda (near Patna) between 415 and 456. Religious sentiment found new forms of expression in temple architecture, sculpture and painting, characteristically to be seen in such outstanding achievements as the rock temple of Ellora, the wall paintings of Ajanta and the carved lions at Sarnath, which have now been

* See Bibliography.

adopted by the Republic as the government seal. To attain self-realization an individual had to follow *dharma*, duty of wisdom in action, which in turn was subdivided into *artha*, economic duty, *kama*, the duty of the preservation of the race, and *moksa*, the duty towards the self. These duties were related to the four stages of an individual's life.[387] The underlying idea was that life is a preparation for salvation—a notion that was further developed by Buddhism. The last message of Gautama the Buddha (d. 483 or 543 BC) was: 'Decay is inherent in all component things, work out your salvation with diligence.'

Social organization was based on the notion of 'caste'. By virtue of birth people became members of a fixed social group, their caste determining both their occupation and their choice of marriage-partners. There were four castes which ranked in hierarchical order. Among Aryans, the Brahman, teacher and preacher of the sacred lore, was at the top, followed by Kshatriya, the soldier administrator, and Vaisya, the farmer artisan. The non-Aryan Sudra was assigned the task of serving the higher castes through menial work. This system was opposed by the Buddhists and Jains. They strongly attacked the caste system—an opposition which was revived in recent times by Gandhi who also attempted to integrate the lowest caste into the general social order. (Today, of course, it is a criminal offence in India to discriminate on grounds of caste.) But Indians with this background experienced a long-drawn-out encounter, beginning in the early thirteenth century, with another group which had a different religion, set of beliefs and social institutions—the Muslims.

'There is no god but Allah and Muhammad is his prophet.' With this message, Muhammad (born about 571) began to call the faithful. His aim was to restore and complete through his religion, Islam (which means 'I submit to the will of God'), the religion of Abraham. This was at a time when people in the land of Abraham had lapsed into polytheism and Christianity. Having consolidated his position in Mecca and Medina through converts and peace treaties with the Jewish and Christian tribal leaders, Muhammad planned to take the message of Islam into neighbouring lands. At the time of his death in 632, the Arabs had found a superior faith and morality.

Muhammad was the last 'messenger of God' to his followers. He prescribed what was right and wrong for his people on God's authority and was the supreme judge of all religious, social and political matters. No wonder, then, that the doctrine of Islam, along with Hadis,[243] the tradition of the Prophet, provides a code of human conduct embracing all aspects of life on earth. Additionally, Muhammad was a practical leader, an organizer and an efficient military strategist. The result was that Islam did not remain simply a religious doctrine, but became a powerful political force as well, with deep socio-economic overtones; religion therefore became all-embracing. From the religious point of view Islam is total submission to the will of Allah, who has stated comprehensively the desirable and the non-desirable aspects of human conduct. His word is embodied in the *Quran* (Koran) which was revealed to Muhammad over a period of time through the archangel Gabriel. Islamic dogmas and beliefs have three aspects: *iman*, religious belief; *ibadat*, act of worship, religious duty; and *ihsan*, right doing. All these are embraced by the term *din*, religion. *Iman* means belief in God, the Quran, the Day of Judgement, and Muhammad as God's messenger on earth. *Ibadat* includes the five religious duties of profession of faith, prayer, alms-giving,[185] fasting[60] and pilgrimage,[381] to which Holy War was later added.

The religious, political and socio-economic totality of Islam remained externally intact between 632 and 661 (the period of the four Caliphs).[206] The orthodox successors to Muhammad, the Caliphs were religious leaders as well as heads of government with total responsibility for political and military affairs. Under their rule Muslims began to extend their power-base; initially to Palestine and Iraq in 632–4, then later to Syria between 633 and 640 and finally to Mesopotamia in 637 and Egypt in 642. Shortly afterwards they spread eastwards and established themselves with the help of local converts in Persia, western Turkestan and part of the Panjab. In less than half a century, half the civilized world from Spain to the borders of China was in the hands of the Muslims, unified by the young, dynamic culture of Islam. At the core of Islamic civilization were religious beliefs which transcended geographical boundaries as well as diverse social and national groups. Islamic obligations, practices and institutions provided the source of supreme values through which Arab, Turkish and Persian traditions could be blended together.

The initial consolidation of the Islamic territories under the Umayyad Dynasty (683–743) was followed by the Abbasides[310] (750–1258) in Baghdad when political stability paved the way for major intellectual and social achievements. This is the Golden Period of Islamic history. The dominant elements helping to shape these achievements were, first, the Arabs, with their social institutions, knowledge of mathematics and astronomy and the Arabic language, which was the language not only of the Holy Book but also of the bulk of Islamic religious literature; secondly, the Turks who brought with them intellectual and social etiquette; and finally, the Persians with their poetic temperament, court manners and ideas about moral and social elegance. 'An Arab henceforth became one who professed Islam and spoke and wrote the Arab tongue, regardless of racial affiliation. This is one of the most significant facts in the history of Islamic civilization. . . . "Arab medicine", "Arab philosophy" or "Arab mathematics" is a body of knowledge in Arabic during the Caliphate held by men who are themselves Persians, Syrians, Egyptians or Arabians, Christian, Jewish or Moslem who may have drawn some of their material from Greek, Aramaean, Indo-Persian or other sources.' (Hitti, p. 240.) This fusion brought forth a rich intellectual harvest with advances in the fields of medicine, philosophy, astronomy, mathematics, alchemy, geography, history and Arabic literature. Along with this a pattern of living evolved which paid due attention to home life, furniture, hygiene and pastimes based upon ideas of elegant living. Both the religious-based intellectualism and the patterns of gracious living were carried by the Muslims wherever they went.

In 710 Muslims began to raid the Indian sub-continent. By 713 they had established themselves permanently in the present regions of Baluchistan, Sindh and southern Panjab. It took them considerably longer to penetrate into the regions of north India. The Ghorids were the first Muslim kings in north India, followed by the slave-kings, the Khiljis, the Tughlas, the Saiyyids, the Lodis and lastly, the Mughals (from 1526/7 to 1857). By the time the Mughal Empire was established, Islam was already entrenched in Indian soil, and in addition to the converts they had made, the Arabs, Turks and Persians who had come in different waves had also made India their home. Traditional Indian and Muslim beliefs, institutions and ways of living encountered each other directly in every-day life. With the establishment of the Mughal Empire and the necessity for an elaborate administrative system—which Akbar evolved—a process of mutual co-operation between the local people and the Muslims began. The complex nature of this relationship and its effects on the life of the people of both groups has been the subject of many studies.* How deep the fusion between them went, however, is problematic. M. W. Mirza,† for instance, has concluded that: (1) the religion of Islam, though it remained substantially the same for the majority, underwent significant changes through Sufi[207] beliefs which were influenced by Hindu Vedantic and Yogic philosophies, and (2) intellectual progress was illustrated mainly by the products of Arabic and Persian literatures produced in India; (3) socially, Muslims from Persia and Afghanistan, unlike the Arabs, held aloof from the local population but these barriers were gradually removed and a process of 'Indianization' began, reaching its climax under the Mughals when Muslims superficially adopted many habits and manners of Hindus. In overall terms Mirza concludes that there was no real cross-fertiliza-tion between the two cultures. 'The ultra-democratic social ideas of Muslims, for instance, remained strictly confined to the Muslim community, while the liberal spirit of toleration and reverence for all religions preached and practised by the Hindus remained confined to them' (Mirza, p. 616). Thus did the civiliza-tion that is the subject of the present work acquire its characteristics: heavily weighted with Islamic beliefs and practices, it was also influenced by elements of the Hindu way of life.

The pattern of life of which Abdul Halim Sharar's *Lucknow: The Last Phase of an Oriental Culture* gives an account began to evolve in the magnificent era of Mughal power, in sixteenth-century Delhi during the reign of Akbar the Great. After the Mughal Empire had begun to disintegrate in the early eighteenth century, certain leading figures left Delhi and eventually found a new home in Lucknow, where the independent court of Avadh (Oudh) was established in 1753. How the already highly developed culture they brought with them was further refined in Lucknow to a level of splendour and sophistication scarcely paralleled in any other Indo-Islamic society is Sharar's main concern in the present work. The high culture of Lucknow was in full flower from the last quarter of the eighteenth century until the collapse of the Lucknow monarchy in 1856. It actually survived, however, as long as the feudal system survived in U.P.—that is, until the British left India in 1947.

This life of Lucknow was sweet and gracious, free from worldly cares and anxieties, a life of affluence, devoted to luxuries and leisured activities. The nobility controlled great wealth through the feudal system and spent lavishly; so too did the comfortable middle classes who were connected with the nobility

---

* E.g. M. Mujeeb, *Indian Muslims*, London 1967; Yusuf Husain, *Glimpses of Medieval Culture*, Bombay 1962; C. H. Buck, *Faiths, Fairs and Festivals of India*, Calcutta 1917; Tarachand, *Influence of Islam on Indian Culture*, Allahabad 1946; K. M. Ashraf, *Life and Conditions of Peoples of Hindustan*, Munshi Ram, Manohar Lal, New Delhi 1970.

† M. W. Mirza, chapter: 'Hindu Muslim Relations' in *The Delhi Sultanate*, ed. Majumdar, Bharatiya Vidya Bhavan, Bombay 1960.

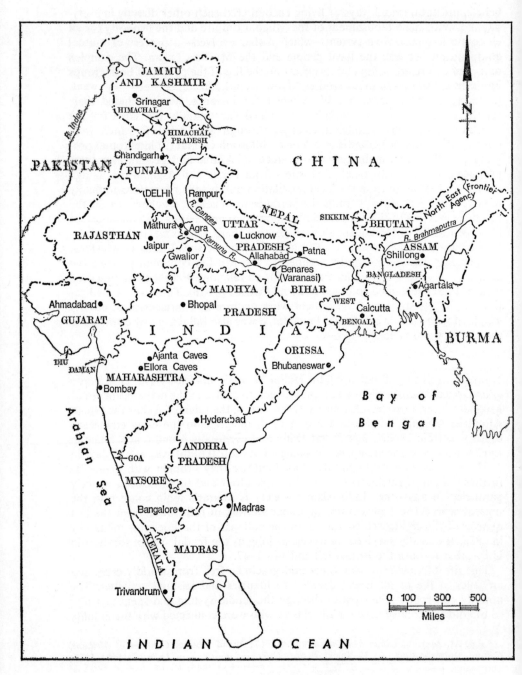

India at the present day

at various levels. Some written accounts suggest that even the peasants led a fairly comfortable life, those who had difficulty in earning a living simply having to look for a patron. They were appreciated for their skills as in the Roman Empire, rather than employed as in a modern industrial society. The life of this period has been the subject of many prose works in Urdu. Rajab Ali Beg Surur (1786–1867),[337] for instance, portrays the contemporary life of Lucknow, which is compared by Saxena (p. 261) with the scene of Tennyson's enchanted city:

> 'Here sits the butler with a flask
> Between his knees half drained and there
> The wrinkled steward at his task,
> The maid of honour charming fair,
> The page has caught her hand in his,
> Her lips are severed as to speak,
> His own are pointed to a kiss,
> The blush is fixed upon her cheek.'

Lucknow: The Last Phase of an Oriental Culture was originally written as a series of articles which appeared under the title of *Hindustan Men Mashriqi Tamaddun ka Akhri Namuna* over a period of years through the second decade of the present century in the Urdu literary journal *Dil Gudaz* which Sharar founded and edited in Lucknow.* The work comprises a history of the court of Avadh and of the development of eighteenth- and nineteenth-century Lucknow's culture and social institutions, and a detailed description of the customs, pastimes, artistic achievements and religious beliefs of its people. The latter constitutes a veritable 'anatomy' of the social and artistic life of Lucknow during the period, covering an astonishing variety of topics: religion, education, medicine; ceremony and social etiquette, dress, the culinary arts, calligraphy, dancing, popular language and the art of story-telling; such pastimes as kite- and pigeon-flying and the arts of combat and self-defence; the development of the Urdu language and its prose and poetry; architecture, music, pottery, theatre and other forms of public entertainment. For the historical part of his work, Sharar drew upon certain rare published sources and manuscripts that he discovered in private hands. His description of everyday life and customs is an eye-witness account of what he himself actually saw in Lucknow, supplemented by information gathered through the oral tradition, passed from generation to generation, that was still very much alive in his time. He would meet regularly with literary friends to discuss and collect information. This part of his account is generally accepted as authentic, and its value is enhanced by the fact that it is the most circumstantial record of Lucknow life of the period in existence.

To determine the causes of decay in a civilization it is necessary to examine its value system in relation to the new political and socio-economic conditions that challenge it. What seems to have been typical of Indo-Islamic societies is the way in which values crystallized into traditions. Over a period of time traditional

---

* See Notes on Abdul Halim Sharar, page 17 and on the present edition, page 25.

values are subject to new pressures which demand new answers. How a society responds to this attack on its established values determines its future. Like an individual, it can respond in two ways. Either it accepts these new challenges and becomes increasingly amenable to reason which opens the door to further evolution. Alternatively, the challenge can be rejected and reason becomes subservient to tradition. In this way society and traditional values ossify and the value system and the civilization based upon it acquire an inward-looking character. In the Kirkegaardian view, it becomes perverted in the sense that it becomes unable to offer a re-statement of its sense of values and ceases to be creative. Kenneth Clark's comment seems meaningful in this context: 'If one asks why the civilization of Greece and Rome collapsed, the real answer is that it was exhausted.'* Such a process, in the civilization described here, seems to have been accelerated by colonialism, which had a debilitating effect on the political and economic values of Indo-Islamic society. Indeed, these values were completely eroded and Indo-Islamic society was left with the mere outer forms of social life and its appurtenances. The value system of the Mughals became, consequently, further stifled, and conformism developed, leading to a search for reassurance either from the external forms of the civilization of the new rulers or relapse into the protective shell of ancient beliefs. The Muslims continued their own practices, rituals and way of life; however, this existence was artificial and lasted only as long as the protective shadow of the colonial power. When this was removed the colonized people were helpless in the face of new challenges from outside, because their value system was not equipped to cope with such problems.

Thus the civilization crystallized in Lucknow collapsed almost totally as soon as the British left India in 1947. The partition of the country into the two separate States of India and Pakistan, the abolition of the Zamindari[211] system, the adoption of Hindi[530] as the State language in U.P., renamed Uttar Pradesh, and a business-like attitude brought about by the beginnings of the new technological civilization—all this caused sudden and violent change in the established order. The younger generation evolved a new outlook compelled by the need to survive. A substantial number emigrated to Pakistan, mainly to Karachi and its neighbourhood, and started a new life.

It may be worthwhile to mention here two works which offer some fictional insight into the process of collapse of the civilization that reached its apotheosis in Lucknow. The first is Ahmad Ali's novel *Twilight in Delhi*,† which describes the life of Mir Nihal and his milieu in Delhi, and the attempts of different individuals to come to grips with the new life-style which had come to prevail, the failure of their efforts and their relapse into traditional habits. The second is Attia Hosain's novel *Sunlight on a Broken Column*,‡ which is set in Lucknow and describes the decay of traditional socio-cultural values under the impact of economic change, family patterns being the prime victim.

Not surprisingly, Lucknow has now changed almost beyond recognition. Yet the past echoes. Could it be that culture is what remains when all else is forgotten?

* *Civilization: A Personal View*, London 1971, page 4.
† London 1940.
‡ London 1961.

A Note on Abdul Halim Sharar (1860–1926)*

In Lucknow during the middle of the nineteenth century lived the hakim[52] Tafazzul Husain, a scholar of Islamic religion and Arabic and Persian literature. He was married to the daughter of Munshi[49] Qamar ud Din employed in the Secretariat of the Court of Wajid Ali Shah (see Chapter 8). Their son Abdul Halim, born in 1860, when he grew up adopted the pen-name[187] of Sharar, the Spark, by which he is most commonly known. His Islamic studies entitled him to use the title Maulana.[95] His full name, then, was Maulana Abdul Halim Sharar.

In 1856 Wajid Ali Shah had been exiled to Matiya Burj, Calcutta. In 1862 Sharar's father also joined the court of the exiled king. After spending the first nine years of his life in Lucknow, Sharar joined his father in Matiya Burj in 1869 and stayed there until 1879. During the last two years of this period he occupied the post formerly held by his grandfather, who had now retired.

In accordance with established custom, Sharar began his studies privately at home. We may reconstruct the following picture. He started to learn the Arabic and Persian languages from his father and continued this along with the study of their literatures and certain subjects of Islamic theology under at least three other scholars. He then began a course of instruction with a hakim in the Indo-Greek medicinal system, but did not complete it.

Even in this period of his early education, Sharar was interested in Urdu literature and in trying his own hand at writing. Urdu newspapers, which were published at this time, attracted him and he started to contribute at an early age to the columns of the Lucknow newspaper *Avadh Akhbar*[343] as its Matiya Burj correspondent. He also found time to be interested in music and in other aspects of the leisure-orientated life around him in Matiya Burj. Sharar's father is said to have been afraid that his son might plunge too deeply into the idle and frivolous life which prevailed in the exiled community. Hence he sent him back to Lucknow in 1879 when he was nineteen years of age. Back in Lucknow, Sharar continued single-mindedly in his course of Islamic religious instruction with the famous Maulvi Abdul Hai at the Firangi Mahal seminary.[96]

---

* The facts about Sharar's life here given have been derived mainly from Saxena (see Bibliography) and from Askari's *Tarikh Adab-e-Urdu*, which is actually a translation of Saxena's *History of Urdu Literature*, in which Askari has incorporated additional information. A note in this translation (p. 425) states that the account of Sharar's life was read and approved by Sharar himself. Hence the dates given there have been considered the more reliable.

In 1880, when he was twenty years old, a marriage was arranged for him, as was the custom. His bride happened to be his first cousin. About this time Sharar became deeply interested in Hadis,[243] the tradition of the Prophet. To pursue his studies in this field he went for a short while to the religious seminary in Delhi where the study of Hadis was more advanced than in Lucknow. The same year he returned to Lucknow and joined the staff of *Avadh Akhbar* as assistant editor at a salary of thirty rupees a month.

He started to write under the guidance of an Urdu writer, Munshi Ahmad Ali, well known for his contributions to the magazine *Avadh Punch*.[341] Ahmad Ali influenced Sharar by his own style, with its emphasis on correct structure of a sentence, elegant and highly stylized prose. It was against this flowery and formalized Persian style that Sharar later revolted and created his own simple and easily comprehensible style, which was better suited to the historical, social and political topics of his essays. His contributions to *Avadh Punch* covered a wide range of subjects and they rapidly became famous. Highly praised by leading men of the time was his essay 'The Soul'.

Having become, through these articles, a writer known wherever Urdu was spoken, Sharar was now offered various appointments in Hyderabad[42] and other Muslim States in India. These he did not accept at this stage, perhaps because, as with most Lucknow inhabitants, the idea of settling elsewhere did not appeal to him.

In 1882 Sharar started his own Urdu magazine *Mahshar*, 'Day of Judgment', taking the pen-name of Abdul Basit Mahshar, which was actually the name of one of his friends (see Chapter 11). This magazine was an important venture, since it was in the pages of *Mahshar* that he perfected and polished his own style, intended, as he himself stated, to adapt the style of Addison to essays in Urdu.

In 1884, however, the journal ceased publication, and Sharar accepted an appointment as *Avadh Akhbar*'s special correspondent in Hyderabad. He stayed there for six months before resigning his position and returning to Lucknow. Here he wrote his first novel, *Dilchasp*, 'Fascinating', describing some of the social evils and customs of his society. Although the first part of the novel received some praise for its style and for the depiction of human hardship, it was generally regarded as rather heavy and didactic. However, the second part of the novel, published a year later, was more polished and enjoyed a much more favourable reception. Sharar next translated into Urdu the English version of the Bengali novel *Durgesh Nandni* by Bankim Chandra Chatterji. By this time his reputation in Urdu prose had become established.

In 1887, encouraged by his two literary friends Maulvi Bashir ud Din, editor of *Al Bashir*, and Munshi Nisar Husain, publisher of *Payam-i-Yar*, Sharar began to publish in Lucknow his famous sixteen-page monthly magazine *Dil Gudaz*,* 'Quickener of the Heart' (see Chapter 11), which won popularity within the first year of publication. Several hundred copies were sold throughout India every month, and some copies managed to reach as far as Mecca, a considerable achievement for an Urdu literary journal of those days. This journal, with its many deaths and re-births, lasted as long as the life of Sharar himself and

---

* Details about *Dil Gudaz*, including citations from Sharar, have been obtained from *Mazamin-e-Sharar*, Vols I–IV, Saiyyid Mubarak Ali, Lahore, n.d. This work in eight volumes edited by Sharar himself is a collection of his short prose works, mainly from *Dil Gudaz*.

became inextricably part of his existence. It was his greatest achievement, and much of his most important work first appeared in it, including his essays on Lucknow which are the subject of the present translation. In an article introducing the journal, Sharar states his aim as being 'To stir people through the imagination by an effective description of their historic past and present-day conditions' (Vol. I, p. 6). In the last issue of 1887 Sharar re-states the purpose of his journal, adding 'to infuse a new style into Urdu prose and to add a new richness to its literature'. He commented further: 'No doubt many people have condemned its style but there are others who have well appreciated it.' *Dil Gudaz* was written almost entirely by Sharar himself and for many years there were practically no other contributors.

The subscription was raised from one to two rupees in 1888 when the journal was doubled in size by the addition of another sixteen pages to each month's issue. These pages were reserved for serializing Sharar's historical novels. The first of these was *Malik ul Aziz Varjinia*, then *Hasan Angelina* in 1889 and *Mansur Mohana* in 1890: many others followed. The plots of these works are woven around events in early Islamic history and the stories are told in such a way as to depict the value of religious teachings and the noble ideals and conduct of the early adherents to the faith. Sharar's deep interest in Islamic history led him to found a second journal in 1890 under the name of *Muhazzab*, 'Refined', the main purpose of which was to publish an account of the life and teachings of leading religious figures of Islam.

In 1891, in order to meet his financial obligations, Sharar was obliged to suspend his literary activities, including publication of both his journals, and to accept an appointment at two hundred rupees per month with a certain dignitary in Hyderabad State who later became Chief Minister. The latter's younger son had been sent to Eton College at an early age, thus missing traditional Islamic religious instruction and education in Indo-Islamic culture. Sharar was employed to go to England in order to provide this education and supervise the boy's upbringing from an Indo-Islamic point of view. The trip did not take place until 1895. In the period between 1891 and 1895 Sharar stayed in Hyderabad but managed to publish a few issues of *Dil Gudaz* from Lucknow in 1893. When he did eventually arrive in England in 1895 the visit was significant for Sharar's own literary activities. During the fifteen months of his stay he improved his English, which he had started to learn on his own in India, and learnt some French. He was able to observe Western civilization at first hand and this influenced his general outlook; he also produced some articles about his specific experiences, such as 'The Eastern and Western Parts of London and Lucknow' (Vol. II, pp. 564–70). In England, too, he completed his novel *Flora Florinda*, later published in India.

Returning to India in 1898 he resumed publication of *Dil Gudaz* from Hyderabad. In it he started to serialize historical materials including his work on the life of the daughter of *Imam Husain*,[106] some points of which agitated members of the Shia community. As a result the Government of Hyderabad discreetly asked Sharar to discontinue the series, which he did by stopping publication of the journal itself. However, he returned to Lucknow in 1899 or 1900, resumed publication of the journal there and completed the controversial life. Sharar remained on the payroll of the State and was allowed to spend his time in Lucknow, working on his writings. This activity culminated in the publication, probably in the pages of *Dil Gudaz* in the first instance, of his novel *Firdaus-e-Barin*, written earlier in Hyderabad; the second volume of *Ayyam-e-Arab*, an account of Arabia before Islam; a translation of Sir John Cox's *History of the Wars of the Crusades* and *Daku ki Dulhan*, a translation of an English novel. This was not all. The same year, in 1900, he started his periodical *Purdah-e-Asmat*, which denounced the custom of purdah[208] as practised by Muslims in India. The journal stopped publication after a year but this concern, and that for some other social evils, became the subject-matter of his two novels *Badrun-nisa ki Musibat* and *Meva-e-Talkh*, as well as of a number of others.

In 1901 Sharar again had to suspend publication of his journals when he was summoned to Hyderabad. On arrival there he found that the political situation had changed and was no longer favourable to him. The Chief Minister had been retired and died a few days later. Another patron had also lost his job. The financial affairs of the State were looked into by the British Government of India. One Mr Walker appointed to this task saw no need of maintaining Sharar on the payroll of the State. The son of the deceased Chief Minister, however, offered Sharar his patronage and maintenance and the new Chief Minister promised to reinstate him to his earlier position when circumstances permitted. Sharar stayed on in Hyderabad until 1904 before he decided to return to Lucknow. By June 1904 he was back in Lucknow and had again resumed publication of *Dil Gudaz* and a new periodical, *Ittihad*, 'Unity', the aim of which was to bring about a better understanding between Hindus and Muslims. This journal lasted only a year and a half. *Dil Gudaz* now had another sixteen pages added to make room for Sharar's additional historical works. His critical account of some Christian institutions, *Tarikh Hurub-e-Saliba*, 'History of the Crusades', was serialized in 1905 in these pages, as was his novel *Shauqin Malka*, 'The Amorous Queen'; the novel *Yusuf-o-Najma* was serialized in 1906 along with the first part of *Tarikh-e-Sindh*, a history of Sindh under the Muslims.

Beginning with the issue of February 1906, besides the sixteen pages reserved for literary and philosophical essays, novels and historical writing, another eight pages were added to the journal under the heading *Biographies of the Heroes of Islam*, making a total of fifty-six pages per number. The journal was suspended yet again in 1907, when Sharar went back to Hyderabad to take up an appointment as Assistant Director in the Education Department on the invitation of the new Chief Minister. In July 1908 *Dil Gudaz* was published again in Hyderabad, together with instalments of the *History of Sindh*, Part II and another new novel, *The Life of Aghai Sahib*. Several months later many changes were made in the form and content of the journal itself, The page size was enlarged in order to allow the use of bigger and clearer lettering, the historical series and the biographies were discontinued and the forty pages allotted to them were given over to essays and articles. As before, sixteen pages were reserved for instalments of Sharar's novels. The publication was suspended yet again in 1909 when Sharar was ordered by the ruling Nizam[42] to leave the State, probably as the result of something he had written.

In 1910 the journal again resumed publication from Lucknow and Sharar invited other writers to contribute to the essay section which had been especially enlarged for this purpose, but the chief contributions to the journal remained the work of Sharar himself. By the end of the year the monthly circulation had risen from four hundred during the first few years of publication to fourteen hundred. The price per copy was further raised. Thereafter the journal seems to have flourished until Sharar's death in 1926. In 1918 the new ruler of Hyderabad invited Sharar to write his biography but later changed his mind in favour of *A History of Islam*, for which Sharar received a salary of six hundred rupees per month. He was allowed to stay and work in Lucknow. This history was in three volumes, and the first volume when published was included in the curriculum of the Osmania University of the State, and probably remained so for a considerable time.

Sharar died in Lucknow in December 1926. After his death his son took over the editorship of *Dil Gudaz* and continued to publish it for a few years in Lucknow though he himself kept his job in Hyderabad. It was still flourishing in 1929 when Askari wrote his account.

Sharar revealed very little about his private life, a characteristic shared with other writers of his generation. As he himself said, 'The world is my story. My own is nothing.' (Vol. I, p. 304.) When he occasionally mentions his own affairs it is to explain delay in the publication of *Dil Gudaz* because of the illness of his son or the suspension of the journal between his different jobs and preoccupations. For him, as for other Urdu writers of his time, wife, children, family and employment to a great extent were private matters not to be shared with outsiders, and in any event they were of secondary importance compared to what really mattered, the world of ideas, religion and literary pursuits.

Nevertheless the picture that emerges of him is that of a strong personality, persevering and daring in his ideas. He was a partisan throughout. He was partisan in his religion and a conformist to the values of his society. This did not, however, overrule the scholar in him. When he had things to say against popularly held religious beliefs he expressed them, even though this meant unpopularity. Similarly, he continued to express his social ideas forcefully though this resulted in long and fierce controversies. In literature, too, he took his own stands and expressed them forcefully.

Sharar was a most prolific writer. A short list of his important works can be found in Askari (p. 134) who calculated the total published books to be one hundred and two in number. Besides his lifelong association with *Dil Gudaz* he edited and published eight other literary journals of varying lifespan. This enormous output, covering an extraordinarily wide range of subject-matter, along with its literary quality, made him unique among his contemporaries.

Apart from the large number of his essays, which cover topics ranging from 'A Pair of Shoes' to 'The Himalayas', Sharar's work can be classified as follows.

1. Histories such as *The History of Sindh* and *A History of Arabia before Islam*, all of which are connected in some way with Islam. Although these show considerable scholarship in Islamic literature, they are not the works of a professional historian and have often been described as lacking in objective evaluation. Some of Sharar's historical works, however, which appeared only in the pages of *Dil Gudaz*, introduced wider horizons to the reader and remain important even to this day. Examples include the translation into Urdu of the Arabic

classic *Memoirs of Ibn-e-Batuta*;[542] extracts from *Ajaib-ul-Hind*, 'The Wonders of India', the memoirs of a Zoroastrian later converted to Islam who wrote about his impressions of India as a traveller in the tenth century; the translation from an Arabic source of the encounter of Alexander the Great with the Raja of Kund in India; and especially the account of the last King of Avadh and his entourage, left incomplete at his death.

2. Biographies of many important figures in the history of Islam, among which accounts of certain less well-known personalities are of special interest.

3. Historical novels, the plots of which are based on heroic or dramatic events in the history of Islam, like *Mansur Mohna* which deals with the early incursions of Mahmud Ghaznavi into India, and *Malik ul Aziz aur Varjina*, dealing with the encounter between Richard Coeur de Lion and his 'noble and chivalrous Islamic rival', Salah ud Din. There are also *Shauqin Malka*, 'The Amorous Queen', which deals with the affairs and intrigues of Louis VII of France and Eleanor of Aquitaine when they led the second crusade against the Muslims after the latter had reconquered Odessa, and *Maftuh Fateh*, 'The Conqueror and the Conquered', set in the year 850 when the Muslims had entered Southern France and their leader won the heart of a French lady by his noble and chivalrous deeds.

Another group of similar novels on the theme of Christianity are *Muqaddas Naznin*, 'The Holy Fair One', set in the tenth century, in which a woman is elected Pope through the intrigues of the priests, and *Flora Florinda*, which describes the supposed moral degradation of Christianity in Spain during the fourteenth century, especially in convents and monasteries. The material of these novels, even when based on historical facts, as with *Flora Florinda*, and not imagination, is heavily influenced by Islamic fervour, and little attention is paid to the details of historical setting. There is additional reason for the glorification of Islam besides Sharar's religious zeal: Saxena (p. 335) describes how Sharar was disturbed by the anti-Muslim bias in Scott's *Talisman* and set out to put things right.

4. Social novels which have as their subject-matter Muslim customs which needed reform. *Badr-un-Nisa ki Musibat*, 'The Tragedy of the Bride', and *Agha Sadiq ki Shadi*, 'The Wedding of Agha Sadiq', describe the tragedies which sometimes occurred as a result of certain practices relating to marriage and purdah.[208]

A general characteristic of Sharar's novels is that they were written more in the spirit of journalism than that of creative writing. But in spite of imperfections in the unfolding of plot and characterization, they were a definite step forward in the historical development of the modern Urdu novel. Sharar developed further the new trend in the Urdu novel along with Sarshar,[342] Nazir Ahmad[344] and others by plotting his stories on the model of English novels. Sequences of events were interlinked and reference was made to actual life, which was a break from the traditional 'romances' based on mythological tales. From this time onwards novel-writing in Urdu became established and flourished, in popular as well as literary form.

5. Sharar's poetry and drama include *Shahid-i-Wafa*, 'Martyr of Loyalty', *Shab-i-Gham*, 'The Night of Sorrows', and *Shab-i-Wasl*, 'Night of Bliss', all written in the manner of the day and offering little that is original.

Sharar's contributions to Urdu literature are many. He introduced a simple style which he adapted to the different types of material he dealt with. The established practice of writing rhythmic prose with repetitious abundance of synonyms and flowery Persianized similes and metaphors was already under attack by some of his contemporaries and he gave it a further blow, modelling his sentences on English syntax. Explaining his point of view in *Dil Gudaz* in 1887, he pointed out that in all developed languages of the world different styles were employed to present different types of ideas, and that any given style was incapable of handling diverse topics. There is no doubt that he succeeded in his efforts and created a style for himself which became popular, and other writers quickly followed his example.

Shrara was an active social reformer, occasionally showing a political conscience as well. The social reforms dear to his heart were the purdah system and education for Muslim women. These he took up not only through his literary works but also by justifying his stand in religious polemics. In this way he contributed strongly to creating an atmosphere which led in 1910 to the founding of a college in Lucknow by Justice Karamat Hussain for the formal education of Muslim girls on modern lines. This school and the one opened by Abdul Rahim Balbalah in Bombay at about the same time seem to have been the first Muslim educational institutions of the kind. Others followed later.

Sharar, a bookish man, like so many of his literary contemporaries remained personally aloof from everyday and political life. However, he seems to have been fully aware of what was happening around him. The pages of *Dil Gudaz* contain frequent references to such events as the Allahabad Exhibition in 1910, King George V's visit to India in 1911, the failure of the Lucknow Municipality to supply the residents with water in 1916, as well as major political developments such as the Russian Revolution of 1917 and the end of the Muslim Caliphate in Turkey at the end of the First World War, but he writes of them in a detached manner. The same lack of involvement appears in his writing about the Indian National Congress, which had begun to be a political force in the country at this time, as well as the Muslim Educational Conference which was the arena for Muslim political activity, though he mentions these from time to time in *Dil Gudaz*. One question, however, with which he seemed very concerned was the problem of understanding between the Hindus and Muslims. He was eager to receive contributions to his journal from Hindus about Hinduism, and to make their history, religion and culture known to the Muslims. Reviewing the work of *Dil Gudaz* at the end of 1887 Sharar writes: 'There is a serious defect in *Dil Gudaz*. It is becoming more and more engrossed in the affairs of Islam to the exclusion of other points of view. We would be grateful, therefore, for the assistance of our Hindu friends in this matter, to add distinction to *Dil Gudaz*.' Although little interested in politics, Sharar seems to have been dissatisfied with the way the Indian National Congress of his time was treating the problem of Hindu-Muslim differences. He wrote in *Dil Gudaz*: 'Whether we support Congress or not, one very sad thing which we do notice about its activities is that it seems to be creating more differences between Hindus and Muslims than existed previously.'

Abdul Halim Sharar is remembered today as a pioneer of the modern Urdu novel, a historian of refreshingly wide horizons, and an essayist equipped with a profound knowledge of Arabic, Urdu and Persian literatures and Islamic theology. *Lucknow: The Last Phase of an Oriental Culture* can be said to be a fulfilment of its author's life's aims. The work has long been recognized by Indo-Islamic scholars as a primary source of great value, a unique document, both alive and authentic in every detail, of an important Indian culture at its zenith. And in many a Muslim household in the Indian sub-continent today this work may be found, read and studied by the older and the younger generations, as a reminder of and an introduction to their past.

The Present Edition

The work here translated is a collection of essays which originally appeared as articles under the title of *Hindustan Men Mashriqi Tamaddun ka Akhri Namuna* (literally, 'The Last Example of Oriental Culture in India') in the Lucknow journal *Dil Gudaz* over a period of years from 1913 onwards. These essays were later included in one of the volumes of the author's collected short prose, *Mazamin-e-Sharar*, edited by him and published in Lahore not long before his death.

The original series of articles seems to have met with a mixed reception. As early as 1915 in the last issue of that year, Sharar writes in *Dil Gudaz* that the series had been started two years earlier and would probably take another two years to complete. In the following year he wrote: 'We do not set out deliberately in these articles to praise Lucknow; any such impression which we may give is unintentional. We do however verify the accuracy of the material put before our readers. Much more remains to be said about Lucknow.' The series in fact continued over a rather longer period than the four years envisaged by Sharar in 1913. With no access to the actual files of *Dil Gudaz*, even if they exist anywhere, I have been unable to ascertain when the series was completed. Possibly it was shortly after 1920. The volume of *Mazamin-e-Sharar* containing these articles has been reprinted many times, mainly in Lucknow, but later in other places too. The text taken for the present translation is that published by Nasim Book Depot, Lucknow 1965 under the title 'Lucknow's Past', which had appeared in earlier editions as a subtitle. Chapter headings have been added to distinguish the various topics treated. These are, however, approximate, as topics tend to overlap between the essays.

The translation of a work such as this poses many problems. The Urdu text is rooted so deeply in the life, religion and culture of the people described that its translation into another language compels the translator to transpose one culture into another. It is not merely a straightforward description which can be restated in simple prose, but rather a record that itself expresses a complex pattern of living and that requires a high degree of precision in translation. For this reason cuts and departures from the original text have been kept to a minimum, and the present translation has been kept as literal as possible, strangeness and all. The reader should also bear in mind that the original was not written according to the conventions of modern dissertation.

The system adopted for annotation is as follows: brief explanations within the body of the translation have been incorporated where necessary to make the text comprehensible to the general reader. At the same time, it was decided to retain the original nomenclature in detail for the sake of accuracy, and this is the subject of much of the extensive annotation that follows the text. In the text itself, square brackets are used to indicate only the most obtrusive editorial interpolations.

Consistency in transliteration is of course impossible to achieve without recourse to phonetic notation. Urdu words and names are spelt as far as possible according to Urdu pronunciation, and with a minimum of diacritical notation. Some older English spellings which have become established—especially proper names—have, however, been retained. In the simplified system of spelling adopted, the reader's convenience has been given priority over strict phonetic consistency.

As early as 1927 the present work was described by Saxena as a 'mine of information' (p. 339). With the passage of time and the disappearance of the civilization described, the comment is still more apt. Sharar's account is today quoted as source material by scholars in a wide variety of fields. Thus in providing descriptive detail in the notes the Editor has been largely concerned with furthering Sharar's aim of recording the special characteristics of Lucknow society before rapid change obliterated them entirely.

Sharar wrote this work in the present tense. It is perhaps superfluous to note that the use of the same tense in the present translation would have been misleading as much of what is described now belongs to the past; the past tense, therefore, has here been used. For the same reason it was considered useful to provide some notes describing the course of events between Sharar's time and the present, especially so in the case of Urdu literature. Reference is also made in the notes to other works that provide additional information about Sharar's main topics.

The present edition is the result of a collaboration between the late Colonel E. S. Harcourt and myself. The late Colonel completed a first draft of the entire text after some discussions with myself. His unfortunate death meant not only that the final text of the translation had to be prepared by myself, but also that I was unable to benefit from his suggestions regarding the introduction and notes. I have revised the translation in order to make it as meaningful as possible to the contemporary reader. Sources of information drawn upon in the notes, wherever obtained from printed works, have been cited. However, much information comes by way of oral tradition through the first-hand experience of some elderly persons remaining in Lucknow. I should like to express my particular thanks to these people for their help in saving this information from oblivion. Thanks are due to many who helped in this in various ways, above all: Saiyyid Akbar Ali Rizvi, Naseer Raza, P. N. Mittal, Mrs C. Egan and Dr R. Rothlach. Special thanks are due to Raja Muhammad Amir Ahmad Khan of Mahmudabad for having given so much of his time to enlightening me on a large number of points. It had been my desire to acknowledge his participation by requesting him to write a Preface, but unfortunately he died before the work was complete. It is for this reason that the book is dedicated to him. I should like to express my gratitude also to Maulvi Malik Khayyam d'Ashkelon and Mrs L. Rosenthal.

Fakhir Hussain

Lucknow: The Last Phase of an Oriental Culture

1

Faizabad and the Early History of Avadh: Burhan ul Mulk and the Predecessors of the Avadh Dynasty

It is unlikely that anyone will question the statement that the late court of Avadh[1] was the final example of oriental refinement and culture in India. There are several other courts[2] to remind us of former times, but the one in which old culture and social life reached its zenith was this court of Avadh which was established not so long ago and, after making astonishing advances, came to an abrupt end. Because of this I wish to write a brief account of the conditions and peculiarities of that court under the title of 'The Last Phase of Oriental Culture in India'.[3] I do not think that anyone will disagree that the fame and importance of the region in which this court was established were greater than those of any other province in India. The great renown and incomparably stirring deeds of some of its ancient families, particularly that of Raja[4] Ramchandra,[5] reached such a pitch of excellence that history is an insufficient receptacle to contain them and thus they have assumed the pure guise of religion. Today there are very few villages in India that are so unlucky as not to be able to stage the yearly religious play *Ram Lila*,[6] which brings back to memory the deeds of Ram.

But the life of this most ancient of divine courts and the grandeur and splendour of Avadh at that time have been portrayed by Valmiki[5] with such wonderful eloquence that they are stamped on the minds of all, whatever their religion, and it is therefore unnecessary for me to repeat them. Those who are already familiar with Ajodhya's era of splendour in the literary chronicle of Valmiki will once again see it portrayed under the name of Faizabad[7] in the pages of *Dil Gudaz*.* I shall begin this account from the time when this final court, whose existence ended about fifty years ago, was first established.

When Navab[8] Burhan ul Mulk[9] Amin ud Din Khan[10] Nishapuri[11] was appointed Subedar[12] of Avadh by the Imperial Court of Delhi, he defeated the Shaikhzadas[13] of Lucknow and came to the ancient habitat of Avadh, that is to say, the honoured and holy town of Ajodhya, and pitched his tent on a high hill

* See Notes on Sharar, page 17 and on the present edition, page 25.

overlooking the banks of the River Ghagra far from any other habitation.* Having no time to build a grand residence because of the exigencies of the administration of the province and also because he was a man of simple tastes and had no desire for pomp and ostentation, he remained in camp for some time. When later he became inconvenienced by the rains, he moved the camp back a little and had a thatched shelter built for himself in a suitable place. After this he had mud walls built around the shelter and made a large square fortress. At each of the four corners, as is usually the practice with fortifications, mud-built towers were erected so that the surrounding country could be surveyed. The enclosure was so big that large numbers of cavalry, infantry, artillery, stables and necessary workshops could all be accommodated inside it with ease.

Burhan ul Mulk had no desire for spacious residences, so mud houses were also built for the ladies of the household and his wives to live in. In short, the ruler of Avadh, when he was not touring his domain about matters of adminis-tration, lived in peace and comfort in his mud-built bungalow and was perfectly happy. His simple abode was soon known as the Bangla.[15]

After the death of Burhan ul Mulk, at the commencement of Safdar Jang's[16] rule this settlement became known as Faizabad.

Such was the origin of the town of Faizabad, which outdid Lucknow in both the rapidity of its growth and its subsequent decay. Most of the Mughal[17] army officers occupied themselves in constructing beautiful gardens and attractive pleasure-grounds to encompass this mud-built, four-walled enclosure and the town soon acquired a new lustre. On the western side of this enclosure was a gate known as the Delhi Gate, outside which Divan[18] Atma Ram's sons erected an impressive market-place and, as an adjunct, houses for people to live in. Similarly, Risaldar[19] Ismail Khan had a market-place constructed, and inside the enclosure many houses were built for *khwaja-saras*[20] [eunuchs] and army personnel.

After Navab Safdar Jang died, misfortune pursued the new settlement for some time and fate destroyed what had been set up over the years. The reason for this was that Safdar Jang's son [Jalal ud Din Haidar], Navab Shuja ud Daula,[21] chose Lucknow as his residence and proceeded to live there, spending only two or three nights a year in his ancestral home. This went on until he was defeated by the British at the Battle of Baksar[22] in 1765, when he fled completely empty-handed to Faizabad, picked up what equipment he could find at the fort and left by night for Lucknow. Here again he stayed only one night, collected any-thing he could lay his hands on and proceeded towards Bareilly in order to take refuge with the Afghans of Ruhelkhand.[23] Nine months after the engagement he made peace with the British, under the terms of which he was responsible for handing over to them about one third of the revenue of his territory.

Before the declaration of peace, it happened that Shuja ud Daula in the course of his journeys passed through the town of Farrukhabad. There he met Ahmad Khan Bangash[24] who was considered to be among the most experienced veterans of his day. His advice to Shuja ud Daula was: 'When you take the reins of government into your hands again do not forget two points. Firstly, put no

* *Author's note:* I have gathered this information about Faizabad from the English trans-lation by W. Hoey of Munshi Faiz Buksh's book *Tarikh-e-Farah Baksh*.[14]

trust in the Mughals but work with your other subordinates and khwaja-saras. Secondly, give up living in Lucknow and make Faizabad your seat of government.'

Shuja ud Daula was impressed by this advice and, after making a treaty with the British, he proceeded towards his own territory in 1765, went straight to Faizabad and made it his seat of government. Here he started to enlist a new army, to organize new cavalry regiments and lay the foundations for new buildings. He strengthened and rebuilt the old fortifications as a protection for the town and these fortifications were now known as 'the Fort'. He demolished the houses of the Mughals that were inside the fortification and gave orders to his family retainers to build houses outside it. For two miles on all four sides of the fortress the ground was left open and a deep ditch was dug around this open space as an additional fortification. Civil and military officers, according to their status, were given plots of land on which to build houses.

As soon as it was known that Shuja ud Daula had decided on Faizabad for his headquarters, crowds flocked in that direction, and thousands came and settled there. The entire population of Shahjahanabad[25] seemed to be making preparations to move there. Most of the eminent people of Delhi bade farewell to their domiciles and turned towards the east. Night and day people kept coming and caravan after caravan arrived to stay and become absorbed into the environs of Faizabad. In no time persons of every race and creed, literary men, soldiers, merchants, craftsmen, individuals of every rank and class had gathered there. All those who came, immediately on arrival, became involved in securing a plot of land and building a house.

In a few years two other breastworks were erected in addition to the fortress, one which adjoined the original square enclosure in the south, the area of which was two square miles, and the other between the fortress and the rampart, the area of which was one square mile. At that time the Tripuliya[26] and Chauk[27] markets were constructed, the road to which started at the southern gate to the Fort and went as far as the turnpike on the Allahabad road. This road was so broad that ten bullock carts could easily pass along it abreast. Whatever the width of the battlements at ground level, they were ten yards wide in the middle and five yards wide at the top. Parties of regular and irregular soldiers would patrol these battlements throughout the night and sentries were posted at various places. The uniform of the regular soldiers was red, and that of the irregulars black. In the rainy season, thatched shelters were erected here and there for the use of the soldiers, but when the rains were over these were demolished because of the fear of fire. In fact, each year about one hundred thousand thatched shelters were erected for the battlement walls alone; after four months they were pulled down and discarded.

In the neighbourhood of the town two tracts of open country were reserved as hunting grounds. The one to the west stretched from the Mosque of Gurji Beg Khan[28] to Gaptar Ghat[29] which is a considerable distance. There were mud walls on two sides and at the extremity was the River Ghagra. Into this many game animals such as buck, spotted-deer, russet-deer and *nilgai*[30] had been introduced and roamed hither and thither, gambolled and bounded about unfettered and in complete freedom. The other hunting ground was to the east of the town and stretched from the village of Janura and the Gushain cantonment to the banks of the river, an area of six square miles. It included eleven villages with the land which pertained to them. But this hunting ground remained incomplete and the time never came for it to be filled with wild animals.

Inside the town were three parks of such an attractive nature that nobles and princes would come and stroll in them and derive much pleasure from their elegance and charm. One was the Anguri Bagh[31] which was inside the Fort and comprised one quarter of its area. The second was the Moti Bagh, which was inside the main Chauk market square. The third was the Lal Bagh, the largest of all the parks. It was furnished with the most exquisite lawns and every sort of delicate and entrancing flower appeared in profusion in its beds. This park was renowned throughout the province and people from far and wide hoped to spend one lucky evening in so delectable a spot. Every evening a crowd of young nobles from the town could be seen here sauntering about and enjoying themselves. The fame of the charm and fascination of this park was so universal that the Emperor of Delhi, Shah Alam,[32] on his return from Allahabad, came to Faizabad to see it and spent some days there before returning to Delhi. In addition to these three parks, there were also the Asaf Bagh and Buland Bagh in the neighourhood of the town on the Lucknow road.

Navab Shuja ud Daula was so interested in the upkeep of the town that he would ride out each morning and evening to inspect the streets and houses. He would take workmen with him armed with mattocks and spades and whenever he saw a house out of alignment or beyond its allotted bounds, or if he found that some shopkeeper had encroached to the slightest degree on the street, he would start digging operations to put matters right.

Navab Shuja ud Daula also paid great attention to improving the army. The highest cavalry leaders were Navab Murtaza Khan Bareech[33] and two Brahmans[34] named Himmat Bahadur and Umrao Gir. These three commanders each had more troops under them than had all the lesser commanders put together. Other military commanders were Ahsan Kambohi,[35] Gurji Beg Khan, Gopal Rao Maratha,[36] the son-in-law of Mir[37] Navab Jamal ud Din Khan, Jumla (a General of Aurangzeb), Muzaffar ud Daula, Tahawar Jang Bakhshi,[38] Abul Barkat Khan of Kakori (a small town on the outskirts of Lucknow) and Muhammad Muiz ud Din Khan, a Shaikhzada of Lucknow. None of these had less than fifteen hundred men under him. In addition, there were khwaja-saras and young novices who were trained under their supervision and had become their disciples and pupils. Khwaja-sara Basant Ali Khan was in command of two divisions, that is, a force of fourteen thousand regular soldiers, in red uniform. Another khwaja-sara also named Basant had under his command one thousand regular lancers and one infantry battalion. Khwaja-sara Anbar Ali Khan was in charge of five hundred cavalry and an infantry battalion in black uniform. There were five hundred cavalry and four battalions of infantry under the standard of Khwaja-sara Mahbub Ali Khan and Latafat Ali Khan had the same number of troops. Raghu Nath Singh[39] and Parshad Singh each had three hundred cavalry and four battalions of infantry under his command, and Mahbub Ali Khan and Yusuf Ali Khan each had a force of five hundred Mughal cavalry and infantry. There was artillery beyond all number.

The total size of the army which was at Shuja ud Daula's disposal and which was stationed at Faizabad was as follows: regulars in red uniform, thirty

Royal portraits by Lucknow artists:

1 (*above*)   Shuja ud Daula.
Water-colour, about 1800
2 (*right*)   Asaf ud Daula.
Water-colour, 1780
3 (*below*)   Sadat Ali Khan. Oil
painting, about 1800

4   Machi Bhavan. Pre-Mutiny photograph

5   Shaikhan Gate, Machi Bhavan. Pre-Mutiny photograph

thousand, and irregulars in black uniform, forty thousand. Their senior officer, that is to say commander-in-chief, was Saiyyid Ahmad, who was known as Bansi Wala.[40] Their muskets could be loaded and fired more rapidly than those of the British soldiers.

In addition to this mass of troops, Shuja ud Daula had twenty-two thousand messengers and informers who would bring news from great distances, every seventh day from Poona for example, and every fifteenth day from Kabul.

Envoys of the rulers of far-off places in India were also present at the court. There was an envoy of the Marathas,[41] one on behalf of Nizam Ali Khan[42] ruler of the Deccan, one on behalf of Zabita Khan[43] and one for Zulfiqar ud Daula, Najaf Khan.[44] These envoys all had their own officers and soldiers. In addition many military officers lived at Faizabad with their troops, as for instance Mir Naim Khan, under whose standard were a number of Sabit Khani,[45] Bundel-khandi, Chandela[46] and Mewati[47] troops.

Muhammad Bashir Khan was commander of the Fort. His cavalry and infantry were spread over the battlements and gates. Inside the Fort he had fine houses for himself and his officers and barracks for his soldiers. When eventually no room was left even within the outermost walls, Saiyyid[37] Jamal ud Din Khan and Gopal Rao Maratha took up their abode outside the Fort in the vicinity of the village of Nurahi where they built houses and set up tents. Owing to limited space in this neighbourhood Navab Murtaza Khan Bareech, Mir Ahmad Bansi Wala, Mir Abul Barkat and Shaikh Ahsan lived in tents in the country between Ajodhya and Faizabad.

Because of the great numbers of people and soldiers the town became so crowded, especially the main market-place, that it was difficult to move and quite impossible to walk normally without bumping into someone. In short, Faizabad was a veritable forest of human beings.

Wherever you looked in the markets there were stacks of merchandise from various countries, for on hearing that Faizabad was the chosen centre for discriminating noblemen and fashionable gentlemen, merchants' loaded caravans came from every direction. As they always found a ready sale, there was a steady inflow of the very best quality merchandise. Merchants from Persia, Kabul, China and Europe arrived with valuable goods and the profits they received encouraged them to make further efforts to bring in fresh articles. Two hundred Frenchmen, such as Messieurs Gentil, Gailliez, Polier,[48] and others who had become domiciled in the town, had entered Government service and had very cordial relations with Shuja ud Daula's administration. They gave the troops military instruction and cannons, muskets and other weapons of war were produced under their supervision.

Munshi[49] Faiz Baksh, author of the *Tarikh-e-Farah Baksh*,[14] to whom I am indebted for having acquainted me with the events of this period, was himself present when they took place and whatever he wrote he wrote as an eye-witness. He says that when he originally left home for Faizabad, as soon as he came to Mumtaz Nagar[50] some four miles from the town, he saw various kinds of sweet-meats, hot viands, kebabs[485] and curries being cooked and *chapatis* and *parathas*[487] being baked under the shade of trees. There were stalls for distributing cold drinking-water. Different sorts of sherbets and *faluda*[51] were sold with hundreds of people swarming to the shops to buy them. The thought passed through his mind that he had entered the town and was in the market-place itself, but he wondered how he had got inside as he had not come upon the city gate. On inquiring about this he was told, 'Sir! The city gate is four miles from here! What are you thinking of?'

Munshi Faiz Baksh was astonished at this answer and entered the town where he found great bustle and activity. On every side was merry-making and excitement. Wherever he looked there were snake-charmers, dancers and jugglers performing their tricks, and people wandering about enjoying themselves. He was lost in amazement at this splendour, tumult and commotion.

There was not a moment from morning until evening when one could not hear the army or the beat of regimental drums. Drums were also beaten to indicate the time and at each period of four hours gongs were struck by mallets, making such a din as to deafen one's ears. In the streets there was a never-ending stream of horses, elephants, camels, mules, hunting dogs, cows, buffaloes, bullocks, bullock carts and cannons. It was difficult for the wayfarer to make any progress.

A town of grandeur and dignity met the eye. In it fashionably dressed persons from Delhi, elegant sons of noblemen, skilled hakims,[52] well-known troupes of men and women dancers and eminent singers from far and wide were employed by the administration, drew very large salaries and lived a carefree life of luxury. The pockets of high and low were filled with rupees[53] and gold coins and it appeared as if no one had ever known poverty and want. The Navab Vazir Shuja ud Daula was constantly engaged in promoting the prosperity and splendour of the town and its people. It appeared that in a very short time Faizabad would claim to be on a par with Delhi.

As the ruler of no country or town lived in such refinement, pomp and circumstance as Navab Shuja ud Daula, and also as it seemed that nowhere else were people so ready to spend money freely on any occasion or for any purpose, all sorts of expert artificers, craftsmen and students from every direction bade farewell to their home towns and made Faizabad their domicile. There was always a large crowd of students from Dacca, Bengal, Gujrat, Malwa, Hyderabad, Shahjahanabad, Lahore, Peshawar, Kabul, Kashmir and Multan who studied in the schools[54] of the local scholars. Then having become satiated at the fount of knowledge existing in Faizabad, they returned to their homes. Would that the Navab Vazir had lived another ten or twelve years. Had he done so, a new Shahjahanabad would have flourished on the banks of the Ghagra and the world would have seen a new and living Delhi.

Such was Navab Shuja ud Daula's achievement in Faizabad after a residence of only nine years, and during this time he honoured the town with his presence only for the four months of the yearly rainy season. He spent the rest of the year touring his realm, amusing himself and hunting. He was by nature attracted to beautiful women and was fond of dancing and singing. For this reason there was such a multitude of bazaar beauties[55] and dancers in the town that no lane or alley was without them. Because of the Navab's rewards and favours they were in such easy circumstances and so wealthy that most of the courtesans had fixed abodes with two or three sumptuous tents attached to them. When the Navab was touring the provinces or travelling, their tents would be loaded with stately grandeur on to bullock carts with those of the Navab and were guarded by a party of ten or twelve soldiers.

As this was the practice of their ruler, all the rich men and chieftains openly adopted it and courtesans would accompany them on their travels. Although this gave rise to a certain degree of immodesty and laxity of morals, there is no doubt that the large number of these bazaar beauties and the nobles' patronage of them added greatly to the splendour of the town of Faizabad.

In the year 1773, Shuja ud Daula travelled towards the west. On this journey it appeared as if a large city were following the Navab's auspicious colours. Passing through Lucknow, he reached Etawa (U.P.), which was in the hands of the Marathas. In one single engagement the Navab wrested it from them and took possession of it. Then entering the domain of Ahmad Khan Bangash, he encamped at Kuryaganj and Kasganj. From here he wrote to Hafiz[56] Rahmat Khan, ruler of Bareilly, to the following effect: 'Last year I handed over on your behalf ten million rupees to Mahaji Sindhia, the Maratha[57] who had seized all your territory in the Doab.[58] On payment of this sum I retrieved your territory from his possession and restored it to you. Please send me at once the five million rupees of my own money which I paid to him.' Hafiz Rahmat Khan assembled all his Afghan chieftains and associates and said, 'Shuja ud Daula is seeking a pretext for a fight. It would be best if the sum he asks for were paid. I will give two million of my own money: you collect the remaining three million.' The short-sighted Pathan chieftains replied, 'Shuja ud Daula's men are of no particular consequence. How can they stand against us? As for the British troops[59] who are with him, when we fall upon their guns with our drawn swords, they will all lose their heads. There is absolutely no necessity for payment.' When Hafiz Rahmat Khan heard this, he said: 'As you wish: but I say this in advance, that if the fighting goes the other way I will not leave the battlefield alive and you will have to suffer the consequences.' Still, Shuja ud Daula did not receive the answer he desired. He therefore attacked and battle was joined. The result of the battle was as destiny had put into the mouth of Hafiz Rahmat Khan, that is to say he was killed and his administration came to an end.

The victory was not however propitious for Shuja ud Daula. The battle took place in 1774. About six months later Shuja ud Daula marched from Bareilly to Lucknow, where he spent the month of Ramzan.[60] The next month he left Lucknow, arriving in Faizabad six days later—nine months and ten days after the victory. He was not granted so long as one and a half months to rest in his home when, still in the year 1774, he was called to his eternal rest. Sadly, his death put an end to all forms of progress in Faizabad.

At that time the person who had most influence over the government of Avadh was Shuja ud Daula's wife, Bahu Begam,[61] who was reputed to be very wealthy. By her consent Navab Asaf ud Daula took on the duties of ruler, but he was an excessively dissolute individual and the courtiers thought that it would be well to keep the mother and son apart. After a few days' hunting, Asaf ud Daula took up his residence in Lucknow, from where he would plague his mother and importune her for money.

Because of Bahu Begam's presence a certain amount of the splendour of Faizabad remained and, although whilst she was alive Asaf ud Daula's iniquities disturbed her peace of mind and consequently affected the tranquillity of

Faizabad, still during the honoured lady's lifetime even the quarrels and disturbances which took place were possessed of some dignity. On her death the history of Faizabad came to an end and the epoch of Lucknow, of which I will now write an account, commenced.

2

The Origins and Early History of Lucknow

No one knows definitely when Lucknow first became populated, who its founder was or how it got its name, but if family traditions[62] and conjectures are taken as a basis, the following account can be given.

It is said that after Raja Ramchandra had conquered Ceylon and completed his term of exile in the wilderness, and when he had honoured the status of kingship by adopting its form, he gave this region as a reward to his devoted brother Lachman [Lakshman], who had accompanied him on his travels. To commemorate the latter's stay, a village was built on a high hill overlooking the river which since that day has been known as Lachmanpur.[63] The hill was called Lachman Hill and in it was a very deep cave with a well of which no one could estimate the depth. People said it went down as far as Shesh Nag.[64] This idea gave impetus to religious feeling and Hindus, inspired by faith, would go there to sprinkle water[65] and offer flowers.

It is also said that Maharaja Yudhistir's[66] grandson, Raja Jaman Ji,[67] gave this region as a reward to holy sages, the *rishis*[68] and *munis*,[69] and that they set up their hermitages throughout the land and became immersed in the contemplation of the Almighty. After some time, realizing that these sages had become weak and defenceless, two hitherto unknown tribes came from the Himalayan foothills and took possession of the region. These tribes seem to have been two branches of the same family—one was called Bhar and the other Pansi.

These people were attacked by Saiyyid Salar Masud Ghazi[70] in 1030 and probably also by Bakhtiyar Khilji[71] in 1202. Therefore the first Muslim families to settle in this region were those that had accompanied these two assailants, especially the former.

From early days Brahmans and Kayasths,[72] in addition to the Bhars and Pansis, lived together in peace and harmony in the small town. It cannot be said when this town changed its name from Lachmanpur to Lucknow. The name which is now current cannot be traced before the days of the Emperor Akbar,[73] but it also cannot be denied that a large population of Hindus and Muslims were settled there before Akbar's reign. This can be proved by an event which is described long before that time in the family records of the Shaikhs of Lucknow. In 1540, when King Humayun was defeated by Sher Shah at Jaunpur, he fled from the battlefield by way of Sultanpur, Lucknow and Pilibheet. He paused to rest for four hours in Lucknow and although he came as a victim of defeat and had no power or authority, the people of Lucknow, purely from feelings of sympathy and hospitality, made him a gift of ten thousand rupees and fifty horses.

That so much was collected in such a short time leads one to imagine that the town must have had a considerable population and that the Lucknow of that era must have been more flourishing and prosperous than most towns of today.

Among the families that came to Lucknow in those early days was that of Shah Mina,[74] whose sacred tomb is still a rendezvous[75] for the masses. He took up his abode on Lachman Hill and, being buried there, he has become, as it were, part of the landscape. Because of his residence the old name of Lachman Hill was changed to Pir Muhammad Hill and in the course of time the ancient cave was filled in. Later on Emperor Aurangzeb,[76] who had come to Lucknow in person, erected on this hill an imposing mosque which to this day calls the faithful to prayer in his name.

When in 1590 Emperor Akbar divided the whole of India into twelve Provinces, Lucknow was, in the first instance, chosen as the seat of the Subedar, or Governor, of Avadh. At that time one Shaikh Abdur Rahim, an impecunious and down-at-heel nobleman of Bijnaur (U.P.), went to Delhi to seek his fortune. Here he acquired some influence with the nobles of the court and was himself accepted as a courtier. Eventually, having become an official in imperial service, he was granted land in Lucknow and a few days later, with great pomp and show, he went to his estate. Here he took up residence on Lachman or Shah Pir Muhammad Hill. He built Panj Mahla, which according to some accounts was a five-storeyed palace and according to others a complex of five palaces, erected the Shaikhan Gate and himself became part and parcel of Lucknow. His tomb is known today as Nadan Mahal.[77] A short time ago the Government of India placed it under their care and protection.

At that time Shaikh Rahim had a small fort built on an eminence close to Lachman Hill. It was stronger than other forts in the vicinity and people in the neighbourhood were much impressed by it. Either because Shaikh Abdur Rahim had been awarded the title of Mahi Maratib[78] at the Imperial Court or because on the twenty-six arches in one portion of the fort the architect had engraved two fishes on each arch, making a total of fifty-two fishes, this fort became known as Machi Bhavan.[79] The word *bhavan*, as well as meaning 'fort', could be a corruption of the word *bavan*, meaning 'fifty-two'. The architect who designed this fort was an Ahir[80] named Lakhna. Some say that because of his name the town was called Lucknow. Others think that Lachmanpur was corrupted into Lucknow. Conjecture as one may, there is no doubt that the town adopted this name after the coming of Abdur Rahim.

Some time later in addition to the family of Shaikh Abdur Rahim, that is to say, the Shaikhzadas, a number of Pathans arrived who settled in the south and were known as the Ram Nagar[81] Pathans. They fixed the limit of their lands at the place where the Gol Darvaza[82] now stands because from that point on towards the river the territory of the Shaikhzadas commenced. After these Pathans, another group of Shaikhs arrived and settled towards the east. They were known as the Benehrah[83] Shaikhs and their land was where the ruins of the Residency[84] now stand.

Although these three groups occupied their own areas and held sway over them, the authority of the Shaikhzadas was paramount and their power over the neighbourhood was supreme. The principal reason for this was that they had influence with the court at Delhi and members of the family had been appointed Subedars of the whole Province of Avadh. Their fort, Machi Bhavan, was so strong that it was said, 'He who holds Machi Bhavan holds Lucknow.'

During Akbar's reign Lucknow made progress and its population grew. But although some of the Shaikhzadas were chosen as Subedars of Avadh, for the most part a Delhi noble was appointed to the post. These officials stayed throughout the year in their own homes in Delhi and came to Avadh only when the time came for collecting taxes. Only their deputies resided in Lucknow, so there was little hope of the town making progress under their administration. On the few occasions that a member of the Shaikhzada family was appointed Subedar, Lucknow certainly benefited by the appointment. It appears as though Akbar took a special interest in Lucknow, for he gave the local Brahmans one *lakh*[85] of rupees for the Bajpai[86] offerings and from that time the Bajpai Brahmans of Lucknow became famous. One can gather from this that the oldest Hindu quarters of Lucknow in existence at this time were the Bajpai, Katari,[87] Sundhi,[88] Banjari[89] and Ahiri *tolas*.[90] All these quarters remain, in the neighbourhood of the then main market-place of Chauk.

Mirza[91] Salim,[92] who was known by the title of Nur ud Din Jahangir when he came to the throne, laid the foundations of Mirza market to the west of Machi Bhavan whilst his father was still alive and he was heir apparent.

Towards the end of Akbar's reign, Jawahar Khan was Subedar. He himself lived in Delhi but his deputy, Qazi[93] Mahmud Bilgrami, built, adjacent to the south part of the Chauk market-place, Mahmud Nagar and Shah Ganj.[94] Between he had a gate erected which was known as Akbari Gate to perpetuate the Emperor's name.

During Akbar's reign, when these buildings were being erected and the town was filling up, Lucknow had become a great centre of commerce. It was so prosperous that a French merchant, who traded in horses, settled there in the hope of reaping a profit. Having received a Certificate of Security* from the Imperial Court for his stay in Lucknow, he set up his stables and in the very first year was so successful that he built four splendid houses in the vicinity of the market-place. At the end of that year he applied for his Certificate of Security to be renewed, but was not granted permission for further residence. When he decided to stay on in spite of this the town authorities, on orders from the Imperial Court, confiscated his houses, made them crown property and evicted him from the town. These four houses remained in Government possession until the reign of Aurangzeb Alamgir when Mulla[95] Nizam ud Din Sehalvi,[96] having become completely frustrated by the disturbances in his own town, decided to live in Lucknow. The houses were presented to him as a Government gift and he came with his whole family and took up residence in them. These houses along with

* *Author's note:* Europeans desiring a domicile in India used to obtain from the Delhi Court a Certificate of Security called the Order of Mastamani (Arabic *mastaman*, seeker of peace), which protected them from the high-handedness of the administrators and local population. As it involved certain Government responsibilities, it was usually granted for a period of one year.

those in their immediate neighbourhood are known to this day as Firangi Mahal.

Owing to the propitious advent of the Mulla, Lucknow became a centre of learning and scholarship and the rendezvous for seekers after knowledge. This influx of scholars increased to such an extent that Mulla Nizam ud Din's curriculum, which was called Silsila-e-Nizamia,[97] was for a long time the course of instruction in use not only in India but in the whole of Asia.[98] In addition to instruction in secular subjects, one may imagine that the course contained sacred tuition. It is easy to understand why in those days many students from a great number of places and from great distances used to gather in Lucknow.

In 1631 at the commencement of the reign of Emperor Shahjahan,[99] a European traveller, Lockett, made a journey to India. He wrote that Lucknow was a great centre for trade.

In Shahjahan's time the Governor of Lucknow was Sultan Ali Shah Quli Khan, who had two sons, Mirza Fazil and Mirza Mansur. To commemorate their names he inaugurated two new quarters, Fazil Nagar and Mansur Nagar, just beyond the southern outskirts of Mahmud Nagar.

A risaldar named Ashraf Ali Khan laid the foundations of Ashrafabad. His brother, Musharaf Ali Khan, built a house on the other side of the drainage stream and erected a new quarter called Musharafabad, the name of which in the course of time was changed to Nau Basta.[100] Another army officer named Pir Khan built a small fort for himself well to the west of all these quarters. It is known to this day as Pir Khan Garhi.[101]

At one time the Emperor Aurangzeb Alamgir had to travel to Ajodhya for some purpose and stopped at Lucknow on his return journey. It was then that he built the Shah Pir Muhammad Hill Mosque. Situated on Lachman Hill, it is at such a height over the surrounding country that no more appropriate place for a mosque could possibly have been found in Lucknow. It is, also, probable that on this occasion Aurangzeb gave the houses of the Firangi Mahal to the great scholar Mulla Nizam ud Din.

In the days of the Mughal Emperor Muhammad Shah Rangeley,[102] the Governor of Lucknow was a valiant Hindu risaldar named Gardhananga whose uncle Chabele Ram had been appointed ruler of Allahabad by the Mughal court. On the death of Chabele Ram, Gardhananga decided to revolt and to assume the rulership of Allahabad in his uncle's place. But thinking better of it, he declared his loyalty and allegiance and was granted the *khilat*[103] of office as Subedar of Avadh by the Government. He came to live in Lucknow and his wife Rani laid the foundations of Rani Katra.[104]

But whoever the Subedar happened to be, however autocratic he was or however much authority was invested in him, the power of the Shaikhzadas was so great that he could never dare enter their circle. Although Machi Bhavan was in the nature of a Government palace, the Shaikhzadas considered it as their own inherited property and the Governor who came from Delhi was not able to intrude in its affairs. The Shaikhzadas had erected two other buildings near Machi Bhavan, the name of one being Mubarak Mahla and the other Panj Mahla. They were built next to each other, and to the south was a great arched gateway called Shaikhan Darvaza. People from the town who wished to visit one of these buildings had to pass through this gate. The arrogant Shaikhzadas had hung a sword from the arch and ordered that if anyone wished to enter, regardless of who he might be or however great a man he was, he would first have to bow down before the sword and salute it. It was impossible for anyone to evade this order and even the Governors appointed by Delhi were obliged to bow if they came to visit the Shaikhs.

This was the state of affairs in Lucknow when, in 1732, Navab Sadat Khan Burhan ul Mulk came to the town after having been appointed Subedar of Avadh by the Delhi Government. It was he who laid the foundations of that fine oriental court whose evolution I consider to be the last example of Eastern culture and of which I wish to write an account. In Chapter 1, I described Faizabad which presents the first portrait of this culture as an adjunct to the court of Lucknow. In this chapter I have drawn a picture of the Lucknow that existed before the formation of this court and have presented to my readers the chequer-board upon which this court arranged its chessmen. In the next few chapters I shall describe the history of the rule of the family of Nishapur and will show the quality and nature of the culture that evolved around it.

3

Burhan ul Mulk, Safdar Jang and the Foundation of the Avadh Dynasty

The family of Navab Sadat Khan Burhan ul Mulk came to India in 1706 during the reign of Bahadur Shah,[105] in the person of one Mir Muhammad Nasir, a Saiyyid of Nishapur who traced his lineage back to Imam[106] Musa Kazim. His eldest son Mir Muhammad Baqir accompanied him and took a wife in India. Father and son lived under the protection of the Governor of Bengal at Azimabad, Patna. God granted Muhammad Baqir a son by his Indian wife; this son was later known as Sher Jang.

Two years after Mir Muhammad Nasir's arrival, his younger son Mir Muhammad Amin also came from Nishapur to India. When he arrived in Azimabad he heard that his father had died. The two brothers then went to Delhi where Mir Muhammad Amin was given the charge of the Prince's personal estate. He showed such efficiency and skill in this appointment that he became renowned in every quarter. Fortune favoured him and in a short time he became one of the honoured officials at the royal court. He then married the daughter of the Governor of Akbarabad[107] and so became numbered among that class of high nobles from whom choice was made for appointments involving the responsibilities of government.

In those days the Saiyyids of Baraha[108] had immense power in Delhi and even the Emperor went in fear of them. Muhammad Amin had them put to death and destroyed their power for ever. In battle he showed such valour that the Imperial Court gave him the rank of Haft Hazari, 'Commander of Seven Thousand'. In addition to being put in command of seven thousand cavalry, he was given the title of Burhan ul Mulk Bahadur Jang and was appointed Governor of Akbarabad. He was then made Superintendent of the Emperor's entourage, which was a post of great honour, and a short time later appointed Subedar of Avadh and Supervisor of the Imperial Artillery. He was an intelligent man with a particularly active mind and was extremely brave and valiant. With the Imperial Artillery under his control he had more power than anyone else in India.

At that time a landowner of Kara (in Allahabad District, U.P.), Bhagvat Singh, insubordinate towards the Government, had become a great nuisance. He had already killed several officers who had been sent to punish him. Eventually Burhan ul Mulk was given the task and advanced against him in a series of forced marches. Bhagvat Singh, with great cunning, surrounded his opponent's forces, and the struggle appeared to be going so badly for them that even the bravest trembled. However Burhan ul Mulk fought with great gallantry and the surrounding enemy was overcome with awe at the sight of his long, lustrous white beard. It was not long before Bhagvat Singh fell a victim to his bow and his forces fled the battlefield.

Burhan ul Mulk's next expedition was even more violent. In those days the Marathas had great power in India. They had forced the crowned head at Delhi into allowing them *chauth*,[109] one-fourth of the regular Government revenue, and even the bravest trembled at the sound of their name. Burhan ul Mulk led a strong army against them and inflicted such a defeat that they were thrown into confusion and fled precipitately, pursued by Burhan ul Mulk. All historical facts being considered, it is probable that if Burhan ul Mulk had not been forcibly stopped he would have advanced[110] and exterminated the Marathas. The influence of the Mughals, such as it had been in their early days, would have held sway over the length and breadth of India. But this unlucky and decaying government was doomed to come to an end and because of the intrigues of the court officials and the jealousies of those connected with the court, Burhan ul Mulk's advance was stopped.

This made him certain that there was now no sense in looking to the Emperor for his own well-being, and that the officials of the court were dishonest and self-seeking. He immediately made peace with the Marathas and resolved to take up residence in his own Province, separate himself completely from the court, and set himself the task of making his domain strong and well-organized. He realized that the Mughal Sultanate was not likely to revive and that it would be more sensible to live apart, leaving the court of Delhi to its fate.

As I have said, the Shaikhzadas had great power in Lucknow and, according to their custom, they tried to stop Burhan ul Mulk's entry into the town. But by exercising great cunning he got in without any bloodshed whatsoever. Two stories became current about his entry into Lucknow. One was that he advanced steadily until stopped at the Akbari Gate. Unlike all former Subedars he was an experienced and resourceful man, so he halted and encamped at Mahmud Nagar. A couple of days later he issued an invitation to the Shaikhzadas and entertained them with great courtesy and hospitality. Whilst the unthinking Shaikhzadas were enjoying the good things put before them, the Imperial Army was silently entering the market-place and advancing steadily until it reached the vicinity of Machi Bhavan.

The second story is that Muhammad Khan Bangash had told Burhan ul Mulk that the Shaikhzadas of Lucknow were very troublesome and it was difficult to get the better of them, but that the other Shaikhs in the neighbourhood were opposed to them and he should therefore enlist their help. So Burhan ul Mulk stopped at Kakori (near Lucknow), got the Kakori Shaikhs on his side and with their help and guidance he pushed forward. On hearing that he would meet opposition at Mahmud Nagar and at the Akbari Gate, he left the main road, went towards the west and crossed the river near Gao Ghat. He advanced cautiously on the far bank and fell upon Machi Bhavan. He took possession of the fort without any trouble.

When he was in possession of Machi Bhavan no one could stand up against him. All the notables of the Shaikhzada family came and humbly bowed before him. Burhan ul Mulk mounted an elephant, rode through the Shaikhan Gate and with his sword cut down that sword which had been the means of humiliation for great and valiant men. Then he said to the Shaikhzadas, 'Relinquish Machi Bhavan to me as my residence.' They tried to evade the issue but to no avail. Eventually they were given a week's notice to quit and in this period they removed as much of their property as they could; what remained fell into the hands of Burhan ul Mulk's soldiers.

Before going to live in the fort, he constructed a *naubat khana* [guard-house][111] near the place where he had camped. Drums were beaten in this guard-house six times a day up to the time when the court of Avadh ceased to exist.

After this Burhan ul Mulk went to Ajodhya and built a bungalow on the banks of the river as I have described (Chapter 1), but from time to time he would go to live in Lucknow, as this city was the seat of government of the Province. In his time several new quarters came into being as people began to construct houses for permanent residence. Most were sites of the camps of his Mughal army commanders—Saiyyid Husain Katra, Abu Turab Khan Katra, Khuda Yar Khan Katra, Katra Bizan Beg, Katra Wafa Beg Khan, Katra Muhammad Ali Khan, Maha Narain Park, Mali Khan Caravanserai and Ismail Ganj (which was east of Machi Bhavan and has now been demolished). All date from that time either as residential quarters or as cantonments of Burhan ul Mulk's army commanders.

Navab Burhan ul Mulk had lived for six years in Avadh and Lucknow when, in 1738, he was urgently summoned to Delhi on Nadir Shah's invasion.[112] He left his nephew and son-in-law, Safdar Jang, as his deputy in Lucknow, and the town was in no way affected by the events of those troubled times.

Nadir Shah had sacked Delhi and perpetrated a general massacre; he was still in the city when Navab Burhan ul Mulk died there. The Navab's nephew had a recommendation sent to Nadir Shah which advised that he, Sher Jang,[113] succeed the late Navab as Subedar of Avadh. However, Raja Lachman Narain,[114] who had been one of Burhan ul Mulk's trusted officers, presented a petition to Nadir to the following effect: 'Burhan ul Mulk was not pleased with Sher Jang, and gave his daughter in marriage not to him but to Safdar Jang who was acting as his deputy and is at the moment representing him in Lucknow. The Government is responsible for Burhan ul Mulk's assets and can bestow them on any-one it wishes because he has no heir.[115] I would also like to plead that Safdar Jang is sympathetic, pious, efficient, reliable and popular with the army. Apart from these matters, Burhan ul Mulk promised to pay His Majesty two *karor*[116] of rupees and Safdar Jang has made arrangements for this payment. The sum will be credited on demand. In view of these facts, I hope that Your Lordship will recommend him to the King.'

Directly he read the petition, Nadir Shah obtained from Muhammad Shah the khilat of Subedar for Safdar Jang and sent it to him in Avadh by the hand of one of his aides-de-camp, accompanied by a retinue of two hundred cavalry. On assuming the insignia of office, Safdar Jang sent the offering of two karor of rupees to Nadir Shah and commenced to rule his Province.

Safdar Jang's full name was Mirza Muqim Mansur Khan Safdar Jang. Although he did not possess the true valour, sincerity, honesty and energy of Burhan ul Mulk, he was very generous, resolute, sympathetic and considerate towards the people and a good administrator. He constructed Fort Jalalabad, three miles from the city, and also took the ancient building of Panj Mahla, situated inside Machi Bhavan, from the Shaikhzadas. In place of this he gave the Shaikhzadas seven hundred acres of land in two villages on the outskirts of Lucknow. Although this may have been tyrannous with regard to the Shaikh-zadas it had the advantage of dispersing the population of Lucknow. Safdar Jang rebuilt Machi Bhavan and had it put into very good order.

Safdar Jang had been in his Province for only five years when he was summoned to Delhi. He went there leaving Raja Niwal Rai as his deputy in Lucknow. Niwal Rai was scholarly, precise, energetic, brave and a very good organizer: to add to this, God had granted him the dignity and generosity of his master. He decided to build a bridge over the river opposite Machi Bhavan. Deep pits were dug for the foundations of the pillars of the bridge, but the erection of these had not commenced when at his master's command he had to lead an expedition against Ahmad Khan Bangash. He took a very strong force on this expedition but was himself killed and the bridge remained incomplete.

Ahmad Khan Bangash was the bravest man of his time; it needed a Burhan ul Mulk to oppose him and Safdar Jang could not possibly rival him in battle. The result was that Ahmad Khan's power and that of the Afghans, who were his allies, continued to increase. Safdar Jang did everything he possibly could and even got the Emperor to oppose him, but to no avail. At Ahmad's instigation, Hafiz Rahmat Khan started to pillage the cities and towns of Avadh and then besieged Khairabad. Ahmad Khan Bangash's son, Mahmud Khan, advanced with an army for the purpose of taking Lucknow.

In 1750 the Pathans established themselves at Malihabad, on the outskirts of Lucknow. One year later an intimate of Mahmud Khan led an army of twenty thousand men against Lucknow. They encamped near the town and Mahmud Khan sent one of his officers as *kotval* [magistrate][117] into the town. None of Safdar Jang's men were there however, and the few that had been there fled on hearing of the Pathans' arrival. The Pathan kotval then entered the town and trouble ensued.

The most important of the Shaikhzadas of Lucknow in those days was Shaikh Muiz ud Din. He went to see the Afghan commander outside the town.

At the very moment of their meeting someone complained to the commander that the people of the town were showing disdain for his officer and that no one would obey his orders. Shaikh Muiz ud Din said: 'How is it possible that anyone should be so impertinent? I will go back and punish the trouble-makers.' Saying this he returned, summoned his relatives and friends and said: 'One cannot trust these Pathans. It would be best if we joined up with Safdar Jang, attacked the Pathans and drove them out of here.' After this Shaikh Muiz ud Din sold his family jewels to raise an army, collected all the Shaikhzadas and attacked the kotval, who just escaped with his life. He then dressed up a Mughal in court uniform, settled him in his own house and issued a proclamation to the effect that Safdar Jang on his own initiative had sent this Mughal as City Magistrate. At the same time he erected a green standard[118] in the name of Ali and people came and collected beneath it.

On hearing this, the Pathans attacked and the Shaikhzadas opposed them with great fury, displaying all their former valour. The Pathans were no match for their onslaught and their army of fifteen thousand fled the battlefield. Having now found their opportunity, the Shaikhzadas drove all the Pathans out of the Province of Avadh.

Two years later peace was signed with Ahmad Khan Bangash and in 1753 Navab Safdar Jang returned to Lucknow and stayed at Mahdi Ghat. He built a special house for himself, decorated it and then set about reforming the army. But he did not have time to complete this work for in that very year, when he was encamped at Papar Ghat near Sultanpur (Faizabad District), he departed this life. His body was taken to the Gulab Bari[119] in Faizabad where it was interred. Soon afterwards the bones were removed and taken to Delhi for burial there. Over them a most imposing tomb[120] has been erected which travellers from all over the world look upon today with veneration.

4

Shuja ud Daula and Asaf ud Daula

In 1753 after the death of Safdar Jang Mansur Ali Khan, his son, Jalal ud Din Haidar, Shuja ud Daula, who has been mentioned earlier in this account, assumed the reins of government. He was restless, impulsive and an ambitious ruler, but unfortunately his régime came at a time of violent disturbances and momentous vicissitudes. Twice the fates of two historically powerful races and forces were decided before his eyes. First of all there was the shattering Battle of Panipat (1761), when on one side were ranged Ahmad Shah Durrani, Shuja ud Daula, Najib ud Daula[43] and all the mighty armies of the Khans of Ruhelkhand, and on the other, the huge hordes of the Marathas. After that came the terrific struggle at Baksar when the orderly British army opposed Shuja ud Daula's myriad forces. This battle took place four years after the engagement at Panipat, and in twenty-four hours it was settled that India would no longer be ruled by the Muslims but by the British.

Although Shuja ud Daula lived in Lucknow before these battles he did not have the time—because of important expeditions, political problems and the carrying out of army reforms—to pay attention to the betterment and embellishment of the town. He erected forts, put up defence works and collected military equipment, but did not have the opportunity to put his own house in order or to beautify his town. After the Battle of Baksar he took up residence in Faizabad and so Lucknow was deprived of the benefit of his presence. In 1774 he died and was succeeded by Navab Asaf ud Daula.

Directly Asaf ud Daula assumed the rulership he quarrelled with his mother and went to Lucknow. It was then that the administrative authority of the court of Avadh started to decline and the visible splendour of Lucknow began to increase.

After having won the Battle of Baksar, the British, by insinuating themselves into the court, acquired a number of rights and privileges. A spoke was thus put into the wheel of army progress and careful watch was kept to see that the government of Avadh did not acquire sufficient strength to oppose the British army. Even so, whilst Shuja ud Daula was alive, he was engaged in army reform and spent night and day planning means whereby he might increase his strength. This is borne out by Munshi Faiz Baksh who in his history, *Farah Baksh*,[14] describes what he saw at first hand: 'from the point of view of rapid loading and firing, the muskets of the British could not in any way compare with those of Shuja ud Daula's forces.'

But with Asaf ud Daula's accession the situation changed. The British, with great intelligence, increased the influence they had already gained and with much wisdom persuaded Asaf ud Daula to pay no attention to army reform and to amuse himself with other things. He himself was not particularly interested in the army; what he wanted was money to squander in giving free scope to his pleasures and this could not be obtained without curtailing the army. For this reason he maintained a small army, having dismissed the rest to embark on a life of debauchery. He was an obedient ally[123] to his Western friends, acted on their advice, and would not listen to anyone who opposed it. As a reward for his friendship and loyalty, the British added Ruhelkhand[124] to his domain and when he solicited their help in persecuting and robbing his mother,[125] Bahu Begam, they very generously gave him their moral support and took his side. In spite of this, during his rulership it was scarcely perceptible either to him or to the people of Lucknow that an external power could interfere in their domestic administration. The principal reason for this was that Asaf ud Daula's public munificence and love of luxury encouraged everyone to lead a life of self-indulgence and frivolity. No one considered it necessary to give a thought to the outcome of this mode of living.

Outwardly the court of Lucknow became so magnificent that no other court could rival it and the town of Lucknow acquired great splendour. The money which Shuja ud Daula had spent on the army and on provision for war, Asaf ud Daula started to spend in satisfying his desire for voluptuous living and on the embellishment and comforts of the town. In a short time he had collected to

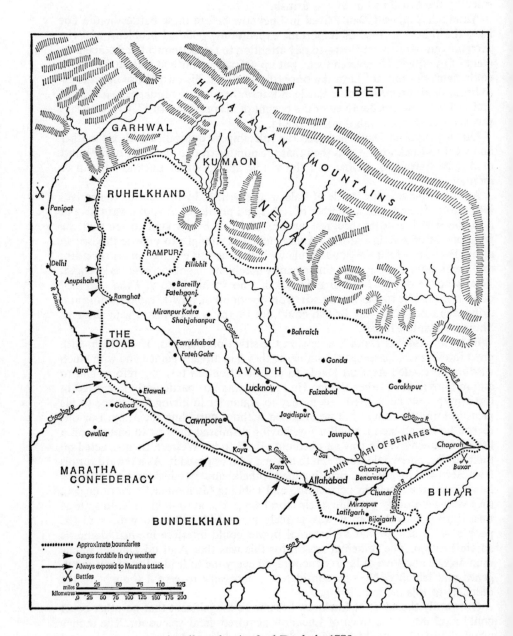

Avadh under Asaf ud Daula in 1775

himself all the pomp and splendour that could be found in the world. His one desire was to surpass the Nizam of Hyderabad[42] and Tipu Sultan[126] and his ambition was that the magnificence and grandeur of no court should equal that of his own.

He showed such zeal and eagerness on the occasion of the marriage of his son, Wazir Ali Khan, that the glitter and magnificence of the bridegroom's procession surpassed any ceremonial that has been recorded in the annals of history. There were twelve hundred elephants in the procession and the bridegroom wore a royal robe on to which had been stitched jewels worth twenty lakhs of rupees. For the reception two elaborate tents were constructed, each sixty feet wide, two hundred feet long and twenty feet high: they were made of such fine, exquisite and expensive cloth that their construction alone had cost the government ten lakhs of rupees.

To the west of Machi Bhavan on the banks of a river, Asaf ud Daula built Daulat Khana[127] as a residence for himself, the Rumi Darvaza [Gate][128] and his incomparable Imam Bara.[129] In 1784 there was a famine in Avadh and even the well-to-do of the town were starving. At that difficult time, the work of building the Imam Bara was started in order to alleviate the sufferings of the population. As the better class people considered it beneath their dignity to work as labourers, the construction was carried on by night, as well as by day, and the impoverished and starving gentry of the town came in the darkness of the night to join with the labourers and work with the aid of torches. The Navab had entered upon the construction of the building from sincere religious motives and, in the same way, the people threw themselves into the work with immense energy and feeling. The result was the creation of an edifice of the most imposing grandeur and matchless character, the like of which could be found nowhere else. Famous engineers and architects had been enlisted to draw up the plans. They all made every effort to ensure that their designs should be better than other proposed designs. The design of the inimitable architect Kifayat Ullah was eventually approved and construction commenced in accordance with it. The building, which is one hundred and sixty-four feet long and fifty-two feet wide, is constructed of brick and very high quality limestone. From floor to ceiling there is no sign of wood. This building is nothing like the Mughal Emperor's stone buildings, for in Lucknow large amounts of marble were not obtainable. But the Imam Bara and Asaf ud Daula's other buildings have a rare beauty and great dignity and distinction.[130] The arched roof of the Imam Bara, which is built without a single beam, is the largest of its kind in the world and the workmanship therefore is counted as one of the world's wonders.[131]

Asaf ud Daula's buildings are in no way influenced by European architecture. In style they are purely Asiatic, without ostentation but with genuine splendour and dignity. Subsequently to Asaf ud Daula's time these buildings were neglected and following the Mutiny the British took possession of them. They demolished the surrounding houses and, except for the side which faced the river, reduced the other three sides to an open plain. They made the Imam Bara into a fort, the gate to which was the Rumi Gate. In the days in which British soldiers lived in the Imam Bara, its great hall was an armoury and heavy guns used to be moved about on the floor. But in spite of this there was never a sign of indentation on the floor and the doors and walls remained intact. Eventually the British Government left the Imam Bara and returned it to the Muslims. In its mosque a *mujtahid*[132] still leads the prayers and Muharram is observed in the Imam Bara itself.

The strength of Asaf ud Daula's edifices can be judged from the fact that although they were built over one hundred and twenty-five years[133] ago they still maintain their original dignity and splendour. Not one brick has become displaced nor has any plaster come away from the bricks. In comparison, the buildings which were constructed by later rulers of Avadh at the cost of millions of rupees are extremely weak, in addition to revealing the decline in national style. If they had not been repaired from time to time they would have long since disappeared.

Asaf ud Daula lived in the Daulat Khana near Machi Bhavan and the Imam Bara. In order to indulge in his pleasures and be far from crowds and worldly affairs he had Bibapur Palace built outside the town on the far side of the river and he usually lived there. Similarly, he built a very elegant and beautiful residence at Chunhat (about eight miles from Lucknow), and in Lucknow itself set up kiosks in Char Bagh and Aish Bagh and erected stables at Yahya Ganj[94] and in its neighbourhood. The Wazir Ganj was then established which, as the residence of Asaf ud Daula's son Wazir Ali Khan, is remembered in his name.

Lucknow had now become the established residence of the Governor and ruler, and ordinary people drifted towards it. Those who had settled in Faizabad in Shuja ud Daula's time left and moved to Lucknow. People from Delhi bade farewell to their birthplace, came to Lucknow and stayed there permanently. There was such a large increase in population that several new quarters were established. For example, there were Amani Ganj, Fateh Ganj, Rakab Ganj, Nakhas,[134] Daulat Ganj, Begam Ganj, Navab Ganj, the Khansama Enclosure (established by one of Asaf ud Daula's household superintendents, to which the former was invited for the opening ceremony), Tikait Ganj, Tikait Rai's Bazaar (ascribed to the Vazir[135] Maharaja Tikait Rai), Tirmani Ganj, Tikri or Tikli, Husain ud Din Khan Cantonment, Hasan Ganj, Baoli, Bhavani Ganj, Balak Ganj and Kashmiri Mahalla.[136] Other quarters were the Surat Singh Enclosure, Navab Ganj, Tahsin Ganj, Khuda Ganj, Nagariya (of which Asaf ud Daula's mother Bahu Begam laid the foundation on the same day as she laid the foundation of Ali Ganj, on the other side of the river), Ambar Ganj, Mahbub Ganj, the Tup Gate, Khayali Ganj and the Jhau Lal Bridge; the founder of these latter two quarters was Raja Jhau Lal who was Vazir-e-Maliat [Minister of the Treasury] in Avadh. All these quarters were established and constructed in the days of Asaf ud Daula. At the same time, Hasan Raza Khan established Hasan Ganj on the other side of the river.

Navab Asaf ud Daula was renowned for his liberality. His bounty was the subject of conversation in cities far and near and his name was everywhere spoken with honour and affection. All his natural faults were effaced under the cover of his generosity. In the opinion of the public he appeared not as a dissolute ruler, but as a selfless and saintly guardian. Until this very day Hindu shopkeepers, on waking in the morning, express the sincerity of their faith in him by saying: 'Hail to thee Asaf ud Daula, our guardian.'

An extremely wealthy French merchant named General Claude Martin[137] was living in Lucknow. He had prepared plans for an exceedingly magnificent house and put them before Asaf ud Daula for his inspection. The Navab was so pleased with these plans that he agreed to buy them for ten lakhs of gold coin. The transaction had not been completed when Navab Asaf ud Daula departed this life and the actual construction of the house had not been finished when Monsieur Martin himself passed away. As he had no heirs and died leaving an immense fortune, he made a covenant on his death-bed according to which he would be buried in the house so that no ruler of Avadh would be able to confiscate it after Martin's death. He called the building 'Constantia', but nowadays it is known to the public as 'Markin Sahib's[138] Kothi',[139] and it is well worth seeing. He was buried in it when he died. The college which he founded is still in existence and many pupils are given food and clothing there as well as instruction. I understand that Monsieur Martin did not leave the school or any scholarships connected with it to persons of any particular race or creed, but stated in his will that Christians, Hindus and Muslims should all benefit equally from it. Now however the school is restricted to European children. It is impossible for Indians to receive scholarships, nor can they even be admitted for education. Perhaps the reason is that at the time of the Mutiny ignorant and hot-headed insurgents dug up Monsieur Martin's grave, removed the bones and scattered them about. After the British had gained control they by chance found one bone which they reburied in the original spot. But ordinary Indians cannot be held responsible for the acts of these insurgents.

In 1798 on the death of Asaf ud Daula, Navab Wazir Ali Khan, the lavishness of whose wedding I have described, assumed the rulership. But in the space of four months he evinced such improper and shocking behaviour that most people became disgusted with him. Bahu Begam herself preferred her stepson Yamin ud Daula Navab Sadat Ali Khan to him and rumours also became current that Wazir Ali Khan was not the son of Asaf ud Daula, whom many thought impotent from birth.

Navab Sadat Ali Khan had been opposed to Asaf ud Daula and during the latter's rule he had had to live outside his domain. He lived for some time in Calcutta and for a long period in Benares. When these feelings about Wazir Ali Khan became widespread, Navab Sadat Ali Khan was chosen as his successor and brought from Benares. The Governor-General himself held a *darbar*[140] at Bibapur Palace where he deposed Wazir Ali Khan and settled Sadat Ali Khan's accession. Wazir Ali Khan was immediately arrested and sent to Benares where he flew into a rage and murdered the Resident, Mr Cherry.[141] In punishment for this crime he was sent to Chunar Garh where he died.[142] A lengthy story of his distress and troubles[143] is well known, although it is not possible to include it in this brief narrative.

5

Sadat Ali Khan and Ghazi ud Din Haidar

Navab Sadat Ali Khan, on assuming the rulership in 1798, presented half his domain to the British. It is well known that he despaired of ever ruling and was living in Benares without hope when news reached him of Asaf ud Daula's death and the succession of Wazir Ali Khan. When he heard this, whatever hopes of ruling he had entertained were completely destroyed. He was in this state of despair when a British official of Benares came and asked him, 'Navab Sahib! If you were made ruler of Avadh, what would you give the British Government?' One does not set much store by what one has lost, so he said without thinking, 'I would give half my country to the British.' Hearing this promise the official said, 'Be of good cheer, I will give you the welcome news that you have been chosen ruler of Lucknow.' Sadat Ali Khan was certainly overjoyed by these unexpected glad tidings but when he thought of his promise he was filled with consternation. Later when he became ruler he fulfilled his promise by giving up half his country, but this rankled in his mind to the end of his days.

There is no mention in English histories of this promise having been taken from him but everyone agrees that in gratitude to the British for giving him the rulership, Sadat Ali Khan ceded half his domain to them.[144] However this may be, when Sadat Ali Khan acceded, only half of Avadh was left under his control. It is well known to the older inhabitants of Lucknow that because of worry on this account he practised excessive economies, and by showing great competence and intelligence in collecting revenue he amassed between twenty-two and twenty-three karor of rupees.

He corresponded with the British Government in England and arranged that the British Government of India should be transferred on contract[145] from the East India Company into his hands. This agreement was about to be finalized when his brother-in-law, who was involved in a plot,[146] poisoned him. As the adage says, 'When the cup is broken, the wine-bearer is no more.'[147]

This incident and scores of others of a similar nature were common knowledge, although based on nothing except rumour and hearsay. There is, however, no doubt that Sadat Ali Khan possessed such sagacity and administrative ability that a ruler of his nature would not readily have given away any part of his domain. From his actions and policies it was clear that he was going to take some important step and that his designs were very far-reaching indeed. The greatest difficulty was that his income was reduced by half; a further embarrassment was that the late Asaf ud Daula had spent money in excess of revenue. As a consequence he had to cut the expenses of court, which was no easy matter. In his efforts to economize he checked accounts and attended to the smallest details. He scrutinized rent-free lands and government grants with the utmost severity and reduced court expenditure wherever possible. In short, by courting disfavour and imposing great hardships on the people, he increased the government's revenue and reduced expenditure.

Intelligent and fair-minded people, on seeing these operations, welcomed Sadat Ali Khan's competence and approved of his planning, but immense discontent spread among the general public. People who had enjoyed rent-free lands and government grants and whose estates had been confiscated complained and those employees who had been dismissed wandered about bemoaning their fate. This was not all, for there were a great number of people in the country who supported Wazir Ali Khan and thought him the rightful and legitimate successor and considered Sadat Ali Khan to be a usurper. In short thousands of enemies threatened his life.

In addition to the people, the army was also exceedingly discontented with the new Navab. The hordes of soldiery established under Shuja ud Daula had begun to be reduced on the advice of the British Government when Asaf ud Daula was the ruler, but the latter's liberality and extravagances kept the men happy and scarcely a word of complaint was heard. When Sadat Ali Khan made further reductions[148] feeling against him increased.

The result was that the British Government thought it essential that a guard of regular British troops should be stationed in Lucknow to safeguard his life. It was also extremely necessary to maintain a powerful force of foreign troops continuously in the town to punish mischief-makers and insurgents and to maintain peace and security. It is said that Sadat Ali Khan agreed to this with extreme reluctance.

In former times the rulers of Avadh had lived very quietly. The first three, that is Navab Burhan ul Mulk, Navab Safdar Jang and Navab Shuja ud Daula, lived in simple houses which did not even belong to them but were rented. They considered their real residence to be either the battlefield or the whole domain which they continuously toured, looking upon all the land they possessed as their homestead. Navab Asaf ud Daula, although he was very wasteful and was in disrepute because of his debauchery and extravagance, contented himself with a simple, old-fashioned residence, the Panj Mahla. This was despite the fact that he took a great interest in building and spent twenty lakhs of rupees on an Imam Bara and a mosque and more money on the Chauk market-place, various bazaars and shopping centres, bridges and rest-houses.

In short, whereas the first three rulers' interests were confined to the building of fortresses and ramparts and to acquiring military equipment, Asaf ud Daula's interests lay in constructing religious edifices and helping the common people. Asaf ud Daula kept up the old style of architecture and his buildings are fine examples of this old architecture.

In Delhi and Agra, Emperor Shahjahan had obtained alabaster and red stone from nearby quarries which gave to the buildings a special delicacy and grandeur. It was impossible to obtain stone in Lucknow and it was very difficult to transport it from Agra and Jaipur. But Asaf ud Daula produced an equal show of splendour with the bricks and mortar that he used.

Although Sadat Ali Khan was frugal, economical and eager to amass money, he was still interested in building. Unfortunately, having lived in Calcutta and

Benares he had been introduced to a variety of architectural styles, and his taste had become so vitiated that buildings constructed in his time are devoid of the old flavour. From his time there was a change in Lucknow's architectural style. Another reason for this change was that General Martin had built one or two houses in his own style in Lucknow which, though comfortable and attractive-looking, from the point of view of strength were poor. Martin's buildings were just like toys which are easily broken and replaced. Europeans remarked that the architectural style of Avadh after Asaf ud Daula was completely vulgar and that all the buildings were like boys' toys or girls' dolls' houses. They did not consider, however, who had caused this deterioration. They said that local style was ruined because it had no strong tradition, but no one gave a thought as to who had ruined it. 'O morning breeze. All this has been brought about by thee.'[147]

Sadat Ali Khan first bought a house, Farhat Baksh,[149] 'Pleasure-Giving', for fifty thousand rupees from General Martin. While living there he had several houses built nearby. Then in the neighbourhood he constructed Tehri Kothi, 'The Crooked House', for the Resident to live in,[84] the ruins of which are in the Residency grounds. After this he built Lal Barah Dari[150] for his court; this is now a library and in those days was known as the Royal Palace. In addition to this he built a new kothi on the other side of the river, called Dil Aram, 'Heart's Repose'. On a high hill, which is now the military cantonment and from where a view of the river and all the country surrounding the town can be had, he erected a beautiful house and called it Dil Kusha,[151] 'Pleasing to the Heart'. He built another kothi called Hayat Baksh, 'Life Giving', but after Sadat Ali Khan no other rulers of Avadh lived in it. Before the Mutiny, Major Milbank[152] and afterwards the high official who was appointed by the British Government as Chief Commissioner[153] of Lucknow, used parts of it as a residence.

In addition to these houses the Navab constructed the celebrated buildings Munavar Baksh, 'Light Giving', Khurshid Manzil[154] and the Chaupar stables. In all these houses the local style of architecture was abandoned and European innovations were adopted. The older houses in Lucknow were not able to rival the new and splendid edifices which had been built and are still being built in various towns in India by the British Government. In short, at this time the old architectural style came to an end in Lucknow.

Navab Sadat Ali Khan erected the large Alam Ganj market to the west of Lucknow and made special arrangements for its population and prosperity. Specific laws were framed in regard to its administration and merchants and shopkeepers were given particular rights. This market flourished and continues to do so to this day. Although it is at a distance and completely separated from the city, it is the most important market for a wide variety of commodities and because of it the Alam Nagar station daily increases in importance.

In addition, Sadat Ganj and other large markets were established during the reign of this Navab, including Rakab Ganj (the largest market for iron, important also for its grain and other commodities), Jangli Ganj, Maqbul Ganj, Gola Ganj and Rastogi[155] Mahalla. Inside the Moti Mahal compound, a building was constructed under the orders of Navab Sadat Ali Khan. This building is to the north of the present Moti Mahal enclosure and has a very beautiful white dome into which craftsmen introduced the sheen and lustre of pearl.[156]

Sadat Ali Khan was the most intelligent of the rulers of Avadh and its best administrator. At the same time he can be considered thrifty, parsimonious and even miserly. He administered the country with extraordinary sagacity and competence and there is not the slightest doubt that if he had had a free hand he eventually would have put to rights the former maladministration, removed the old evils and completely reformed Avadh. But the trouble was that his relations with the East India Company were not good; he was disillusioned[157] with his rule as he had been forced to hand over more than half of his domain to the all-powerful British Government. He had thought that he would be able to rule over the territory which remained in his possession without interference. Unfortunately, he was not left in peace even then. British army camps had been set up in various parts of Avadh that remained in his hands and many British troops were stationed in Lucknow and its neighbourhood. The troops were difficult to control and their large numbers greatly burdened the government of Avadh. To offset this, Sadat Ali Khan had to make large reductions in his own forces.

In spite of these worries and anxieties he carried out some most praiseworthy reforms. However, the most extraordinary thing about this period is that in addition to prosperity in the markets and a rise in trade, there were more eminent and distinguished persons at this court than could be seen in any other court in India.

Such individuals normally congregate in places where the person in authority has evinced more than the usual generosity but, as I have said, Sadat Ali Khan was thrifty and even miserly. However, his own efficiency caused him to acknowledge competence in others and because of this he was wont to extol the merits of capable people. The result was that Lucknow became the rendezvous for more distinguished people than ever before. Any talented person, wherever he lived, on hearing of Sadat Ali Khan's appreciation of merit, left his own town for Lucknow where he lived in such ease that he never thought of returning home.

In 1814 Navab Sadat Ali Khan departed this life and was succeeded by his son Ghazi ud Din Haidar. The tombs of Sadat Ali Khan and his wife Murshid Zadi[158] are within the rectangular structure of Qaisar Bagh. In the place where these tombs are situated there used to be a house in which Ghazi ud Din Haidar lived while he was heir apparent. Immediately after his father's death he went to the royal palace and said, 'I have taken my father's house, so I must give him mine.' Therefore, he had his father's body buried in his house, then demolished the old house itself and had these tombs erected.

Ghazi ud Din Haidar showed no signs of his father's intelligence and appreciation of the value of money, nor had he the interest of the former rulers in the army. To be true, there was certainly the same indolence and sensuality as in the time of Asaf ud Daula, but the difference was that whereas Asaf ud Daula's extravagances had been for the benefit of the country and the people, now there was nothing but self-indulgence.

Ghazi ud Din Haidar had received the karor of rupees[159] which his father had amassed in the treasury and this now began to be dissipated to satisfy his royal desires.

I have described how Sadat Ali Khan had a house constructed on the northern side of Moti Mahal. Ghazi ud Din Haidar had two other houses built within the enclosure and these were called Mubarak Manzil and Shah Manzil.[160] Near Shah Manzil there was a bridge of boats and Mubarak Manzil lay back from it to the east. Facing Shah Manzil on the other side of the river was a park known as Hazari Bagh where for miles there stretched pleasing, verdant pastures in which elephants, rhinoceroses and wild beasts of prey were often made to fight each other. The ruler used to honour Shah Manzil with his presence and watch the fights across the river. Fights between tigers also took place and strong palisades and a stout enclosure had been erected for these. When fights were arranged between small and harmless animals, they would take place in the Shah Manzil enclosure itself.

The sport of making beasts of prey and wild animals fight each other had not been heard of before in Lucknow. It seems as if Ghazi ud Din Haidar had acquired a predilection for it from learning about the Roman amphitheatre from Residents and other Europeans who came to court. However, I understand from Maulana Habib ur Rahman Sherwani[161] that fights between beasts of prey had been customary under the Mughal Emperors.

Ghazi ud Din Haidar had a European-style house built for one of his wives who was a European and named it Vilayati [European] Bagh, and near it he constructed the edifice Qadam Rasul.[162]

In accordance with Ghazi ud Din Haidar's wishes, the British Government bestowed on him the title of King. Before then the rulers of Avadh had held the rank of Vazir,[135] and were given no honorific title except that of Navab. The country had been divided among independent and absolute rulers and until this moment only the Mughals in Delhi had been called emperors or kings even though their empire was confined to Delhi itself and the land surrounding it. Except for those who sat on the throne in Delhi no one in India had the right to be called king and to bestow titles upon people. It was to hurt the pride of the Delhi kings that the East India Company conferred the title of King on Ghazi[163] ud Din Haidar, who had loaned the British much of his father's wealth.[164] The court of Avadh greatly appreciated this honour and from that time on the rulers of Avadh, who were puppets in the hands of the Resident, were classed as kings. This continued to be a source of pride to them until the death of the last ruler, Wajid Ali Shah.

Ghazi ud Din Haidar, to commemorate the title of King, established a new market on the other side of the river opposite Machi Bhavan and called it Badshah Ganj. At the same time Hakim Mahdi established Mahdi Ganj. Because the royal residence of the Vazir Agha Mir stretched so far, the threshold of the Agha Mir Quarter was established right in the centre of the town and at the same time the Agha Mir Caravanserai was built.

Royalty, and especially queens, showed great enthusiasm for religion. From the days of the Safavi dynasty[165] the religion of Persia had been that of the Asna Ashari Shia[166] sect of Islam, but most of the Muslims in India were Sunnis.[167] As Navab Burhan ul Mulk had recently come from Persia, his sect and that of his family was Shia. In spite of this, for a time in Lucknow the government followed the old practices which had prevailed in India since the start of Muslim rule. But from Ghazi ud Din Haidar's time, owing to the religious fervour of the King and his household, the Shia faith became an important element in the Lucknow government. The ruler disregarded the religious heads of the Firangi

Mahal, and the family of Shia priests,[168] who had gained ascendancy, established a close contact with the court.

It would not have mattered so much if the Shia faith had been left in its true form. The trouble was that because of the Queen's strange and autocratic religious fervour, various heresies were introduced. These not only gave rise to all kinds of childish squabbles among rulers and nobles but also made the Shia practices of Lucknow distinct from the Shia faith in the rest of the world.

First of all the Queen arranged for *chhati*,[169] the sixth day after the birth ceremony, to be celebrated in honour of the Present Imam.[106] No harm would have been done if particulars of the esteemed Imam had been recounted and religious merit thus obtained. But no, the whole lying-in room was reproduced as in the case of the Hindu Janam Ashtmi[170] ceremony. In addition to this the beautiful daughters of Saiyyids were taken and made the imaginary wives of the twelve Imams and were called the 'undefiled'. Because they were the wives of Imams, Imams had to be born to them and the birth ceremonies of the twelve Imams were celebrated with great pomp and solemnity.

Ghazi ud Din Haidar was an extremely irritable and bad-tempered king and inspired much awe but his relations with the British were good. Vazir Agha Mir gained great influence at court and even the Queen and the heir apparent were not free from his molestations. Ghazi ud Din Haidar would strike and kick him. He accepted these blows with pleasure and in return would take his revenge on favourites of the court and friends of the royal family.

This first king of Avadh, because of his faith and religious fervour, reproduced on the banks of the river near Moti Mahal a sacred Najaf,[171] a holy mausoleum, to be a copy of Ali's burial place. He gave the British a large sum of money for its embellishment, lights and maintenance[172] and for this reason it is today in excellent condition and an object of splendour. When he died in 1827 he was buried in this mausoleum.

6

Nasir ud Din Haidar and Muhammad Ali Shah

In 1827 Ghazi ud Din Haidar's son, Nasir ud Din Haidar, ascended the throne. As I have described, from the time of Ghazi ud Din Haidar, the rulers of Avadh ceased to be navabs and became kings. At first, ministerial rank from Delhi had been the status of the administrators of Avadh and influential rulers had been called 'Navab Vazir'. Now, however, when they had no influence at all, they had become kings.

One would have imagined that in conferring the honour of royalty on these rulers of Avadh, the British would have helped them to increase their authority and would have made them kings in reality and not in name only. But no, it seems that at that time they had no power whatsoever outside the confines of Avadh and even in their own domain they were not as free as their predecessors. No one could succeed to the throne without British consent and British troops were quartered throughout the country. No important matter could be settled without the intervention of the Resident. The royal throne was a stage where it appeared as if the actors were responsible for whatever happened but where in reality their actions were determined by another, more powerful personage hidden in the wings.

But God in his mercy decreed that the later rulers of Avadh and almost everyone connected with them at the seat of government had lost all sense of reality and because of this did not realize the weakness of their position. Directly Ghazi ud Din Haidar became king he plunged into a life of dissipation and now Nasir ud Din Haidar was heir to the throne. Of the wealth amassed by Sadat Ali Khan, some went to prolong their debauchery and to assist in their lives of luxury, some was given to the British as a loan, some was spent on those new practices which the King and his Queens created with great assiduity according to their inclinations, and the rest was squandered in needless extravagance and intemperance. At least Ghazi ud Din Haidar reproduced Shah Najaf and destined it for his place of burial. Without relying on his heirs, he handed over some money to the British so that they could maintain Shah Najaf on the interest which would accrue. As a result lamps are lit on his tomb to this day, people assemble, passages[173] are read from the Quran and the place is beautifully illuminated during Muharram, thus providing employment for the poor and needy. But there was not much divine guidance to set against Nasir ud Din's excessive debauchery. He reproduced a Kerbala[174] on the far side of the river in Iradat Nagar which was destined to be his place of burial, but since he did not pay the slightest attention to its upkeep, it is now a piece of derelict waste land near Dali Ganj railway-station and it is unlikely that anyone ever lights a lamp there. In his time the new quarters of Ganesh Ganj and Chand Ganj were established in this neighbourhood on the far side of the river.

Nasir ud Din Haidar believed in astrology. He studied the science of astronomy and decided to set up an observatory in the city. For this purpose he had a house constructed between the tomb of Sadat Ali Khan and Moti Mahal which was known as Tarunvali Kothi,[175] 'The House of Stars'. It housed some very large telescopes and exceptionally good astronomical instruments. Their proper maintenance, organization and supervision was entrusted to Colonel Wilcox, who was a skilled astronomer.

The reign of Nasir ud Din Haidar commenced in 1827 and the observatory was probably established four or five years later. From that time until his death in 1847, when the last king of Avadh, Wajid Ali Shah, came to the throne, the observatory remained under the colonel's supervision. No other astronomer was appointed in his place and Wajid Ali Shah showed no interest in the observatory. I have heard some reliable Lucknow people say that Wajid Ali Shah considered the biggest telescope a toy and gave it to a courtesan named Haideri. However, one understands from the *Gazetteer*[176] that the observatory was in existence until the fall of the Avadh monarchy. It was probably destroyed by insurgents during the Mutiny since Ahmad ullah Shah, who was also known as Danka Shah and who evinced a great zeal and ardour in fighting the British army, used Tarunvali Kothi as his residence. He had his headquarters in the house and officers of the insurgents used to meet there.

At that time Raushan ud Daula, who was Vazir, had his magnificent house built. It is now the court of the Deputy Commissioner because it was confiscated by Wajid Ali Shah when he was constructing Qaisar Bagh, and when the British took over the territory it was already Government property.

Nasir ud Din Haidar's reign was really a period of danger. There was maladministration[177] in the country. The King was never free from his debaucheries and his invented religious rites. The administration of the kingdom was left in the hands of a Vazir but none could be found to direct the affairs of state in good faith or with sound policy. First Hakim Mahdi was summoned to the post. He was an excellent administratoɩ but his one desire was to increase his own wealth. After him, Raushan ud Daula became Vazir. He had neither ability nor wits and was incapable of accomplishing anything. Because of the King's excessive extravagance all Sadat Ali Khan's amassed wealth had vanished and the country's income was insufficient to cover the expenses of the palace. To crown everything, quarrels started between the King and his mother, Ghazi ud Din Haidar's chief consort. She said that Munna Jan was the King's son but the King refused to acknowledge[178] the fact. Such incidents created a state of affairs in which it appeared that the rulers were totally unfit to govern or to exercise any control over the country.

The Resident and Governor-General of India on various occasions admonished the King and warned him of the consequences, but to no avail.[177] Nasir ud Din Haidar, through living continuously with women, had become so effeminate that he spoke like a woman and dressed like a woman. This, combined with his religious ardour, made him revive and exaggerate the ceremonies initiated by his mother in connection with the imaginary wives of the twelve Imams and of the births of the Imams themselves. These exaggerations were carried to such an extent that in the ceremonies in connection with the births of the Imams, he himself played the part of a pregnant woman, sat in the lying-in room and by his demeanour and actions portrayed the pain of childbirth. He then gave birth to an imaginary child for whom the ceremonies of the sixth day after birth and the ablutions were observed in the usual way. There were so many of these ceremonies that the King was never free from them throughout the year. Who was to look after the kingdom?

When one considers the relations between the court of Avadh and the British Government, it seems likely that if the Governor-General and Residents had not shown their favour and had the Board which supervised the East India Company in London not restrained it, the monarchy would have ended at that time. But this childish court remained in existence as the British wavered in their intention to take over the territory.

Older residents of Lucknow assert that Nasir ud Din Haidar, in addition to his effeminate and puerile behaviour, was also extremely tyrannical and that because he spent the whole of his time with women the objects of his tyranny were mostly women. He immured scores of women for the smallest faults or merely on suspicion. They say that once when he saw a man in the street touching a woman's breasts, he had the woman's breasts and the man's hands cut off.

At last after ten years of this injustice and confusion, when the courtiers had reached a state of desperation, the King himself became a prey to his friends and favourites and in 1837 he was poisoned, thus putting an end to the whole sorry story. Nasir ud Din Haidar died without offspring and Ghazi ud Din Haidar's queen, Badsha Begam,[169] put forward Munna Jan, whom she had always considered to be her grandson and heir to the throne. Both Ghazi ud Din Haidar and Nasir ud Din Haidar had refused to acknowledge[178] him as belonging to the royal family. Accordingly the British Government had arranged for the accession of the late Navab Sadat Ali Khan's son, Nasir ud Daula Muhammad Ali Khan. However the Begam would not agree and brought Munna Jan to Lal Barah Dari, the throne-room.[150] The Resident tried his best to stop her and argued with her but she would not listen and forcibly placed Munna Jan upon the throne. As soon as he ascended the throne he accepted gifts of homage and then started to take revenge on his enemies. The houses of many were plundered, others were imprisoned or killed and the town became the scene of tumult and uproar.

The Resident and his assistant hurried to the court and emphasized to the Begam that Munna Jan could not be considered as an heir and that she would never be successful in her efforts. Then they showed her a written decree from the Governor-General and said, 'It would be best if Munna Jan were to vacate the throne and action were taken for the accession of Nasir ud Daula.' But no one listened and moreover somebody attacked the Assistant Resident, leaving him streaming with blood. The Resident had beforehand summoned British troops from the cantonment in Mandyaon. They had set up guns outside the throne-room and the troops were drawn up in readiness. There was nothing left for the Resident but to take his watch in his hand and say, 'I will give you ten minutes. If within that time Munna Jan does not vacate the throne, I will have to use force.' No one paid any attention although the Resident continued to warn: 'Now five minutes are left . . . now only three minutes . . . please note there is less than one minute left . . .'

No one paid any heed to these warnings. Then the guns started to roar and thirty or forty people fell. The bewildered courtiers started to flee. Several of the dancing troupe who had remained behind were wounded. Glass was shattered all around. When several of the loyal and gallant people who were shielding him had been killed, Munna Jan stumbled from his throne intending to escape, but was seized.

The British arrested both the Begam and Munna Jan and at the same time arranged for Nasir ud Daula's succession. He was installed as King of Avadh with the title of Muhammad Ali Shah. Munna Jan and his grandmother were sent under guard from Lucknow to Kanpur and from there to Chunar Garh[179] Fort. A monthly allowance of 2,400 rupees was allotted them from the Lucknow treasury.

Muhammad Ali Shah was sixty-three years of age when he ascended the throne. He was an experienced man who had known good and bad fortune and who had watched the childish antics of the court. Above all he was the son of Navab Sadat Ali Khan and had seen with his own eyes what his father had accomplished.

He proceeded very carefully, started to economize and as far as possible made efforts to set right the administration, but he was getting on in years. Directly he became king he sent for Hakim Mahdi from Farrukhabad and conferred on him the khilat of Vazir. When Hakim Mahdi died a few days later Zahir ud Daula was appointed Vazir; but after two or three months he died as well. The post was then given to Munavar ud Daula who a few months later resigned and went to Kerbala. After that Ashraf ud Daula Muhammad Ibrahim Khan was appointed Vazir and proved himself more intelligent and vigorous than his predecessors.

When Muhammad Ali Shah came to the throne a new treaty[180] was signed between the British Government and the Kingdom of Avadh. Under it, the forces which the British Government had appointed for the supervision of Avadh were increased and the governing body of the East India Company was given authority to hold under its jurisdiction, for as long as it liked, the whole region of Avadh or any part of it which was badly administered. The King signed this treaty reluctantly and set to work to reform the country to the best of his ability.

In the second year of his rule he started to construct his famous Imam Bara,[181] Husainabad, and near it an imposing mosque. For this mosque preparations were made to ensure that it should be more magnificent and greater in size than the Jamey Masjid[182] mosque in Delhi.

In those days the population and splendour of Lucknow increased to such an extent that it would not be out of place to call it the Babylon of India. In fact the status of the town at this time was that of a living Babylon.

Perhaps because this similarity had been suggested to him by the British or by a courtier, Muhammad Ali Shah was determined to make Lucknow into a veritable Babylon and to leave for himself a memorial representing him as the greatest of all the kings of Avadh. He started to build, in the neighbourhood of Husainabad near the present clock tower,[183] an edifice similar to Babylon's minaret or floating garden. Each circular storey was composed of arches, a second storey of arches being superimposed onto the first, a third onto the second, and so on from the ground level to the top. He intended there to be seven storeys and a lofty tower from whose summit a view of the whole of Lucknow and the surrounding country could be obtained. If this edifice had been completed it would certainly have been unique. The name destined for it was Sat Khanda,[184] Seven Slices, and it was being built with great care and diligence but had reached only the fifth storey when in 1842 Muhammad Ali Shah died.

In his short time as king, Muhammad Ali Shah made Lucknow into a very beautiful city without provoking any internal quarrels or any complaints about the maladministration of the kingdom. He built a road called Chauk along the river from Husainabad Gate to Rumi Gate. There were lofty buildings on either side of the road and at one end were the Rumi Gate and Asaf ud Daula's Imam Bara with its mosque. At the other end were Sat Khanda and Husainabad Gate. The new Imam Bara had many tall buildings and the main mosque, Jamey Masjid, was adjacent to them. Taken together, all these buildings presented a beautiful sight. Even though the private houses have been demolished, this scene is still one of the finest in the world.

7

Amjad Ali Shah, Wajid Ali Shah and the End of the Dynasty's Rule—Urdu Drama

After Muhammad Ali Shah, Amjad Ali Shah ascended the throne. Muhammad Ali Shah had made every effort to ensure that the heir apparent received an excellent education. He had therefore entrusted him to the company of religious scholars and learned men. The result was that Amjad Ali Shah, instead of making an outstanding advance in learning, became a *maulvi*, a devout Muslim. After taking over the reins of government his energy was concentrated on making the people become, like himself, true followers of the religious leaders. But it goes without saying that spiritual leaders or those learned in religion cannot be concerned with politics, neither can they be counsellors to the state or statesmen. The only guidance to be got from them was that service should be rendered to Saiyyids,[37] and that the country's money should be spent on helping and supporting the faithful. In the opinion of the deeply religious, circumspect and abstinent ruler of Avadh, Amjad Ali Shah, this could only be satisfactorily accomplished if done by the blessed hand of the leading prelate[168] of the time. For this reason, lakhs of rupees of the country's revenue were given over to him as *zakat*,[185] alms for the poor, and he received other large sums for charitable purposes.

For Amjad Ali Shah, considerations of piety and sanctity had become obsessive. He was so tied to his convictions that he had no time to attend to the affairs of state. The inevitable result was that the method and system of administration introduced by Muhammad Ali Shah became completely disorganized. Matters had reached such a state that according to Qazi Muhammad Sadiq Khan[186] (pen-name[187] Akhtar) all the officials were vicious, evil-minded and self-seeking. The people were oppressed, terrorists had their own way, tyrants and criminals were never punished, bribes were the order of the day and no one could put a stop to any mischief that arose. But in spite of his carelessness towards worldly affairs, his negligence and lack of concern for cultural matters, Amjad Ali Shah established the Hazrat Ganj quarter, which is today the finest, most populated and most splendid part of the Civil Lines.[188]

He constructed a road from Lucknow to Kanpur and it was in his reign that the erection of the iron bridge was finally completed. The circumstances regarding the building of this bridge dated back to Ghazi ud Din Haidar who had sent for its component parts from England, but before the parts arrived the King had departed this life. In the reign of Nasir ud Din Haidar the parts arrived from England and the King gave the contract for assembling them and erecting the bridge to his court engineer, Mr Sinclair. He gave orders that these iron parts be stacked on the other side of the river opposite the Residency, where there now stands a bathing place and *shivala*.[189] Mr Sinclair had deep wells dug in the river bed for the pillars and even had the pillars erected, but after this he vacillated and the bridge was not completed. Under Muhammad Ali Shah the bridge remained incomplete. Then Amjad Ali Shah became king; he paid attention to it and the bridge was completed. The present iron bridge is not that of Amjad Ali Shah's time. The original one had been a suspension bridge, the whole weight of which was supported on four strong iron pillars. Later, under the British, parts of this bridge became rusty and weak and it became dangerous. It was pulled down and replaced by another iron bridge which exists to this day.

In Amjad Ali Shah's reign his Vazir, Amin ud Daula, established Aminabad, the population and magnificence of which are at present increasing day by day. Amjad Ali Shah did not accomplish much and did not have the desire to construct any building that would serve as a memorial to him; nevertheless, perhaps as a reward for his piety and self-restraint, he has achieved fame. The most celebrated, densely populated and richest quarters of the town today, Aminabad and Hazrat Ganj, are there to perpetuate the memory of his reign.

Eventually time turned over a page of the book of his life and in 1848, when he was just over forty-eight years of age, he became the victim of cancer and breathed his last. He was buried inside Risaldar Mendu Khan's cantonment in Hazrat Ganj, the quarter which he had himself established. His Imam Bara, Sibtainabad,[190] in which he is entombed, is situated at the side of the road in the western part of Hazrat Ganj. It was built after his death by Wajid Ali Shah at the cost of ten lakhs of rupees. This Imam Bara is a bad imitation of Husainabad—but if it were illuminated[191] like Husainabad at the time of Muharram then the eastern part of Lucknow would also become a blaze of light. Although it has no *vasiqa* [endowment], its income is not inconsiderable. Many of the shops outside the enclosing walls of the building are those of prosperous tradesmen and inside the enclosure many of the houses are occupied by Eurasians and others from whom large rents are collected. A benevolent act on the part of the rent collectors is that at the time of Muharram they light some lamps on the grave itself and in the Imam Bara.

Amjad Ali Shah's eldest son, Wajid Ali Shah, had honoured the royal throne by ascending it. His era forms the last page of the history of this Eastern court and the last stanza of the old elegy. Because the monarchy came to an end during his reign he became the target for the abuse of all thinking people and it was almost universally agreed that he was the cause of the downfall of the kingdom. But at the time when his kingdom came to an end the national powers throughout India were breaking up and their rulers and governments, both good and bad, were disappearing. What caused the destruction of the Sikhs[192] of the Panjab and the Marathas of the Deccan, who are considered brave, strong and intelligent people? Why should the Mughal Emperors of Delhi and the Governor, Navab Nazim[193] of Bengal, have been uprooted, even though they did not display the childishness ascribed to the crowned heads of the Kingdom of Lucknow? There was no Wajid Ali Shah at any of these four courts, yet their ruination was not in any way less complete than that of Lucknow.

The truth of the matter is that the cup of negligence and foolishness of the people of India was near to overflowing. To add to this, the power of the British

Government and the British people's far-sightedness, efficiency and forbearance were day by day proving that they were entitled to reap the fruits of their efforts and their advanced civilization. It was impossible for the intelligence of these foreigners and their good planning and methodical ways not to prevail against the ignorance and self-effacement of India. At this time the world had assumed a new pattern of industrialized civilization, and this way of life was crying aloud to every nation. No one in India heard this proclamation and all were destroyed. Among them was the Kingdom of Avadh, but it is highly unfair to lay the blame for its downfall on poor Wajid Ali Shah.

Wajid Ali Shah's father was a slave to religious law and placed his son in the company of religious leaders, hoping to make him what he was himself. Wajid Ali Shah was influenced to a certain extent and as he got older became further interested in religion, but Amjad Ali Shah could not prevent the natural inclinations of his son, heir to the throne, from being turned towards sensuality and the pursuit of pleasure and amusement. On his father's insistence he had received a good education, but music was still uppermost in his thoughts. As heir apparent, because of his natural desires and contrary to his father's designs, he was a patron of singers and musicians and learned to sing and play. His association with dissolute women, singers and dancers, continued to increase. Consequently he could not get nearly as much pleasure from learned and refined society as he did from the company of beautiful women and talented singers.

Unlike his father he was interested in architecture. When he was heir apparent he set out a very fine park and in it he built one or two small, beautiful and elaborate houses to be used as the meeting places for his gay parties. Also at this time he met, in the house of a courtesan,[194] Ali Naqi Khan, on whom he conferred the khilat of Vazir on ascending to the throne. He was attracted by Ali Naqi's youthful cheerfulness and when the park and houses which had been constructed under the latter's supervision were approved by him it seemed to him that no one more suitable could be found to be Vazir and to administer the country's affairs.

The first part of Wajid Ali Shah's reign was characterized by the dashing young King's paying more than usual attention to the dispensation of justice and army reform. When he went out riding, two small silver boxes were borne ahead of him and anyone who had a complaint would write out a petition and put it into one of the boxes. The King kept the keys to the boxes and when he returned to the palace, he took out the petitions and wrote instructions concerning them in his own hand. In this manner several new cavalry regiments and infantry battalions were formed. According to his temperament the King gave poetic names to the cavalry regiments such as Banka, Dandy; Tircha, Fop; Ghanghur, Dark; and the infantry battalions Akhtari, Lucky, and Nadiri, Rare. His Majesty, on his own initiative, would mount a horse and sit for hours in the sun watching parades and exercises in the art of war. He showed his pleasure by rewarding deserving soldiers and honouring them with favours. He himself ordained the use of Persian idiom and words of command for military parades: for instance, *Rast rau*—To the right; *Pas biya*—Retire; *Dast-chap bagard*—Left turn. Later a small army of beautiful girls was formed and they learned their drill in the same manner.

But this early routine of the new reign did not last. In less than a year Wajid Ali Shah had become tired of these things and the old tastes which he had had as heir apparent returned. He started to consort more frequently with beautiful and dissolute women and soon dancers and singers became the pillars of state and favourites of the realm. If the King had retained any scholarly or noble taste at all, it was for poetry. He himself wrote poems and had great esteem for poets.

At that time in Lucknow Urdu poetry was very much the fashion. In Lucknow alone there were more poets than in the rest of India. The *ghazals*[195] and *qasidas*[196] of Mir[197] and Sauda[198] had become outdated and heads were now filled with Nasikh's[199] compositions and Atish's[200] thoughts. Coupled with these, the *rindi*[201] of Rind[202] and Saba[203] and the *masnavi*[204] of Navab Shauq[205] stirred the souls of the sensually inclined and the King, because of his natural proclivities, liked and approved of this taste.

Up to the end of the first century of the Muslim Caliphate,[206] it was characteristic of Islamic poetry to show the poet as being in love with a particular woman. He would mention her name, describe the glory of her beauty and the allurement of her coquetry, and addressing her, he would describe his agitation and anxieties. Occasionally he would meet her secretly but would never go beyond the bounds of morality and chastity. In a much later period this loved one became an abstraction in Arabia and as a rule the poet's beloved was an idol of his imagination. Drink-loving libertines took this to be either a beautiful woman or a good-looking boy. Sufis[207] gave spiritual meaning to her, describing her as part of the 'Absolute Beauty', that is, the Creator of the Universe. This indefinite, ambiguous form of narrative existed in Persian poetry and up to that time in Urdu poetry as well. Navab Mirza Shauq in his poems became the lover of beautiful veiled women[208] and made his poetry the scourge of conventional morality. The trouble was that the language of his masnavis was so beautiful, frank, pure and clean in spite of its erotic allure, that even honourable and decent people could not abstain from reading and enjoying it.

Wajid Ali Shah also read these masnavis, and because he was a poet himself, he adopted this style and versified his love-affairs and hundreds of the amorous escapades of his early youth. He made them public throughout the country and became to a conventional, moral, world a self-confessed sinner. Few ministers and nobles in their early youth have not given full rein to their sexual desires. None of them, however, like Wajid Ali Shah, has made public his sensuous transgressions. Wajid Ali Shah could not outdo Navab Mirza in the realm of poetry, so he decided to surpass him by proclaiming to the world his unchaste predilections, thoughts and deeds. He even had no hesitation in showing shamefully low taste and in using obscene language.

He would fall in love with female palanquin-bearers, courtesans, domestic servants and women who came in and out of the palace, in short with hundreds of women, and because he was heir to the throne, he had great success with his love-affairs, the shameful accounts of which can be read in his poems, writings and books. His character, therefore, appears to be one of the most dubious in all the records of history.

As he was very interested in architecture he started to build Qaisar Bagh[209] as soon as he came to the throne. His buildings, although not as strong as those of Asaf ud Daula, were certainly beautiful and splendid. He constructed a large oblong enclosure of elegant and imposing two-storied houses, one wing of which, in the direction of the river, was pulled down after the Mutiny;[210] the other three are still in existence. These have been subdivided and handed over to *taluqdars*[211] [wealthy landowners] of Avadh by the Government with instructions that they are to live in the houses and maintain[212] them in their original state.

The inner courtyard of the Qaisar Bagh, with its lawns, was called Jilo Khana, the Front House. In the centre were a Barah Dari which is now Lucknow's Town Hall[213] and some other buildings which are no longer standing. Outside the Qaisar Bagh were many nearby royal houses which made this plot of land one of the wonders of the age. These buildings were outside the eastern gate of the Qaisar Bagh. People on passing through this gate found fences on either side. They then came to Chini Bagh, the Chinese Garden, and turning left they entered Jal Pari, the Mermaid Gate. The Vazir Navab Ali Naqi Khan lived near this gate so as to be always near the King and within immediate call if necessary. On the other side of the Mermaid Gate was Hazrat Bagh and inside it to the right there was the Chandi Wali Barah Dari. This was an ordinary building of bricks and mortar but because there were sheets of thin silver on the roof [and walls and columns] it was known as The Silver House. The house next to it, Khas Maqam, the Residence, was a private residence in which the King himself lived and which was quite near to Badshah Manzil built by Navab Sadat Ali Khan.

At the end of the fences there was a complex of buildings known as Chau Lakhi, 'Worth Four Lakhs', that were once owned by the royal barber, Azim Ullah. The King bought them from him for four lakhs of rupees and in them lived the King's chief wife Navab Khas Mahal[214] and other honoured royal ladies. During the Mutiny Hazrat Mahal lived and held court there.

A road led from these buildings to the Qaisar Bagh and at the side of it stood an enormous shady tree around which a circular marble platform had been erected. At the time of the Qaisar Bagh fairs the King would dress himself up as a *yogi*[215] in red-coloured garments and sit there. In front of this platform there was a fine gateway which was called Chau Lakhi Gate because lakhs of rupees had been expended on its construction: going through it you again came to the Qaisar Bagh. The Government had spent eighty lakhs of rupees on the houses in the Qaisar Bagh for the wives and ladies of the King. Nowadays, on seeing commonplace faces in lieu of them older residents say with the Persian poet, 'The fairies have hidden their faces and the demons are showing their coquetry and blandishment.'

Outside the western gate of the Qaisar Bagh was Raushan ud Daula's kothi. Wajid Ali Shah confiscated it and called it Qaisar Pasand,[216] 'Favourite of Qaisar'. One of his favourite ladies, Navab Mashuq Mahal, used to live in it. Nowadays it is the Deputy Commissioner's court. Opposite to it on the western side of Qaisar Bagh was another Jilo Khana.

Once a year a great fair was held in the Qaisar Bagh to which the public was admitted and they could then see the voluptuous style of living to which the King was addicted. The King had seen the *rahas*,[217] theatrical representations of Sri[218] Krishna's[219] dance, and was so pleased with Sri Krishna's amatory dalliances that he devised a drama about them in which he himself played the part of Kanhaya (Krishna) and decorous and virtuous ladies of the palace acted as *gopis*, milkmaid loves of Krishna. There was much dancing and frolicking. Sometimes the ardour of youth impelled the King to become a yogi. Pearls were burnt and the King would cover his body with the ashes. Thus abstinence,

6   The Residency. Engraving

7   Panj Mahla Gate. Drawing by T. Daniell, 1789

Water-colours by a Murshidabad   8   Mosque of Asaf ud Daula
artist, about 1800:   9   Imam Bara of Asaf ud Daula.

too, acquired the flavour of royalty. At the time of the fair, ordinary people of the town were allowed to take part in these pastimes, but only on condition that they came wearing clothes dyed in red ochre. The result was that even old men of eighty would put on red garments and become young sparks, filling the cups of their old age with the joyous wine of the King's youthfulness.

This atmosphere prevailed in Lucknow and gaiety and merriment were the order of the day. Successive Residents informed the British Government in England of the local state of affairs. The Board of the East India Company decided that Avadh should be included in the region under British control and, to achieve this, a British armed force came to Lucknow. Quite unexpectedly the following instructions were issued to the King: 'Your country has been included in that administered by the British. Twelve lakhs of rupees a year have been allocated to you and three lakhs of rupees to your ceremonial troops, which will be paid monthly. This will be amply sufficient for your needs and those of your immediate entourage. You will be free to live at your ease and without a care in the city, free from any anxiety about the populace, and to pursue your pleasures in peace and comfort.' The receipt of these orders dealt a stunning blow to the city. The King, weeping and wailing, made every effort to exonerate himself. The King's mother and the chief consort pleaded, but the Resident was power-less to alter the orders given by the Governor-General. The Government of the East India Company had, without any difficulty, taken possession[220] of Avadh. The King, his mother, his heir, his chief wives and faithful friends departed for Calcutta with a view to going to England to lodge an appeal, to establish the King's innocence and to have the order for the dissolution of the monarchy repealed.

8

Wajid Ali Shah in Matiya Burj—the Mutiny

Wajid Ali Shah was extremely fortunate in that immediately after losing his crown and throne he was able to leave Lucknow for Calcutta to put forward his case in an orthodox manner. If he failed with the Council of the Governor-General of India, it was his intention to go to London and plead his case before Parliament and the British Queen. Accordingly, when he had no success in Calcutta he decided to go to London, but his doctors thought the sea journey would be harmful to his health and his advisers stopped him from going. The result was that he stayed in Calcutta but sent his heir, his mother and his brother to England. On this journey my grandfather, the late Munshi Qamar ud Din, was in the retinue of the ruined family. The King refused to accept the allowance allocated by the British Government and insisted on claiming his crown and throne which had been taken from him unjustly.

The King was in Calcutta, his family in London and his case under consideration when suddenly in 1857 the strife about cartridges and the Government's opposition led to the Mutiny.[221] From Meerut to Bengal there was a general conflagration which destroyed the houses of friend and foe. So great was the trouble which arose that it appeared as if the very foundations of the British Government were tottering. In the same way as the insurgents from Meerut and many other places had concentrated in Delhi and made Zafar Shah[222] Emperor of India, so in May 1857 the mutineers from Allahabad and Faizabad went to Lucknow. As soon as the mutineers arrived many idle residents joined them. They could not find any other member of the royal family in Avadh, so they placed the ten-year-old son of Wajid Ali Shah, Mirza Birjis Qadar, on the throne, and his mother Navab Hazrat Mahal became regent of the monarchy. The British troops quartered in Lucknow, and all the European officials of the administration who had managed to escape from the mutineers, fortified themselves in the Baillie Guard.[223] Wajid Ali Shah had left Lucknow, otherwise he would have been proclaimed King and his lamentations would have been more bitter than those of Zafar Shah. The temporary refuge of the Matiya Burj court, which allowed him and his entourage to survive for a while, would never have been the fate of the unfortunate people of Avadh.

In addition to the mutinous soldiers of the British Indian army, most of the landowners and taluqdars of Avadh and the dismissed soldiers of imperial days had collected in Lucknow in great numbers. They had been joined by a mass of bad characters and every class of person in the town was engaged in despicable activities. It appeared as though the encircled small numbers of British had to face the attack of the whole mass of people. But in fact the besiegers consisted of the disreputable elements of the town and unprincipled and headstrong combatants. There was not a single man of valour among them who knew anything of the principles of war or who could combine the disunited forces and make them into an organized striking force. The British, on the other hand, who were fighting for their lives, stood their ground. Facing the gravest danger they repelled their assailants and proved themselves skilled in the latest arts of war.

At that time Birjis Qadar, with the royal consort, Hazrat Mahal, had become effective ruler in Lucknow. The authority of Birjis Qadar was acknowledged, coins were issued in his name, officials were appointed to the State, taxes began to be collected and the siege itself was continued only as a sort of pastime. People praised the efficiency and good intentions of the Queen, who had great regard for the soldiery and would reward them highly for their work and prowess. But to what avail? It was impossible for her to discard her purdah and become commander-in-chief of the army. Her advisers were bad and her soldiers useless. Everyone was a slave to his own desires and no one agreed with what anyone else said. The mutineers of the British Indian army were so arrogant that they thought that everything happened by their grace and considered themselves the true rulers and the only 'king-makers'.

A religious mendicant, Ahmad Ullah, popularly known as Shah Sahib, who had come from Faizabad with the insurgents and who had fought in several engagements, wished to establish his authority by force and even to establish his rule. He set up a separate court in Lucknow in opposition to that of Birjis Qadar. In addition to political differences between the two courts there arose quarrels and prejudices in connection with the Shia and Sunni sects of Islam and the rivalry between King and Shah increased. Eventually, in November of that year, when Birjis Qadar had been on the throne for six or seven months, a British army unit advanced on Lucknow. With the British army were Sikhs from the Panjab and hillmen from Bhutan who were reputed to have committed many atrocities. After two or three days' bombardment the new kingdom disintegrated[224] like a spider's web. The royal consort and Birjis Qadar fled to Nepal with thousands of other fugitives. The Shah Sahib fought on for two or three days and, although this prepared the way for Birjis Qadar's safe escape, he was unable to save his own life. Defeated, he fled through Bari and Muhammdi, arriving at Puwain (Pilibhit District, U.P.) where he was shot dead. The Raja of Puwain cut off his head and sent it to the British, who in gratitude gave him a reward and a grant of land.

In order to clear the town of insurgents, the British put up a massive bombardment and all the inhabitants were terrified. Men and women left their houses and fled and such confusion and distress ensued that people who saw it tremble even today at its memory. Women who had lived all their lives in purdah, whose faces had never been touched by the sun, now stirred up the dust of the countryside with their bare feet and in their forlorn state clung to each other. Whoever they met proved an enemy and the hemistich of Sa'di,[225] 'At the time of famine . . . our friends have forgotten love', was fully substantiated. Whilst these conditions prevailed, the victorious army looted the city.

After much hardship and with immense difficulty the people got permission to return to their homes and the peace that ensued after this time of panic exists to this day by the grace of the Almighty. But those connected with the old government and the royal favourites, who were unemployed after the revolution and who could not derive any benefit from the new government, were gradually effaced from the scene. That is to say that for a period great, rich and honoured families, one after another, continued to disintegrate and then were finally destroyed. One section of the town after another fell into decay, family after family disappeared and most people thought that Lucknow would remain only as a memory. But in the end the methods of the British Government, similar to those used in establishing new colonies throughout the world, prevailed and Lucknow escaped from the calamitous disaster of that era. Those who were to be ruined were ruined and those who remained became capable of taking themselves in hand. If Lucknow continues to receive the services of Governors like the present Mr Butler[226] I am convinced that there will be much improvement in the future.

It appears to be necessary that I give my readers an account of the remainder of Wajid Ali Shah's life and of his sojourn in Calcutta, without which this history would be incomplete. I spent my childhood in Calcutta under the King's protective shadow. I have described events until now through having heard of them from others or having read about them in the pages of history. I will from now on describe events mostly as I saw them for myself.

About three or four miles south of Calcutta on the banks of the Bhagarthi River, popularly known as Houghly, there is a quiet quarter known as Garden Beach, and because there is a raised plateau there, ordinary folk called it Matiya Burj, the Earthen Dome. There were also some very fine houses, the grounds of

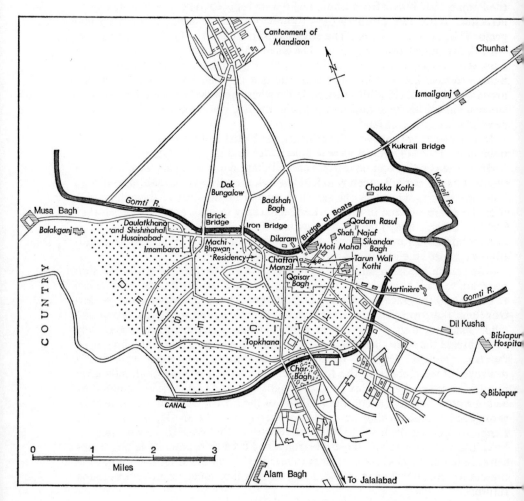

Lucknow and its environs at the time of the Mutiny

which stretched for two to two and a half miles along the river bank. When Wajid Ali Shah came to Calcutta the British Government of India gave him these houses; two for the King himself, one for his chief consort and one as a residence for Ali Naqi Khan. Around them a large expanse of land, stretching on one side for a mile or a mile and a half from the river bank and with a perimeter of not less than six or seven miles, was given over to the King for his personal use and that of his retinue. The municipal road traversed the area from one end to the other.

Of the two houses which had been given to the King, he called one Sultan Khana, King's House, and the other Asad Manzil. When he took possession of the house of his chief consort, he called it Murassa Manzil. Ali Naqi Khan's house remained in his ownership to the last and then was passed on to his family, more particularly to Navab Akhtar Mahal, who was Ali Naqi Khan's daughter and the King's honoured wife and mother of his second heir, Mirza Khush Bakht Bahadur.

During the Mutiny, the rebel Indian officers of the British Indian army decided that if Wajid Ali Shah would become their leader they would start a rebellion in Calcutta. But the King, on losing his crown and throne, had not adopted this course towards the British Government of India and did not wish to do so now. On the contrary, he informed the Governor-General of these people's plans and received his thanks for the information. However after a few days it was thought advisable that the King should be domiciled in Fort William[227] so that the rebels could not contact him again. His case, which was proceeding in London, was suspended on the grounds that the country to which the claim referred was not in British hands. Further consideration would be given to it when the British Government had regained possession of the region.

The King was still in detention when the rebellion in Lucknow subsided and his plenipotentiary in London, Masih ud Din Khan, resubmitted the claim. On the face of it he had every hope that he would succeed and that the monarchy would be restored, but unfortunately the King's advisers and companions in Fort William, either because of outside interests or on their own initiative, hatched a plot. They thought that if Masih ud Din Khan won the case and thus became the honoured one, they would become of no account. Therefore they started to make suggestions to the King on the following lines: '*Jahan Panah*,[228] Your Majesty, has anyone ever heard of a country which has been taken over being restored? Masih ud Din Khan has misled you, obviously nothing will result and Your Majesty is merely being put to unnecessary inconvenience. No allowance has been received for nearly two years. There is scarcity of everything and we, your servants, are destitute. It would be appropriate if you agreed to the proposals of the British Government, took the allowance and led a happy, carefree life with your noble ladies and devoted servants.' The King was short of money and those around him were in a much more distressed condition than he was, so when his companions continued to make these suggestions, he wrote to the Viceroy: 'I am willing to accept the monthly allowances sanctioned by the British Government. Therefore the allowances due up to date should be credited to me and the case which is proceeding in London should be annulled.' He received the reply: 'In the first place, you will not receive credit for the period which has elapsed, the monthly allowances will only start from now onwards.

Secondly, only twelve lakhs a year will be paid. It is no longer considered necessary to pay the annual allowance of three lakhs which was proposed for your retinue.'

It is not difficult to imagine that the King by himself would not have agreed to this, but his companions made him accept it. The British Government of India informed England that Wajid Ali Shah had accepted their proposals and that his case therefore should be annulled. I heard of these events myself from my grandfather, Munshi Qamar ud Din, who was chief clerk in the Queen Mother's secretariat, deputy to Maulvi Masih ud Din Khan and responsible for all matters of procedure. When news that the King had accepted the monthly allowance reached London, Masih ud Din Khan nearly went off his head. The King's mother, his brother and his heir were in a state of consternation over the calamity which had overtaken them. All that had been accomplished so far was ruined. At last Masih ud Din Khan, after much thought, devised a plan and put the following legal point before Parliament: 'The King is now under the close supervision of the British Government of India and under these circumstances nothing which he puts on paper can be trusted.' The point was reasonable and it was accepted. The British Government of India was then informed of the plea put forward by the King's plenipotentiary and at the same time Masih ud Din Khan and all the important people connected with the royal family wrote to the King, 'What are you starting? We fully expect to have the country of Avadh restored to us.'

The Mutiny was at an end. The Government released the King who was very pleased to leave Fort William and return to Matiya Burj. No sooner had he gained his freedom than his companions said, 'Huzur[229] [Sir], Masih ud Din Khan is saying in London that Your Majesty only accepts the allowance because you are a prisoner.' On hearing this the King flared up and wrote, 'I was free and from my own desire and volition I accepted the Government's proposals. It is quite wrong for Masih ud Din to say that I accepted them owing to force or coercion. Therefore from now on I revoke his power of attorney.'

What was to happen now? All transactions had come to an end, the King had started on a life of revelry and orgies, money was flowing like water in the houses of his companions and the unfortunate members of the royal family in England were practically ruined and were deserted by most of those who had been with them. Janab-e-Alia, Her Highness the King's mother, became ill from the shock and whilst still unwell she left England intending to pass through France, make a pilgrimage to the holy places of Mecca and Kerbala and then return to Calcutta. But death did not permit her to do this and she died in France. She was buried in the Muslim cemetery adjacent to the mosque of the Osmani Legation[230] in Paris. The death of his mother was such a blow to Mirza Sikander Hashmat that he fell ill and two weeks later he too died, and was placed near his mother to await the Day of Judgment. The only one to return to Calcutta and rejoin his parents was the heir apparent.

They say that when the King first came to live in Matiya Burj he displayed much sagacity and his outlook on life became serious. On seeing this, his entourage collected various musical instruments. Immediately the King was reminded of his old fancies and love for song and dance and as a result troupes of artists started to congregate at his court. The best singers in India were enlisted into the King's service and there was a larger concourse of musicians in Matiya Burj than could be found anywhere else in India.

There was the same desire for collecting together good-looking women and concentrating on beauty and love in Matiya Burj as one hears there had been in Lucknow. In Matiya Burj, however, when embarking on these desires, due regard was given to religious considerations. The King belonged to the Shia sect of Islam, and according to Shia law, *muta*,[231] temporary marriage, is legal. Taking advantage of this religious freedom the King pursued his inclinations to his heart's content. He made it his rule not to look at a woman who was not temporarily married to him, and carried his religious caution to such lengths that he even entered into a temporary marriage with a young female water-carrier who would pass him when she was taking water to the women's quarters; he gave her the title of Navab ab Rasan Begam, Her Highness the Lady Water-Provider. There was also a young sweeping-woman who used to come into his presence. She too joined the ranks of the temporarily married and was honoured with the title of Navab Musafa Begam, the Lady Purifier. In the same way, the enjoyment of music was also confined to those women who belonged to him. It was very seldom that a courtesan danced before the King. These temporarily married women were formed into various groups and taught diverse forms of dancing and singing. The following are the names of some of these groups: Radha Manzil, Sardha Manzil, Jhumar ('Earring'), Latkan ('Dwindling'), Nath ('Nose-ring'), Ghunghat ('Veil'), Rahas ('Dance'), and Naqal ('Mimic'). There were scores of similar groups who had been given the best instruction in the dancing and singing in which the King delighted. He had entered into temporary wedlock with all of them and they were called Begams. In some of the groups, there were a few young girls who had not reached the age of puberty. They were not in a state of temporary wedlock and they would be admitted to that state immediately on reaching puberty. Most lived near the King in Sultan Khana but some of them lived in separate women's apartments in other houses. Those temporarily married women who bore children were given the title of Mahal. They were given separate women's apartments as their residences, received enhanced allowances and were greatly honoured.

From what has been written above it is clearly evident that, except for music,[232] the King was in every way extremely devout, abstinent and a strict observer of Muslim religious law. He never missed offering up his prayers. He observed the fast for the whole of the thirty days in the month of Ramadan. He was a life-long abstainer from opium, wine and other intoxicants and he performed the mourning ceremonies at the time of Muharram with sincere devotion.

His other interest was building. Scores of women's apartments were constructed on all four sides of Sultan Khana and many new houses with their own female quarters were built. The King had received only Sultan Khana, Asad Manzil and Murassa Manzil from the British Government of India, but in a very short time he built several more houses which were surrounded by beautiful gardens and pleasing lawns. When I saw them, the King possessed the following fine houses which, taken from south to north were: Sultan Khana, Qasr ul Baiza, Gosha-e-Sultani, Shahinshah Manzil, Murassa Manzil, Asad Manzil, Shah Manzil, Nur Manzil, Tafrih Baksh, Badami, Asmani, Tahaniyat Manzil, Had-e-Sultani, Sad-e-Sultani, Adalat Manzil. In addition to these, there were several other houses, the names of which I have forgotten.

There were also many single rooms, bungalows and small kiosks on the banks of the pools inside the parks. In all of these there were spotless, ornate carpets covering the floors and silver bedsteads with bedding and pillows. They were further decorated with pictures and a variety of fine furniture. In order to help support the people, more housekeepers than were in fact necessary had been appointed to look after the houses. These people used to sweep them every day and ensure that they were kept clean and in good order. In short, all these houses, in their separate settings, were so decorative and trim that no one could help admiring them. Surrounding them were gardens and lawns set out in geometrical designs with such engineering skill that those who beheld them marvelled at the King's talent and sense of proportion.

In Lucknow the King had constructed only the Qaisar Bagh, a few houses in the neighbourhood, an Imam Bara and a tomb for his deceased father, but in Matiya Burj he had established a beautiful town of fine houses. On the other side of the river, exactly opposite Matiya Burj, are Calcutta's famed Botanical Gardens. But they were as nothing compared to the earthly paradise of Matiya Burj and the entrancing wonders it contained. There was a high-walled enclosure surrounding all these houses, lawns and markets.

For about a mile along the municipal high road there were some fine shops. Lower-class employees, whose duties necessitated them being there, were allowed to live in them. One could enter the enclosure only through the main gates on which guards were mounted; there was no means of entry through any of the shops. Near the gate to Sultan Khana there was a very imposing guard-house in which *naubat* [drums] were beaten and the hours of the day and night were announced by gongs according to the old fashion.

Many kings have been interested in architecture but scarcely any other monarch can have built so many houses or established so many parks as did Wajid Ali Shah during his unfortunate life and the short period of his so-called reign. Second to Shahjahan in this respect, if one can mention anybody's name then it must be the name of this afflicted king of Avadh. Some of Shahjahan's buildings have remained standing for hundreds of years while hundreds of buildings constructed by others have soon been demolished by fate.

Apart from architecture, the King took an interest in animals and he developed this interest to an extraordinary and unsurpassed extent. I do not suppose that any other individual has ever made half the efforts in this direction that he did.

In front of Nur Mahal there was a large open space, enclosed by a neat iron fence, into which hundreds of spotted deer, buck and other wild quadrupeds had been turned loose. In its centre was a well-built marble pool which was always filled to the brim with water. This was the habitat of partridges, ostriches, turkeys, sarus cranes, geese, herons, demoiselle cranes, ducks, peacocks, flamingoes and hundreds of other birds, and tortoises. Such care was given to cleanliness that droppings or shed feathers of a bird were never to be seen. On one side of the pool there was a cage containing tigers and near the meadow there was a row of large wooden cages into which scores of different species of monkey had been collected from far-flung places. These monkeys performed comic antics which people could not help lingering to watch.

In various places there were pools filled with fish which would gather at a signal and if anyone threw in some food it was wonderful to see them leaping from the water.

The most amazing thing of all was a large, long and deep tank in front of Shahinshah Manzil. All four sides of the tank had been made very slippery and in the middle was an artificial hill, sloping downwards at the front and into which hundreds of pipes had been run, some of which were open at the top to act as fountains. Thousands of large snakes, six to nine feet long, had been released on this hill and would crawl about it. They would go to the top and then come down to the bottom and catch the frogs which had been put there. Round the hill there was a sort of moat where the snakes would swim and chase the frogs. It was quite safe for people to stand by the tank and watch what was happening.

Below this hill were two cages in which there were two large leopards. Normally they lay quiet but if a fowl was given to them they would spring on it and gobble it up whole.

It is unlikely that arrangements for keeping snakes in captivity had ever been made anywhere before and Wajid Ali Shah was the first person to think of it. European travellers were amazed at the sight and would take pictures and write down details.

Apart from these animals, there were thousands of shining brass bird-cages in Sultan Khana itself. There were also scores of large aviaries enclosed by wire netting, which were called *kunj*. A large number of birds of various kinds were let loose in these and all possible arrangements were made for their upkeep and breeding.

The King's desire was to collect as many kinds of animals as possible. It is unlikely that there has ever been such a perfect example of a living museum in all the world as the one he possessed. Money was spent without restraint in acquiring these animals and if anyone brought in a new species he was given exactly what he asked for it. It is said that the King paid 24,000 rupees for a pair of silk-winged pigeons and 11,000 rupees for a pair of white peacocks. There was also a pair of giraffes, very large and strange animals from Africa. The two-humped camel of Baghdad is never seen in India, but the King possessed one in his zoo. There were even a couple of donkeys let loose in a meadow, so intent was the King that all sorts of animals should be included. Beasts of prey such as lions, Indian tigers, cheetahs, leopards, bears, lynxes, hyenas and wolves were all kept in cages and carefully tended.

Arrangements for the pigeons were different from those for the other birds. In his various pigeonries, the King had, in all, twenty-four or twenty-five thousand birds which the pigeon fanciers showed great skill in flying.

It is possible to form an idea of the amount spent on the animals from the fact that there were over eight hundred attendants and about three hundred pigeon fanciers; about the same number looked after the fish and there were thirty or forty employed for the snakes. These attendants received from six to ten rupees a month as pay. Officers received a monthly salary of twenty to thirty rupees. Apart from the pigeons, snakes and fish, a little less than nine thousand rupees a month was spent on food for the other animals. The building arrangements for the zoo had mostly been entrusted to Munis ud Daula and Raihan ud Daula who received twenty-five thousand rupees a month for this purpose.

Besides the staff at the zoo there were about one thousand watchmen whose pay was normally six rupees a month although some received up to eight or ten rupees. The same pay was received by the housekeepers who numbered over five hundred. There were some eighty clerks who received a monthly salary of ten to thirty rupees. The number of favoured companions and high officials was probably not less than forty or fifty and each received eighty-eight rupees a month. There were also more than one hundred palanquin-bearers.

In addition there were scores of minor departments dealing with the kitchens, vegetables, *abdar khana* [water-cooling], *khas khana* [house cooling] and so on.[233] Then again there were the relations and male members of the family of the temporary wives, all of whom received salaries in proportion to their standing.

All these people had built houses for themselves outside the area of the original houses. These new houses were for the most part on the land which had been given to the King but many were on other land nearby. So a town had grown up with a population of more than forty thousand souls, all of whose livelihood derived from the King's monthly allowance of one lakh of rupees. No one could understand how such a large population could live on such a small sum and it was commonly thought in Bengal that the King possessed the philosopher's stone, and that whenever necessary he rubbed iron or brass and turned it into gold.

From the time of the King's arrival in Calcutta, a second Lucknow had arisen in its neighbourhood. The real Lucknow had ended and was replaced by Matiya Burj. There was the same bustle and activity, the same language, the same style of poetry, conversation and wit, the same learned and pious men, the same aristocrats, nobles and common people. No one thought he was in Bengal: there was the same kite-flying, cock-fighting, quail-fighting, the same opium addicts reciting the same tales,[238] the same observance of Muharram, the same lamentations at the recital of *marsiya* and *nauha*,[234] the same Imam Baras and the same Kerbala as in former Lucknow. But the ceremony, pomp and circumstance with which the King's Muharram procession was invested probably could never have been equalled in Lucknow even in the days of his rule. After the Mutiny, a Muharram procession of *tazias*[129] could never have been carried out in Lucknow with the former glory, but in Calcutta thousands of people, even the British, came to Matiya Burj as pilgrims.

Although the King was a Shia he was without religious prejudice of any sort. He could say: 'Of my two eyes, one is Shia and the other is Sunni.' On one occasion two people came to blows over some religious difference. The King gave orders that both be dismissed and refused to have them readmitted to his service, saying, 'I cannot have such people near me.' Later on, some unpalatable words had been printed in one of the King's books which caused an uproar among the Sunnis of Calcutta, but no one knew that these words were not actually of the King's authorship but that they had been taken by him from another source. When the King heard about the matter he was ready to apologize without any prompting from others.

What greater proof of this lack of prejudice could there be than the fact that the whole administration was in the hands of Sunnis? The Vazir, Munsarim ud Daula Bahadur,[235] was a Sunni. The Chief Secretary, Munshi ul Sultan, who at one time had been the person nearest to the King and was the senior officer in charge of the zoological gardens, the secretariat and various other departments, was a Sunni. The Paymaster, Bakhshi Amanat ud Daula, at whose hands all the retainers and even the royal ladies and princes received their salaries and allowances, was a Sunni. Attar ud Daula and the Superintendent, Motabar Ali Khan, who were in fact the highest of officials and in charge of all organization, were both Sunnis. How could one imagine any greater proof of impartiality than that the management of the Sibtainabad Imam Bara and the royal Imam Bara, called the Baitul Buka, the House of Lamentation, as well as the arrangements for *majlis*[129] and other religious ceremonies were all in the hands of Sunnis? No one even noticed who was a Sunni and who a Shia.

Even the shopkeepers and money-lenders in Matiya Burj were from Lucknow and there was not a single product of Lucknow which was not there in its very best form. Wherever one went one saw great magnificence and activity. All were so charmed and fascinated by their pleasurable existence that they gave no thought to the future. The people of Lucknow, all the royal servants and even other residents of Matiya Burj, had free access to the palaces and meadows. You could not find a more pleasant place to walk in than the parks. If you stood on the bank of the river you obtained a most wonderful view. Ships going to and from Calcutta passed in front of you and as they did, dipped their standards in salute to Fort William; people, however, thought they were being dipped in salutation to the King. If you stood at the threshold of the palaces or at the doors of the female apartments you were filled with a pleasurable emotion. Sometimes you might catch a glimpse of a lovely face and sometimes you heard eloquent, attractive speech and sometimes such delectable talk that it remained in the memory for a very long time afterwards, if not for ever.

How could this beautiful and entrancing scene ever be destroyed! But alas, fate destroyed it and destroyed it so completely that it might never have existed. In 1887 the King suddenly closed his eyes for ever and it seemed as though 'all one had seen was a dream and all one had heard was a story'. Everything was fantasy and illusion, a myth, the origin of which had all at once become effaced. That beautiful spot which European kings and Indian rulers had longed to visit was now reduced to an uncouth void and a place of ill-omen. Whoever had seen its previous state and now witnessed the wilderness it had become, could only heave a deep sigh of grief and sorrow and exclaim, 'Only God is eternal!'

9

Mirza Birjis Qadar—Urdu Poetry

As regards the history of this court, it is left to relate how Mirza Birjis Qadar fled from Lucknow and halted at the Nepal border. He had with him about one hundred thousand men. These people had decided to take refuge in the Himalayan valleys and, should opportunity offer, come out again and attack the British. If they were victorious they would go back to their own country and if they were defeated they would retreat and live in the hills. But this was not to be. The state of Nepal could not give refuge to such a large number of people nor could she fight with them against the British as she did not have sufficient strength. Therefore the government of Nepal gave asylum only to Mirza Birjis Qadar and his mother and issued definite orders to the inept rabble that had accompanied them that they go back immediately: Nepalese territory must be cleared at once and anyone who did not leave would be expelled by force. The result was that all of them fled the country. Many were killed and many disguised themselves and disappeared. Mirza Birjis Qadar and his mother went on into Nepal, were domiciled there and granted a small allowance by the government. It is said that all the jewellery they had with them was presented to the Nepalese government. Eventually the royal consort, Hazrat Mahal, died in Nepal in 1874. After her death, on the occasion of the jubilee of Queen Victoria (1887), the British Government pardoned Birjis Qadar and he was allowed to return home. Without informing anyone, he hurried from Nepal to Calcutta where Wajid Ali Shah had already died and where Qamar Qadar, since he was the eldest son (in Matiya Burj at the time), was receiving the biggest allowance. However, Birjis Qadar put in a claim which stated that of all the King's sons he was the favourite and had the greatest rights (being now the eldest son) and that legally therefore he should receive a pension equal to two thirds of the allowance allotted to the King and should be made responsible for looking after the King's heirs and dependents. He was preparing to go to England to further his claim when one of his family invited him to a meal. On returning from this meal he became ill with food poisoning and his condition rapidly deteriorated. In a single day he, his wife and several of his sons came to an untimely end and no member of that family was left who had ever had direct contact with the crown and throne of Lucknow.

Even so, the activities of Matiya Burj and the splendour and prosperity of the new town had assumed such proportions that if they had escaped they would for a long time have served as a reminder to the world of the style and taste of the court of that luckless king and his dependents. But the British Government thought that the best way of administering justice in the distribution of Wajid Ali Shah's effects was for all his property and houses to be sold and proportionate shares given to each heir in cash. The inevitable result was that Matiya Burj was destroyed to the last brick. Property which was worth thousands of rupees was sold for cowries[236] and that place which in a short time had become an earthly paradise was now a veritable hell. If you should happen to wander about there, you will see nothing. If you are searching for the former splendour and activity, summon an Umara ul Qais.* He will come weeping to you and point out: 'Here was Murassa Manzil, here was Nur Manzil, here Sultan Khana and here Asad Manzil. In this place *mushairas*, poetry recitals,[237] were held, and in that place erudite scholars used to meet. In one place sophisticated friends would exchange pleasantries and in another, eloquent narrators would recite tales which held people spellbound. Here was a gathering of the chosen beauties of the world and there a group engaged in song and dance. In this place *houris*, nymphs of the Muslim paradise, were given instruction in singing and dancing and there the King used to enjoy himself sitting amongst his coquettish temporary wives. Here stories would be narrated by a group of opium[238] users and there quail-fighting would take place. Here pigeons would be flown and there kite-flying competitions were held. At this threshold moon-faced and entrancingly beautiful women could be seen peeping from behind curtains, and at that there was a constant bustle and activity with the continuous coming and going of male and female servants. At this threshold there was always a gathering of eminent poets because the lady of the house took a great interest in poetry, and at that there was a daily search for youthful, spirited writers of flowery language with a view to the composing of *todu nama*,[239] love letters, to be sent every second or third day to the King.'

Even with the disappearance of Matiya Burj countless memories of the former court remain. The town of Lucknow, its society and every corner of the domain of Avadh is a memorial to its greatness and bears the stamp of the glory of the old monarchy. Every deed and gesture of the people of Lucknow is a living historical record of the members of the court. One cannot help saying, 'O rose, I love thee for thou hast the same scent as the one I love.' In order to refresh the memory with regard to these relics of the past I should like to describe how Lucknow society developed as a result of the establishment of that court, and in what respects that society influenced Indian social life in general.

In those days Persian was the court language and the people of India had adopted the best Persian social customs. At the time of the Safavid dynasty, the main faith in Iran was Shia[166] while the ruling family in India, the Mughals, were Chugtai Sunnis. The result of Persian influence on society was such that in spite of religious differences, whenever a Persian came to the country he was treated with respect.[167] This general preference had made Nur Jahan Begam[240] the real occupant of Jahangir's throne and because of this since the early seventeenth century most of the esteemed officials in Delhi were Shias. For the same reason, as soon as Amin ud Din Khan of Nishapur came here, he was created Navab Burhan ul Mulk and became master of the whole vast Ganges plain. As Burhan

* *Author's note:* Umara ul Qais was a prominent Arabic poet of the pre-Islamic era, who described the ruination of his old home in heart-rending language.

ul Mulk's influence and power increased, so his court came to be regarded more and more as a refuge for the distinguished people from Delhi. As both he and Safdar Jang had spent their lives laying the foundations for a new monarchy, they had very little time to devote to culture and social matters. They were more concerned with leading armies and gaining victories than living a peaceful life of luxury.

Shuja ud Daula, after the Battle of Baksar,[22] was forced to live quietly in Faizabad, and thus the foundations for a new culture were laid in Avadh. As I have described earlier, a great number of distinguished people left their homes in Delhi and came to Faizabad. There was a very large influx of people of every trade and class and in the short period of nine years Faizabad, from being of little account, became a town of repute. Following Shuja ud Daula, when Navab Asaf ud Daula took up residence in Lucknow, all those who had gathered in Faizabad uprooted themselves and settled here. Eventually some nobles and accomplished persons who had remained in the Bahu Begam's service came to Lucknow because Asaf ud Daula was spending such vast amounts of money that no one could help being attracted to his court.

There were of course at that time many Hindu states, but the Muslim courts were the only ones which were considered refined and cultured. The Hindu rajas themselves admitted that they could not surpass the Muslim courts as regards culture and social status. The idea of reviving their old civilization and providing for themselves a new culture and literature came to them only later as a result of British education. Because of this, if any distinguished scholar, poet or soldier left the service of a Muslim noble and went to the territory of Hindu nobles he was received with respect and accorded the highest rank and dignity.

The first and foremost Muslim court was the Mughal court of Delhi. Because of its antiquity and past grandeur, it was the centre for distinguished men and noble families who were now scattering themselves in distant areas and establishing themselves in new states. Of these there was the court of the Nizam Asaf Jah in the Deccan and further afield the courts of Tipu Sultan and the Navab of Arcat.[241] Going north from Delhi you came first to the region of the valiant Khans of Ruhelkhand, then to the court of Avadh and further on the court of Navab Nazim of Bengal in Murshidabad. The courts of the Deccan were at a very great distance from these Muslim courts and were difficult to reach because the roads leading to them passed through jungles and over mountains. Moreover, even if anyone had the courage to take these roads, he might lose his life because of the thugs and dacoits[242] who infested the whole countryside. It was also difficult to reach the country of the Nizam of Hyderabad. Therefore, when Delhi started to fall on evil days and its Mughal crowned heads were in a bad way talent was no longer appreciated there and most people turned towards other regions of the north. There is no doubt that Ruhelkhand was very close and if the Khans had had any appreciation of the fine arts they would have had the first opportunity to secure these people. They were religious and brave and had many excellent qualities, but they were completely devoid of any taste for learning or for the niceties of society. In evaluating them one realizes that their tastes were purely military. Apart from bringing together their fellow countrymen to add power to their military strength, they had no other interests. Their attitude towards polite society and the embellishments and etiquette of cultured life did not allow them to appreciate poets, men of letters and other accomplished persons. As a consequence, whoever entered their country moved on quickly and arrived in Lucknow. Here he received a warm welcome from every class of person and all were eager to help him in any way they could. Would anyone reaching such a place wish to leave? All who went there remained. Members of every ruined family from Delhi, immediately they got there, decided to stay permanently. They had no further thought of their birthplace nor had they the desire to see any other court. A few people moved on to the territory of the Navab Nazim of Bengal, but they were those who had not been appreciated in Lucknow. These were few in number. It was not long before all the great and distinguished men of the most refined social classes of the day had congregated in Lucknow.

Before the establishment of the court in Lucknow only Arabic scholarship existed. The foundations for this were laid when the Emperor Aurangzeb presented the houses of Firangi Mahal to Mulla Nizam ud Din Sehalvi.[96] The presence of this scholarly maulvi and his family had in a short time made Firangi Mahal into such a fine university that this small quarter of Lucknow became the centre for learned men from all over India. After Shaikh Abdul Haq of Delhi (1551–1642), no outstanding scholar emerged in Delhi itself. Certainly the family of Shah Wali Ullah (1702–63) eventually achieved greatness, but their academic fame was limited to *hadis*,[243] the traditions of the Prophet. Lucknow was the university for all forms of [religious-based] learning. In those days Lucknow was little known internationally and it was astonishing that such a place should develop a great university, before which not only India but Bukhara, Khwarazam, Herat and Kabul bowed their heads. The whole Islamic world took pride in acquiring knowledge here and at their own universities following the syllabus[97] of Mulla Nizami. In short, before the establishment of this new court, the learned men of Firangi Mahal had made Lucknow the centre for the study of medicine (*hikmat*), doubt and religious principles (*kalam*), religious jurisprudence (*fiqh*), Islamic philosophy, logic, social and physical sciences and theology.[351]

Now I wish to describe in detail all that came from Delhi to Lucknow and developed here. First the Urdu language, the language of the nobles and army officers who came to Lucknow with Navab Burhan ul Mulk Bahadur.

The Urdu language had its origin in Delhi and its poetry originated in the Deccan. Wali[244] of Gujrat came to Delhi with his collection of poems and awakened those who spoke the language to its charm. There was such magic in the melody of these poems that they were immediately on everyone's tongue and Urdu poetry made its début in Delhi.[245]

At first there were only a few eminent persons who started to promote and give value to the language in Delhi, but at that time even if the Urdu language was not in its infancy, it was certainly in its childhood. The most learned, erudite and distinguished of the original pioneers was Khan-e-Arzu,[246] whose work the late Maulana Azad[247] classed as belonging to the second phase of Urdu poetry. In the ensuing period, among the greatest and most illustrious can be counted Sauda,[198] Mir,[197] Mirza Mazhar Jan,[248] and Khwaja Dard,[249] all of whom were *shagirds*[250] [pupils] of Khan-e-Arzu. Khan-e-Arzu laid the foundations of poetry and expert linguistic knowledge in Lucknow. Navab Shuja ud Daula's uncle, Salar Jang, had great admiration for his achievements and had invited him to Lucknow. He lived in Avadh for some time and died in Lucknow itself two years after Shuja ud Daula's accession in 1756. He was the first preceptor of Urdu poetry and it was he who sowed the seeds of Urdu poetry and Urdu speech in Lucknow. But alas, his bones were snatched from the fond embrace of the Lucknow countryside and handed over to the soil of Delhi.

After Khan-e-Arzu, the most renowned man of letters of this phase was Ashraf Ali Khan Fughan.[251] He was a *koka*[252] [foster-brother] of King Ahmad Shah and came to Lucknow in the hope of recognition. Shuja ud Daula received him with great honour and the utmost respect and for a while made him a member of his court. But poets are by nature both sensitive and imaginative and he became annoyed because of some minor matter and went to Azimabad where he died two years before Shuja ud Daula himself left this world.

In the third stage of Urdu poetry, as defined by Maulana Azad, the pupils of Khan-e-Arzu reigned paramount over Urdu verse. Mirza Rafi Sauda, Mir Taqi Mir and Saiyyid Muhammad Mir Soz[253] were the leading men of letters of this phase. All had left Delhi for Lucknow.

Other distinguished men of letters who at this time came to Lucknow and stayed there were Mirza Jafar Ali Hasrat,[254] Mir Haidar Ali Hairan,[255] Khwaja Hasan Hasan,[256] Mirza Fakhir Makin,[257] Mir Zahik,[258] Baqa ullah Khan Baqa,[259] Mir Zahik's son Mir Hasan Dehlavi,[260] author of the famous *masnavi* and scores of similar poets. Mir Qamar ud Din Minnat,[261] Mir Zia ud Din Zia[262] and Ashraf Ali Khan Fughan came from Delhi to Lucknow, stayed and shone there for a time but were eventually enticed away by other courts who were on the lookout for talent. They went to Calcutta and then Azimabad, where they eventually died. Although Shaikh Muhammad Qaim[263] died in his native Nagina (in Bignor District, U.P.) he too had been a member of the Lucknow circle.

Only a few great men like Mirza Mazhar Jan-e-Janan and Khwaja Mir Dard who led ascetic lives and cared nothing for worldly possessions remained in Delhi. They were, furthermore, tied to Delhi because both were *sajjada nashin*,[264] leaders of their sects. In short, during this third phase of poetry the concentration of poets in Delhi broke up and started to reassemble in Lucknow. There was more enthusiasm and appreciation of talent in Lucknow than had ever been known before in India.

Now the fourth phase commenced. Although its exponents came from Delhi and Akbarabad, their poetry reached its zenith in Lucknow. Here they became famous and here they were the principal figures at the mushairas. Here they lived, here they gained repute and here they died. The most notable poets of this era were Jurat,[265] Saiyyid Insha,[266] Mushafi,[267] Qatil[268] and Rangin.[269] All were masters of the language of the time and their poetry acquired such fame that no other Urdu poet could surpass them. Where are the bones of all these men? In the soil of Lucknow.

One can judge the number of cultured people who came from Delhi to Lucknow from a story told by Saiyyid Insha. He describes a conversation between an elegant old nobleman of the time and a courtesan named Nuran. The nobleman and courtesan were both from Delhi but the conversation took place in Lucknow. Nuran said, 'Welcome Mir Sahib! You are like the Eid Moon,[270] which shows up only once a year. In Delhi you used to come and stay with me until late at night. What has happened to you in Lucknow that you never show your face? How I searched for you recently in Kerbala without finding a trace of you! Do not forget to go there on the eighth day[271] of Muharram. For Ali's sake I implore you to go there on the eighth day of mourning.' The answer which Mir Sahib gave was extremely interesting, though too lengthy to include here. But he commented on contemporary fashions in Delhi and Lucknow and criticized the poets of the day. I have no argument with what he said and merely wish to point out that in addition to well-bred and distinguished people, even courtesans were continuously coming to settle in Lucknow and those who once found delight in the Delhi flower shows[272] now found enjoyment in Kerbala and the celebrations of the eighth day of Muharram.

The late Shams ul Ulema[273] Maulana Azad, without discriminating between poets or their period, placed all the later poets of Delhi and Lucknow into one category which he called the fifth phase. But this is not fair; the real fifth cycle belonged only to Nasikh and Atish and in it the language acquired a new form, old ideas were discarded and new constructions were created. The foundations were laid for the language which was unanimously accepted by the poets of Delhi and Lucknow and which is, to all intents and purposes, the language which is now firmly established in India. This is the period when Lucknow, for the first time, exercised its authority over the domain of Urdu poetry.

After this came the sixth phase when in Lucknow, Wazir,[274] Zia,[262] Rind,[202] Goya,[275] Rashk,[276] Nasim Dehlavi,[277] Aseer,[278] Navab Mirza Shauq[205] and Pandit Daya Shankar Nasim[279] demonstrated their talents. The last two acquired great fame as the authors of masnavis, whilst in Delhi, Momin,[280] Zauq[281] and Ghalib[282] were causing their melodious poetry to be acclaimed. It is certainly true that the poetry of this phase enriched the language more than any other.

Then followed a seventh cycle which consisted of the works of Amir,[283] Dagh,[284] Munir,[285] Taslim,[286] Majruh,[287] Jalal,[288] Latafat,[289] Afzal,[290] Hakim[290] and others.

When carefully considering these latter phases one realizes clearly what a strong tradition[291] of linguistic eloquence and poetry had been established in Lucknow. In a short time it became the fashion to compose poetry and it is unlikely that there has ever been a greater concourse of poets in any other language. Women also started to discuss poetry and language and even in the speech of the uneducated one could find poetically inspired thoughts, similes and metaphors.

10

The Development of Urdu Poetry— *Masnavi, Marsiya* and Forms of Humorous Verse

The real starting-point of Persian poetry was the *masnavi*[204] and this form of poetry has always been considered the most important and most forceful. Firdausi's[292] martial masnavi *Shah Nameh* led the way and Nizami,[293] Sa'di,[225] Maulana Rum,[294] Khusrau,[295] Jami,[296] Hatifi[297] and others achieved the highest renown in this field. Mir Taqi Mir wrote many short masnavis when he was in Delhi and Lucknow but they are so abridged and commonplace that it seems inappropriate to include them in the category of masnavis.

The first poet to write masnavis in Urdu was Mir Ghulam Hasan Hasan,[260] the son of Mir Zahik, who came to Lucknow in his childhood with his eminent father. He grew up as one of the community in Lucknow, he was nurtured here and his poetry developed in the local atmosphere. The society which influenced the writing of his masnavi *Benazir-o-Badar-e-Munir* was of Lucknow pure and simple. At the time, Mirza Muhammad Taqi Khan Havas wrote his masnavi *Laila Majnun* and taste for masnavis increased in Lucknow. At the time of Atish and Nasikh there was a waning of interest, until Pandit Daya Shankar Nasim[279] wrote *Gulzar-e-Nasim*, Afatb ud Daula Qalaq[298] wrote *Tilism-e-Ulfat* and Navab Mirza Shauq[205] *Bahar-e-Ishq, Zahre-e-Ishq* and *Fareb-e-Ishq*. These achieved such fame and prominence that their verses were on the tongues of all. At an earlier period an author had written the masnavi *Lazat-e-Ishq* in reply to Mir Hasan's masnavi. As this was published with the masnavis of Navab Mirza Shauq, it is usually ascribed to the latter. But in reality it is not his, nor is it of his period.

Compared with all these other masnavis *Gulzar-e-Nasim*, in spite of its universal popularity, contains hundreds of mistakes.[299] It appears as the work of a recondite novice who wished to introduce into his composition every sort of poetical charm but who, lacking the power of expression, stumbled at every step and was unable to achieve his object. In answer to it Agha Ali Shams, who was a poet of long experience, wrote a masnavi in the same metre which was free from errors and showed perfection in the use of simile and metaphor and in command of language. But unfortunately that masnavi was lost and could not prove its superiority over *Gulzar-e-Nasim* which had already acquired fame. Also at this time, in Delhi, Momin Khan[280] wrote some incomparable short masnavis which became popular and famous.

Momin Khan's poetic taste was a mass of recondite ideas. He built the edifice of his diction on fanciful similes and metaphors and in his masnavis defined imaginary desires and qualities in a way that rendered his style most attractive. One of Momin Khan's shagirds,[250] Nasim Dehlavi,[277] came to Lucknow and proved his worth to such an extent in mushairas that many people became his disciples.

Nasim Dehlavi added great lustre to the name of his master when he came to Lucknow and one of his pupils, Taslim[286] Lakhnavi, reproduced the beautiful thoughts of Naziri,[300] Urfi[301] and Saeb[302] in an Urdu masnavi and made Faizi[303] and Ghanimat[304] live again in Urdu poetry. At the end of this period Maulvi Mir Ali Haidar Tabatabai[305] Nazm Lakhnavi placed before the Urdu reading public an incomparable ethical poem censuring the drinking of wine, which he called 'Saqi Namah Shaqshaqia'. In short, if one disregards certain short masnavis of Momin Khan, the composition of Urdu masnavis began in Lucknow and also developed there.

Some scholars illustrate the difference between the speech of Delhi and that of Lucknow[306] by comparing Mir Hasan's masnavi with *Gulzar-e-Nasim*. Maulvi Muhammad Husain Azad[247] lent great weight to this idea but although *Gulzar-e-Nasim* acquired some renown, as did Nazir Akbarabadi's[307] *Banjari Nama*, to compare it with Mir Hasan's masnavi is an insult to Urdu poetry. A true comparison would be between Mir Hasan's masnavi and *Tilism-e-Ulfat*. However, if the language of *Gulzar-e-Nasim* is (unjustifiably) regarded as a true example of the language of Lucknow, the comparison between the masnavi of Mir Hasan and *Gulzar-e-Nasim* is not a comparison between the poetry of Delhi and that of Lucknow but one between the earlier and later speech of Lucknow. Mir Hasan's masnavi is an example of the early language of Lucknow and *Gulzar-e-Nasim* that of a later period.

An important early form of poetry is *marsiya*,[234] the elegy. In ancient Arab poetry the recital of elegies and *rajaz*,[308] battle hymns, was the means of displaying perfection in verse and eloquence. The recital of elegies in Persian had become rare until the time of the Safavi dynasty when the Shia religion had prominence in Persia. Then, in order to revive the memory of the calamities which overtook the members of the Prophet's family, poets turned their attention to the composition of elegies. Maulana Muhtashim Kashi composed a noteworthy marsiya consisting of a few verses which became universally popular. After this it became the custom for poets occasionally to compose a marsiya in order to lament the death of Imam Husain, but marsiyas were so scantily valued in the world of poetry that there was a saying, 'A down-at-heel poet turns to composing marsiyas.' However, as the Shia kingdom of Avadh became the religious successor to the defunct Safavi monarchy, a great impetus was given in Lucknow to mourning assemblies.[129] The composition of marsiyas was accorded such value that this art reached exceptional eminence. In fact these Shia practices are the source of Lucknow's cultural rise. In India the Mughal government had made Persian the court language. The social life of the Mughal nobles was that of the Persians and they considered it to be the acme of perfection. The result was that any Persian, immediately he came to India, was the cynosure of everyone's eye and his actions and mannerisms were watched with approbation. In Delhi, because the religion of the kings was Sunni, the Persians concealed many of their customs and so were unable to reveal themselves completely. The court of Avadh had emanated from Khurasan and adhered to the Shia faith. Hence the Persians here showed themselves in their true light. The more brilliantly they revealed themselves, the more their co-religionists at this court began to adopt their mannerisms and deportment. Thus Persian culture, which had been nurtured in the stately and majestic laps of the Sassanide[309] and Abbaside[310] dynasties, permeated the society of Lucknow.

At the time of Sauda and Mir, Mian[311] Sikander, Gada, Miskin and Afsurda were the composers of marsiyas. They wrote short poems on the martyrdom of Imam Husain which they recited at assemblies of mourning. After them Mir Khaliq[312] and Mir Zamir[313] greatly enriched the art of marsiya composition and the present style was developed in their day. Mir Zamir's pupil Mirza Dabir[314] and Mir Khaliq's son Mir Anis[315] both reached the heights of fame and showed such poetical perfection in their composition of marsiyas that they shone like the sun and the moon in the firmament of poetry and letters. The controversy which had existed over the merits of Mir and Sauda and Atish and Nasikh was now centred on Mir Anis and Mirza Dabir. Mirza Dabir displayed a grandeur of language, lofty ideas and great erudition. Mir Anis's style had those fine attributes of simplicity, frankness and human allurement that cannot be learned but are obtained only from the Almighty. Both these great men composed marsiyas superior to any other form of poetry and made the innovations in Urdu literature that people had been seeking as a result of the influence of British education.[316]

Anis and Dabir had improved the composition of marsiyas to such a degree that instead of being despised the form was now considered the finest in poetic art. People of Lucknow praised these two great men to such an extent that the city was divided into two factions. Every literary man was the champion of either Anis or Dabir and the controversy between these two groups was unending.

Mir Anis made an art of the reciting of marsiyas, known as *marsiya khwani*,[317] in addition to composing them. One hears that some Greek orators made special efforts to render their speech effective and by raising and lowering their voices and varying their mannerisms and gestures gave force to their diction. In the long life of Islam, Anis was the first to introduce such techniques of oratory. The art of making desirable changes in the sound of words, of adjusting one's facial expression to the subject, of moving one's limbs in a way befitting the discourse and of making it forceful through minute gestures is distinctive to Lucknow, which is directly attributable to the family[318] of Mir Anis. The family is still making efforts to improve this technique, and if our speakers would take instruction from these accomplished people, they would achieve great success as orators.

Arabic and Persian literatures did not include the art of drama which is the life-blood of Western poetry. Urdu, being the pupil of Persian literature, has never paid any attention to the subject. There are several very fine Sanskrit dramas, but latter-day Indian society has become completely unacquainted with them. Certainly the exploits of Ramchandra Ji and Sri Krishna are depicted among Hindus with religious reverence, but Urdu poetry was not in the least concerned with them. Ramchandra Ji's adventures are depicted in martial dramas in open spaces. Sri Krishna's adventures are reproduced in song, dance and music in religious gatherings. They are like operas and are known as Rahas.[217] Wajid Ali Shah became absorbed in the Rahas, and used their plots to compose a drama in which he himself played the part of Krishna, as well as that of a love-sick yogi who sat in meditation and was pursued by many beautiful women and lovelorn milkmaids. Then, when the gates of the Qaisar Bagh fairs were opened to the public, dramatic art made great headway in the city. The enthusiasm was such that some famous poets, in deference to the taste of the time, took to writing dramas. At the same time as Wajid Ali Shah was showing his love for Rahas, Mian Amanat,[319] a practised poet, wrote *Indar Sabha* and, in the manner of present-day theatrical companies, several associations in various parts of the city gave performances of it on the stage, young boys sometimes taking the parts of women. The *Indar Sabha* had attractive tunes especially composed for it and townspeople were eager to see the play. Because of Mian Amanat's success, others attempted to emulate him and many dramas of the same nature were produced. All were called *Sabha* and *Madari Lal* and others staged many *Sabhas* with different versions of the same plot. These were so attractive to the people that they became the only form of singing and dancing in which they took any interest. Old love stories were retold in pleasing verse with additional subject-matter and put before the public to suit the taste of the moment.

There is no doubt that the Parsi theatre,[320] with its excellent organization and engaging ostentation, superseded the Sabhas, but it should not be forgotten that this taste for drama originated, became popular and developed in Lucknow. For a start, the Parsis had taken their cue from Lucknow and the first play which they produced was Amanat's *Indar Sabha*. But despite the Parsi theatre even up to the present time plays like *The Snake-Charmer*, *Harish Chandra* and scores of others continue to be performed in Lucknow. A company of actors has been established which continues to delight the public even though cultured people have turned away from drama. In any case, there is no doubt that the foundations of Urdu drama[321] were definitely laid in Lucknow and from there became current throughout India.

One form of Urdu poetry is *vasokht*. It consists of a special kind of *musadas*, a six-lined verse, of an erotic nature. The subject of these poems usually involves a lover who first proclaims his love, then gives a description of the beloved and her infidelities. After this the lover becomes offended and tells the beloved that he has become enamoured of some other charmer. He praises the beauty and fascination of this imaginary loved one, thus making his true love jealous, teasing and tormenting her until her pride is broken and there is a reconciliation. This form of Urdu verse originated in Lucknow in the middle period when poets wrote very beguiling vasokhts. At a later period, various vasokhts were composed in Delhi; those of Momin Khan in particular are excellent. But their place of origin was Lucknow.

The voluptuous temperament of the nobles encouraged the development of several other forms of poetry that had originated in Delhi and flourished in Lucknow. Of these *hazal goi*, comic verse, was the most senseless of all, and another, having some attraction, was *rekhti*,[322] verses written in the language of women. Jafar Zattali,[323] who probably lived at the time of Muhammad Shah, started hazal goi in Delhi. I have read his work from beginning to end and, except for lewdness and the height of immodesty, there is nothing in it; one can find neither poetic refinement nor beauty of language. Then a writer of hazal goi originally from Bilgram, U.P., called Saiyyid Imam Ali with the pen-name of Sahib Qaran, came from Delhi to Lucknow. He arrived in Lucknow at the time of Asaf ud Daula and kept company with degenerate and showy young nobles. Copies of his work are still in existence and although it is vulgar and obscene, it has some poetic beauty and a command of language and refined idiom. In the final poetic phase of Lucknow, Mian Mushir, who was a pupil of Mirza Dabir, brought hazal goi to perfection.

Now, ignoring any bigoted views held by either Shias or Sunnis, I want to say something about these faiths. The Shia faith is based on two canons. The first is *tawalla*, affection, that is to say showing affection to the family of the Prophet. The second is *tabarra*, condemnation, or showing unforgiveness, towards the enemies of that honoured family. This precipitated prejudice and led to abuse and vilification. On principle, Sunnis share this belief with Shias but differ in that they believe the first three successors to the Prophet to be the most pre-eminent of mankind after the Prophet himself and the true vicars of the apostleship. The Shias, however, consider them usurpers and tyrants and as such enemies of the Prophet's family—hence *tabarra*, objects of condemnation. Cultured and learned men minimize this distinction, but common Shias heap insults and abuse upon the first three Caliphs. This is the basis for antagonism between the Shias and the Sunnis.

These two religious doctrines had a very good and welcome effect on Lucknow, poetry. Tawalla took the art of *marsiya*, elegy-writing, into its embrace and made it the greatest form of poetry. Tabarra, the desire to condemn enemies of the Prophet's family, adopted *hajo goi*, satire, and from it developed *harzia goi*, frivolous poetry. Several brilliant men in Lucknow gained repute through it but unfortunately it was especially displeasing to members of the Sunni sect. At the time of the rule of the Navabs swords were drawn, and under the British, even to this day, there are sometimes quarrels and court actions because of it. The result has been that the composing and reciting of this form of poetry has not dared to emerge from the four walls of the house in which it originates. If the general subject had not become a matter of contention then that period would have shown the extent to which the writers of harzia goi had proved the excellence of their immodest utterances and obscenities.

The person who acquired the highest renown in this art was Mian Mushir, a pupil of Mirza Dabir. There had been satire and obscenity before, but the ways in which Mushir employed idiom, picked his words, formed his style and introduced humour into his similes were beyond description and his language and technique convulsed his readers with laughter. To introduce elegance into despicable subject-matter and to make it worthy of being placed before cultured people was a talent he alone possessed and one that has not been seen in anyone else either before or after him.

In considering hazal goi one should also mention the name of Mirza Chirkin.[324] Near the middle period of Navabi rule in Lucknow, there lived a learned nobleman of good taste named Ashur Ali Khan. At that time, to be numbered among his friends signified admission to the highest society. He discovered Jan Sahib[325] and Chirkin and some say that Sahib Qaran rose to fame because of his patronage. All Chirkin's poems deal with urine and latrines and they are all so disgusting that his name would offend the senses of my readers. I have mentioned him however as he had a particular aptitude of his own. There is a certain amount of poetic beauty and apt metaphor in his writing, though even this is ruined by the filth and squalor of his thoughts.

The art of *rekhti*, verse couched in woman's language, although vulgar, is interesting and it is not offensive like Chirkin's verse. In every language there are certain differences between the idiom and cadence of a man's speech and that of a woman. These differences, while they are present in Persian and Arabic, are more pronounced in Urdu.

The old custom in Persian and Arabic was that if a woman wrote poetry, she wrote it in her own form of speech. If a man expressed an idea through a woman it was done in woman's speech and this added charm to his diction: the same applied in English. Urdu poetry has always been written exclusively in the masculine form, so much so that if women compose verses they do so as if they themselves were men.[326] They use men's speech and even apply masculine pronouns to themselves. If the poet's name is unknown, it is not possible to say whether the work is by a man or a woman.

In the third or fourth phase of Urdu poetry some humorous young persons created the form known as *rekhti*, women's speech, to approximate to *rekhta*, the usual masculine form. Mir Hasan, in his masnavi, used this form of speech where necessary and to good effect. Mian Rangin,[269] who lived in Delhi and would attend Lucknow mushairas, always employed this style, which was at first considered immodest and uncultured by people of polite society. I have written elsewhere of Saiyyid Insha's account of the conversation that took place in Lucknow between a refined elderly gentleman of Delhi and Nuran, a celebrated courtesan of the same place. The old gentleman says: 'Above all, listen to this. The son of Sadat Yar Tahmasp—adopted name Anvari[327]—whose nom de plume is Rangin and who considers himself rekhta personified, has written a masnavi and given it the name of "Dilpazir". It is couched in the language of harlots and makes bitter criticism of Mir Hasan and his masnavi "Badar-e-Munir", asking how anyone can call it poetry. And indeed, the late Mir Hasan was not much good. Still, everyone in Delhi and Lucknow reads Rangin's masnavi which goes something like this: "There she goes, corner of dress in hand, jingling her bangles." The wretched Rangin tells his tale in the same way. One wonders how a boy, the son of an army risaldar, more used to sword and lance, can have turned to poetry. The fact is that he degenerated by associating with prostitutes and so gave up rekhta and invented this new form of rekhti with a view to exciting the female members of decent families and corrupting their morals. He says, "Be sure of the address of Rangin: how far it is, O palanquin-bearers!" and he takes the trouble to collect the language of the prostitutes in a notebook.'

But such cultured old men died complaining and the young made Rangin popular. Thus rekhti became established as a form of Urdu poetry which, although created by a Delhi poet, was used by him in Lucknow and achieved prominence here. After the era of Mir Hasan, the heights to which Navab Mirza Shauq raised this form of poetry are beyond all praise. One can go on reading page after page without finding anything forced in the versification, as if this form of language came quite naturally to the author. Jan Sahib was Rangin's successor as a writer of hazal goi. He was an ordinary resident of Lucknow who had gained polish and perfection at Ashur Ali Khan's court. After Jan Sahib, there were other writers of rekhti in Lucknow, but he was the best and the most famous. He wrote ghazals, vasokhts, and other forms of poetry in this style.

If rekhti had refrained from obscenity and immorality and had dealt in ideas of virtue and chastity, the art would have been worth cultivating to a certain extent. But it failed. Rekhti always marched outside the path of culture and moderation and, although it may have added something to the language, it certainly had a harmful effect on morals.

11

The Development of Urdu Prose

Urdu prose has not been in existence as long as Urdu poetry. For a considerable period it was usual among educated people to write verse in Persian as well as Urdu. However, the preference and inclination of the majority was towards *ghazal sarai*,[328] the chanting of odes, in Urdu, and in India the number of Urdu poets was much greater than that of Persian poets. But as regards prose, the whole country[329] preferred reading and writing in Persian. Books on science and the arts were in Persian, religious books were also produced in that language and things had reached the stage where old and young were corresponding in Persian. Children at school were given Persian lessons and were taught to write letters in that language. The result was that however sweet and eloquent Urdu might have been for conversation, immediately it came to writing people seemed to be struck dumb.

Mir Amman Dehlavi, with the encouragement and guidance[330] of the British, wrote his *Chahar Darvesh*, 'The Four Dervishes'. At the same time Mirza Ali[331] produced his treatise on Urdu poets which was printed through the efforts of Abdullah Khan, a resident of Hyderabad. Also about this period Maulvi Ismail Shahid[332] wrote his *Taqwait-ul-Iman*, 'The Strengthening of the Faith', on the subject of the unity of God and allegiance to the Sunni faith. However one likes to look upon these two books today, they were not written with a view to displaying literary perfection: their only objective was to present the subject-matter in unaffected and simple language so that the general public might benefit. If these distinguished men had wished to show literary perfection in Urdu, then in accordance with prevailing principles, they would have adopted the style of Zahuri,[333] Nemat Khan-e-Ali,[334] Abul Fazal[335] and Tahir Wahid,[336] who in those days held sway over the world of literature, and without reference to whom no writing was considered worthy of praise. In conversation, culture and refinement were shown by adopting a style similar to that demonstrated by Saiyyid Insha when he copied out some of the utterances of Mirza Mazhar Jan-e-Janan.

The fact is that Urdu prose-writing originated in Lucknow with the publication of Mirza Rajab Ali Beg Surur's[337] *Fasane-e-Ajaib* and other works. A little later *Nau Ratan* was also published in Lucknow. Its author was Muhammad Baksh Mahjur,[338] a pupil of Jurat, and a product of Lucknow society.

It is true that Rajab Ali Beg Surur showed the highest skill as a writer and when his book appeared it was received with admiration in Urdu circles. Unfortunately the author made an attack on Mir Amman in his preface, with the result that he was a failure in the eyes of the people of Delhi—so much so that a refined and distinguished man like Maulvi Muhammad Husain Azad called him 'that vagabond from Lucknow'. It is impossible to say how long it will be before the late Rajab Ali Beg is forgiven for his impertinence. Although the skill of Mir Amman as a writer may have come to the notice of the British in those days, it had not been recognized by any Urdu-speaking person. This was so because the effects of British education had not yet changed the country's literary style and oriental taste in literature.

In regard to literary style, I have often written that this is closely connected with one's upbringing and education. It is acquired in the same way as discrimination in matters of food, scent, colour and other similar things. Because of differences between countries and races the most delightful and best-loved thing in one person's estimation can be tasteless or even the object of disgust to another. Literature and literary taste are no exceptions. A style which has been fostered by one country and has become popular with its people might in the view of another be insipid, absurd and tasteless. Truth to tell, no one can come to a final decision as to which style is good and which is bad.

In pagan times in Arabia it was considered eloquent to employ rhyming sentences, to combine related and common words in uninterrupted sequence, and to repeat one subject several times over to render it effective and interesting. As the Quran was in the national language it had a miraculous effect in bringing this style to the pitch of perfection and it became the greatest work in Arabic literature. If considered by present-day standards, the best written Arabic books, like *Muqamat-e-Hurari* and *Tarikh-e-Timuri*, contain nothing but artificial rhyming and unjustifiable prolixity. It was a style, however, which had for centuries been a source of pleasure to all.

Persian writers also adopted this style and as literature progressed it became firmer and stronger. Because this style was very popular it was adopted by early Urdu writers and was acclaimed by all. Therefore to think that when *Chahar Darvesh* was written, except for its popularity with the British, who did not even understand Urdu, it was accorded any literary merit by learned men of India, is completely unrealistic.

Undoubtedly English influence had created a period when old Urdu literature discarded the jewels and clothing it used to wear and adopted the garments of the West. *The Four Dervishes* and other similar books became popular with the public, not because they had any particular merit but because they had discarded the old literary style which, having been universally popular, was not now in favour.

At that time Maulvi Ghulam Imam Shahid[339] wrote his celebrated *Maulud-e-Sharif*, 'The Birth of the Holy Prophet', in Lucknow. It conformed to such a degree with contemporary literary taste that everyone was very pleased with it.

Because of its acceptability from a religious point of view it is still popular today.

Present-day Urdu prose actually originated in Delhi and will always owe a debt of gratitude to that city. Mirza Ghalib adopted a stimple style in writing Urdu which is very near to the style of today. Although he sometimes made use of rhyming sentences, this use is so unaffected that the reader has to think twice before he realizes that he is reading rhyme. Present-day education has done a great deal to make this style acceptable to the public and it has been acclaimed by all classes of society. After Ghalib, Sir Syed[340] added some vigour to this simplicity but always with the aim that his writing should be in no way abstruse. Maulvi Muhammad Husain Azad added greater charm to this vigour at a time when the people of Lucknow, being unfamiliar with British influence, were still enamoured of the old-fashioned style. In Lucknow up to the end of Wajid Ali Shah's lifetime, flowery and rhymed composition was the order of the day and people had had no chance of acquiring a taste for simple style.

During this period the journal *Tahzibul Ikhlaq* was appearing from Aligarh, *Terwhin Sadi* from Agra and *Avadh Punch*[341] from Lucknow. The language of all these was the highest quality Urdu prose. In *Tahzibul Ikhlaq*, sorrow in regard to national tribulation was portrayed with seriousness and scholarly dignity. The phrasing was clear and analytical, incorporating ideas taken from the latest Western philosophy and literature together with impressive discourses. *Terwhin Sadi* with great skill preserved the old literary style whilst adorning it with new ideas. Old Eastern literature was portrayed with its ancient garments remodelled so that adherents to both the old and the new styles could not help acclaiming its contents. *Avadh Punch*, although humorous in content, was written in a dignified style. There were several contributors whose style possessed both charm and beauty. The wit of the editor, Munshi Sajjad Husain, the crystal-clear language of Mirza Machu Beg, the Persianized style of Munshi Ahmad Ali Ksamandavi and the Hindi verses of Tribhavan Nath Hijr, as well as his beautiful prose—all infused new life and elegance into Urdu prose.

At that time Pandit Ratan Nath's[342] novel *Fasana-e-Azad*, 'The Adventures of Azad', began to be published in the newspaper *Avadh Akhbar*.[343] It made a great impression on its readers, and through it the Urdu world acquired a taste for novel-reading that even became a passion. In *Fasana-e-Azad*, when the author described a scene or wrote about an incident, he employed the old style of Surur's *Fasana-e-Ajaib* and improved upon it. When he recorded conversations between two characters he used very simple and homely language; the language of the women is particularly lucid. Although the novel has some faults, it is true to say that his efforts achieved a higher standard than those of anyone before him.

This was also the time when Maulvi Nazir Ahmad,[344] on Government instructions, translated the Indian Penal Code. In this and in his other works, he gave his country a style which in terms of fluency and clarity is incomparable. In other respects it is difficult, recondite and ponderous because it is so full of Arabic words.

The writings of Maulvi Muhammad Husain Azad were also in a popular style. In particular his history of the Urdu language and treatise on Urdu poets made him famous.

In 1882 I started the weekly journal *Mahshar* under the pen-name of Maulvi Muhammad Abdul Basit Mahshar. It reproduced Addison's style in Urdu in such an attractive way and with such suitable wording and ideas that it was universally admired among Urdu-speaking people. At the same time my articles began to appear in the columns of *Avadh Akhbar* and presented an entirely new style of writing that became very popular. It became apparent that most essayists had adopted this style and that it was given general preference. I then presented to the public my novel *Dilchasp* and a touching and interesting drama *Shadid-e-Wafa* and received encouragement from every direction.

Eventually realizing the feeling throughout the country, I produced my journal *Dil Gudaz* at the beginning of 1887. Its style appealed both to those who knew English and to people with old-fashioned tastes. From 1888 a series of historical novels was published in the journal. The first of these was *Malik ul Aziz aur Varjinia*. Readers eagerly took to these novels, and through them the foundation was laid for an increase in the reading of books. An appetite for reading history and for taking an interest in world affairs was engendered and these novels and the *Dil Gudaz* achieved a style on which present-day Urdu prose literature is based.

Urdu prose,[345] as far as the old literary style is concerned, had its origin in Lucknow. Certainly the new style originated in Delhi but wherever possible Lucknow vied with Delhi in efforts at improvement. Humorous and witty writing in particular was initiated in Lucknow and came to perfection here.

12

Dastan Goi—The Art of Story-Telling

The development of the Urdu language in Lucknow was not confined to the efforts of men of letters alone. Contributions were made at all levels of society that caused the language to improve, broaden and assume new aspects which were sources of interest to all classes.

The subject most worthy of attention is *dastan goi*, story-telling, which is in fact the name for extemporary authorship. This art actually originated in Arabia where in pagan times assemblies were held for the telling of tales. We do not know whether the recital of tales in India has any connection with that of Arabia. *The Tale of Amir Hamza*,[346] which is the basis for all raconteurs, was in fact in the Persian language. It is said to have been composed by a most gifted person named *Amir Khusrau*[347] in the days of the Tughlaq dynasty.

Famous raconteurs from Delhi came to Lucknow and here opium addicts so much appreciated their art that they made listening to stories an important element of their gatherings. In a short time the practice had such a hold on Lucknow that there was no rich man who did not appoint a story-teller to his entourage. Hundreds of them soon appeared on the scene. There are still one or two distinguished raconteurs in Delhi but in Lucknow their name is legion.

Their eloquence has had a great effect on the language of the general public. After the taste for reading novels had developed, attention was paid to writing tales in the language of these raconteurs, and Lucknow was able to produce most worthy exponents of the art. They wrote bulky volumes for distribution to the Urdu-reading public.[348] Among these were Jah and Qamar who are regarded with great appreciation throughout the country.

The art of telling stories is divided under four headings: 'War', 'Pleasure', 'Beauty' and 'Love', and 'Deception'. The raconteurs of Lucknow have shown such perfection in telling tales under these headings that one must hear them in order to realize the extent of their skill. The painting of pictures with words and the ability to make a deep and lasting impression on the minds of their audience are the special skills of these people.

For entertainment, wit and merriment, several devices were developed in Lucknow to enrich the language. One of these devices is *phabti*, pleasantry, to give an appropriate name in jest. It is connected with poetic simile and metaphor but has the peculiarity of making a target of its victim, revealing his faults and producing an apt, mirth-provoking simile to castigate him. In Lucknow even the humblest boys, courtesans, illiterate shopkeepers and tradesmen are so expert in producing apt phabtis as to amaze the stranger. A gentleman had returned from making a pilgrimage to holy Kerbala and was sitting with his friends dressed in resplendent white attire when a boy said: 'Well I never. Where has this Euphrates heron appeared from?' An old bridegroom, having dyed his hair, came to marry his bride and brought with him a most imposing bridal procession. Having emerged from the women's quarters he was going towards the reception. He bent down to take off his shoes and for a short distance advanced in this position. Someone asked 'Where is the bridegroom?' and a witty courtesan who was entertaining said laughingly, 'There goes the baby on all fours.'

A street-vendor was selling sugar-cane in the market. His cry was, 'O brother, who needs to hook in his kites?'[349] Can any metaphor be more apt than that? The most delicate metaphor is that in which neither the name of the object itself, nor the object to which similitude is given, is mentioned. What better example could there be than this case where there is no mention of sugar-cane nor of the pole by which the kite is hooked in? There could not be a more appropriate phrase to appeal to the sense of humour of the people of the bazaar. Thousands of similar examples may be heard at all times in everyday conversation.

Another device is *zila*, double meaning. This really is to prose what *riayet* is to poetry, a way of handling words in which most, if not all, the ideas introduced link up with what is suggested by the first word. When used by ordinary people, this device gives a special flavour and adds wit to conversation. Efforts are made with zila to bring in everything connected with the matter discussed from one point of view or another. Azad Faqir, who had a particular style of his own, is considered to have reached mastery in his employment of zila. In his poetry, Amanat concentrated to such an extent on the pursuit of riayet that he made it his primary objective, completely disregarding all other forms of poetical niceties. The result is that his diction left the field of poetry and entered the category of zilas. Most of the ordinary folk in Lucknow have advanced this art to such a degree in their everyday conversation that Amanat's poetry has been left far behind. Nowhere else have people attained one-hundredth the proficiency of the inhabitants of Lucknow in uttering zilas. A book has even been published on the subject.[350] A third device is *tuk bandi*, rhyme-forming. This is poetical rhyming, and many unlettered people when they give their attention to this will, in competition with someone else, produce extempory rhymes which amaze the greatest of poets. In my schooldays I used to see a Hindu sweet-meat seller who came out of his house in the early morning carrying his wares on a tray. As soon as they saw his face, hundreds of bazaar boys surrounded him and he would put down his tray and sit by the side of the road. Immediately a rhyming competition commenced, he on his own competing against all of the boys. There was a flood of abusive repartee between them, but the understanding was that the words of abuse must rhyme and as many words as possible must be used. I saw him scores of times. People would contest against him for hours on end but I never saw him at a loss for an answer. He used to produce some form of rhyme on every occasion.

In this way, in badinage and in ordinary conversation, many new ideas were formulated and ignorant people sometimes put forth ideas that left great poets dumbfounded. This period was in fact Lucknow's golden age. The beauties of poetry and literature had penetrated into the very hearts and souls of the people. Everyone who was more or less educated would try his skill. Even unlettered and common people of the lowest grades of society as well as stay-at-home women realized the sweetness of poetry and the elegance of literature. Illiterate vegetable-vendors were poets and the speech of the ignorant was so refined and polished, so full of words expressive of ethics and etiquette and so overflowing with cultured views on correct behaviour that the majority of learned men were astonished on hearing their conversations and no one could look upon them as ignorant. The cries of the street-vendors were so decorated with poetic conceits and eloquent obscurities that it was sometimes difficult for others to understand them.

Lower-class people had also evolved special literary interests according to their tastes. For instance, one practice arose which was known as *khayal* [lit. 'imagination']. People composed extempory verses and recited them when sitting in a circle. The name *khayal* was given to the feat of everyone producing a masterpiece from his imagination and creating some new idea. Several exponents of this art achieved great success and although they had no connection with the best society or with educated people, still, if one considers the matter, one must admit that they produced real and natural poetry. It was the equivalent of the poetry produced in Arabia in pagan times.

In this manner there developed a style known as *danda* [lit. 'club-wielding']. The aim was to compose poems about important and well-known contemporary events, with complete freedom of expression. With the greatest temerity these poems would show up a person exactly as he was, no matter how influential and rich that person happened to be. They would reveal the good he had done for the country or the great harm he had inflicted on it. Then the verses would be sung in a special way to the accompaniment of the beating together of sticks.

In every country and in every race the speech of women is purer and more attractive than that of men. In Lucknow the speech of noble women and honoured ladies, in addition to having femininity and allure, was imbued with literary and poetical refinement. When they spoke it seemed as though 'flowers were dropping from their lips'. One realized from the perfection of their words, their pleasing constructions and the delicacy of their enunciation the excellence that language had attained in this part of the country.

13

Islamic Studies

At the same time as it achieved perfection in language and poetry, Lucknow advanced further in the field of academic studies[351] and erudition than any other city in India. As regards learning, Lucknow was the Baghdad and Cordova of India and the Nishapur and Bokhara of the East.

Those responsible for the introduction of this scholarship and erudition were the learned men of the Firangi Mahal, whose circumstances I mentioned earlier in this book (Chapter 2). There is little doubt that learning came to Lucknow from Delhi in the first instance, although in the past only one person, Abdul Haq (1551–1642), among the learned men of Delhi emerges as having achieved lasting fame in regard to the Hadis[243] [the sayings of the Prophet], and religious lore. At no time can one find a centre of learning in Delhi like the Firangi Mahal. It is undoubtedly true that after the Firangi Mahal became famous the family of Shah Wali Ullah (1702–63) in Delhi gained great renown. It is because of their favour and blessing that instruction in the lore of the Hadis has become current throughout India today. But if instruction in the lore of the Hadis is a memorial to that famous Delhi family, it must be remembered that grammar, logic, philosophy, eloquence of language and expression and instruction in other academic fields are memorials to that renowned university of Lucknow, the Firangi Mahal.

At no other period or place in India has it been possible to find such erudite scholars as those who existed in Lucknow and particularly in the Firangi Mahal. The proof of this is that manuals used for religious instruction are the product either of famous Persians of bygone times or of members of the Firangi Mahal or their pupils.

The highest authorities on religious jurisprudence of the Shia faith, the Mujtahids, were products of the Firangi Mahal. The first Mujtahid, Maulvi Dildar Ali, started his studies at the Firangi Mahal, then went to Iraq and studied at the feet of the religious leaders of Kerbala and Najaf. On his return he was appointed Mujtahid, spiritual leader of the Shias by the ruling family of the time, with the approbation and ratification of the members of the Firangi Mahal. As he had studied in Iraq he brought with him the taste for new Arabic literature, with the result that he became more prominent in this field than the members of the Firangi Mahal school. The continuing interest of the later Shia religious leaders in literature made Lucknow a very important centre for literary studies and produced such an eminent man of letters as Mufti[352] Mir Abbas.[353]

The learned men of the Firangi Mahal had acquired special fame in the field of Islamic religious knowledge for *fiqh* [Islamic jurisprudence], *usul-e-fiqh* [principles of jurisprudence], the Quran, and *kalam* [doubt in religious tenets]; in the field of literary knowledge[354] for grammar and eloquence of language and expression; in the field of scientific knowledge for logic, philosophy, natural science and metaphysics and in the field of mathematical knowledge for geometry and astronomy. Lucknow was the centre of India for the study of these subjects. Shia religious leaders and Mujtahids of Lucknow had made literature, poetry and Arabic prosody their own particular subjects.

Munazirah [public debate] between Shias and Sunnis became an established custom in Lucknow. It started in India with the arrival of Qazi Nur Ullah Shustri who had come specially from Persia to contradict the Sunni interpretation of some points of Islamic doctrine. From that period quarrels arose between Shias and Sunnis and eventually after Qazi's time, Shah Abdul Aziz Muhaddis (died 1824) of Delhi wrote *Tuhfa-e-Asna Ashari*, in refutation of Shia doctrine. Maulvi Dildar Ali, however, contradicted some of its chapters. Then Maulana Haidar Ali entered the dispute. He actually belonged to Faizabad but became famous in Lucknow. He wrote *Muntahi-ul-Kalam*, which was considered to be the best book in confutation of the Shia doctrine. At this time Maulvi Lutf Ullah, who had been educated in Lucknow and had become an inhabitant of the place, wrote several books which had an amusing style as well as investigating and refuting the rival doctrine. Mian Mushir violently opposed his arguments but his book exceeded the bounds of controversy and entered the realms of satire and obscenity. Eventually Maulvi Hamid Husain, an expert on theological literature, wrote several long books in confutation of the Sunni doctrine. At present Maulvi Abdul Shakur is gaining recognition in this art through his championship of the Sunni doctrine.

Although religious dispute may appeal to some people, it is, to my mind, completely pointless and there is more harm than good in it. But I wanted to show here that the heights which this practice attained in Lucknow had never previously been attained in any other city.

Lucknow was not strong in the fields of theological science, *tafsir* [the interpretation of the Quran], *hadis* and *rijal* [investigation of hadis]. Tafsir was understood to a certain degree, but no more than in many other places. The study of hadis has always been associated with Delhi. In recent times the late Maulana Muhammad Abdul Hai was granted a diploma in this subject by the hierarchy of Holy Mecca itself. On his return he started a course of instruction but the subject was never satisfactorily developed in Lucknow.

The subject of rijal is subordinate to that of hadis and the more knowledge a man acquires in regard to the hadis, the greater is his mental perception of rijal. Therefore the learned men of Lucknow were as wanting in this subject as they were in hadis. As regards history, India never achieved great distinction. There is no doubt that Persian scholars gave it their attention both as an intellectual pursuit and a social record, but Muslim religious leaders in India paid no more regard to it than if it were a collection of legends and for that reason most of these men must be found wanting. Thus even in children's minds the idea grew,

'What reason have religious leaders to concern themselves with knowing what happened at a certain time? Their concern is purely and simply paradise.'

Realizing the necessity of the times, the religious leaders of both factions have started to make appropriate additions to their manuals. The university of Nadvat-ul-Ulema[355] has also been inaugurated and is paying particular attention to these necessary subjects which have so far been neglected. In spite of these shortcomings, Lucknow has done much more than any other place to remedy these defects.

14

The Development of Yunani Medicine

This most noble of all sciences, concerned with preserving and developing humanity, was practised in every country in the past in a spontaneous and elementary manner. But in ancient times in the West, the people of Greece achieved notable success in advancing medicine and in the east talented Hindus also developed the science.

When the Muslim court of the Caliphate was established, the doctors of Baghdad included skilled physicians coming from both of these regions. For one or two centuries all the regular doctors at the Abbaside court were either Hindus, Christians or Jews; there was not a single Muslim. The eminent physicians of this era, whatever faith they embraced, were supported by the Muslims and were famous in the Islamic world. In their hands the science of medicine began to be based on efficient collation and classification of information. Basic Greek medicinal methods, with a few improvements and alterations, were adopted, incorporating the experience gained in other countries. Later, distinguished Muslim physicians appeared who developed the science of medicine experimentally on their own lines. This culminated in Abu Sina (Avicenna, 980–1037), who presented to the world an incomparable book of codes to which all nations of the East and West bowed their heads in admiration. The court of Andalusia[356] made great progress in development and experimentation and the science of medicine became the special prerogative of the Muslims. They became the fount of medical science, and every nation acquired knowledge from them. Present-day European medicine is founded on these early studies which were closely connected with the Muslim medical school of Andalusia.

But when this Muslim society started to disintegrate, the effects were felt in the arts and sciences and especially in the science of medicine. In most countries medical knowledge had reached only early Greek levels. Persons of ordinary capability, without access to the best books on the subject, used their limited experience to treat their patients. The result was that in a short while Egypt, Arabia, Asia Minor and Iraq were devoid of physicians. Among the Islamic countries the science remained in existence only in Persia and India. In the last century, Persia, too, has lacked physicians. There has been such ignorance in all Muslim countries regarding their ancient science that when French and British doctors appeared from Europe they were regarded by all as a blessing from heaven. No one ever considered that the science had originally belonged to the Muslims or that they had ever possessed competent physicians.

If Muslim medicine survived at all it was only in India where today physicians of the Yunani school are more numerous than doctors of the European school.

In former days in Delhi there were many who achieved distinction in the field of medical science. Hakim Arzani, Hakim Shafai Khan, Hakim Alavi Khan and Hakim Muhammad Sharif Khan—all acquired great fame as physicians. From the time of Burhan ul Mulk, skilled physicians started to come from Delhi into the Province of Avadh. When Shuja ud Daula was ruling, not just one or two but all the best physicians left Delhi to come to Lucknow. One learns from the history of Faizabad that every noble there had his own physician of the Yunani school who was treated with great consideration and respect and who would be honoured with favours and rewards in addition to his monthly emoluments.

From the days of Asaf ud Daula, when Lucknow became the cultural centre of India, many Delhi families[357] whose profession was medicine became domiciled here. Just as language and poetry were regarded as local arts, so the science of medicine was adopted as a local science. As a result, Lucknow produced eminent and celebrated physicians such as Hakim Masih ud Daula, Hakim Shafa ud Daula and Hakim Mirza Muhammad Jafar, all of whom were renowned experts. As time went on, the science progressed to such a degree that there were few quarters in Lucknow which did not contain a celebrated family of professional physicians. Apart from those existing in the hundreds of quarters of the city itself, thousands of clinics had been set up in neighbouring villages and small towns. All the famous physicians practising at the courts or in the towns of India had come from Lucknow or its neighbourhood. There was one physician at the court of the Gaekwar[358] of Baroda who was accorded such honour as rarely falls to the lot of any member of his profession. In short, Lucknow produced such eminent men of medicine that their achievements are remembered even today.

In the final days of the court of Avadh, there was an exemplary pupil of Saiyyid Muhammad Murtaish, Hakim Muhammad Yaqub, who established his own clinic and through it gained great renown. His family and descendants have continued the tradition and they are, without exaggeration, unrivalled. Among the distinguished members of this family who are now deceased are Hakim Muhammad Ibrahim, Hakim Hafiz Muhammad Abdul Aziz and Hakim Hafiz Muhammad Abdul Wali. Hakim Abdul Hafiz, Hakim Abdur Rashid and Hakim Abdul Moid are still displaying[359] their skills. It is a pity that some members of the family, because of other interests, are not concentrating whole-heartedly upon their traditional profession.

The family of Hakim Muhammad Sharif Khan, which included such distinguished men as Hakim Mahmud Khan and Hakim Abdul Majid Khan, still exists in Delhi. Haziq ul Mulk[360] Hakim Muhammad Ajmal Khan is today upholding the family tradition.

In Delhi Hakim Muhammad Ajmal Khan has set up a medical college[361] and, having established contact between exponents of the Muslim and Vedic schools[362] of medicine, is giving great impetus to medical knowledge. Hakim Abdul Aziz has set up a college in Lucknow called Takmil ut Tib,[363] the Perfection of Medicine, from which scores of hakims graduate every year, go to different parts of the country and demonstrate that Lucknow is the centre of medicine.

The Muslim medical system known as Yunani is now dead everywhere in the world except in India, where its only two centres are Delhi and Lucknow. In Delhi there is only one family, that of Mahmud Khan, which still practises it, whereas in Lucknow there are scores of such families. In Delhi one sees mostly hakims who have recently established themselves. In Lucknow, although there are many such practitioners as well, there are also many from old families who have continued and improved the science for centuries.

There is another difference between the hakims of Lucknow and Delhi. I do not know whether the present medical text-books were drawn up by the physicians of Delhi or those of Lucknow, but whereas the latter rigidly adhere to them, the former do not. Instruction from these text-books is given in Delhi but the Delhi physicians' medicinal system diverges to a great extent from the original. They have adopted Vedic remedies, using them indiscriminately and without integrating them properly into their own system. Delhi's Madarsa Tibbia, the College of Medicine, apart from the method of diagnosis, includes so many European medical practices that the original science of Muslim medicine, instead of advancing, seems to be heading for disaster. The Delhi physicians showed this carelessness in adopting the principles of Vedic medicine and are now doing likewise in adopting the principles of European medicine. With this state of affairs, the future of our ancient medical science in Delhi appears to be greatly endangered.

Unlike those of Delhi, all the medical families of Lucknow, particularly that of the late Hakim Yaqub, and the Takmil ut Tib College, make every endeavour to preserve and improve upon the principles of Muslim medical science. Their medical system does not diverge in the least from the original science. It is progressing so smoothly that one can hope that Islamic medicine may survive the difficulties of the age, although our physicians are still far from doing full justice to it. The essence of medical art is the preparation of remedies, which is a branch of the ancient science of alchemy. The European science of chemistry is based on alchemy and ancient books on the subject, written by Muslim authors, have not all disappeared. Many still exist and it is the duty of preceptors of medical science to study them continually. They should give them deep thought and analysis and incorporate them in manuals of instruction. New discoveries should be added to the original principles, bringing them up to date and making full use of them. If such action is not taken, medical progress will be retarded and good results will not be obtained.

In spite of some defects, Lucknow has improved and strengthened[364] Muslim medical science to a much greater degree than Delhi, and in this respect it has no equal anywhere in the world.

15

The Significance of the Persian Language

In spite of the fact that Lucknow produced great and distinguished scholars of Arabic lore, it must be said that Arabic learning was confined to religious leaders and their followers. In India, the court language was Persian. To gain employment and to shine in refined and honoured company, a knowledge of Persian was considered quite sufficient. Not only in Avadh, but throughout India, Persian alone was the road to literary and social advancement. Apart from Muslims, the leanings of élite Hindus were towards Persian writing and literature, so much so that distinguished Persian compositions flowed from the pens of Hindu authors. Tek Chand Bahar was the author of *Bahar-e-Ajam*, which is an unequalled and unique storehouse of Persian idioms and which presents, in support of each idiom, numberless verses composed by Persian writers. When Lucknow started to develop, Mulla Faeq and later Mirza Qatil[268] who had been converted to Islam were famed as Persian scholars. The latter would say jokingly that the smell of kebab[365] had turned him into a Muslim, but the truth is that instruction in Persian, his inclinations and his keen desire to become truly proficient in the language forced him to embrace Islam. Because of this he travelled in Persia and lived for years in Shiraz, Isfahan, Teheran and Azerbaijan. He reached such heights in Persian literature that it is not surprising that even people whose mother tongue was Persian envied his mastery of the language.

Mirza Ghalib made occasional attacks on Mirza Qatil. No doubt the former was an extremely good judge of Persian and he often stressed the point that no one could be an authority on the subject if it was not his mother tongue. But in his day people from Avadh to Bengal were devotees of Qatil and were always mentioning his name with reverence. This would enrage Ghalib, and once when Qatil's devotees criticized him, he wrote the following verse:

> This language belongs to Persians,
> 'tis hard for us and not for them.
> The matter is plain and not obscured,
> Delhi and Lucknow are not Persia. . . .

But this does not show that the efforts Qatil made in acquiring a knowledge of Persian and the lifetime he spent in gaining erudition were completely in vain. One will agree that no claim of Qatil regarding Persian was worthy of acceptance without the support of a native speaker and Qatil himself would have agreed. But this is not confined to Qatil. No one in India can be an authority on Persian usage. Even Mirza Ghalib could never employ a Persian idiom without the authority of Persian sources. If the authority of any Indian scholars of Persian can be established it is only on the basis that they had an extensive knowledge of the language and had mastered the use of each word in its correct significance. In this respect, Qatil's standing was much greater than Ghalib's: Ghalib had never left India in his life and had always been busy with problems of livelihood. Qatil had lived a life of ease and for many years had spent his time wandering from village to village in Persia.

The study of Persian in Lucknow began with Qatil. Shortly before him Mulla Faeq, whose family had come from Agra and had become domiciled in the environs of Lucknow, was the author of excellent books on Persian literature, poetry and prose. There had been other Persian speakers and Persian scholars in India before him, but the desire to assemble the principles and rules of the language and its grammar in order to perfect knowledge of it arose in Lucknow. Qatil's books are of a very high order, indeed, they are incomparable.

After Qatil Persian became an ordinary subject of instruction and an intense and complex course of studies was introduced which was more advanced than the curriculum in Persia itself. In Persia, as in all countries, people like their language to be straightforward and simple. Their courses of studies are designed to this end. However, in India the intricate poems of Urfi, Faizi, Zahuri and Nemat Khan-e-Ali were included in the syllabus of instruction along with the works of abstruse writers like Mulla Tughra and the author of *Panj Ruqub*. It may thus be claimed that knowledge of the Persian language in the late eighteenth and nineteenth centuries was greater in India than it was in Persia itself and people of this country wrote learned commentaries on all the Persian manuals of instruction. The most remarkable result of this was that whilst poets of all countries of the world normally write in their own language—and even if a few write in a foreign language they are not taken seriously by those whose mother-tongue they have adopted—there was as much if not more Persian poetry written in India as there was in Persia itself. This was particularly the case during the last century when Lucknow was famed throughout the world for its progress and education, when every child could speak Persian, when ghazals were on the lips of all, even the uneducated, the courtesans and bazaar workers, and when even a *bhand*[366] [entertainer] would jest in Persian. A refined pastime and means of livelihood for better-class people in the small towns of Avadh was the teaching of Persian. The streets and alleys of Lucknow were filled with excellent local teachers whose knowledge of the language evoked the praise of native Persians themselves. Their accent and intonation may not have equalled those of native speakers but they had acquired a mastery of Persian idiom, construction and the exact and finer meanings of words.

One can judge how far a taste for Persian has developed in Lucknow from the Urdu spoken in the town. Persian forms, constructions and genitives are on the tongues of all, even the uneducated and the women. If there is one fault with the Urdu of Lucknow it is that it has been influenced by Persian to an excessive degree. But judging by present-day standards this enhances the beauty of Urdu speech. Persian influence was greatest in the latter phases of the Urdu language.

Like the Muslims, Hindus also gained prominence for their knowledge of Persian, a fact that became evident in the early days of the Mughal Empire when there were several famous Hindu scholars and speakers of Persian. This vogue reached its zenith in Avadh, when there were more Hindus with an eminent knowledge of Persian in the environs of Lucknow than anywhere else. Kayasths[72] and Kashmiri Pandits[367] considered it obligatory to learn Persian and progressed to such a degree that Urdu became their mother-tongue. There was little difference between their knowledge of Persian and that of the Muslims. As the Kayasths were natives of Avadh their language was Bhasha,[368] but the idea of learning Persian was engrained in them and they were in the habit of using Persian idiom without discrimination. This affinity with Persian, however, was not shared by Hindu sects in other parts of the country. Sometimes people would laugh at the Kayasths' speech, but actually instead of laughing at them they should have appreciated their efforts because these were proof of academic progress. In the same way nowadays people consider that bringing English words into their conversation, either in or out of place, is a sign of their advance in education, although in actual fact their use of English is characterized by a complete lack of discernment and discrimination.

In Lucknow of this period there were hundreds of writers of Persian prose and poetry and there were mushairas for Persian poetry just as there were gatherings for Urdu poetry. Persian was a mark of distinction not only for the better classes but also for the masses. Despite the fact that Persian has ceased to be the court language and that Urdu has become predominant and in standard use in Government circles,[369] Persian has set its seal on polite society up to the present day. Persian has been eliminated from the syllabi of schools and colleges and knowledge of it is no longer considered necessary as a means of obtaining a livelihood, nevertheless one unacquainted with Persian cannot be considered worthy of moving in refined circles nor can he be regarded as a person of any intellectual consequence.

French used to be the court language of England. It has long since ceased to be so. Yet no one can achieve social advancement in England today without a knowledge of French. French still holds sway over food, drink, manners, clothes, gaiety and speech; in fact, over everything that goes to make up life, and young ladies cannot take their place in refined society without having acquired a knowledge of the French language. The same standards obtain in Lucknow. Persian has ceased to be the court language and is no longer used for correspondence but it is still paramount over all departments of society. Without a knowledge of Persian our sentiments cannot be correctly expressed nor can we correctly achieve polished conversation.

Of the few people who lived in Matiya Burj, Calcutta, with the ill-fated last king of Avadh there was not a single educated person who did not know Persian. The language of the secretariat was Persian and there were hundreds of Hindus and Muslims who wrote Persian poetry. Even women composed Persian verses and every child could make himself understood in the language.

In present-day Lucknow Persian teaching has been very much curtailed and Hindus have given it up to such an extent that the speech of the Kayasths[72] and the semi-Persian language of the bhands[366] are now no more than a dream. Nevertheless a great taste for Persian remains among older scholars, particularly Muslims, because their knowledge of Urdu is, to a certain extent, a means towards their acquiring a knowledge of Persian. Among Muslims, an authority of the calibre of Khwaja Aziz ud Din is with us to remind us of the old Persian literary tradition. There are many Persian scholars, now advanced in years, among Hindus, an outstanding example of whom is the Raja of Sandela (District Hardoi, Avadh), Durga Parshad.[370] We should revere him as we would the moth-eaten pages of some ancient holy manuscript, and place the brow upon him.[371]

16

Scripts—Calligraphy and the Urdu Press

Calligraphy and penmanship are connected with learning. The old Muslim script was the ancient Arabic Naskh.[372] Until halfway through the time of the Baghdad Caliphate (750–1268) this script was used by the whole of the Islamic world. It had evolved from the old Armenian Hira[373] through the Kufic.[374] From the time of the Tahira dynasty[375] in the ninth century, intellectual pursuits that had developed in Baghdad were introduced into Iran and Khurasan. By the time of the Deylamites (945–1055) and Seljuks (1037–92), most of the knowledge of Baghdad had found its way to Persia. In particular, Azerbaijan, the western province of Persia situated in the bosom of Persian and Arabian Iraq, became the cradle for all the perfections and improvements resulting from the Deylamite love for learning.

In that region, writing started to take on a new form. Script, advancing beyond the boundaries of mere writing, entered the realm of engraving, and the finesse of painting was introduced. To Persian lovers of delicacy the robustness of the old Arabic script appeared crude and so its original form started to disappear. In Naskh the writing of each letter and each word from beginning to end was the same. There was a lack of symmetry and badly-proportioned unevenness in each letter; the circles were not round but elongated and crooked and here and there took the form of angles. The delicacy of engraving was added to the script, fastidiousness was cultivated and the circles became beautifully rounded. The first person to introduce these new accomplishments was Mir Ali Tabrizi, a native of Deylam. He laid down formal rules and principles for the script, which he called Nastaliq, and made it current throughout Eastern Islamic countries. The name he gave his script is actually formed from *Naskh* plus *taliq*, hanging on, in other words an adjunct of Naskh.

It is not known at what period Mir Ali Tabrizi lived. Munshi Shams ud Din, who is a famous and established calligraphist in Lucknow at the present time, puts his period as before that of Tamerlane.[376] However, one finds old books written in Nastaliq and I think that this script must have been invented before the time of Mahmud of Ghazni. There is no doubt that at the time of Mahmud's onslaughts, Persian calligraphists started to come to India and it was through them that this script became current here. A large number of Nastaliq calligraphists sprang up in every district and province of India. Therefore either Mir Ali Tabrizi lived a very long time ago or he was not the actual inventor of the script. There is however no doubt that the present-day calligraphists of Delhi and Lucknow and the rest of India consider him to be their master. Many years later the name of Mir Amad al Hasani became famous as a master of Nastaliq in Persia. He is recognized to be the most eminent of calligraphists and the best exponent of the art. His nephew Agha Abdur Rashid of Deylam came to India at the time of Nadir Shah's invasion and lived in Lahore. He had hundreds of pupils there who spread throughout the country and proved themselves if not the Adams, then certainly the Noahs of calligraphy in India. Two of his most renowned pupils, who were Persian, came to Lucknow: Hafiz Nur Ullah and Qazi Nemat Ullah. It is said that Abdullah Beg, a third distinguished pupil of Agha Abdur Rashid, also came to Lucknow. All these probably came at the time of Asaf ud Daula when no eminent newcomer wanted to leave the city. Immediately Qazi Nemat Ullah arrived, he was appointed to improve the princes' handwriting and Hafiz Nur Ullah was also attached to the court of Avadh. Both of them stayed in Lucknow and taught calligraphy.

Apart from these distinguished men there were already some other calligraphists here in Lucknow, such as the celebrated Munshi Muhammad Ali. The pupils of Agha Abdur Rashid had acquired such fame that all those desiring to learn calligraphy, in fact the whole city, turned to them and anyone interested in scripts became their pupil. Earlier calligraphists were forgotten and drowned in the shoreless seas of anonymity. It must be admitted that these distinguished men, because of their great skill, deserved all the fame they had acquired.

The respect with which Hafiz Nur Ullah was regarded in Lucknow cannot be judged from the fact that he had become a government servant; a true indication of the appreciation accorded to him was that people bought passages written by his hand at enormous prices. Even rough copies of his work were sold from hand to hand in the bazaars at one rupee per letter of the alphabet.

In those days both the wealthy and the not so wealthy would decorate their houses with *qatat* [usually four-lined verses] instead of pictures. Because of this there was a very great demand for qatats, and whenever a specimen of the writing of a good calligraphist came to light, people fell upon it like moths and put it reverently to their brows.[371] Society benefited because ethical quotations and sentences or verses giving moral advice were constantly before the people and there was always moral instruction in the home. Calligraphy benefited because calligraphers and penmen of repute dedicated their skill to producing *katbas*[377] on pure and noble subjects which they wrote out in their own houses and from which they acquired wealth. But unfortunately this vogue for qatat and katbas is disappearing and is being replaced by pictures. With the dying out of this delicate and refined religious taste, calligraphy has also disappeared from India. Now there are *katibs*,[378] clerks, not calligraphers. If one or two well-known penmen have remained, they are forced to earn their living by *kitabat*, the copying out of documents and manuscripts, which is actually inimical to the art of calligraphy. To counteract this a group was established whose aim was to adhere to the principles of calligraphy and occasionally to make suitable improvements. Earlier calligraphists thought that getting involved in writing a manuscript was beneath their dignity as it would be impossible for anyone who wrote out a whole book to maintain throughout the principles and standards of calligraphy.

One can judge the amount of effort involved from the fact that Navab Sadat Ali Khan once asked Hafiz Nur Ullah to write him out a copy of the *Gulistan*. Navab Sadat Ali Khan was extremely fond of Sa'di's[225] *Gulistan* and it is said he always kept it at hand. If anyone else had given such an order, Hafiz Nur Ullah would have taken it as a personal insult. But as it was an order from the ruler of the day he agreed and said, 'Please order eighty *gadis* [reams] of paper, and one hundred penknives for fashioning and sharpening goodness knows how many thousand bamboo quills.' Sadat Ali Khan asked in amazement whether all these things would be necessary for just one copy of the *Gulistan*. He received the reply, 'Yes, sir, I always use this amount.' It was not difficult for the Navab to collect the articles and he ordered them. Now Hafiz started to write out the *Gulistan* but he never finished it. He had written out seven chapters and the eighth chapter was still to be written when he died. After his death, when his son Hafiz Ibrahim was presented at court and given a black khilat to mourn his father, Sadat Ali Khan said to him, 'I asked Hafiz Sahib to write out the *Gulistan* for me: goodness knows what has happened to it.' Hafiz Ibrahim said, 'He has completed seven chapters, the eighth remains. Insignificant as I am, I will write it out and make it so similar in quality that Your Excellency will not be able to recognize the difference. But certainly, if some expert calligraphist saw it he would recognize the discrepancy.' The Navab agreed and Hafiz Ibrahim finished the *Gulistan*.

The most eminent of Hafiz Nur Ullah's pupils was his own son Hafiz Muhammad Ibrahim and the next was a distinguished Hindu, Munshi Sarab Singh, who according to some was a Kayasth and according to others a Kashmiri Pandit. The third was a Lucknow calligraphist named Muhammad Abbas. Hafiz Ibrahim acquired great fame and trained hundreds of calligraphists. He made innovations in the art and created a technique different from that of his father. Hafiz Nur Ullah's curves were completely rounded whereas Hafiz Ibrahim made them slightly oval. It is said of Munshi Sarab Singh that he had assimilated his teacher's style to such an extent that he was able to distribute hundreds of tablets as having been written by Hafiz Nur Ullah. The most eminent calligraphists could not tell the difference in spite of the fact that distinguishing a copy from the original was in those days their speciality.

Eminent pupils of Hafiz Ibrahim included his own son Hafiz Said ud Din. In addition to him were Munshi Nazir Hamid and Munshi Abdul Majid who was employed by the government to write royal edicts, memoranda and correspondence with the British Government. Two of Hafiz Ibrahim's pupils acquired great prominence and were in their own time recognized as masters in the whole of Lucknow. One of these was Munshi Mansa Ram, a Kashmiri pandit who excelled greatly in his art, and the other Munshi Muhammad Hadi Ali, who in addition to writing Nastaliq had no equal in Lucknow in the writing of Naskh and Tughra[379] scripts. Besides these there were two pupils of Qazi Nejat Ullah, one of whom was his son Maulvi Muhammad Ashraf and the other Maulvi Qul Ahmad.

In short, these people were masters in writing Nastaliq and through them calligraphy reached perfection in Lucknow. Then after printing-presses[380] had been introduced, *kitabat*[378] became the vogue. Thanks to the latter thousands of Muslims and Kayasths in Lucknow, who abound in the Nau Basta and Ashrafabad quarters, as well as hundreds of Kashmiri pandits, became calligraphists. Unfortunately Kashmiri pandits became interested in British culture and seeing the decline in calligraphy, gave up this art altogether. Nowadays all good penmen are either Muslims or Kayasths.

In recent times, Munshi Abdul Hai of Sandela was a very distinguished calligraphist. Among his pupils were Munshi Amir Ullah Taslim, his elder brother Munshi Abdul Latif, Munshi Ashraf Ali and some others. At the present time Munshi Shams ud Din and Munshi Hamid Ali are famous writers of Nastaliq and Naskh respectively. They are both pupils of Munshi Hadi Ali.

In India the first expert to whom the writing of Naskh script can be attributed is considered to be a man popularly |known as Yakut-e-Mustasmi and called Yakut the First. One cannot find any accomplished scribe of that name at the time of Mustassim Billah. It would not be strange if Amad Katib Juvaini, entitled Fakhr al Kitab, who died about 1167, was intended. He wrote the well-known book *Kharida* and was scribe to Sultan Atabak Nurud Din Zangi in Asia Minor and later scribe to Sultan Salah ud Din Ayubi, the conqueror of Jerusalem, in Egypt. He is certainly considered the greatest of the later Naskh penmen. Subsequently, in the days of Emperor Aurangzeb Alamgir, a distinguished calligraphist of the Naskh script named Muhammad Arif made his appearance and was given the title of Yakut the Second. It is generally agreed that he evolved a new form of Naskh writing and made it more beautiful than before. The Lucknow masters of Naskh claim that the whole Islamic world acknowledged his supremacy. I am not ready to agree with this. Whatever supremacy Yakut the Second may have gained in India, his name was unknown in countries where the national writing is Naskh and the national speech Arabic. People of those countries do not copy his style.

At the time of Muhammad Arif, Yakut the Second, there was a man called Abdul Baqi, who was an ironsmith by trade. Seeing how Yakut had become universally popular he too wanted to become adept in the art. There was another Naskh penman famous at the time, named Abdulla Tabagh. The ironsmith enrolled as one of his pupils and worked so diligently that he became renowned as a master of the art of calligraphy. After these two had passed away, Yakut's nephew, Qazi Ismat Ullah, took his place and the ironsmith's two sons, Ali Akbar and Ali Ashghar, also became experts.

After that many distinguished calligraphists came into being and the Naskh script in India continued to improve. Eventually Shah Ghulam Ali, who was adept in the Naskh script, became famous and after him Maulvi Hadi Ali gained great renown in Lucknow as a writer of Tughra.

A contemporary of Maulvi Hadi Ali was a famous Naskh calligraphist named Mir Bandey Ali Murtaish. His instructor was Navab Ahmad Ali, a well-known nobleman and distinguished master of Naskh. Mir Bandey Ali's hands were palsied but directly they touched paper it seemed as if they were made of iron and he could not lose control. He was so perceptive in the recognition of handwriting that even the greatest bowed to his expert opinion.

Munshi Hamid Ali tells how on one occasion Munshi Muhammad Yahya, an accomplished Naskh penman who was the first man in Lucknow to write out the Quran for printing, Munshi Abdul Hai of Sandela (U.P.), Munshir Mir Bandey Ali Murtaish and he himself were together. It was like a congress of the best Naskh calligraphists. Someone put forward a Naskh script for sale and although the name of the writer was not on the script, all these experts immediately recognized it as the work of Yakut. They all wanted to have possession of it. Munshi Hadi Ali said, 'Let me keep it for a day and I will go into the matter carefully and satisfy myself whether it is really Yakut's handwriting or not.' The owner handed it over and he took it home. The next day he brought it back and said, 'This is assuredly by the hand of Yakut. I had another similar excerpt by Yakut and compared the two. I found them exactly the same and I am convinced that this is truly the work of Yakut.' Then he placed both excerpts before the assembly and all agreed without hesitation that both had been written by Yakut. But Mir Bandey Ali scrutinized Muhammad Hadi Ali's excerpt carefully, then smiled and wrote beneath it, 'This comes from your hand. Let people say what they like.' Munshi Abdul Hai looked at what was written and said with annoyance, 'Have you any doubt in the matter?' Mir Bandey Ali said, 'This excerpt cannot have been written by Yakut.' Munshi Abdul Hai and others present who did not agree with him said, 'This is certainly Yakut's writing.' Mir Bandey Ali pointed out the top of a *waw* [letter *v*] and said, 'This cannot be Yakut's.' At this everyone began to feel uncertain and Munshi Hadi Ali tore off a corner of the tablet and showed his own name on the bottom sheet. Now all were assured that the work was that of Munshi Hadi Ali and gave him unlimited praise. He himself said, 'I, for my part, salute Mir Bandey Ali's fine perception.'

In accordance with the general practice of calligraphists, it was unprofessional for Mir Bandey Ali to engage in any form of writing except the production of excerpts. He never once wrote out even the shortest of books. When Haji[381] Harmain Sharifain inaugurated a printing-press, after much exhortation he got Mir Bandey Ali to agree to write out *Panj Sura*, five sub-sections of the Quran. Mir Bandey Ali put in an immense amount of work and took many days to accomplish the task. When he took it to the Haji and had a last look at it in his presence, something about it displeased him and instead of handing it over to him, he tore it up and said, 'I can't do it.'

In discussing these accomplished men it is not my intention to prove that Lucknow attained a distinction in calligraphy which was unrivalled throughout India. On the contrary, I think that the writers of Lucknow did not have a fraction of the skill of the Naskh penmen who lived in India before the days of the Mughal Empire. Besides, in the period under discussion, Naskh writing was already a thing of the past. As regards Nastaliq, this much can be said: the recognition given throughout India to the qatat of Hafiz Nur Ullah and Hafiz Ibrahim had probably never been accorded to the work of any other calligraphist. Even so, the art of penmanship in Lucknow was of much the same standard as that of other cities of culture.

The benefit that Lucknow's calligraphy conferred on the printing-press is probably unrivalled. I am not certain where the first printing-press in India was established. Great attention was given in Calcutta to the promotion of Urdu literature and also to supporting Eastern sciences in general. But I have never seen old books there which were lithographed; all I have seen is type-printing.

At the time of Ghazi ud Din Haidar, a European named Archer came to

Lucknow and popularized the idea of the printing-press. When learned people became interested, he opened Lucknow's first press. He constructed the press and all the materials required for it and started to print. He produced *Zad ul Miad, Haft Qulzum* and *Taj ul Lughat*, the latter a dictionary which ran to several volumes. Learning from him, other people started to open up presses, the first of which was probably that of Haji Harmain Sharifain. In those days a rich glass merchant named Mustafa Khan took something to Haji Harmain to be printed. The Haji was so rude to him that when Mustafa Khan got home he decided to start his own press, and the Mustafai Press subsequently proved a great success. Soon afterwards, Ali Baksh Khan started the Alvi Press and many printing firms opened in Lucknow.

At first printing was not undertaken on a commercial basis but purely as a private pursuit. The finest quality paper, highly appropriate for lithography, was used and the best calligraphists were employed at high salaries. They were shown great favour without any stipulations as to working conditions or how much they wrote in a day or even whether they wrote anything at all. In the same way the printers were never asked how many pages they had printed in a day. For the ink, thousands of lamps of mustard-oil were lighted to produce fine-quality lamp-black. Instead of acid, fine-skinned lemons were used and sponges took the place of cloth. In short, only the finest materials were employed. As a result, Persian and Arabic educational and religious books in the days of the monarchy could not have been printed anywhere else but in Lucknow, where they were produced irrespective of cost for discriminating eyes. Books printed at that time represent a fortune to those who possess them. People search for them but cannot find them.

My father's uncle, Maulvi Ahmad, was very fond of travel and trade at a time when people were frightened of leaving their homes. He went as an agent for Haji Harmain Sharifain from Lucknow as far as Rawalpindi, taking thousands of books with him in bullock carts and other similar conveyances. He used to say that in those days books were very rare. On seeing books printed in Lucknow, people would open their eyes wide and be drawn to them like moths to a candle. They were so eager that at whatever town or village Maulvi Ahmad arrived, his coming was known beforehand and his arrival was attended by great pomp and ceremony. When he came to a village, he was surrounded by people, a crowd would collect and any book he offered, at whatever price, was willingly accepted and reverently placed on the brow of the purchaser. He used to sell *Karima* and *Ma Muqiman* at a few annas a copy and each volume of *Gulistan* or *Bostan* at three or four rupees. Even so he could not meet the demand. Between one town and another the supply of books would run out and he had to wait months for further supplies. In those days it was difficult for goods to be transported but he eventually made arrangements for a regular supply from Lucknow.

Towards the close of the rule of the Navabs the printing of the Mustafai Press had no equal. When the monarchy collapsed, Munshi Newal Kishore opened his press.[382] Although its printing could not compare in elegance with that of the Mustafai Press, it was run on such sound commercial lines that it produced a greater quantity of Persian and Arabic books than any other press would have had the courage to attempt. The fact is that the interest taken in the printing-press in Lucknow was such that it needed an energetic and ambitious man like

Munshi Newal Kishore to take full advantage of it. Eventually the Newal Kishore Press gained such pre-eminence that it revived all Eastern literatures and Lucknow acquired great distinction in this field. Lucknow benefited in that it was able to meet all the literary demands of Central Asia, including those of Kashgar, Bukhara, Afghanistan and Persia. Consequently the Newal Kishore Press is still the key to the literary trade. Without using it no one can enter the world of learning.

But sad to say, in spite of the number of presses in existence, the printing situation in Lucknow is bad and is getting worse every day, so that now other cities have taken precedence over it. Lucknow printers' standards have deteriorated, and I think that printing in Lucknow is now inferior to that of most other towns. But we can comfort ourselves with the thought that in Kanpur, because of Munshi Rahmat Ullah, the printing-presses are in a good state and Kanpur is actually an adjunct to Lucknow's progress.

When printing-presses started, the art of *musleh sangi*, stone correction, was invented in Lucknow. The technique of making an impression on stone and scraping and correcting with a pen probably originated in Europe. But to correct Naskh and Nastaliq letters in this way so that the calligraphist's art remained unspoilt was an invention of Lucknow. At first this art was confined to putting right letters and designs that had become obliterated, overlaid or spread out. Soon the desire for improvement increased and expert stone correctors came to hand who could write out whole books in inverted script, or mirror-writing. The letters were so perfectly formed that no one realized they had been written in reverse on stone. The first expert was a veteran stone corrector who was responsible for the fame of the Mustafai Press. His many pupils were of benefit to the Lucknow printing-presses, much improvement was made and the number of stone correctors increased.

When the art of musleh sangi became common Munshi Jafar Husain, a famous stone corrector, persuaded the printing-presses to dispense with taking impressions in the ordinary way, that is, from the copy prepared by the katib. It was he who originated mirror-writing on stone. This work was initiated in small bazaar presses and then was adopted more or less by all presses. Now Munshi Saiyyid Ali Husain has made such progress that few eminent calligraphists can vie with his inverted scripts. One example of his mirror-writing is our *Dil Gudaz*, the copy of which Munshi Ali Husain writes on stone in inverted script. Readers of *Dil Gudaz* can judge the excellence of the art of musleh sangi in Lucknow for themselves.

Although in most Indian towns the stone correctors are from Lucknow, up to now no other presses have succeeded in printing from mirror-writing and the art is confined to Lucknow. Unfortunately,[383] owing to the fact that wages and conditions in printing have greatly deteriorated, Lucknow cannot derive as much benefit from the art of musleh sangi as it should.

17

The Arts of Combat and Self-Defence

I shall now deal with many subjects that are peculiar to Lucknow. While these mostly concern cultural and social affairs, it nevertheless appears appropriate that I should also make brief mention of some matters connected with the art of war.

It is true that this last Eastern court was established at a time when soldiering among Muslims and among Indians in general was on the ebb. It would be more accurate to say that the old military arts had not quite disappeared but that old methods and weapons of war had become useless in face of new military tactics and modern weapons. As a result these old arts of war, instead of being passed on by Muslims and other Indians to other valiant people, were completely lost to the world. In fact they were so lost that the present generation knows absolutely nothing about the courageous deeds and military prowess of its ancestors. When I lift up my pen to describe these arts, I can find scarcely anyone from whom I can get information. I am extremely indebted to Prince Mirza Masud Qadar Bahadur and to a very venerable Lucknow sage of long standing, Suleman Khan, of the family of Hafiz Rahmat Khan the famous ruler of Bareilly. All that I write with regard to these ancient arts of war is due to their help.

The military arts that developed in Delhi and later in Lucknow actually emanated from three different races, and their progress was determined by the intermingling of the three traditions. The extraordinary thing is that in spite of this intermingling the distinctive characteristics of these arts remained. Some of these arts were derived from Aryan military sources, some were brought to India by Turks and Tatar warriors, and some belonged to the Arabs and came to India by way of Persia. The arts of combat which were practised in Lucknow, and of which there were past masters in the city, appear to have been as follows: *lakri*, combat with long wooden sticks; *pata hilana*, with wooden swords; *bānk*, with knives; *binaut*, with staves; *kushti*, wrestling; *barchha*, with spears; *bana*, with cudgels; *tir andazi*, archery; *katar*, with stilettos; and *jal bānk*, underwater bānk.

Lakri

This art which they called *phankainti*, akin to single-stick fighting, is Aryan in origin and was common among the Aryans in India and Iran. After the Arab conquest, Arabian belligerence had its effect on Persian phankainti, more advanced that that of India. These two arts always remained in their separate forms in India and schools for both were established in Lucknow. The Persian phankainti which had been influenced by the Arabs was known in India as *ali mad*, and the pure Indian as *rustam khani*. In ali mad, the left foot of the fighter is fixed to one spot and only by moving the right foot forwards or backwards is the stance changed. In contrast to this, in rustam khani the fighter can change his stance and move forwards or backwards, right or left, as much as he likes or finds room to do so. By advancing or retreating, he falls unawares on his enemy. Another difference is that ali mad was only for aristocrats and nobles. Its teachers never accepted people from the lower classes as their pupils and would not permit them to learn anything of the art. On the other hand, rustam khani was common among the lower orders.

A great teacher of ali mad is mentioned in *The Delightful History*[14] as having been attached to the government of Shuja ud Daula and subsequently to the court of his widow Bahu Begam. It appears that he was the first teacher of the art to live in Faizabad and that he then came to Lucknow. The second teacher of the art was Muhammad Ali Khan who used to live in my own quarter, Katra Bizan Khan, and who is generally accepted as the inventor of ali mad. The third teacher was Mir Najam ud Din who first went with the Delhi princes to Benares and from there came to Lucknow. His custom was to accept only nobles as pupils. When he accepted a pupil he used to take money from him if he were a prince and only sweetmeats if he were a noble. None of this did he keep for himself; he would present it in person to the Saiyyids.[384] He lived at the time of Navab Asaf ud Daula. A very great expert was Mir Ata Husain who was a companion of Hakim Mahdi. Another great teacher was Patey Baz Khan who, because of his prowess, was popularly known at the time of Ghazi ud Din Haidar as the originator and inventor of ali mad. It is said that he was a convert to Islam. He also confined the teaching of his art to nobles and never taught the lower classes. To commemorate his name he left a mosque in Lucknow which is still standing in the neighbourhood of Alam Nagar beyond the Dhanya Mahri bridge.

Rustam khani remained for the lower classes, and for this reason it was particular neither to the Hindus nor to the Muslims. Hundreds of teachers of the art were to be found throughout the villages and towns of Avadh but none of them acquired the skill and renown of Yahya Khan in Lucknow. Navab Fatehyab Khan, in addition to being a nobleman, was a great calligraphist and also attained perfection at rustam khani. A well-known and dashing athlete, Mir Langar Baz, was likewise a rustam khani expert. The art is still carried on to a certain extent. Since ali mad was particular to the aristocracy and since none of them now has any interest in military matters, the art has died out. Rustam khani was confined to the lower classes and as these people go on squabbling and fighting, they have preserved the skill to this day.

I saw one or two teachers of ali mad at Matiya Burj; lastly there was Mir Fazal Ali who lived in the Mahmud Nagar quarter.

Pata hilana

The object of this art was that if a man were surrounded by enemies he could, by swinging his *pata* (wooden sword) like a stick in every direction, drive them back and escape, having inflicted blows on all of them. To fence and protect oneself with a pata required great skill, the height of which was the ability to leap with one end of the pata on the ground as a lever. Praise was accorded a man who, if he were shot at by ten arrows, could cut through them all with his pata. This skill did not exist in Delhi; it came to Lucknow from the eastern part of the Province (U.P.) and was most practised by weavers although eventually it was adopted by a number of nobles, particularly the Shaikhzadas who lived in the neighbouring townships. Gauri was considered the best exponent of the art in Lucknow. Hundreds of his deeds were well known to all and sundry, but alas, even these tales are being forgotten by the present generation.

Mir Rustam Ali had a double-edged sword, and by swinging it he would cut his way through hundreds of opponents. A Shaikhzada of Asaun, Shaikh Muhammad Husain, would grip his sword with both hands when swinging it. At the time of Ghazi ud Din Haidar, the Resident and some other European visitors wished to see some expert exponent of the art. Shaikh Muhammad Husain came forward and as he had no wooden sword at the time he was given a grand pata encrusted with jewels from the royal armoury. He showed such prowess with it that he was acclaimed on all sides. Excited by the acclamation, he left the assembly still swinging the sword, and went home. It was common knowledge among masters of the art that anyone who could swing a pata could stop ten swordsmen from getting near him.

In Lucknow there was one expert in the art, Mir Vilayat Ali, who was known as 'the Club Breaker'. It was said of him that however strong his opponent's club, he could cut through it.

Bānk

Bānk was an extremely important and useful combative accomplishment considered superior to all such arts. Young noblemen would make great efforts to learn it. The aim was to defend oneself with a knife when faced with an antagonist. From ancient times this art was practised by both Hindus and Arabs but their knives were different. Hindu knives were straight and double-edged whilst Arab knives curved like a dagger and had only one edge. Later the Arabs developed a knife called *junbiah* which had a four-sectioned tip that could inflict a clover-shaped wound extremely hard to sew. The method of instruction was that the instructor and pupil knelt opposite each other. In training with the straight Hindu-knife, the two opponents knelt opposite each other with one knee raised. In training with the Arab knife, the opponents crouched with both knees on the ground. Then they were taught blows, and very complicated holds, compared with which the holds of wrestling are as nothing. One difference is that in the Arabian style there were seven forms of blows and in the Indian style there were nine. In the Arabian bānk, when there was a complete hold, it was not in the power of the man who had pinioned[385] his opponent to set him free; in the Indian style one had the option up to the end to release the hold and let one's opponent go.

This art was not only a matter of administering blows; there were also the most intricate holds and both opponents would remain interlocked for hours, continuously trying to make the hold more complicated and inflict a wound.

The holds and tricks of this art were so sure, so reliable and so well-founded on principles of human physiology, that it is said all the tricks of wrestling and single-stick fighting originated from them. Bānk experts asserted that the full art was practised in the lying position, half in the sitting position and only one quarter in the standing position. One should not imagine that the essence of this art was confined to wounding one's adversary with a knife; the real object was to pinion him alive and to make him a helpless captive.

The exponents of bānk tried to conceal their art as far as possible, so that from their habits and deportment one could not possibly realize that they were combat men. A reliable bānk fighter appeared to be an ordinary gentleman and he dressed accordingly. He never carried arms and even took a vow not to keep a metal penknife or needle on his person. He carried a handkerchief in one corner of which a lump of iron was tied, and this was a sufficient weapon in times of necessity. If he was more highly cultured he carried in his hand a *tasbih*[386] [rosary] to which a small but heavy iron bead was attached in the centre, and this was sufficient.

Among the Hindus in ancient days, the art was confined to the Brahmans. The Rajputs knew nothing of it, neither did the Brahmans teach it to them, nor did the Rajputs try to learn it as they considered it contrary to their nature. The probable reason was that a prerequisite for bānk was secrecy, and Rajputs were openly soldiers. Brahman exponents of bānk did not carry an iron weight; instead they had a key attached to the *janeu*[387] [the sacred thread] which they wore and with which they used to finish off their enemies most politely and firmly. Prince Mirza Harun Qadar says that the art came to Lucknow at the time of Shah Alam when Mirza Khurram Baksh went to Benares and brought back one or two experts. But I know from reliable sources and from having studied the history of Faizabad that the first expert in the art was Mansur Ali Khan who came to Faizabad at the time of Shuja ud Daula.

In the days of Navab Asaf ud Daula, Shaikh Najam ud Din was a master of bānk in Lucknow. About the same time there was another expert in Lucknow who went by the name of Mir Bahadur Ali. His claim was: 'Put a wild pigeon under a bed and see the fun. If it manages to fly out in any direction I am no bānk expert.' This was an attribute of bānk and was not confined to him; any expert could have made the same claim. There was a third instructor in Lucknow, Wali Muhammad Khan, and at the time of Nasir ud Din Haidar the name of Mir Abbas, a pupil of Najam ud Din, was famous. He had four accomplished pupils; one of them became a dacoit but the other three were refined men of good breeding. The last instructor in the art was Mir Jafar Ali who went with Wajid Ali Shah to Matiya Burj after the collapse of Lucknow. I knew him and in my childhood became one of his pupils, but gave up the lessons after a month or two. Whatever I learnt is now no more than a dream and I do not know whether anyone still exists who knows anything of the subject.

Binaut

The primary object of this art is to disarm one's opponent of the sword, staff or whatever weapon he is carrying and to deal him such a blow, either with a

10 Old Chauk. On the left is the entrance to the Imam Bara of Asaf ud Daula; at centre, the back of the Rumi Gate. Pencil sketch by Robert Smith, 1814

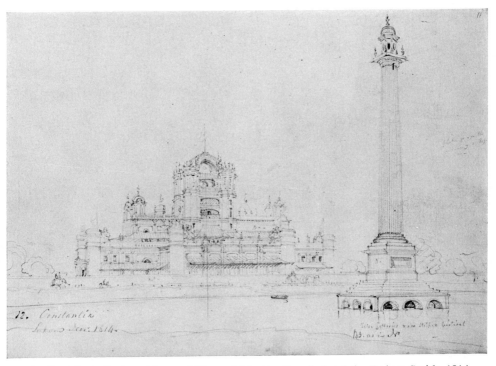

11 'La Martinière', residence of General Martin. Pencil sketch by Robert Smith, 1814

12 Farhat Baksh, Lal Barah Dari, with Chattar Manzil in the foreground. Pre-Mutiny photograph

13 Dil Kusha. Pre-Mutiny photograph

14 Palace of Raushan ud Daula. Photograph taken in 1859

15 Chau Lakhi Gate, Qaisar Bagh. Pre-Mutiny photograph

16 Rumi Gate. Pre-Mutiny photograph

17 Part of a procession by Muhammad Ali Shah and the British Resident from the Rumi Gate to Husainabad Imam Bara. Detail from an unfinished water-colour and pencil scroll by a Lucknow artist, 1848

18 Husainabad Imam Bara. Pre-Mutiny photograph

handkerchief into which a coin is tied, or with one's bare hand, that he becomes powerless. It was known from the outset in Lucknow that the greatest experts in the art were in Hyderabad Deccan and on making inquiries I discovered that this art is still alive there to a certain degree. People who know something of the subject say that if the opponents face each other standing unarmed it is *kushti*[388] (wrestling), if they have knives it is bānk, and if they carry about two-yards-long staves or handkerchiefs it is binaut. Exponents of binaut also keep their art secret and have a mutual pact that they will give instruction only to well-bred persons. They also make their pupils swear that they will never fight anyone who is particularly weak or who is inoffensive. The exponents of binaut always aim to make their movements, which they call *paule*, movements of the feet, highly dexterous, swift and clean. This is not possible for a man who is at all advanced in years. In addition to this they have knowledge of the nerves and muscles of the human body and are well aware of how to render an opponent powerless or breathless by pressing on a certain spot with a finger or by inflicting a very slight injury.

Although Hyderabad was famed for this art, there were many accomplished exponents in Lucknow. It is said that the first of these was Muhammad Ibrahim Khan who had brought it from Rampur. In Lucknow there was a very dashing and expert swordsman named Talib Sher Khan. When he heard of Ibrahim Khan's claims he wished to oppose him with a sword and Ibrahim Khan accepted his challenge. As soon as Talib Sher Khan struck the first blow with his sword, Muhammad Ibrahim Khan cast his handkerchief, into the corner of which a coin had been tied, with such dexterity that the sword left Talib Sher Khan's hand and fell with a crash some distance away. He was left standing in bewilderment and all the onlookers acknowledged Muhammad Ibrahim Khan's prowess.

This art flourished in Lucknow until the end of the Navabs' rule and was continued in Matiya Burj by a man named Muhammad Mahdi who was *darugha*[389] [supervisor to the household] of the lady Navab Mashuq Mahal, and who was recognized as an expert instructor in the art of binaut.

Kushti

This art belonged especially to the Aryans. The Arabs and Turks in India and Persia knew nothing about it, neither did the pre-Aryan inhabitants of India. In Lucknow various types of holds and methods for throwing one's adversary developed rapidly but the real essential in wrestling is bodily strength. The people in Lucknow, however hard they tried, could not possibly compete with people of other parts of the country, especially those of the Panjab. Providence has not accorded the climate of Lucknow the quality to produce brawny wrestlers like Ghulam. For this reason Lucknow wrestling could rely only on tricks whereby victory might be obtained over a man twice one's size, but an extremely strong man could never be thrown. There are many famous stories about the Lucknow arenas and former wrestlers, but all concerning tricks and holds and having nothing to do with superiority of strength. On one occasion I saw a bout between a famous local wrestler, Saiyyid, and a Panjabi wrestler of twice his size. There is no doubt that from the start Saiyyid's wrestling was very pretty to watch. His movements, nimbleness and agility were worthy of praise but after an hour he was bathed in perspiration, his strength had given out and he could scarcely breathe. The Panjabi wrestler on the other hand was not in the least affected and was completely fresh. Eventually Saiyyid fled from the arena and acknowledged defeat without finishing the bout.

Barchha

Fighting with spears is an ancient art which was equally prevalent among the Aryans, the Turks and the Arabs. The Arab spears were long and their heads triangular. The Turkish spears were short and their heads rounded and pointed, that is to say, conical. The spears of the Aryans in India were long with fine-edged heads of the shape of a betel leaf. All three types of spear were to be seen in Lucknow. The long spears were expected to be very flexible—the best of them could be bent double—while the short ones had to be stiff and not resilient at all. A well-known and genuine spear-man of Lucknow was Mir Kallu, who was famous at the time of Burhan ul Mulk. After him Mir Akbar Ali became famous and several other experts began to come to Lucknow from Bareilly and Rampur. At the time of Ghazi ud Din Haidar, when the King was interested in hunting elephants, much was thought of those who were practised in the art of spearmanship and the weapon was used in hunting. It is a pity that the use of this old weapon which gained fame for great nations in the past and which is still known in Lucknow, is now employed only on the occasion of wedding processions.

Bana

Fighting with cudgels is common among the lower classes and still exists to a certain extent. The art of inflicting blows and strokes in fighting developed from this. The object and limit of bana was that a person swinging his stick should escape from his encircling enemies. Bana was the name of a long stick at the end of which was an iron knob; some sticks had knobs at either end. It would be swung so that no one could approach. Some would tie cloth around the knobs, soak them in oil and set them alight. They would then swing the staff so that while they themselves were not in the least affected by the fire their adversaries had to remain at a distance to avoid it.

Tir andazi

This is the old weapon of all the warlike races of the world and is the gun of ancient times. Great prowess can be displayed in archery and both the noble and humble considered it essential to acquire the art. With this weapon Raja Ramchandra and his brother Lakshman are said to have slain Ravana, the chief of the demons and ruler of Sri Lanka, Ceylon. Although the invention of fire-arms curtailed its value, archery is still considered a jewel among military arts.

Bows were made so stiff that it was not easy for everyone to pull them. The stiffer the bow, the further the arrow went and the more effective it became. In their conquests the Arabs showed astonishing prowess at archery. At the time of the taking of Damascus, Um Ayan, an Arab bride of a few days' standing, shot two arrows in revenge for her martyred bridegroom with such effect that the first slew the enemies' standard-bearer and the second pierced the eye of the valiant enemy leader Thomas so deeply that it could not be removed. Eventually the shaft had to be cut off and the arrow-head left in the eye.

The Pansis and Bhars of Avadh had been well acquainted with the art for a long time. Then various experts came from Delhi and during the rule of Asaf ud Daula one of them, Ustad Faiz Baksh, at the King's instigation, shot an arrow with such rapidity at Mir Haidar's father, who was coming towards him on an elephant, that no one even saw him take aim and his victim felt nothing. Although the arrow had passed through his cloth belt and come out on the other side, he knew nothing of it at the time. When he got home and took off his belt he discovered that it was covered in blood and a fountain gushed from the wound. In a few minutes he was dead.

Instruction in this art was difficult and now it has ceased to exist among all civilized nations because present-day firearms have made it completely useless. However, the wild tribes of India generally still use arrows for hunting game and killing beasts of prey and also sometimes in their inter-tribal warfare.

Katar

This was an ancient weapon like a stiletto, peculiar to the Aryan race, and recently has been made use of by thieves and brigands. It was not used when meeting an antagonist in open fight but rather to attack him when caught unawares. For this reason most of the better-class people in Delhi and more particularly those in Lucknow completely abandoned its use. All used to carry it but no one knew how to fight with it or use it as a weapon. It was extolled as a weapon of attack because, if desired, the attack could be stopped before any real injury, or it could be driven home to the hilt. Thieves generally used it at night to take their victims unawares or when asleep and so silently finish them off.

Jal bānk

This was the bānk which had swimming as one of its attributes. The object was to gain mastery over one's enemy in deep water and either to tie him up and bring him out or to destroy him in the water. It does not appear ever to have been practised anywhere else but in Lucknow where it was invented by a master of swimming named Mirak Jan who taught it to hundreds of pupils. Even today there are some Lucknow swimmers who are recognized in other parts of the country as masters.

18

Animal Combats—Beasts of Prey and Other Quadrupeds

There is an Urdu adage: 'In old age a man's sexual powers go into his speech.' In the same way, experience shows, with regard to the bravery of valiant and intrepid men, that, when weakness comes and the power of their limbs gives out, courage and strength are concentrated in tongue and eyes. One tells stories of past courage and fame. Unable to display deeds of valour one looks for them through the medium of fighting animals. One enjoys watching courageous acts and seeks acclaim by causing others to watch animal combat.

This is what happened in Lucknow. When men had given up territorial conquest and no longer had the ambition to face the foe on the battlefield, then their warlike instincts led them to initiate the pastime of causing animals to fight. This gave them the opportunity of witnessing intrepidity and bloodshed. To a certain degree a predilection for this sport existed everywhere, but the diligence with which the people of Lucknow applied themselves to this wanton, cruel form of pleasure-seeking and the pitch of perfection to which they brought it could never have entered the dreams of people from any other place. The scenes that were witnessed in Lucknow were probably never seen in any other city of the world, let alone in Delhi or any other Indian court.

The desire to vent spleen through the courage of animals was fulfilled by three methods in Lucknow: combat between beasts of prey and other quadrupeds, fighting between birds, and matching small and large kites against each other. Combat between beasts of prey and other quadrupeds included fighting between tigers, cheetahs, leopards, elephants, camels, rhinoceroses, stags and rams. This interest in fights between beasts of prey, unknown in ancient India, originated with the ancient Romans, where men and beasts of prey were sometimes pitted together and sometimes against each other. Interest waned with the rise of Christianity, but even today in Spain and some other European countries wild bulls are set to fight each other and human beings.

It is probable that in Lucknow, British friends interested Ghazi ud Din Haidar in fights between beasts of prey. The King took to it and in a short time royal interest in these terrifying and savage contests had greatly increased and all possible efforts were made to further the sport. In Moti Mahal, right on the bank of the river, two new houses, Mubarak Manzil and Shah Manzil, were erected. Opposite them on the other side of the river, beautiful park-land stretched for miles and in it an extensive preserve had been enclosed with iron railings. Into this hundreds of animals of various kinds were let loose, the beasts of prey being shut up in cages. At one end of the preserve, on the river bank, large expanses of land were enclosed by bamboo fences or iron railings for wild animal combat. These were exactly opposite Shah Manzil on the other side of the river, which is very narrow at this spot. The King, his guests and his companions would sit in the shade of elaborate marquees decorated with gold and silver thread on the upper terrace of Shah Manzil. In ease and comfort they watched the uproar and confusion of combat across the river. It was easy enough to make beasts of prey and rutting elephants fight each other but it was a very difficult matter to control these fights. If a rutting elephant or a tiger escaped from a cage all was confusion and many lives could be lost. But the people had become so adept at these dangerous operations that European travellers who were present at the court have testified in their diaries that there were none in the world better at looking after, training and controlling the wild animals than these keepers. They brought the elephants and beasts of prey into the arena, let them loose and exercised control over them. When the combat was over they took charge of both victor and vanquished. For these duties hundreds of men with goads and spears were appointed who prodded the beasts and warded off any attacks. They were equipped with red-hot, iron-tipped staves and torches with which they could turn the animals in any direction or drive them to any place they wished and also were responsible for locking up the tigers and leopards in their cages. One may say that the movement, agility, skill and presence of mind of the keepers was as interesting to watch as the fights themselves.

Tigers

The King had collected a large number of tigers from the foothills of Nepal. Some were extremely large and he had become very fond of several because they had been the victors in numerous encounters.

For the fights their cages would be brought up to the enclosure of the preserve and then opened. Directly they were freed, both antagonists would spring roaring at each other, and would close together and inflict wounds with tooth and claw until one succeeded in forcing the other to the ground and getting on top of him. After a long and terrifying battle one of the antagonists sometimes lost its life or became so badly wounded that it lost heart and being weakened by excessive loss of blood, it would turn to flee. It was then that the skill, efforts and proficiency of the trainers in bringing the animals under control could be seen.

Tigers were often pitted against leopards, but the leopards were so powerful that the tigers could hardly ever beat them. These fights followed the same pattern as those between two tigers. Sometimes tigers and elephants fought each other but they were not evenly matched and the result was often contrary to what had been expected. If an elephant was alert, the tiger could rarely put up a fight against it.

The most interesting battles were those between a tiger and a rhinoceros. Except for the underpart of its belly, the rhinoceros is brazen-bodied and the tiger's teeth and claws have no effect on it. With the assurance of this strength, the rhinoceros cared nothing for the strongest of foes and, lowering its head, was able to get under its adversary's belly and rip it open with the horn on its snout; all the entrails came tumbling out and the adversary's days were over. Only rarely did a tiger knock a rhinoceros flat on its back and then tear open its belly with teeth and claws. Generally the rhinoceros managed to kill the tiger with a thrust of its horn.

At one time during the reign of King Nasir ud Din Haidar the tigers were completely defeated by a certain horse. This astounding animal was more dangerous to man than were beasts of prey. It was impossible for anyone to come near it. Its fodder was thrown to it from a distance and if it got loose it was capable of killing people. It would kill any other animal in its path, chew up its bones and mutilate its body to such an extent that it was unrecognizable. With no other solution in sight, plans were made to have it attacked by tigers. Accordingly a tiger named Bhuriya, of which the King was fond and which had been victorious in many combats, was let loose upon it. The horse, instead of being frightened by the tiger, prepared to fight and, immediately the tiger sprang, lowered the front part of its body so that the tiger landed on its back and dug its dagger-like claws into the horse's hind quarters. The horse lashed out so violently that the tiger was turned head over heels and struck the ground some distance away. When the tiger had recovered it sprang on the horse again. The horse employed the same tactics as before and, lowering its forehead, the tiger landed on its hind quarters again. The tiger's instinct was to knock the horse over with its paws and then kill it, but the horse kicked out with its hind legs so powerfully that the tiger landed flat on its back some distance away with a broken jaw. This injury so disheartened the tiger that it turned its back on the horse and started to run away. The onlookers were amazed and another, larger tiger was let loose. It would not face the horse and had to be removed. Now three wild buffaloes were brought in. They too refused to attack the horse which, without being provoked, advanced on one of the buffaloes and kicked it so hard with both hind legs that it fell over. Its two companions started shaking their heads as if in appreciation of what had happened. Eventually the horse was granted its life and Nasir ud Din Haidar said, 'I will have an iron cage made for it and make arrangements for it to be looked after. I swear on my dear father's head that it is a very valiant animal.'

Cheetahs

All beasts of prey were starved for a couple of days before a fight, but with cheetahs great care had to be taken because, fierce and blood-thirsty as they were, they sometimes proved to be cowardly. It was generally believed that they had a desire for adulation like the spoilt sons of rich men. Therefore in the arena, when they wished to fight, they would fight, but if they did not wish to, nothing on earth could make them do so; they would flinch and shrink away when advancing on an adversary. When they did fight, first they sprang with the hope of inflicting wounds but after one or two such attacks they stood up on their hind legs and started fighting with their paws. Their contests were very bloody, with both contestants roaring the whole time and striking out with their claws. Eventually the stronger one brought the weaker to the ground and tore it apart with its teeth, though itself covered with wounds from head to tail.

Leopards

The leopard is small but despite its size it is said that most of the leopards that fought against tigers in Lucknow were such marvellous fighters that they often were victorious. Fights between leopards were exactly the same as those between tigers. In the course of the fight both antagonists were grievously wounded. The one that was vanquished either fell down and died in the arena or, acknowledging defeat, fled from its enemy.

Elephants

In Lucknow people were particularly fond of elephant fighting. Such was the interest taken that at the time of King Nasir ud Din Haidar there were one hundred and fifty fighting elephants which were never ridden. For fighting purposes it was essential that an elephant should be ruttish, because it would not fight until it was in rut, and even if it should fight, it would not be truly angry or have any urge for victory over its opponent.

Before two elephants were put to fight, a rope was tied around the neck and tail of each. Both contestants, when confronting one another, raised their trunks and their tails, and trumpeting loudly, charged to meet with a terrific impact. They then continued to butt and jostle each other, pushing and thrusting with their tusks, and one realized from the contortions of their bodies what force they were putting into their blows. The mahouts kept striking them with an *ankas*[391] [goad] to excite them to further efforts. Eventually one of the elephants would weaken and, no longer able to stand up to the jostling, fall to the ground. The victorious elephant then usually gashed its victim's belly with its tusks and finished it off. Often when an elephant weakened, it would avoid its antagonist's tusks and run away. The victor then pursued it and if it succeeded in catching up, knocked it to the ground and killed it by tearing open its belly. The only way a vanquished elephant could save its life was by escaping.

Rhinoceroses were often pitted against elephants, but usually these animals did not like fighting each other. If it came to a fight, however, that fight was certainly ferocious. If the elephant managed to push the rhinoceros over the latter would be killed by the elephant's driving its tusks into its belly. If the rhinoceros got the chance to thrust its horn into the elephant's belly it would make a wide gash in the hide. But the elephant with the help of its trunk could stop the horn penetrating too deeply and would thus escape a mortal wound.

Camels

Although as a rule any animal is capable of fighting, none could be less suited to it than the camel. In Lucknow even camels were made to fight each other when ruttish and excited. The camel's bite is well known, but the clumsy way in which they fall is very dangerous for them. They would show their excitement by discharging froth and saliva. They started their fights by rushing at each other, foaming at the mouth, spitting froth at their adversary's head, discharging mucus and vilifying each other. If one got the chance, it seized its adversary's drooping lower lip with its teeth and pulled at it. The camel whose lip was seized usually fell down and was defeated. Thus the battle ended.

Rhinoceroses

No animal is more powerful than a rhinoceros. It has been fashioned with such a brazen body that neither the tusks of an elephant nor the claws of a tiger are effective against it. Only the skin of its belly is soft, and if any animal managed to attack that part of its anatomy it could destroy it. Otherwise an animal would expend its strength in vain and eventually tire. Then the rhinoceros would drive the horn on its snout into the adversary's belly and kill it.

In Lucknow, rhinoceroses were pitted against elephants, tigers, leopards and against each other. At the time of King Ghazi ud Din Haidar, some rhinoceroses, besides being made to fight, were so well trained that they were harnessed to carts and, like elephants, used to carry people on their backs. The rhinoceros is not by nature a pugnacious animal and avoids fighting whenever possible. If, however, it is baited, it will face an opponent and fight with great ferocity. At the time of Nasir ud Din Haidar there were fifteen or twenty fighting rhinoceroses which used to be kept at Chand Ganj. When their keepers prodded them and set them to fight they would lower their heads, charge and butt at each other. Each tried to rip open its adversary's belly with its horn. They bellowed loudly and banged their horns together. In fighting, their heads met and their horns became interlocked. Then they both started pushing and the one who weakened started to retreat slowly, giving up its ground. If this didn't save the animal, it tried to run away. The stronger continued butting until the weaker one disengaged its horn, turned from the contest and swiftly took flight. If the arena was limited in size, the victorious opponent attacked its antagonist as it fled, knocked it over and killed it by driving its horn into its belly. In large arenas, the vanquished rhinoceros was often able to escape by running away. The keeper, by prodding and beating with burning staves, got control over the victor, stopped its pursuit of its adversary and drove it back. A fight between rhinoceroses depended upon the animals keeping their heads down and protecting their bellies. The minute one raised its head, its opponent could take full advantage of the lapse. On one occasion, a rhinoceros had won a fight and its antagonist started to run away. Seeing this, the victor raised its head. The vanquished rhinoceros immediately ran in like lightning, lowered its head and ripped its opponent's belly.

Stags

Lucknow is probably the only place where these delicate animals were made to fight in order to provide entertainment.* Their fights were very interesting to

---

* *Author's note:* Maulana Habib ur Rahman Sherwani[161] points out, and I have confirmed this from historical sources, that combats between beasts of prey as well as elephants were staged in Delhi. (This was probably under the later Mughal Emperors.)

watch. Poets liken the beloved to a deer, and even when these beasts are in combat, one is reminded of loving gestures. Confronting one another, both antagonists showed very graceful footwork. Eventually they would strike at each other using their horns both as swords and shields. After this had gone on for some time, their horns would get inextricably locked together and they started pushing and shoving each other until one of them weakened. The one who weakened became so overcome with fear that its delicate legs would shake and its whole body tremble. Its opponent, on the other hand, would become violent and push its adversary right across the arena until they both reached the fence. The defeated stag gave up all hope, tears would fall from its eyes and blood drip from its horns. Disengaging its horns, it would turn from the fight. Then the victor started to gore its body with its horns and the vanquished stag ran for its life. But however swiftly it ran, its adversary kept up the pursuit. This was a race worth seeing, both animals moving at such a pace that it was difficult to keep them in view. The victor showed no mercy and continued to gore its opponent until the latter died of its wounds. Even then it went on striking the corpse with its horns. Eventually it turned away, preening itself upon its victory.

Rams

These are extremely gentle and harmless animals but their butting is terrific. When they fight it is as if two mountains collide, and people made them fight in order to watch them butting. This was not a new practice but had been going on since ancient times. It was started in India by the Baluchis and interest in it spread from Baluchistan to other places. Looking after these animals and training them to fight was usually the duty of butchers and lower-class persons. Nobles and gentlefolk used to send for rams and watch the fights. It is said that Navab Asaf ud Daula and Sadat Ali Khan were fond of watching ram-fighting and Ghazi ud Din Haidar and Nasir ud Din Haidar would often watch the sport. When Wajid Ali Shah was in Calcutta he derived a certain amount of pleasure from it and the Munshi ul Sultan, his Chief Secretary, kept several pairs ready, in the charge of butchers. I have myself seen a strong ram butting so violently that it has split its opponent's skull. When a ram is worsted and cannot stand up against the butting of its adversary, it escapes by swiftly dodging its opponent's attack and running away.

I remember that once a year crowds of British from Calcutta came to see the King's park. On one such day the King, contrary to his custom, came out riding on a sedan chair, and in order to please his guests, ordered that some rams be brought out and made to fight. Soon the noise of butting could be heard but it was nothing in comparison with the noise made by the Europeans in their 'hurrahs' and shouts of acclamation.

In Lucknow, even after the fall of the monarchy, Navab Mohsin ud Daula used to take a great interest in watching ram-fighting. Recently nobles and better-class people have given up the pursuit and now it only exists among the lower classes.

19

Bird-Fighting and Pigeon-Flying

Organizing fights between beasts of prey in Lucknow was confined to the royal family and nobles of the court. Keeping the animals, training them, controlling them after the fight and protecting spectators from injury were beyond the means of the richest men, let alone the impecunious. For this reason fights between beasts of prey were only witnessed in Lucknow whilst the court existed, and when the court disappeared so did the terrifying amphitheatres.

But bird-fighting was different. Rich and poor alike could indulge in it. Any interested person, if he took the trouble, could train cocks and quails to fight. The birds that people in Lucknow used for fighting were cocks, bush quails, partridges, *lavway, guldum, lals,* pigeons and parrots.[392] Lucknow pigeon-flying and quail-fighting were famous throughout the country, but nowadays educated people, who make a show of modern culture, are apt to ridicule these sports. They are totally unaware of the degrees of perfection to which their devotees have raised them, having in fact made them a fine art. However, when they go to Europe and see that these 'frivolous' sports are also practised there, they will at least be sorry for their utterances in regard to the interest taken in them in their own country.

Cock-fighting

Although every sort of breed of cock will fight, the best fighter is the *asil*, the thoroughbred, and it is a fact that there is no braver beast than the thoroughbred cock. Braver than tigers, they would sooner die than turn away from a fight. Experts believe that the breed came from Arabia and this appears reasonable, as thoroughbreds are found mostly in Hyderabad Deccan, the area in India where Arabs came to settle in greatest number. The breeds of cock in the mountainous regions of India originated in Persia.

A well-known Lakhnavi cock-fighter used to tell the tale that his cock was unluckily beaten in a fight. He was distressed and went to the Sacred Najaf in Iraq where he spent some months in divine worship. He prayed day and night that God, as *sadqa*[393] [charity] for the sake of his Imams, might grant him a cock which would never be beaten in a fight. One night in a dream he received a revelation: 'Go into the wilds.' The next morning when he awoke he went into the desert taking a hen with him. Reaching a valley he heard the sound of crowing. He approached and released his hen. A cock, hearing the hen, came out of the scrub and the man managed to seize it. Its progeny was such that never again was he put to shame in a cock-fight.

Interest in cock-fighting dates from the time of Navab Shuja ud Daula, who was extremely fond of the sport. Navab Sadat Ali Khan, in spite of the fact that he was very abstinent, also enjoyed cock-fighting. His interest had a great effect on society and in addition to the Lucknow nobles, Europeans at the court also became its devotees. General Martin[137] was an expert at cock-fighting and Navab Sadat Ali Khan used to bet his cocks against those of the General.

For fighting purposes in Lucknow, the cock's claws were tied so that they could not cause much damage, whilst their beaks were scraped with penknives and made sharp and pointed. When the two cocks were released in the cock-pit, their owners stood behind them, each trying to get his own cock to deal the first blow. When the cocks started to fight with beak and claw their owners incited and encouraged them, shouting, 'Well done my boy, bravo! Peck him, my beauty!' and 'Go in again!' On hearing the shouts of encouragement the cocks attacked each other with claw and beak and it seemed as if they understood what was being said to them.

When they had been fighting for some time and were wounded and tired out, both parties, by mutual consent, would remove their birds. This removing was called *pani* [literally water] in cock-fighting idiom. The owners would wipe clean the wounds on the cocks' heads and pour water on them. Sometimes they would suck the wounds with their lips and make other efforts, whereby the cocks were restored to their former vigour in the space of a few minutes. They were then once again released into the cock-pit. This method of *pani* was continued and the fights would last four to five days, sometimes even eight or nine days. When a cock was blinded or was so badly hurt that he could not stand and was unable to fight, it was understood that he had lost. It often happened that a cock's beak was broken. Even then, whenever possible, the owner would tie up the beak and set the cock to resume the fight.

In Hyderabad the sport is much more violent. There they do not tie up the claws but scrape them with penknives and make them like spearheads. As a result the fight is decided within the space of an hour or so. The practice of tying up the claws in Lucknow was probably adopted to lengthen the fight and thus to provide longer entertainment.

When preparing cocks to fight, the owners would show their skill not only in the feeding and upkeep: they also massaged the bird's limbs, sprinkled it with water, tended its beak and claws and displayed their dexterity in tying up the claws and removing any signs of fatigue. From fear that the beak might be injured by pecking food from the ground they sometimes fed grain by hand.

Great interest was taken in the sport until the time of Wajid Ali Shah. In Matiya Burj cock-fights were held in Navab Ali Naqi's residence and some English people from Calcutta would bring their birds to fight there.

In addition to kings, many nobles were interested in cock-fighting. Mirza Haidar, the brother of Bahu Begam, Navab Salar Jang Haidar Beg Khan, and Major Soirisse, who lived at the time of Nasir ud Din Haidar and used to set his cocks against the King's, and Agha Burhan ud Din Haidar, were all fond of the sport. The last-named nobleman always kept, throughout his life, two hundred to two hundred and fifty birds. They were kept with scrupulous care and cleanliness and ten or eleven men were employed to look after them. Mian Darab Ali Khan was a great devotee, as was Navab Ghasita.

The respected Pathans of Malihabad were also adherents of the sport and had very good breeds of game-cock. In Lucknow there were many who were considered outstanding experts: Mir Imdad Ali, Shaikh Ghasita and Munavar Ali had acquired such skill that they could tell from the noise a cock made whether it would win its fight. Safdar Ali and Saiyyid Miran, a *vasiqa dar*,[394] were also famous. In latter days the names of the following were well known: Fazal Ali Jamadar,[395] Qadir Jawan Khan, Husain Ali, Nauroz Ali, Muhammad Taqi Khan, Mian Jan, Dil, Changa, Husain Ali Beg and Ahmad Husain. None of these men is now alive.

These were the people who perfected the sport of cock-fighting in Lucknow but nowadays I think that interest in the sport is greatest in Hyderabad Deccan. Many noblemen, landowners and officers are devotees. They have an unequalled stock of game-cocks and give great care to breeding.

Quail-fighting

The interest in quail-fighting came to Lucknow from the Panjab. Some gypsies from this area, whose women were of easy virtue, went to Lucknow in the days of Sadat Ali Khan and brought bush quail with them, which they used to cause to fight. (Some well-known courtesans of today are descended from these gypsies.) There are two kinds of quail, bush quail and button quail.[396] In the Panjab there is only the bush quail, which is bigger and stronger than the button quail. In Lucknow both the bush quail and the button quail exist. The button quail is small and delicate but it is the more powerful fighter and its fighting the more interesting to watch. In Lucknow, the button quail was considered more suitable for fighting.

Quail-fighting does not require a large arena nor does one even need to leave one's house to watch a performance. One can sit comfortably in a room on a nice clean carpet and watch the fight. For this reason the sport was very popular in Lucknow society. Dainty bamboo cages adorned with strips of ivory were made to keep the quails.

To prepare a quail for fighting it is first necessary to keep him wet with drops of water and to hold him in one's hand for hours. He then becomes quite tame and starts chirping and chirruping. After this he is starved and subsequently given a purgative containing a large amount of sugar so that his inside is thoroughly cleansed. Then late at night his trainer shouts the word 'ku' into his ear and this is known as *kukna*, winding up. By these methods the quail loses his surplus fat and any awkwardness and his body becomes very active and strong. The more diligently these details are carried out the more efficient is the quail when the bird begins to fight.

For the fight, grain is sprinkled over the floor and the quails are taken out of their cages, their beaks having been previously sharpened with penknives. When they are set against each other their fight is much the same as that of cocks. They strike with their beaks and feet. With their beaks they wound and lacerate their opponent's head and with their feet they sometimes split open his crop. The fight usually lasts fifteen to twenty minutes but it can go on longer. Eventually the vanquished quail turns and runs. When he has once run away he will never stand up to another quail again.

There are three stages in the development of a quail which are considered landmarks in the bird's career. The first is when he is originally caught, tamed and then has his initial fight. If he wins several fights and never runs away, he is put into a cage at the end of the fighting season. This is the time when he sheds his old feathers and moults, which is known as *kuriz*, the first moult period. When this period is over, he enters his second year and his second stage of progress. The bird is then known as *nau kar*, an apprentice. After this, when he has moulted a second time, known as the second kuriz period, and is trained for the third year's fighting, the bird himself is known as *kuriz*. This is the third and final stage of a quail's progress. It is generally acknowledged that a nau kar is stronger than a newly-entered quail and that a kuriz is stronger than a nau kar. A newly-entered quail could scarcely stand up to a kuriz even if the bird had two beaks. Expert quail-fighters and enthusiastic noblemen use only kuriz for fighting; they consider fights between first-year birds to be a very poor form of sport.

Many artifices and harsh practices can be employed in quail-fighting. Some people occasionally put bitter and poisonous oil or *etar*[397] on their quail's beak so that the other quail after a few encounters moves back and abandons the fight. Should the bird go on fighting, he will die after the encounter. Some people introduce intoxicants into the sport and a few hours before a fight, administer such a strong drug to their bird that he does not realize when he is injured in the fight and never thinks of running away. He goes on fighting like one possessed until he has driven his opponent from the pit.

Interest in quail-fighting in Lucknow produced such expert fighters that they were unrivalled elsewhere. Some people seeing a famous and successful quail could produce a very ordinary quail and make it resemble the other in every detail. Then when they got the chance they changed the birds round in the course of conversation. This was of course a sharp practice amounting to theft.

Some experts acquired the ability to re-train a quail which had run away and make it fight and beat very good third-year birds. There was also an expert in intoxicants who used to prepare such efficient pills that he received one hundred rupees for ten of them and people were only too willing to buy them. These people showed their highest skill in the field of the medical treatment of quail. They cured quail which were very sick, and on the point of death. They diagnosed their ailments with accuracy and used such suitable ingredients in their medicine that physicians were astounded. They even made great efforts to breed quail from eggs which were kept in dried grass, but without success.

Quails were given high-sounding names such as 'Rustam', 'Sohrab' (Persian fairy-tale heroes), and 'Shuhra-e-Afaq', World-Famed. Large bets were made on the encounters and I myself have seen a fight on which one thousand rupees were wagered. Some kings took an interest in the sport and Nasir ud Din Haidar was fond of watching quail-fighting on a table set before him.

The memory remains of old quail-fighters such as Mir Bachchu, Mir Amdu, Khwaja Hasan, Mir Fida Ali, Changa, Mir Abid and Saiyyid Miran. I remember, forty years ago in Matiya Burj, finding Darugha Ghulam Abbas Chotey Khan and Ghulam Muhammad Khan Khalispuri, both very old men, adept at the sport. Ghalib Ali Beg, Mirza Asad Ali Beg, Navab Mirza Mian Jan, Shaikh Mumin Ali and Ghazi ud Din Khan attained great fame in later days.

The hunting of quails is also interesting. At first it was merely an interest which led to some carefree people, who never otherwise left the town, going into the country and fields to get some fresh air; but now many make their living by it. They say that quails leave the mountains at night and fly about at great altitudes. Hunters get hold of a certain kind of quail having a loud call which they then train to call throughout the night: these are known as call-birds. Nets are erected round a field of pulse and call-birds are put into it. On hearing them, the quail in the sky come down into the field, where many of them collect during the night. In the early morning they are driven into the nets where they become enmeshed and are then put into cages.

Partridge-fighting

Partridges, when fighting, leap into the air more than other birds. Interest in the sport is taken only by villagers and lower-class people. Noblemen and gentlefolk never go in for it.

The birds are trained by being rolled in the dust and made to race. They are fed with termites to make them worked up and excited. But this is really no sport and was never taken up by refined society, though the lower classes in Lucknow took it up quite extensively and still indulge in it.

Lavwa-fighting

The *lavwa* is a variety of partridge, smaller than a quail. While other birds fight over grain, they fight over a female. A fight would begin, therefore, with a cage containing a female lavwa being placed before two male birds to make them angry. The sport was more popular in the State of Rewa and other regions of central India, but people in Lucknow followed it to a certain extent. Lavwas are usually trained by being starved and rolled in the dust and their fighting is more attractive to watch than quail-fighting. The lavwa spreads his wings, closes with his opponent, rises like a blossoming flower and then descends. Some rich men in Lucknow took an interest in the sport and there was also an expert at the late Wajid Ali Shah's court at Matiya Burj. Lavwa fighting began before quail-fighting but eventually the latter became more prevalent and the former died out. The method of catching the birds is quite interesting. Like quails, they have the habit of flying about at great altitudes. People tie an earthenware pot on top of a pole, cover the mouth of the pot with a dried animal skin, drive a stick through the skin and fasten it inside the earthenware pot. A cord is tied to the stick and when this cord is pulled a loud humming sound is emitted from the skin. This noise attracts the lavwas so that at night they fly down to the nets around the pole. In the early morning they are caught in the nets in the same way as quails.

Guldum-fighting

Most people call the *guldum* a nightingale, but this is incorrect. The nightingale is a song-bird from Badakhshan and other parts of Persia, whereas the bird in question is called *guldum,* Rose-Tail, because it has red feathers like a rose beneath its tail. Villagers and lower-class people often make them fight but better-class people have never taken much interest in the sport.

Guldum-fighting is not unattractive to watch. During training the birds fight over grain sprinkled on the ground. When they fight, both birds fly into the air as they close with each other, become enmeshed and then descend still entangled.

Lal-fighting

Lals are really only suitable as cage-birds, but in order to get some short-lived pleasure, people also used to make them fight. In the first place, it is difficult to tame the lal sufficiently to ensure that it will not fly away directly it is released from its cage. Secondly, it is not easy to work these birds up to a pitch of excitement sufficient to make them attack and fight. However, when they do fight, they fight very well. They become entangled as they fly into the air, close with each other and go on fighting for a long time; in fact their fights last longer than those of other small birds. Lal-fighting was never popular in Lucknow. There were only one or two experts and as a general rule people were opposed to the sport which, in any case, was confined to the lower classes.

Pigeon-flying

Pigeons can be classed among those tame animals in which human beings everywhere have always taken interest, from ancient times until today. There are several varieties. Among the fliers are *girah baz* and *goley* which are kept merely because of their beauty and bright colours.[398] The best-known varieties are *shirazi,*[399] *guli,*[400] *peshawari,*[401] *gulvey,*[402] *laqa,*[403] *lotan,*[404] *choya* or *chandan*[405] and some others. The *yahu*[406] never stops cooing night and day and because they utter the sound 'Yahu, O God', they were very popular with the pious Muslims and holy men.

I believe that tumbler pigeons were first brought to Lucknow from Kabul. These were the first variety to be flown. After these came the goley, a variety which was originally bred in Arabia, Persia and Turkestan. The tumbler pigeon, if it is released in the morning, will fly for hours. They rise up into the sky, vertically, and encircle the house. If water is put into a basin in the courtyard their reflection can always be seen in it. Sometimes they fly about all day and only come down at night. They recognize their cots and are particularly home-loving. As an example of their intelligence, I once had a tumbler pigeon which was caught by someone who clipped its wings. Three years later, when it got the chance and its feathers had grown again, it returned, went straight into its cot and attacked the pigeon which was occupying it at the time.

Tumbler pigeons only fly in flocks of ten or twelve. Those who preferred to fly flocks of one or two hundred kept goleys. Pigeon-flying reached such perfection in Delhi that they say when the last Mughal king, Bahadur Shah, went out in procession, a flock of two hundred pigeons would fly in the sky above his head, thus providing shade.

Pigeons are extremely fond of their homes. In Delhi pigeons were taken by cart to distant places where they were released at any given spot and then called back to the cot.

From the start, the ruling family in Lucknow practised pigeon-flying. Shuja ud Daula took a great interest in it and an inhabitant of Bareilly, Saiyyid Yar Ali, was attached to his court as an expert in pigeon-flying. Navab Asaf ud Daula and Navab Sadat Ali Khan were also interested and at the time of Ghazi ud Din Haidar and Nasir ud Din Haidar the art had reached a high level. Mir Abbas, an expert pigeon-flier, could go by invitation to anyone's house and for a payment of five rupees would release a pigeon from a cot and call it back by whistle. By no chance would the pigeon come down anywhere else.

So great was the interest taken in this sport that some rich men would fly up to nine hundred female pigeons in one flock and some nobles flew the same number of male pigeons without mixing the two flocks.

From Khost, a territory on the borders of Afghanistan, came some special-coloured pigeons called *tipait*. They were extremely costly and nobles used to spend thousands of rupees on these birds.

An old gentleman in Lucknow who was fond of novelties produced an unusual phenomenon with two young pigeons. He cut off the right wing of one and the left wing of the other and then stitched them together, thus making them into a double pigeon. Then he nurtured it with such care that when it matured it was able to fly. He produced many such composite pigeons.

Nasir ud Din Haidar, when he crossed the river from the Chattar Manzil in his boat and sat in his kothi,[139] Dil Aram, admiring the river scenery, would make a habit of watching these extraordinary composite pigeons. They were released from the far bank by this same old gentleman. They used to fly across the river and sit near the King. This pleased him very much and the owner was rewarded.

Another old gentleman named Mir Aman Ali invented something fantastic. He could produce a pigeon of any colour he desired. Pulling out most of the original feathers and inserting different coloured feathers into the apertures, he could fix them so that they held as firmly as the original ones. Sometimes he used to paint them in a way that was so lasting that the colours did not fade throughout the year. But after the bird had moulted, the original feathers returned. These pigeons used to be sold for fifteen or twenty rupees each and wealthy men were eager to buy them. The same man could produce coloured designs and floral patterns on the wings which were extremely rare in nature and unequalled in beauty.

Navab Paley was a great expert. He used to fly tumbler pigeons like goleys. His speciality was that with a given signal at any place he could make his pigeons show off their tricks and turn somersaults in the air.

Wajid Ali Shah collected many new varieties of pigeon in Matiya Burj. It is said that he paid twenty-five thousand rupees for a silk-winged pigeon, and that he developed the breed of a certain form of green pigeon. When he died he had more than twenty-four thousand pigeons with hundreds of keepers to look after them. Their darugha was Ghulam Abbas who was unrivalled as a pigeon expert.

Interest and skill produced the most wonderful varieties of pigeon, not only for flying but for raising as well. I myself saw a shirazi pigeon which was large enough to fill the whole of a cage a yard in breadth and a guli pigeon which could pass through the bracelet of a twelve-year-old girl.

20

Parrots and Kite-Flying

An interest in training and watching birds fight became extremely common among carefree people in Lucknow, and the art of training pigeons was so perfected that nobles from all over India who took an interest in such matters—and this frivolous interest became common among the leisured wealthy—sent for experts from Lucknow. These are now the superintendents of everything having to do with the management of these activities.

Parrots

The abundant interest in pigeon-flying led to the development of means whereby other birds could be made to perform like pigeons. An old gentleman named Mir Muhammad Ali was very successful in getting parrots to behave like pigeons.

A parrot is by nature without fidelity. You can keep and nurture one all its life but if it gets out of its cage it will fly away and never return. A parrot's second name is 'infidelity'.[407] It will copy other animals and talk if it is taught a sentence or two but it is useless for flying purposes because directly it leaves its cage it is completely out of control. However, Mir Muhammad Ali managed to change the parrot's nature and would fly a flock of ten or twelve. As soon as he blew a whistle for their return they would, without fail, descend from the sky and enter their cages. In the evenings he brought these parrots to the Husainabad quarter and flew them from there.

Having described the training of these birds, I feel impelled to say that if the people of Lucknow had paid as much attention to the training of themselves and their bodies as they did to the training of animals, things would have been very different.

Kite-flying

Interest in kite-flying remains throughout India, and nowadays most boys and youths are extremely fond of this pastime. Seeing this, one would imagine that it has existed in India for a very long time. But this is not so and it is unlikely

E

that it has been in existence for more than a hundred years. The centre in which it developed was Lucknow.

Boys in Europe fly cloth kites which remain in the air as long as they run holding the string. Immediately they stop, the kite comes down, unless there is a high wind. I cannot say when these kites originated or whence they came. However, in India, I believe that interest was first taken in this pastime in Delhi at the time of King Shah Alam I and that it was limited to a few select people.

Great care was taken in the construction of a kite. It was composed of two *tukkals,* paper kites, joined together back to front. The tukkal had three rounded edges arranged in the shape of an inverted triangle; a batten was fixed to the centre of the frame and was called a *thaddi,* back-stick, and two curved battens, scraped and softened, were fixed to the top and bottom of the frame and called *kamps,* bows. Between these light paper was inserted, and this made up a tukkal. Two such tukkals were put one in front of the other and joined together by fixing supporting battens in various places. Then paper was fastened round the tukkals making a sort of triangular Chinese lantern. Into this a ball of cloth soaked in oil was hung by a wire and set alight. People used to fly the kite at night, holding it by a strong cotton or silken thread. The beauty of the kite was that it looked like a lantern flying in the sky, which could be left flying or pulled down at will. Sometimes it turned upside down, but it could then be righted.

At that time some people used to fly effigies of human beings in this manner and reliable elders state that these effigies were the first kites to be invented in Delhi and that *changs* were invented as an improvement. As these changs were equal in length and breadth, they were easy to fly and to keep in the sky. Hindus took a greater interest than others in these kites and it is likely that they were associated in their minds with something pertaining to religion, probably *akas diyas,*[408] Lamps in the Sky. Then tukkals gained popularity, as they could cut down the strings of the changs in kite-fighting and be flown in the daytime. They were actually half or one side of a chang. The tukkal was easier to fly than a chang. It could dance in the air and fly far away into the sky. The chang stayed in one place, whereas the tukkal moved about and was so easily controlled that whenever one liked one could cut down someone else's chang by fraying its string with that of the tukkal.

People soon gave up the idea of Chinese lanterns and illuminated effigies and took to flying this new kite, which was easier to control than the chang and could move about in the sky. Interest in tukkals increased among rich Muslims and élite Hindus and money started to be lavished upon the sport. The best type of tukkal was known as *patang.* Its back-stick was made of bamboo from Murshidabad (Bengal) and cost eighty rupees, its decorations cost twenty rupees, paper two rupees and labour about five rupees. That is to say, it cost one hundred and seven rupees to make a patang.

After tukkals and patangs had become popular in Delhi, the patrons and others interested in this sport came to Lucknow. Later kite-fighting instead of kite-flying became the vogue. Such strong tukkals were made that a man of normal strength had difficulty in controlling them. Eight strands of strong cord would be rolled into a kind of pulley in order to cope with the tukkals. For the fight, the cords of two tukkals would cross with each other and the tukkals would rise twisting and knotting into the sky, the cord coming from the pulleys on either side.[409] One may judge the interest taken in Lucknow from the fact that Navab Asaf ud Daula's tukkals were decorated with five rupees' worth of gold and silver fringes. Whoever brought one of the Navab's tukkals back was given five rupees. Whoever retrieved one but did not bring it back to the Navab could still sell it for five rupees anywhere.

Experts of former times in Lucknow at these kite competitions were Mir Amdu, Khwaja Mathan and Shaikh Imdad. There was also a weaver who achieved such distinction in the art that he was received with respect among elegant kite-fliers.

In the time of Amjad Ali Shah a paper kite named *guddi* was invented which was shaped like an upright diamond and was easier to construct than a tukkal. In a tukkal there were two bows and one back-stick. In a guddi there was only one bow and one back-stick.

In Wajid Ali Shah's time kites were produced with one and a half bows and a back-stick. They were shaped like the present-day kite except that, like the tukkal, they had a small paper tassel at the bottom. Then Muhammad Husain Khan of Salar Jang's family, Agha Abu Tarab Khan and one or two other interested noblemen produced a kite which had a *patta*, triangle, cut out of paper, instead of a tassel at the bottom. This is still in use today and it appears that it has come to stay. Nowadays kites with pattas, called *kankava*, or with tassels, called *dehr kana*, are flown all over India. They were invented in Lucknow. In fighting with these kites a string was fed as with tukkals. Very large kites were made which carried a large amount of cord.

Towards the end of the Navabi rule there was a famous expert named Mir Vilayat Ali, who was popularly called Vilayati. Then there was Ilahi Baksh Tundey, who went to Matiya Burj and became renowned there as well. There were hundreds of other experts in Lucknow but the greatest of them all was undoubtedly Lamdur.

At the commencement of the British period *khinch*, the dragging-pulling style of kite-fighting, was established. It was really begun by small boys who had very little cord and would put their indigence to rights by recklessly cutting down other people's kites. In those days experts would look on them with contempt and keep their kites at a distance. But eventually this art became very popular in kite competitions and many experts sprang up. Today in Lucknow there are scores of people who have frittered away lakhs of rupees on this pursuit and have ruined themselves but have achieved prominence and have become honoured and revered in kite-flying circles.

21

The Origin and Growth of North Indian Music

Now I will describe the art of music and the circumstances of the people in Lucknow who were connected with this art.[410]

Singing is one of the skills that human nature evolved in very early times. People sang words that they wished to emphasize, and danced when their emotions were aroused by deeds or actions. Since religious sentiments arouse more fervour than any others and since among wordly affairs the most important emotions are those of love and affection, singing originated, in the first instance, with worship and with love. In India it was with worship that singing was connected at first. The first singers were Brahmans, who at worship sang hymns of praise to their deities. Later love for Krishna became divine adoration and amorous music was established. It is for this reason that poetry is written in the feminine gender, and song and dance in India are expressed by women.

Originally Brahmans would sing *git*,[411] devotional songs, either solo or sometimes accompanied by *sangit*,[412] instrumental music. As a result of the intermingling of this with Egyptian, Babylonian and Persian traditions, a characteristic style evolved in India. It was noticed that every sound, as it alters pitch, changes in quality, and having made an exact estimate of these changes, experts determined seven *surs*,[413] fixed notes.

Later in India *ragas*,[414] musical modes, were sung during worship in glorification of Brahma, the divine creative element, or in praise of Vishnu, the divine element of preservation, or in homage to Mahesh or Mahadeo, the divine element of destruction.[415] On these lines three distinct groups of ragas evolved. Of the first it is said that the Brahmans divulged nothing and kept its secrets with them until death. The second was concerned with aspects of life such as childbirth, marriage and worldly affairs. The third was concerned with life after death, religious merit and final chastisement. It was designed to inspire awe and to emphasize the transitory nature of this world. Amorous musical modes were included in the third category simply to show how a lover longs for death and because Sri Krishna was an incarnation of Mahadeo. These ragas were given the names of *barog*, which included *bhairun* and *saras*, and their *raginis*[416] were called *bhairvin, parach, kalangra, soni, sindhi, pilu* and some others.

In later days when Brahmans had to sing odes in praise of rajas at their courts, ragas suitable to express dignity and splendour were created and were given the names *malkus, darbari, shahana* and *adana.*

The Muslims brought their own music with them to India. This had originally been perfected by Ibn-e-Mashaj [Ibn-e-Mushajjah]. After this, when the Abbaside court was established in Iraq, Arabian and Persian music were added to it and a very fine art was evolved called *ghena*, vocal music, which spread throughout the Islamic world and was finally known as the music of Persia. This was the art that Muslims brought with them to India and present-day *qavvals*[417] are the musical descendants of these Muslim singers. The instruments they play are *sarod,*[418] *chang,*[419] *shahnai* or *sinai,*[420] *barbat* and *rabab.*

The Muslims made their influence felt on almost everything in India. They brought about changes in the arts and sciences and in all aspects of social life, but far less did they influence the music of the sub-continent. It is generally thought that the reason for this is that Indian music was already so well organized and of such calibre, so firmly established and so elaborately developed, that it could not be affected by outside influence. The real reason, however, is that the music or musical system of a country rarely receives real attention from anyone unless he is a long-term resident or is born in that country and has assimilated its language and culture. The Muslim invaders, mainly Arabs and Persians, paid no attention to local music. When they did start to devote attention to it they had become so completely Indianized that they forgot their own traditional music and became enamoured of local airs. By then they were incapable of influencing Indian music in any way or of offering the slightest form of criticism.

But the music of the qavvals from Persia had a certain effect on Indian music, and several of their ragas became incorporated into the local Hindu music. It is thought that *zangula* (or *jangla*), *zaif,*[421] *shahana, darbari, zila* or *khamach* and others were airs of the Persian ghena system which have become included in the Indian ragas.

Amir Khusrau[422] mastered both of these traditions and made great efforts to blend the two together. It is said that he invented the *sitar*[423] and it is certain that he originated many *dhuns,*[424] but his actual contribution to the development of Indian music is difficult to establish.

It appears that among Muslims, the Sufis gave their attention to music earlier than the courts. Their *hal-o-qal,*[425] musical assemblies of the devout, which were established in Iraq and Persia as part of the form of worship, became established in India as well. Singers who formerly used to sing hymns in Hindu temples sat in the circles of these Muslim devotees and mystics and chanted odes of worship.

Indian singers and courtesans who sang and danced were attached to the courts, but they were always under the direction of a Persian singer who had a certain amount of influence over the music they produced. In the reign of Muhammad Tughlaq[426] the greatest court singer was Amir Shams ud Din Tabrizi, who was in charge of all male and female musicians. In those days, in the vicinity of Deo Garh, that is to say, Daulatabad, there was a village known as Tarabadad,[7] City of Entertainment, which was inhabited only by musicians. In the centre of its market-place was a tower in which the *chaudhri*[427] [village headman] would take his seat every evening and all the troupes of singers and courtesans would collect and take their turn to sing. Some of them were Muslims and practised their religion. In the village there were mosques in which *taravih*[428] [special prayers in the holy month of Ramzam] were held. Great rajas came to listen to the singing, as did some Muslim crowned heads. The musicians' leader and supervisor was usually a Muslim, and thus the Arabic, Persian and Indian arts of vocal music were blended together.

The centres of Hindu music in northern India were Mathura, Ajodhya and Benares (U.P.). The art of music developed in these places as they were the main centres of pilgrimage. Of the Sharqi Sultans of Jaupur, Sultan Husain Sharqi was very fond of music and he was himself a great singer.[429] Because both Ajodhya and Benares were in his territory, it is certain that he did a great deal to improve this noble Indian art.

Akbar had such a great appreciation for the art that he included the most famous singer of his time, Tan Sen,[430] among his *nau ratan*,[431] Nine Jewels. Seeing such consideration and favour from a Muslim Emperor, Tan Sen or, according to some accounts, his son Bilas Khan, became a Muslim. As a result of the appreciation of the court, Hindu music reached great heights through the medium of this family, and at later courts singers of this lineage continued to be honoured.[432] Members of the family today still consider themselves to be connected with the Mughal court. It is generally thought that the accomplishment of Hindu music was acquired by Muslims through the Tan Sen family, but from what I have written it is abundantly clear that Muslims acquired it long before the family existed. Nowadays the greatest experts of Hindu music and all its famous singers are Muslims.[433]

The first book to be written on this art in Delhi is entitled *Shamul Aswat* and appeared in the reign of Emperor Shajahan. It is no longer procurable anywhere. Later at the time of Akbar Shah II a distinguished man named Mirza Khan, with the help of pandits and Sanskrit scholars, wrote a book called *Tuhfat ul Hind* of which a few copies are still in existence. It is a collection of Hindu arts and sciences[362] and deals with such subjects as astrology, palmistry, sexual pleasure and magic. There is also a description of Hindu music.

Such was the stage that music had reached in Delhi when the art came to the court of the Navabs. Navab Shuja ud Daula's approbation of it and his liberality attracted musical experts from all over India who came together in Avadh. Some fruits also remained of the enthusiasm of the Sharqi Sultans of Jaunpur, so that when accomplished singers and musical experts from Tan Sen's established school in Delhi gathered in Lucknow, a great impetus was given to music and one can say that it started a new era.

The author of *The Delightful History* states that Shuja ud Daula took great interest in musicians. Thousands of courtesans who were singers had come to Lucknow from Delhi and other places. It had become the custom that when the Navab Wazir or any of the nobles or army officers set out on a journey, the tents of the musicians and courtesans accompanied them.

At the time of Asaf ud Daula, a book was written in the Persian language entitled *Usul un Naghmat ul Asafiya,* 'Principles of the Melodies of Asaf'. No better book has ever been written about the art of Indian music. Although very few copies of this book are available, I possess one and have read it. The author was an extremely intelligent and erudite man who appears to have had a complete mastery of Arabic, Persian and Sanskrit and who made very successful efforts to impress Indian music on the minds of all with great clarity.

The late Asad ullah Khan Kaukab, who died very recently, was an expert and a noted professor of Indian music in Calcutta. With reference to this book he wrote me a letter in which he said: 'I have a copy of this Persian treatise on music. Its subject-matter has been taken from those esteemed books that contain the essence of the ancient knowledge of this science and it was written after much research and in great detail.' It is a great pity that this incomparable book has never been reprinted. There are so few copies in existence that there is a danger of the book's complete disappearance. If some wealthy man would give his attention to the problem, he would be conferring a great favour on our country and its history.

The book describes to what heights music had risen in the days of Asaf ud Daula. Its learned author begins by discussing a work of Avicenna, *Shafa*, and gives further expositions of the principles of Arabic and Persian music. In order to complete the subject for *Dil Gudaz*, I asked the late Professor Kaukab for his help. I reproduce word for word what he wrote in his reply, from which one may appreciate exactly the conditions of the art of music at the time when it was introduced to Lucknow. It is sad that the professor is no longer in this world, otherwise I should have been able to get much more help from him especially as he wished to have his new book, an excellent exposition of musical science, printed by our press. After affirming that music had made great advances at the time of Asaf ud Daula, he writes:

In the days of Sadat Ali Khan a blight fell on music. When Ghazi ud Din Haidar was reigning, there lived in Gola Ganj quarter in Lucknow a man who was inimitable and unparalleled in the art. His name was Haidari Khan, and owing to his supine nature he was known as 'Crazy Haidairi Khan'. Ghazi ud Din Haidar very much wanted to hear him sing, but never got the chance.

One evening Ghazi ud Din Haidar was taking a ride along the river bank in his *havah dar* [carriage]. People saw Crazy Haidari Khan walking through the Rumi Gate and said to the King, 'Your Majesty, that is Haidari Khan.' As the King was interested, he gave the order 'Bring him here.' The musician was brought before the King, who then said, 'Mian Haidari Khan, why don't you ever let me listen to your singing?' Haidari Khan replied, 'Well, why not? I will sing to you but I don't know where you live.' The King could not help laughing and said, 'All right, come with me, I will take you to my house.' 'Very well', said Haidari Khan, and calmly accompanied the King. When they got near to the Chattar Manzil, Haidari Khan appeared annoyed and said, 'I will come with you, but you must give me *puris*[434] [pancakes] and *balai*[435] [cream]. Then only will I sing.' The King promised to do this and, seating himself in the palace, began to listen to the singing. After listening for a while he became enraptured and ecstatic. Seeing this Haidari Khan fell silent. The King told him to sing again, but he said, 'Sir, the tobacco in your *pichvan*[436] [*huqqa*, hookah] appears to be excellent. From whose shop do you get it?' Ghazi ud Din Haidar was temperamental by nature, and this question irritated him, so his companions replied, 'Your Majesty, this man is quite mad, he hasn't yet realized to whom he is talking.'

At a sign from the King, Haidari Khan was taken to another room, given pancakes and cream to eat and a pichvan to smoke. He asked for a *pao*[437] [half a pound] of pancakes, a quarter pound of cream and a *paisa* [a farthing's worth] of sugar. These he sent to his wife as was his practice everywhere.

While he was thus employed, the King was drinking wine. When he was really happy he remembered Haidari Khan; he sent for him and ordered him to sing. As soon as he started to sing the King stopped him and said, 'Listen, Haidari Khan, if you only make me happy and don't make me weep, I will have you drowned in the River Gumti.' Haidari Khan was confounded and realized that this was the King. He said, 'Sir, everything is in the hands of God.' He then began to sing as he had never sung before. The power of the Almighty was such, that Haidari Khan was destined to live, for he so affected the King that in a short time he could not refrain from weeping. To show his pleasure he said, 'Haidari Khan, ask for whatever you wish.' Haidari Khan replied, 'Will you give me anything I ask for?' The King promised to do so, then Haidari Khan made him confirm his promise three times and said, 'Sir, I wish that you will never send for me again to listen to my singing.' The King was surprised and asked, 'Why not?' Haidari Khan replied, 'What is it to you? If you have me killed the world will never know another Haidari Khan. If you die someone else will immediately become King.' Ghazi ud Din Haidar was angry at this answer and turned his face away. Seizing the opportunity, Haidari Khan fled for home still in possession of his life.

In short, Haidari Khan was the only distinguished musician in Lucknow at the time of Ghazi ud Din Haidar. In Nasir ud Din Haidar's reign there were a large number of singers, but none was of the standard of Haidari Khan. In Muhammad Ali Shah's and Amjad Ali Shah's reigns little interest was taken in these worldly affairs: the former had no energy because of his advanced years and the latter did nothing without referring to religious authority. Therefore, in their days enthusiastic nobles of the city, even if they enjoyed musical entertainment, could only listen to it in private. So whatever appreciation was given to the art dates from the time when Wajid Ali Shah ascended the throne as a young man and the cup of luxury in Lucknow was about to overflow, the time when the lamp which was about to be extinguished flared up for the last time.

22

The Development of Light Classical and Instrumental Music

I should like to say something more about the music of Nasir ud Din Haidar's time and in the years after him, but before doing so, I think it would be to the point to present the remaining part of the late Asad ullah Kaukab's letter, which is an expert's evaluation of music in Lucknow. He states:

> During the reign of Wajid Ali Shah there was a large number of musical experts in Lucknow, but the singers who had influence at court and received royal titles were not among the most adept. One Qutub ud Daula, a resident of Rampur, was certainly an expert sitar player and was proficient at the art, but Anis ud Daula, Musahib ud Daula, Vahid ud Daula and Razi ud Daula, although good singers, were not excellent and had only become title-holders because of royal favour. The real experts were Piar Khan, Jafar Khan, Haidari Khan and Basit Khan, all of whom were of Mian Tan Sen's family. Nowadays two well-known members of this family still remain, Wazir Khan[438] who lives in Rampur state and Muhammad Ali Khan who is employed in Puranda state.[453] Muhammad Ali Khan's father was the above-mentioned Basit Khan.

The late Kaukab Khan relates that his deceased father, Nemat ullah Khan, learnt the science of music from Basit Khan. For about eleven years Nemat ullah Khan was with Wajid Ali Shah in Matiya Burj and then spent thirty years at the court of Nepal. Then he writes:

> There was much talk of music at the time of Wajid Ali Shah, but the art had fallen from favour and only the commonplace aspects were in vogue. In Lucknow, Kadar Piya[439] composed *thumris*,[440] which became popular with the masses with the result that music was cheapened. Most music-lovers lost interest in the classical forms of ragas and raginis and began to enjoy Kadar Piya's thumris.
>
> The deterioration of the music had commenced at the time of Muhammad Shan Rangeley when Mian Sarang composed his *khyals*,[441] which were a departure from the original musical principles. Far more harm however was done by Kadar's thumris. Matters got to the state that if by chance someone listened to pure classical music, he could not appreciate it nor take any interest in it. In fact he often disliked it.

Of the singers at Wajid Ali Shah's court, Anis ud Daula and Musahib ud Daula had learnt their music from Piar Khan. He was an excellent master and what he taught these two pupils was certainly of a very high order. However this music had no place in the court and was not appreciated and the rahas and gopis of the day were full of cheap music.

But whilst little interest was taken in pure classical music, expert musicians were much esteemed at the royal court. The reason was that Wajid Ali Shah had been taught the science of music by Basit Khan and had a very good understanding of it. Being highly talented, the King had evolved new raginis to his own liking. These he named *jogi, juhi, jasmine,* or *Shah pasand,* 'favourite of the King', according to his predilections. Wajid Ali Shah was a master at the art and possessed the knowledge of an expert but he cannot escape the criticism that it was his conventional and cheap tastes that made the music of Lucknow frivolous and easily understandable by all. In accordance with popular tastes even the most discriminating singers omitted difficult techniques and based their music on light, simple and attractive tunes which could be appreciated by everyone. Ghazals[442] and thumris were the vogue and no one paid any attention to heavy intricate ragas such as *dhurpad* and *hori.* Short attractive raginis, such as *khammach, bhairvin, jhanjhauti, sendura, tilak* and *pilu,* were selected for entertainment. As they were pleasing to the King and the connoisseurs of Lucknow society, these modes flourished. Today Lucknow's *bhairvin* raginis, sung in the early morning, have become as famous throughout India as Lucknow's melons. Bhairvins belong to Lucknow and this style of singing is its own contribution to music. None to equal them are sung anywhere else in India. By adopting them in *soz*[443] [laments], singers rendered them still more popular. With their religious undertones they became popular even with stay-at-home noble ladies. Expert singers were astounded when they heard these songs of lamentation sung by the noble ladies of the house. Most singers of soz were the pupils of Piar Khan and Haidari Khan.

Lai, rhythm, more commonly known as time-beat, is an integral part of music. Wajid Ali Shah possessed in full measure this natural gift, which is present to a greater or lesser degree in everyone. The metres, which have been established by poets, are connected with lai and the science of prosody is really a perfected form of lai, for poetical metre is based on rhythm. A person in whom this faculty is developed will automatically make rhythmic movements and start to move. His whole body will respond to the rhythm. Others may think that these movements are senseless and absurd, but the person who makes them cannot help doing so. His limbs start moving on the impulse of lai. When Wajid Ali Shah acted in this manner, people would say he was dancing, but in actual fact Wajid Ali Shah had never danced at any time. He was more affected by rhythm than the musicians themselves. I have heard from reliable court singers who were his companions that even when asleep, the King's big toes used to move rhythmically because of the influence of lai. *Nirat,* which is to depict inner feeling through bodily movements, is also an important part of the science of music. Important speakers and lecturers practise this and no one ever criticizes them, whilst the same habit was criticized in Wajid Ali Shah.

From the above account by Professor Kaukab, it is clear that although Lucknow gave no encouragement to pure classical music, its society was instrumental in developing a variety of light classical styles and making them popular throughout India.[444]

At the time of Ghazi ud Din Haidar, Lucknow was famed for possessing eminent qavval musicians. Jhagu Khan and Ghulam Rasul Khan were recognized as experts in the art. Shori was such a great innovator in the art of qavvali that the invention of *tappa*[445] is ascribed to him. Both Bakshu and Sulari were considered outstanding at playing the tabla. At Muharram thousands of enthusiasts came to Lucknow from other places and sat hopefully in Haidar's Imam Bara waiting for the courtesan Lady Haidar to commence her song of lamentation.

In later days the most expert tabla player was Muhammad Ji who was renowned throughout India. About thirty years ago I met a Maratha gentleman in the Chauk market-place, dressed in European-style clothes, who had some respected employment. As we met he said, 'I have come to Lucknow to find out about the proficiency of the musical experts here.' 'Who are you?' I asked. He said, 'I come of a family of singers and my ancestors were singers at the court of Shiva Ji. Although I have now taken up other employment and have received a British education, I still know my family art.' Another gentleman, who used to visit the famous singer Muhammadi, joined us at that moment. He said, 'Come along with me.' The Maratha gentleman took hold of my arm and we all went to Muhammadi's house together. As chance would have it, Sadiq Ali Khan was there and they all showed off their skill; the Maratha also sang. After that we went to the house of the Chaudarayan,[427] the chief courtesan, which was considered to be the principal meeting-place of the local artists. From there both Munney Khans were sent for. They came and displayed their skill at singing. Eventually the Maratha gentleman said, 'The real reason for my coming here is to sing a *tarana*,[446] with Muhammad Ji accompanying me on the tabla.'[447] Muhammad Ji was immediately sent for and the Maratha's singing and Muhammad Ji's playing were much appreciated and applauded by all present. Finally the Maratha admitted, 'I have been everywhere but I have never heard a more accomplished tabla player.'

Music has made such great strides in Lucknow that in contrast to the richer classes in other places, those of Lucknow are genuinely fond of it. They understand it, recognize tunes, raginis and dhuns, and after listening to one or two notes, they can judge the standard of a vocalist so that an indifferent singer will get nowhere. Boys from the bazaar who go about singing in the streets sing tunes with such accuracy that one would think they were trained musicians. In most towns one meets many people who cannot read poetry rhythmically. But in Lucknow one would not be able to find anyone, however illiterate he may be, who is unable to give proper rhythm to verse. A feeling for rhythm is ingrained in everyone, including children. Sometimes bazaar boys have been heard singing *bhairvin, sohni, behag,* and other ragas with such excellence that those who heard them were entranced and the greatest singers envied them.

Whilst on the subject of music, it would seem appropriate for me now to say something about musical instruments. To spoil either of the two elements in music—*sur*, notes, and *lai*, rhythm—in singing is an unpardonable fault. Therefore, two instruments were found necessary for their correct maintenance: to help keep the tune, the *sarangi*,[448] a stringed instrument, and to keep time, the *tabla*, a pair of small drums.

The old Indian instrument to help keep the tune was the *bin*,[449] which consisted of a hollowed-out, wooden tube, with a gourd affixed to each end. It had seven strings for the seven surs and when these were struck the sound, running along the tube, echoed in the gourds. The Muslims brought the *rabab*, the *chang* and the *sarod*. The rabab was probably an Arabian instrument which had been greatly improved upon at the time of the Abbasides. The chang and sarod were non-Arabian instruments. The chang was a very ancient instrument which can be traced to Assyria, Babylon, Egypt, Greece and Asia Minor; in fact it was used by all the earlier races. The sarod is a purely Persian instrument which the Abbaside musicians adopted and improved to a great extent. After the Muslims came to India and their music joined forces with that of the Hindus, the *tamboura*[450] was invented. This was actually a smaller version of the bin and was used only to accompany a singer. It was not an instrument which could be played by itself. Soon after this, Amir Khusrau invented the sitar, which was a simple instrument reminiscent of both the bin and the tamboura. But whether it was the bin, the tamboura, or the sitar, none proved a perfect accompaniment to the human voice. Seeing this deficiency, Mian Sarang, who was an accomplished and famous musician at the court of Muhammad Shah Rangeley, invented the sarangi, which was named after him. The sarangi forced the bin, tamboura and sitar into the background and received such a welcome in singing and dancing circles that the older instruments disappeared. Among the old instruments played in Lucknow was also the *qanun* which the Muslims brought with them from Syria and Iraq. Today one rarely comes across people who can play this instrument. The sarangi replaced all these instruments at joyous gatherings. Occasionally, however, a die-hard among experts still achieves distinction by playing the bin or sarod, the rabab or qanun. The sitar has remained an instrument to give pleasure to the young. They usually play it and listen to it without singing, but sometimes they sing to its accompaniment.

There remains the tabla. Although this instrument is extremely important in maintaining tempo and rhythm, no trace of anything of its kind can be found among the ancient races of any other country. In ancient days in other countries, drums were beaten in war-time and the chang was played, and in guard-houses kettle-drums were beaten. But only in India was the tabla found to aid dancing and singing. Arabs used the *daf*, a tambourine, to accompany their singing. It would appear that in India too, the daf was an early instrument to accompany singing. It used to be played along with the bin as an aid to maintaining tempo. After that, still in very ancient times, the *mardang* was developed, although it could have already existed at the time of Sri Krishna, assisting the tunes of his flute in the Braj forests on the banks of the Jamna. After the mardang, an improvement was made with the evolution of the *pakhavaj*,[451] which could be used effectively to accompany classical music. Subsequently it became customary for ordinary people and women in the home to use the *dhol*,[452] which had been evolved from the mardang and the pakhavaj, and which had become widely popular. Finally, for the most sophisticated musical gatherings the tabla was invented. It was made by dividing the pakhavaj into two separate drums, one being called 'right' and the other 'left'. The tabla was certainly invented after the Muslims came to India, but I do not know precisely when or by whom the improvements were made in these percussive instruments.

23

Dance and the Development of the *Kathak* School

Together with music, dance in Lucknow developed strongly and became a preeminent art. Dance is common to every nationality and has existed since time immemorial. Sophisticated, attractive women danced to music in the presence of the Pharaohs of Egypt. At the time of Christ, Herod's daughter danced before having St John the Baptist decapitated. But it appears indisputable that, like singing, dancing in India was connected with divine worship and that this art was always nurtured by religion. For instance, the people who knew and practised it were the Brahmans and their centres were Ajodhya and Benares where the *kathak*[454] dancers lived, just as the *rahas* dancers flourished around Mathura and Braj. An extraordinary thing is that in all the old Indian temples, although a large number of women danced every day before the image of the gods, and in all the important centres of worship there have always been from earliest times a large crowd of female dancers, instruction in dancing was always given by men. It was they who would teach the young women.

Dance is essentially the regulation of bodily movements. If this regularity of movement is the same among several people, it amounts to drill or military exercises or to the performances of European music hall, now often seen in Indian theatres. But if these movements are to the accompaniment of musical tempo and the rise and fall of sound, it is dance. Genuine Indian dance occurs when the movements of the body conform to and fit in with the treble and bass notes of songs and intoned poems. This evolved into a great art for which hundreds of new *gats*[455] and *torey*[456] were created. Later mime and gesture were added to portray thoughts and emotions with the result that dancing interpreted the singing. Then when the dancing of beautiful women gave pleasure to the spectator, the portrayal of amorous dalliance and coquetry became part of the art. In this respect the Lucknow school differentiated between the functions of male and female dancers. To portray amorous dalliance with elegance and grace in all their movements and to display feelings of love were the functions of women. This could on occasion become tedious for the onlooker. Therefore as a contrast it became the function of male dancers to show sprightliness and vigour in their movements in accordance with the rhythm and to display their emotions with poetic allure. Although there is a certain relationship between the art of both groups, male and female, there is a palpable difference between them.

I have already mentioned the enormous influx into Avadh and Lucknow of musicians and troupes of singing courtesans in the days of Shuja ud Daula. Besides these, kathaks from Ajodhya and Benares, seeing the interest which was taken, were attracted to the court. The forgatherings of these people advanced the art of dance and gave it great local importance.

There are two groups of male dancers in Lucknow: the Hindu kathaks and rahas dancers, and the Kashmiri Muslim bhands. The real dancers are the kathaks, and the Kashmiri dancing troupes, in order to give life to their performances, have apparently introduced a young boy who wears his hair long like a woman and dances with such animation and vivacity that his activities arouse the spectators.

There have always been accomplished Hindu kathaks in Lucknow. These people believe that Mahadeo or Shiva, Parvati his consort, and Krishna were the founders of their art.[415] At the time of Shuja ud Daula and Asaf ud Daula, Khushi Maharaj was a very expert dancer. In the days of Navab Sadat Ali Khan, Ghazi ud Din Haidar and Nasir ud Din Haidar, Hallal Ji, Parkash Ji and Dayalu Ji were celebrated dancers. From the time of Muhammad Ali Shah until Wajid Ali Shah's reign, Durga Prashad and Thakur Prashad, the sons of Parkash Ji, were famous. It is said that Durga Prashad taught Wajid Ali Shah to dance. Later the two sons of Durga Prashad, Kalka and Binda Din, became renowned and nearly everyone acknowledged that no one in the whole of India could rival either of them at dancing. The older experts achieved fame because of some particular aspect of the art but these two brothers, especially Binda Din, were masters of every aspect. Most of the well-known dancers of today are the pupils of these two brothers and their house is the greatest school for dance in the whole of India.[457]

Kalka died a short time ago and his death undoubtedly had a detrimental effect on Binda Din's dancing. Binda Din is now seventy-seven years of age but even now devotees of the art consider that to watch him is one of the greatest pleasures in life. His dancing to a gat, his portrayal of delicate technical aspects of *tora* and *tukra*,[45] the superb control with which he makes as many bells on his ankles as he likes resound, is individual to him and beyond all compare.[459] He gives to every step and gesture a hundred fascinations and embodies in them a variety of subtle perceptions. His deft movements and originality are such that the onlooker, unless well-versed in the art, is unable to follow them.

Binda Din used to perform *batana*,[460] depiction through bodily movements, and Kalka[461] used to give a verbal interpretation. From this commentary people were able to realize how perfect Binda Din was in displaying his art. When dancing, his feet touched the ground so lightly that he used to dance sometimes on the edges of swords and come to no harm.

24

Light Entertainment

The second category of male dancing is that of the *bhands*. In these performances, a handsome adolescent boy with long hair in the chignon style, wearing gaudy-coloured male clothes and with bells on his ankles, dances and sings. The accompanying music is rhythmic and gay. In the dance itself musical nimbleness, playfulness and fun are displayed and the singing is suited to the style of the dance. Apart from the instrumental musicians present there are about a dozen bhands who loudly applaud the boy's dancing and singing. They become excited at the beat of the *tals*[462] and make amusing and frivolous remarks about the postures, movements and gestures of the dancer. When the boy has performed for some time, they come forward and mimic him, showing great skill in their witticisms and imitations. There are two groups of these people in Lucknow: the Kashmiris who originated in Kashmir and the local people who formerly followed another trade but who have now adopted this form of acting as a profession.

Acting, especially mimicry with song and dance, was a very ancient art in India and achieved great heights at the court of Raja Bikramajit,[463] before the time of Christ. In those days, serious dramas were enacted in this manner and it was certainly a very refined and cultured form of acting. Today it is the custom among the lower classes in India to accompany their dancing and singing in celebration with a droll form of mimicry.

There is no trace of bhands or actors of that kind in the Muslim era before the time of the Mughals. It is possible that they existed and that the recorders of events in those days did not think them worthy of mention. But in the time of the Mughals, the bhands had certainly achieved fame. They are known to have existed after the days of Aurangzeb Alamgir when the nobles and kings of Delhi felt free from the cares of war, conquest and government and started to think that to care for their courts and live a life of luxury were their birthrights. In actual fact, these bhands did wonderful work for local society. They were the national critics and satirists and did much for India.

The first well-known bhand in Delhi was Karela, who lived in the reign of Muhammad Shah. Muhammad Shah, becoming annoyed over some matter, gave orders that all the bhands should be expelled from his dominion. The next day, when the King was out with his cortège, the sounds of dhols and the singing of bhands became audible overhead. The King, amazed, looked up and saw that Karela and some other bhands had climbed to the top of a date palm and were beating drums and singing. The King halted the cortège and said, 'What impudence is this? Why have my orders not been carried out?'

Karela replied, 'Mighty King, the whole of this earth is under your control and there is nowhere left for us to go so we thought of seeking a place in the regions of the atmosphere and this is our first stage.' At this answer the King and his companions had to laugh and the bhands were pardoned.

After they came to Lucknow, these people were so appreciated that they made the city their centre. As far as I know there are no bhands in Delhi at the present time. If there are any, they are very much in the background. Certainly there have been troupes of bhands in Bareilly from the earliest days and some of the *doms*[464] and *dharis*[465] in Lucknow came from there. From this it would appear that the Khans of Ruhelkhand had an appreciation for music and that, because of their generosity, musicians were able to prosper in Bareilly and Muradabad. From there too the most expert doms and dharis came to Lucknow and made the city their home.

Their jokes, witticisms, innuendos and great skill in mimicry are well known in Lucknow. One incident comes to mind. Some noblemen had given a shawl as a reward, but the shawl was old and worn out. One of the bhands took it in his hands and looked at it carefully, giving his whole attention to it. Another asked, 'What are you looking at?' The first said, 'I see something written on it.' The second asked, 'Well, what is it?' Putting on his spectacles the first bhand, after much scrutiny, read out with difficulty, 'There is no God but God.' The other said, 'Is that all? Is it not written that Muhammad is his Prophet?' The answer came, 'How could it be written that Muhammad is the Prophet of God? This thing dates from before our Holy Prophet.'

In Lucknow there was a Navab who was known as the Navab of Garhiya, the Lord of the Pond, because there was a pond near his residence. On one occasion he arranged a party with dancing and singing in his house. A bhand, looking perturbed, came forward and said to his companions, 'Get up and make your salutation.' They all said, 'Whom shall we salute?' He said, 'The Navab Sahib is coming.' Saying this, he took the lid off an earthenware pot and a large frog jumped out and joined the party. He then said, 'Get up quickly, get up quickly. Don't you see the Navab of the Pond?'

It was well known that these people used to mock the person at whose house they went to entertain and it was impossible that they should not make a jibe at him in some way. It is true that the manner in which they made their hosts aware of their shortcomings would not have been possible otherwise. In their acting, personifications and mimicry, they showed great perfection and received much applause. They used to ridicule the Persianized Urdu of the Kayasths in the same way that Babu[466] English is ridiculed in British circles today. Their acting in playing the role of *divanji*[467] [a Hindu bookkeeper] was so accomplished that spectators were amazed.

There was a bhand in Lucknow, also called Karela, at the time of Nasir ud Din Haidar. Then Sajjan, Qaim, Daim, Rajbi, Nau Shah and Bibi Qadar also became famous. Ali Naqi Khan and his wife, who were very influential people, came to see Qaim's *sabil* [stall that distributed free cold drinks as a religious gesture].[468] It was beautifully decorated and sherbet flowed freely. On seeing the distinguished pilgrims, Qaim came forward, pressed his hands together respectfully and said, 'May God preserve the Navab and keep the Begam young forever.' In order to avoid further remarks of this nature both the Navab and the Begam were obliged to offer gratuities. One of Qaim's most outstanding feats was the occasion on which for three and a half hours he did nothing but make various kinds of grimaces.

Later the troupes of Fazal Husain, Khilona and Badshah Pasand became famous, as is that of Ali Jan at the present time. These troupes were unrivalled in the art of this kind of entertainment.

But Lucknow society was more affected by *domnis*[464] [female entertainers] than by any of these people. In towns of all sizes from time immemorial, *mirasans*[469] and *jagnis*[470] have attended weddings as singers. Their performances never vary. The domnis on the other hand were great innovators. Giving up dhols they adopted tablas, sarangis and cymbals, as was the practice with male and courtesan musicians. They advanced from mere singing to dancing as well and, not content with this, started to give personifications in the manner of bhands at female festivities. They became the most important feature of all wedding celebrations and so fascinated the ladies of wealthy families that there was no household which did not employ a troupe of domnis. As they were unequalled at dancing and singing, female celebrations became much more lively and interesting than those of men. Their witticisms and innovations were so entrancing that most men had a strong desire to get some chance of witnessing their performances—but the domnis themselves were averse to dancing and singing before a male audience. There are still a large number of domnis here who perform in the traditional way, but the quality of their performance has been lost.[471] It is unlikely that there have been singers anywhere else to equal the accomplished domnis of Lucknow.

25

Courtesans and Theatre

Dance instruction is in the hands of men, and they are the masters of this art. However, the widespread popularity that the art attained could never have been achieved by men. Dancing is more natural to women and they display more grace in the art. This can be observed in every city in India, but it is unlikely that anywhere else were there more perfect demonstrators of the art of dance than the courtesans of Lucknow.

Forty years ago a celebrated courtesan, Munsarim Wali Gohar, went to Calcutta and achieved fame. At one performance I witnessed her skill in *batana*[460] on the same theme for a full three hours. All those present at the gathering, including the most expert dancers and distinguished people of Matiya Burj, were spellbound. There was not even a child who was not impressed by the performance. Courtesans, Zohra and Mushtari, were not only poetesses and accomplished vocalists, but were also incomparable dancers. And Jaddan, also a courtesan, had entranced people for a long time with her dancing and singing.

The courtesans of Lucknow were usually divided into three categories. The first were the Kanchanis, women of the Kanchan tribe, who were actually harlots and whose primary and regular profession was to sell their virtue. They were actually inhabitants of Delhi and the Panjab, whence they had started to come at the time of Shuja ud Daula. Most of the well-known prostitutes of the town belonged to this category. The second category were the Chuna Walis. Originally their work was to sell lime but later they joined other groups of bazaar women and became well known. Chuna Wali Haidar, who was renowned for her voice, belonged to this category and collected a large group of courtesans of her caste. The third category were Nagarnt, from the Gujrat area. These three classes were the queens of the bazaar. They established themselves and worked in groups. Some women who had already gone astray joined these groups.

In addition to these courtesans who sang and danced, another group of similar character developed in Lucknow. Perhaps it would not be wrong to say that these courtesans are peculiar to Lucknow. This is the group which performs rahas. The art of rahas belongs to Mathura and Braj and the constant flow of dancers from these areas made it popular in Lucknow.

After Wajid Ali Shah came to like rahas, he produced a new representation of Krishna according to his own taste and with a plot of his own imagination. Directly they saw it, the people became extremely enthusiastic about it, because amorous tales, which in those days were mostly concerned with supernatural love and beauty, were now portrayed by living human beings. Realizing the feelings of the public, Mian Amanat, who was a famous poet, wrote his *Indar Sabha*, which is the first example of the mixture of Muslim Persianized taste with the ideas of Hindu mythology.

When *Indar Sabha* was performed in Lucknow, it completely charmed and captivated everyone. In no time scores of *Sabhas*,[472] theatrical societies, were established in the city and became so popular that for some time courtesan musicians lost favour. Later, in addition to Amanat, many others, less talented, wrote their Sabhas in simple language. Still, this popularized the Urdu language, for the unpolished language in these plays came to permeate the speech of people as far away as the eastern part of the Province, as well as local trades-people. This interest in Sabhas laid a strong foundation for drama and the theatre. If the monarchy had existed a little longer *natak*,[473] the traditional Indian stage-play, would have evolved further along new lines while retaining its Indian character.

But suddenly refined society lost interest in these new plays. Love for the art of music made the élite turn their attention again to troupes of singers and dancers and forms derived from natak were patronized only by the masses and the people of the bazaar. Former enthusiasm had however produced a group of people who, according to present idiom, are called actors. These actors of ours, because they were esteemed in refined society, used good language and continued to improve their Urdu. But now because their audience consists only of the masses their refined speech no longer exists: they give scores of different sorts of performances, but their language is that of the bazaar.

The most important cause of the deterioration in our tastes in drama was the Parsi theatre[320] which was set up in Bombay on British lines, in which no musical art was displayed, nor any real acting. But its expertise in stagecraft, its organization and its magical scenery with marvellously painted stage properties strangled our national drama which was at the time still in its infancy. The élite became enamoured of the splendour of these plays and forgot their former tastes.

These theatres[474] certainly did India incalculable harm as far as the arts of singing and dancing are concerned. First of all, they ruined music by adopting tunes which spread throughout the bazaars without reference to musical principles. Nothing could have been more vulgar. Then they tried to put an end to our dance, which was a highly developed art, by staging European 'drill' in the name of dance and by introducing boys who gave it interest by changing their appearance and dress.

Although both the music and acting of the rahas are imperfect, they are permeated with national colour and taste. They should not be abandoned but should be improved.

26

Soz—The Chanting of Dirges

I shall now discuss *soz khwani*,[443] the chanting of dirges, in a musical framework. Although it is presumptuous to include this new religious art in the arts of singing and dancing which are contrary to Muslim religious law, the fact remains that it is definitely music. It was begun by the Shias in India to keep fresh the memory of the martyrdom of the Prophet's family, especially during the period when this faith became the national religion of Persia and people coming from that country were gaining influence at the Indian court.

Just as religious fervour created for poetry *marsiya goi*, the recital of elegies, and *taht ul lafz khwani*, so did it create *soz khwani* for music. In *taht ul lafz khwani* an elegy is read out and explained simply and forcefully, just as a poet reads out his odes in a *mushaira*. A soz khwan sings an elegy to sad melodies. Both these accomplishments advanced to such an extent that they became distinct art forms which were from start to finish peculiar to Lucknow.

The old and original *marsiya khwani* was actually *soz khwani*. In *majlises*, gatherings of mourning, marsiyas were recited to melodies. These gatherings were held not only in Delhi, but in all the cities of India where Shias lived, even as far distant as Madras and the Deccan. *Nauhas*,[234] dirges, which were composed about two hundred years ago still exist. To recite elegies in poetic cadence was the special talent of Lucknow and I have already described the heights to which Mir Anis, Mirza Dabir and a few others rose in the art.

Although soz khwani dates from ancient times and was widely known, Lakhnavis brought it to such perfection that they made it an art peculiar to themselves. They raised its standards in India to such a degree that they became more accomplished than the professional singers.

Like many other artists, these cantors came to Lucknow with Navab Shuja ud Daula or during the time that he was ruler. In *The Delightful History* it is written that Bahu Begam used to hold majlises at her residence and that Khwaja Sara Javahar Ali Khan, who was the superintendent of her household and personal estate, listened to the chanting of elegies. At that time the standard of the art in Faizabad was the same as anywhere else.

Some people say that Khwaja Hasan Maududi created the art. Instructor to the author of *Naghmat ul Asafiya*, he was a self-taught man and such an expert musician that none within miles could rival him. One can judge his musical skill from the following anecdote. He was travelling from Lucknow to Etawah (U.P.) by palanquin at the time of the Maratha raids. As he was passing through a certain village, news came that the Marathas were on the point of attacking it. The palanquin-bearers, who had covered a great distance, suddenly put down the palanquin and said they were too tired to go any further. They were told over and over again that the place was in danger but they would not listen. The Khwaja gave up all hope of life, made his ablutions, said his late afternoon prayers and sitting on the ground, commenced to sing. His song so affected the bearers that they recovered their strength and took him to a place of safety.

Although he was by religion a Sunni, he harmonized some special *dhuns* [airs] to the singing of dirges, and taught them to his pupils. The foundations were thus laid for this art on a regulated and defined basis. Later,'Crazy' Haidari Khan chanted dirges during Muharram to tunes suited to his taste. As he was a great singer and was held in esteem by the court, his efforts met with outstanding success. It was realized that if further improvements were made, this art could achieve a dignity of its own. From the thousands of existing dhuns those tunes were selected that were expressive of grief and sorrow and were used for hundreds of dirges. Eventually Haidari Khan taught this art to Saiyyid Mir Ali who came of a noble Saiyyid family and who gave great impetus to the art because of his religious fervour. He became so well known in the days of Sadat Ali Khan that on one occasion, when he was annoyed about something and had decided to leave Lucknow, Insha Allah Khan exerted his influence and the Navab consoled him, assured him of his esteem and stopped him from going.

Later a singer of the family of Tan Sen named Nasir Khan came to Lucknow and became famous. Seeing the vogue for dirge-chanting here, he lent his musical skill to the art and achieved popularity and fame. Taking pity on the indigent widow of a Saiyyid who lived in the neighbourhood, he gave her two children, Mir Ali Hasan and Mir Bandey Hasan,[475] instruction in the chanting of dirges. These two outstripped in skill all former experts and brought the art of chanting dirges to the level of a raga. Although even some singers may not remember the exact notes of certain ragas, these notes, when interpreted through a dirge, are so comprehensible that people can recall their ragas and dhuns.

In emulation of these distinguished individuals, people of good families became interested in the art and the chanting of dirges in Lucknow passed from the hands of professional singers. Numerous persons who were not musicians came to be able to chant so excellently as to eclipse professional singers.

At the moment Manjhu Sahib[476] and a few other accomplished individuals are so expert at chanting dirges and have become so well known that they are welcomed with open arms everywhere in India. The appreciation shown to them by people of other places robs Lucknow of their presence at the time of Muharram and other days of mourning.

This enthusiasm had its greatest effect on the women of Lucknow.[477] As soon as the impressive and heart-rending notes of dirges were chanted by Mir Ali Hasan and Mir Bandey Hasan, hundreds of men from élite families began to sing them, and then the women of noble Shia families also intoned them with their matchless voices. Women are naturally more fond of music and singing than men and their voices are usually more attuned to rhythm. When women began to practise this regulated form of music it became incredibly attractive and in a short time not only Shias but some Sunni women as well were attracted to the chanting of dirges. Matters have now reached the stage that during Muharram and on most other days of mourning, heart-rending sounds of lamentation and the melodious chanting of dirges can be heard from every house in every lane in old Lucknow. In every alley one will hear beautiful voices and melodies which one will never forget. There is silence in the houses of Hindus and also in those of some Sunni families; otherwise desolate sounds of lamentation can be heard from every direction.

As mourning for the Prophet's family is the pretext for the chanting of dirges, this religious enthusiasm existed in the houses of both Sunnis and Shias. But thousands of Hindus also chanted these dirges. From this it can be seen that the desire for chanting was the main reason for the development of the elaborate practices of mourning celebration in Lucknow.

In Lucknow there are many refined and educated women who are so good at chanting, that were they not hampered by the limitations of purdah, no male cantor could excel them.

Many years ago, on the occasion of Chehlum [the fortieth day of mourning], I went with some friends to the local Tal Katora shrine and we spent the night there in a tent. I awoke suddenly at about two in the morning and the most entrancing melody greeted my ear. This sound had also aroused my friends and made them restless. We left the tent and saw in the still and silent night in the light of the moon a procession of women approaching carrying *tazias* [paper models of the shrines of Husain]. All were bare-headed and their hair hung loose. In the centre was a woman carrying a candle. By its light a beautiful, delicately formed girl was reading from some sheets of paper and chanting a dirge and several other women were singing with her. I cannot describe the emotions that were aroused by the stillness, the moonlight, these bare-headed beauties and the soul-rending notes of their sad melody. As the graceful company passed through the gate of the shrine the beautiful girl started a lament in a dhun called *parach*:

> When the caravan of Medina, having lost all
> Arrived captive in the vicinity of Sham

Foremost came the head of Husain, borne aloft on a spear
And in its wake, a band of women, with heads bared.

This elegy, so suitable to the occasion, made one wonder whether through this verse the lady was describing the present mourning procession entering the Kerbala, or whether she was referring to the historic procession of Husain's family.

The truth is that nothing produced so great an effect on the women of Lucknow, and on their men, as the chanting of dirges. The first beneficial result of this was that many women have become good singers and have learnt to chant dirges according to true musical principles. The second is that all the people of the city, men as well as women, have become attuned to music. One can see humble boys and people of the bazaar going about the streets and alleys singing as they walk along. They sing so well and are able to master the most difficult tunes with such ease as to astonish strangers to the city. The basic reason for this is the taste for chanting dirges and elegies. One can take pride in the fact that although this chanting spread among the masses and illiterate people, it maintained its standards and did not deviate from the true principles of music. This is contrary to the usual process, when anything adopted by the masses becomes mutilated and deteriorates.

Although the ordinary Shia considers soz khwani the road to salvation, their religious leaders have not yet sanctioned it in view of the Muslim religious law. At majlises where mujtahids and maulvis are present there are only recitals of the hadis and *taht ul lafz khwani*, the spoken recital of elegies; dirges are never chanted in their presence. But it cannot be denied that the chanting of dirges, because of its widespread popularity, has in practice achieved complete victory over the decrees of religious leaders.

In Sunni belief and for the Sufis there is room for broad views on the legality of singing. Probably Shia theology is less broad-minded, otherwise this art would by now have been given the seal of legality.[478]

27

Bands, Processions and the Telling of Time

I have written a great deal about musicians, the art of music and the arts that developed from it. But an account of band music is still lacking. I shall therefore describe now what effect Lucknow had upon these bands and with this I shall conclude my discussion of music.

The bands that accompany marriage and other processions are of six kinds: *dhol tasha*, large drums and semi-spherical drums; *raushan chauki*, the pipe and tabor; *naubat*, kettle drums; *narsi* and *qurna*, horns and trumpets; *danka* and *bugal*, large kettle drums and bugles, and Scottish bagpipes, a British instrument of increasing popularity.

Dhol tasha is the ancient Indian national band which the British call the 'Indian tom-tom' and, in their utter ignorance, make a subject of ridicule. In England at the Earls Court Exhibition of 1896 where there were many demonstrations of Indian ways of life, arts and occupations, I saw with my own eyes an example of what was described as a dhol tasha. An extremely black-visaged individual wearing nothing but a filthy loin-cloth stood practically naked before the assemblage. A dhol was tied to his neck which he proceeded to beat violently in a wild manner without any regard to musical rhythm, shaking his head from side to side like a madman. This they called the Indian 'tom-tom'. In fact, this merely displayed these people's ignorance, for the dhol is a most excellent instrument and to play it is an art that requires a highly developed sense of rhythm.

In Lucknow bands there are usually three or four large dhols and at least one man, though occasionally two or three, beating tashas. There is also at least one man playing the *jhanjh*, cymbals. The jhanjh can be traced to Persia and neighbouring countries and the tasha is common in and around Egypt, but the dhol is purely Indian. This type of band was introduced into Lucknow from Delhi mainly by the military. In Delhi there were only dhols and jhanjh; tashas were added in Lucknow and very soon were considered so important that a band without them seemed to lack life. Although there are only dhols and jhanjh in most cities, in Lucknow bands dhols are never played without tashas, and the men who play the tasha require the highest degree of skill. They give the rhythm and the dhol players follow them. The method of playing the tasha is to beat it with such rapidity that one stroke cannot be distinguished from another and from these continuous and incessant strokes, high and low notes, bass and treble, rhythm and melody are produced. In Lucknow the musicians in this type of band were so expert that they made an ordinary band, which was not conducted on any particular lines, into a well-regulated and concerted whole.

After the fortieth day of mourning there is a tazia[129] procession in Lucknow known as the Bakhshu's Tazia. Nowadays, because of the quarrels between Shias and Sunnis, this procession has lost its original form. This procession was initiated by a devout Shia of the royal family who had subsequently become poor. About ten years ago, all expert band musicians joined in out of sympathy for them. They were surrounded by admirers and stood in one place for hours on end, issuing challenges to all and sundry to rival them at playing music. Great singers used to praise them and this incited them to play even more expertly. Among these musicians, the tasha players were the most skilled and were always introducing innovations into their music.

What greater proof can there be that the dhol and the tasha were played according to correct principles, than that Wajid Ali Shah, who was an incomparable musician, was an exponent of the art. I have seen him with my own eyes in Matiya Burj, coming out of Asmani kothi with the procession on the seventh day of Muharram playing a tasha which was tied round his neck. Expert singers carrying dhols accompanied him and he was surrounded by his court favourites. He played the tasha with such delicacy and skill that even people who did not understand music applauded him. I have also seen him playing the dhol.

Lucknow society has taken full advantage of this most ancient of Indian bands, which is popular and at the same time maintains traditional standards. If anyone should come here and see the skill of the tasha players he will fully realize the degree of instrumental improvisation and the extent to which it has raised the level of dhol and jhanjh playing.

The raushan chauki is also a very ancient form of band. Most if not all of its important elements were brought by the Muslims. The *shahnai* is its most essential accompanying instrument and is considered to be the invention of Avicenna. No other instrument can come so close to the sound of the human voice as the shahnai. In raushan chauki bands there are at least two shahnai players and one percussion player who has two small drums tied around his waist. The drums establish the rhythm, one shahnai player is responsible for maintaining the basic melody and the other improvises on the musical themes of ghazals and thumris.

The raushan chauki in India was a special court band which used to play at the dinner parties of kings and the highest nobles. During the silence of the night its players marched around the royal palace and it was delightful to listen to its notes in the distance. At the time of the Mughal dynasty this band was considered very important and attractive. It had existed in Delhi for a very long time and there is no doubt that raushan chauki bandsmen came to Lucknow from there. However, there have been expert players of this sort in this vicinity for some time. In Benares, raushan chauki bands are played in most temples in the early morning. It is most pleasing to listen to them before dawn.

In Lucknow weddings, raushan chauki bands usually march near the bride-groom. In Hindu marriage processions they are given money for their perfor-mance on the road. The timing and the attractive melodies produced by the musicians here cannot be rivalled. Their skill and art can be understood only if one listens to them attentively. In the Bakshu's tazia procession, the raushan chauki bandsmen showed their skill and played with such fervour that after hearing them one could no longer derive pleasure from listening to any other shahnai players.

The third type of band, the naubat, is the best suited to our traditional joyful melodies. In it there are two or three shahnai players and a *naqaras* (kettle drum) player who carries two very large naqaras in front of him which he beats at the same time with sticks. The naqaras produce a very large volume of sound which echoes over a great distance. There is also a jhanjh player in the band.

The naubat is a traditional band and for many years has been employed on ceremonial occasions. In Islamic history traces of it are found at the courts of Damascus, Baghdad and Egypt. In the middle period of the Abbaside dynasty in Baghdad, naubat bands played at the residences of all the nobles and were considered a mark of honour and distinction. It appears that these bands came to India with the Muslims, although it is possible that they were in existence here before then. However there were no shahnai at the time, only naqaras and jhanjh. The present form was established in Persia and Iraq and came here from those countries.

It was customary for a naubat band to accompany the processions of kings and exalted nobles. These bands, playing from the backs of elephants, would precede the processions of important crowned heads. Victors in war used to proclaim their success by making them play lustily. When the Emperor Aurangzeb Alamgir conquered Hyderabad he had a naubat band play from the top of a hillock in the vicinity. This hillock is still called Naubat Hill. Only the highest officers and nobles of the Mughal court were given the right to keep naubat bands, which played outside their residences and in their processions. An elevated position was selected for their performance and bandstands were often erected on the tops of the gates of royal residences. Examples of these may be seen in any large city where there has been an important court.

It is the custom in Lucknow, at the time of marriages or on other joyous occasions, for wealthy people to erect at their gates high platforms on poles covered with red cloth or tinsel to act as temporary platforms for the naubat band. The band remains on the platform all day and plays from time to time. Similarly, in marriage or tazia processions, temporary bandstands are erected on planks and carried on the shoulders of palanquin-bearers in front of the procession while the band plays continually.

In early days, especially at the Lucknow court, the naubat was used to announce the time. The day was not then divided into twenty-four hours as is now the Western practice. Day and night were then divided into eight *pahars*, watches, four for the day and four for the night, and these sections were each divided into eight *gharis*. In every bandstand there was a copper or earthenware vessel filled with water, on top of which floated an empty cup with a small hole in the bottom. The water seeped in slowly through the hole, which was so designed that the cup was full within the space of one ghari, and then sank. When the cup sank for the first time one ghari was struck, and for the second time two. This went on until eight gharis had been struck. With the eighth ghari there were chimes, and a gong was struck, first eight times sharply and then for some time with rapid strokes. This was a signal that a watch was over and the gharis started again from one.

In houses that had bands at their gates, the naubats were played for about the period of a ghari (twenty minutes) at the end of each watch. According to this system naubats should have been played eight times in all. However, the custom was that only seven were played and the last one was omitted so as not to disturb the people's sleep in the second half of the night. At that time only chimes were heard. The naubat for each watch had a name appertaining to the time of day or night—'early morning naubat', 'sunrise naubat', 'midday naubat', 'afternoon naubat', 'evening naubat', 'early night naubat', and 'midnight naubat'.

Time was reckoned in this way at the Mughal court and in Lucknow until the eclipse of the monarchy. In Calcutta up to the time of Wajid Ali Shah's death naubats announced the watches and gharis. Since then this method of reckoning time has been abandoned and now there is scarcely anyone who understands it. However in spite of the new division of time the old system has become such an integral part of our language that we still say, 'I'll come in a ghari', 'I will sleep in the second pahar', and 'I will have my food when the first pahar is over'. But we do not know what a pahar is or what a ghari is. We often hear: 'The pahra has come on duty', or 'the soldiers of the pahar', but we do not realize that the word *pahra* is derived from *pahar*, meaning watch, and that the watchmen were on duty for the period of one watch at a time. Today a pahar is simply considered to be a period of three hours. This old method of reckoning time belonged to the Hindus but it was also employed in Persia and naubats used to be struck there also.

The naubat players of Lucknow were of a very high order and they or their pupils could be found in every district and town. The bands, the number of players and the method of playing did not alter. They simply played the popular tunes and melodies of Lucknow society. The picture that Amir Khusrau paints in his poetry of naubat-playing gives one a very good idea of the art at his time. It was very much the same in more recent times.

Turhai, the horn, and *qurna*, the trumpet, are very old Indian instruments which were for the most part played by the military. From its shape it would appear that the turhai is of British origin and was adopted in India at the time of their arrival. But the qurna is essentially a Persian instrument. Its sound is so awe-inspiring that it is particularly suitable for intimidating an enemy in battle. Neither of these instruments, though used in Lucknow processions, belongs to established musical use. A turhai or qurna player accompanies military detachments or regiments and plays his instrument at short intervals to announce their presence. A similar instrument is the old Hindu *narsingha*, a sort of horn, which was blown in battles and is now played in Hindu religious processions. All these instruments came from Delhi and have remained unchanged through time. Perhaps it has been impossible to improve upon them.

The bugles and the dankas, which are seen today in Lucknow wedding processions, are a poor combination of early and modern instruments. The dankas are supposed to replace those naqaras which in ancient times were carried on horseback with the armies of great conquerors and inspired great awe. The bugle is a British military instrument which conveys instructions to change position, to make some movement or perform some other duty. Therefore the bugle was combined with the danka to form the band that is now seen in marriage processions. Its bandsmen are hired from people of menial occupations and their clothes, horses and general appearance are so mediocre that instead of conveying any idea of splendour, they display a pitiful and ignominious spectacle.[479]

The final and most modern instrument is the bagpipes, brought to India by the British and unknown before their arrival. In Lucknow, the only people to play it are sweepers, who do this in addition to their usual duties. The probable reason for this is that initially both Hindus and Muslims felt such social revulsion towards Europeans that anything they had touched was considered defiled. This instrument had to be learnt from the British and one had to put one's mouth to it. Therefore no one except a sweeper could be expected to learn it. In any event, it has now become to all intents and purposes a pursuit of sweepers. As these people never had any connection with music there was little hope that the art would progress. The result however was most unexpected. The sweepers were eager to improve their playing and as they knew and liked popular local and Indian tunes they began to play them on their Western instrument. The British had only taught them a few Western tunes but they soon started to play current Indian airs, and their success increased.

I have heard British bands in many places: everywhere British melodies are played and the band never attempts an Indian melody. On the other hand, hundreds of Indian bands have now been established which make use of the amorous compositions set to music by the raushan chauki bands of shahnai. Some of them have twenty-five to thirty bandsmen. They wear coloured uniforms according to Indian taste which are cut like the uniforms of British soldiers. This special uniform has improved their appearance and greatly increased their popularity. But other bandsmen never think of making a uniform for themselves and wear the most filthy clothes.

28

Gastronomy

The most important activity in human life is eating. As any community or nation progresses, its diet is the most salient guide to its refinement. For this reason I should like to discuss the attitude of the court of Lucknow towards its cuisine and the extent to which the people of Lucknow improved the art of gastronomy.

At the time of Shuja ud Daula, the supervisor of the court kitchens was Hasan Raza Khan, who went by the name of Mirza Hasanu and came of a respectable Delhi family. A Shaikhzada, Maulvi Fazal Azim, had come to Lucknow from Safipur (Unao District, U.P.) to study. By a stroke of fortune he had been received into Mirza Hasanu's house. The two had grown up together and Mirza Hasanu appointed him assistant supervisor of the kitchens. It was Fazal Azim's custom to prepare the trays for dinner, then put his seal on them and take them to the Navab's antechamber. He would personally hand them to Bahu Begam's special maidservants and thus ensure that nothing detrimental was done to the food. He also kept on good terms with the maidservants.

Navab Shuja ud Daula had his meals inside the Palace with his wife Bahu Begam. The maidservants brought the trays to the Begam, uncovered them in her presence and placed the food on the *dastar khwan*[480] [tablecloth]. Each day food for the Navab and the Begam came from six separate kitchens. Firstly, there was the Navab's own main kitchen supervised by Mirza Hasanu. In this two thousand rupees a day were spent on food, so that, apart from the wages of cooks and other servants, 60,000 rupees a month were spent on food and delicacies. The second was the subsidiary royal kitchen, the supervisor of which was originally Mirza Hasan Ali, but later on was Anbar Ali Khan, a eunuch; here three hundred rupees a day were spent on food. The third kitchen belonged to Bahu Begam's apartments, supervised by Bahar Ali Khan, also a eunuch. The fourth was the kitchen of Navab Begam, Shuja ud Daula's mother, the fifth, Mirza Ali Khan's, and the sixth that of Navab Salar Jang. These last two were Bahu Begam's brothers.

All these six kitchens were excellent and every day produced the most sumptuous and delicious food for the dinner of the ruler. One day a fly emerged from the Navab's dish which had been prepared in the royal kitchen. The Navab was very annoyed and asked, 'Where has this food come from?' The maidservant thought that if she mentioned the royal kitchen, her adopted brother the Maulvi would get into trouble, so she said, 'Sir, the meal has come from Navab Salar Jang's kitchen.'

After Shuja ud Daula's time Asaf ud Daula gave Mirza Hasan Raza Khan the title of Sarfaraz ud Daula and honoured him with the khilat. Hasan Raza then thought that supervising the kitchens was beneath his dignity and appointed Maulvi Fazal Azim for the task, who now took the dinner trays to Asaf ud Daula's antechamber. He then collected some of his relatives to help him, amongst whom were his brother Maulvi Faiq Ali and his two cousins Ghulam Azim and Ghulam Makhdum. The four used to take turns to convey the meals to the antechamber. Following Asaf ud Daula's reign, during the short period of Wazir Ali Khan's rule, Tafazul Husain Khan became Vazir. He sent these relatives back to Safipur and appointed Ghulam Muhammad, popularly known as Bare Mirza, to be supervisor of the kitchens.

Thus from the time of Shuja ud Daula a very high standard of cooking was maintained. The very best cooks were enlisted, elaborate efforts were made in the preparation of foods and innovations were introduced. Expert cooks from Delhi and other places polished up their skills and invented new delicacies and special savours.

Sarfaraz ud Daula Hasan Raza Khan would prepare the most wonderful meals. He himself was extremely fond of good food and entertaining and as supervisor of the main royal kitchen he had every opportunity of displaying his talents. Scores of nobles became connoisseurs of good food, though Navab Salar Jang's family was the most celebrated for its innovations and delicacies.

Reliable sources tell us that Navab Salar Jang's cook, who prepared food for him alone, received a monthly salary of 1,200 rupees, an amount greater than the salary of any cook in the highest courts in the history of India. This cook used to prepare the most enormous *pulaus*,[481] which no one except Salar Jang could digest. One day Navab Shuja ud Daula said, 'Why have you never offered me any of those pulaus which are cooked for you?' Salar Jang replied, 'Certainly, I will have one sent to you today.' Accordingly he asked his cook to prepare a pulau, but of twice the usual amount. His cook replied, 'I am responsible only for your meals and I cannot cook for anyone else.' Salar Jang said, 'The Navab has expressed the desire, can't you possibly make him a pulau?' The cook continued, 'I can't cook for anyone else, whoever he may be.' After much persuasion on the part of Salar Jang, the cook finally agreed on condition that he himself would take the pulau to the Navab, who would eat it in his presence, that he would not allow the Navab to eat more than a few mouthfuls, and that Salar Jang would provide the Navab with plenty of cold water. Salar Jang agreed. The cook prepared the pulau and Salar Jang himself placed it on the dastar khwan. As soon as he had tasted the pulau, Shuja ud Daula was full of praise and began to eat heartily. He had taken only a few mouthfuls, however, when Salar Jang tried to stop him. Shuja ud Daula looked at him with annoyance and continued eating. But after a few more mouthfuls he became exceedingly thirsty and was happy to drink the cold water that Salar Jang had brought with him. Finally his thirst was quenched and Salar Jang went home.

In those days the best food was considered to be that which appeared light and delicate but was in fact heavy and not easily digestible. People with old-fashioned taste still have a penchant for this sort of food but today it is not generally popular.

A special art was to produce one particular substance in several different guises. When placed on the table it looked as if there were scores of different kinds of delicacies, but when one tasted them, one found they were all the same. For instance, I have heard that a Prince Mirza Asman Qadar, the son of Mirza Khurram Bakht of Delhi, who came to Lucknow and became a Shia, was invited to dine by Wajid Ali Shah. *Murabba,*[482] a conserve, was put on the dastar khwan which looked very light, tasty and delicious. When Asman Qadar tasted it he became intrigued because it was not a conserve at all but a *qaurma,*[483] a meat curry, which the chef had made to look exactly like a conserve. He felt embarrassed and Wajid Ali Shah was extremely pleased at having been able to trick an honoured Delhi connoisseur.

A few days later, Mirza Asman Qadar invited Wajid Ali Shah to a meal. Wajid Ali Shah anticipated that a trap would be laid for him, but this did not save him from being taken in. Asman Qadar's cook, Shaikh Husain Ali, had covered the tablecloth with hundreds of delicacies and many varieties of comestibles. There were *pulau, zarda,*[484] *qaurma, kababs,*[485] *biryani,*[486] *chapatis,*[487] chutneys,[488] *achars,*[489] *parathas, shir mals*—in fact every kind of food. However, when tasted they were all found to be made of sugar. The curry was sugar, the rice was sugar, the pickles were sugar and the bread was sugar. It is said that even the plates, the tablecloth, the finger bowls and cups were made of sugar. Wajid Ali Shah tried everything and became more and more embarrassed.

I have said that trays of food for Navab Shuja ud Daula's dinners came from six different kitchens. This practice was not confined to him alone. It continued after his time and the honour was also accorded to some chosen nobles and especially to the royal relations.

My friend Navab Muhammad Shafi Khan Nishapuri tells me that his grandfather, Navab Agha Ali Hasan Khan, an eminent noble, used to send *roghni roti,*[487] a rich bread, and *metha ghi* [ghee],[490] clarified butter, from his house to the King. This bread was so fine and cooked with such care that it was not thicker than paper. The metha ghee was a very special product which had to be prepared with great care.

In Delhi the most popular food was biryani, but the taste in Lucknow was more for pulau. To the uninitiated palate both are much the same, but because of the amount of spices in biryani there is always a strong taste of curried rice, whereas pulau can be prepared with such care that this can never happen. It is true that a good biryani is better than an indifferent pulau, for the pulau may be tasteless and this is never so in the case of a biryani. But in the view of gourmets a biryani is a clumsy and ill-conceived meal in comparison with a really good pulau and for that reason the latter was more popular in Lucknow. There are seven well-known kinds of pulaus in Lucknow. I can remember the names of only *gulzar*, the garden, *nur*, the light, *koku*, the cuckoo, *moti*, the pearl and *chambeli*, jasmine; but in fact scores of different pulaus are served. Muhammad Ali Shah's son Mirza Azim ush Shan, on the occasion of a wedding, invited the parents of the bride and bridegroom to a dinner at which Wajid Ali Shah was also present. For that occasion there were seventy varieties of savoury pulaus and sweet rice dishes.

At the time of Ghazi ud Din Haidar, Navab Husain Ali Khan of Salar Jang's family was a great gourmet who had scores of different varieties of pulaus prepared for him. These were so light and delicate that no other nobleman could compete with him. Even the King envied him and gourmets would call him 'the rice man'.

During the reign of Nasir ud Din Haidar, a cook came to Lucknow who made *khichri*[491] using pistachio nuts and almonds instead of rice and lentils. He cut the almonds into rice-shapes and the pistachio nuts into the shape of lentils so perfectly that when cooked the dish looked exactly like khichri. Once savoured, the taste could never be forgotten.

At the time of Navab Sadat Ali Khan there was an expert cook who made nothing but *gulathis*,[492] rice puddings. This was the splendour of the royal table, the favourite dish of the ruler and such a delicacy that the noblemen all longed for it.

There is a story about a new cook who came before Navab Asaf ud Daula. He was asked, 'What do you cook?' He answered, 'I only cook lentils.' When he was then asked what wages he required he replied, 'Five hundred rupees.' The Navab agreed to employ him but the cook said, 'I will only take on service under certain conditions.' When asked what those were, he said, 'When your Excellency wishes to eat my preparation of lentils, you must order it the day before and when I tell you it is ready you must eat it right away.' The Navab agreed to these conditions and some months later ordered the cook to prepare his lentils. The cook did so and when it was ready informed the Navab who said, 'All right, put it on the dastar khwan, I am coming in a minute.' The dastar khwan was laid but the Navab became engaged in conversation. The cook reminded him again but the Navab tarried. After a third reminder, when the Navab still did not appear, the cook took the pot of lentils, emptied it on the roots of a withered tree and departed. The Navab regretted this and instituted a search but no trace of the cook was found. Some days later it was seen that the tree under which the lentils had been thrown was now blossoming. There is no doubt that this incident has been exaggerated. Still, one can judge from it the esteem accorded to cooks at the court and realize with what liberality an expert chef was treated.

Seeing the interest that the wealthy took in matters of food, cooks tried various innovations. One invented a pulau which resembled an *anar dana* [pomegranate seed] in which half of each grain of rice was fiery red like a ruby and the other half was white and sparkled like a crystal. When the pulau was put on the table it looked as if the dish had been filled with coloured jewels. Another cook produced a *nau ratan*[431] [nine-precious-gem] pulau, in which the rice was coloured to reproduce the nine well-known gems and the colours were so pure and so polished that they were a delight to the eyes. Many more delicacies of this nature were created which became known to different houses and kitchens.

Of the noblemen interested in food, one was Navab Mirza Khan Nishapuri, who was reputed to have a vasiqa of 14,000 rupees a month. He showed such talent in producing delicious food and enlisting the services of expert chefs that his dastar khwan became famed throughout the city. Another was Mirza Haidar, also of Nishapur. He was such an honoured and respected nobleman that the Nishapuri community in Lucknow acknowledged him as their leader. It was his practice whenever he accepted an invitation to take with him all the items necessary for the preparation of betel leaf and a hundred or more *huqqas* [hookahs], as well as the necessary equipment for cooling drinking-water. This was a great help to people of moderate means, who would make sure to invite him. In this way all arrangements for huqqas, betel leaf and drinking-water would be his responsibility and these arrangements were always perfect.

Three classes of people were employed in preparing food. First there were the scullions who cleaned enormous pots and dishes and worked under the cook. Second was *bavarchi*, the cook, who prepared the meals in large quantities. Third was *rakabdar*, the chef, who was the most expert and usually cooked in small pots for a few people only. He considered it beneath his dignity to produce food in large quantities. Cooks, too, like to prepare in small quantities, but chefs never do otherwise because in addition to cooking, they are occupied with the presentation and serving of the food. They adorn the dishes with dried fruits cut into the shape of flowers, edible silver foils and other embellishments. They prepare light, delicious conserves and pickles and exhibit their skill in the gastronomic art in subtle ways.

Ghazi ud Din Haidar was fond of parathas. His chef used to cook six parathas a day and put five seers [approximately ten pounds] of ghee into each, that is to say, he used thirty seers of ghee a day. One day the Vazir Motamad ud Daula Agha Mir sent for him and asked, 'What do you do with thirty seers of ghee a day?' He said, 'Sir, I cook parathas.' The Vazir asked him to cook a paratha so that he could witness this. The chef did so and put in all the ghee it would hold and threw the rest away. Motamad ud Daula said with astonishment, 'You have not used all the ghee.' The chef said, 'What is left over is not worth keeping for another meal.' The Vazir could not understand the answer and said, 'Only five seers of ghee a day will be given to you, one seer for each paratha.' The chef said, 'Very well, I will cook with that much ghee.' He was so angry at the Vazir's interference that he started to cook very indifferent parathas for the King's table. After a few days the King remarked, 'What is wrong with these parathas?' The chef said, 'Your Majesty, I cook the parathas as Navab Motamad ud Daula Bahadur has ordered.' The King asked for details and was given a full account. He immediately sent for the Vazir who said, 'Your Majesty, these people rob you right and left.' On this the King became angry and slapped him, saying, 'Don't you rob? You who rob the whole monarchy and the whole country and think nothing of it? He only takes a little too much ghee for my meals and you don't like it.' The Vazir repented, showed his contrition and the King, exercising his clemency, gave him a khilat. The Vazir never interfered with the chef again and the latter continued to take thirty seers of ghee as before.

29

Delicacies and Confectionery

Navab Abdul Qasim Khan was a nobleman of taste. Very rich pulaus were cooked in his kitchen and the broth from thirty-four seers of meat was used to stew the rice. It was so tasty that if you took a mouthful you felt as though the rice had melted as it went down your throat and there was no question of heaviness. A pulau as rich and nutritious as this used to be cooked every day for Wajid Ali Shah's principal wife.

Munshi ul Sultan, the Vazir at Matiya Burj, was among the more stylish enthusiasts and was very fond of his food. Although there were some excellent cooks available, he never enjoyed a meal unless he had cooked some of it himself. He became so famed for his good food that Wajid Ali Shah used to say, 'The Munshi ul Sultan eats well. I wish I were as lucky.' I lived with him as a child for six or seven years in Matiya Burj and used to have my meals with him. I saw thirty to forty different pulaus on his dastar khwan and scores of curries, the like of which I have never tasted since. He was very fond of *halva sohan*,[493] a round confectionery, which I shall describe later.

In recent times since the Mutiny the late Hakim Banday Mehndi, who lived in Lucknow, was extremely interested in his food and clothes. Only a few people were able to eat as well or dress as well as he did. An honoured friend told me that his family were on very good terms with the hakim. He said:

'One day the hakim sent a message to my father and uncle to say that he had invited a wrestler to his house and that they should come to see the fun. My father went and took me with him. When we got there we discovered that the wrestler drank twenty seers of milk every morning and that he ate five or six pounds of dried fruit, almonds and pistachio nuts. At midday and in the evening he ate five pounds of bread and an ordinary-sized goat. The size of his body was in proportion to this amount of food. We found him impatient for his breakfast and he went on demanding that the food should be sent for, but the hakim made him wait. This continued until hunger made him so impatient that he became irritated and started to get up. Then the hakim promised to send for the food and went into the house. He kept him waiting a little longer and when he saw that the wrestler could not bear his hunger any longer he sent for a tray. On seeing this the wrestler revived, but when he opened up the tray he found there was only a small dish containing an ounce or two of pulau. This small amount of rice was scarcely a mouthful for him, and he became enraged and decided to leave. But he was persuaded to stay. He turned the dish upside down into his mouth and swallowed all the contents with scarcely a gulp. A few minutes later he asked for water and after another five minutes drank again and proceeded to belch. Trays of food now came out of the house and the dastar khwan was set out. The hakim himself appeared and the food was served. A plate containing about half a pound of rice of the same pulau as before was put in front of the hakim who handed it to the wrestler and said, "Look, is this the same pulau or not?" The wrestler agreed that it was and the hakim said, "Eat it now. I am sorry it took so long to prepare and that you have been inconvenienced." The wrestler said, "Please excuse me. I have become so satiated by the first mouthful that I cannot swallow a single additional grain." However much he was entreated he stayed his hand and said, "How can I eat when there is no room in my stomach?" The hakim took the rice, ate it all and said to the wrestler, "To swallow twenty or thirty seers is not the human way of eating: that is how cows and buffaloes feed themselves. A human being should eat a few mouthfuls but those mouthfuls should give him more strength and nourishment than twenty or thirty seers of corn. You were satiated by this one mouthful. Come again tomorrow and tell us whether you feel you have not gained as much nutrition from this as you do from twenty seers of milk and many seers of fruit, meat and corn." The hakim also invited the rest of us to come on the following day. The next day when he came the wrestler said, "Never before have I felt so vigorous as I do today."

During the later period of the Navabi rule, Navab Mohsin ud Daula and Navab Mumtaz ud Daula, both of the royal family, were acknowledged to be unrivalled in their enthusiasm for gastronomical pleasures. It was their cook who used to prepare these pulaus for Hakim Banday Mehndi.

At that time one of the ladies of the royal family maintained a very large household. Her kitchen was famous and food to the value of three hundred rupees was cooked there every day. Also at that time there was a cook in Prince Yahya Ali Khan's household named Alim Ali whose incomparable preparation of fish was well known to all the nobles. Cooks of other households made every effort to equal him but without success.

At the time of Nasir ud Din Haidar, a non-Lakhnavi who was generally known as Mahumdu, opened a food stall in the Firangi Mahal quarter. His *nahari*[494] [breakfast curry] was so celebrated that even the greatest nobles and princes used to show their appreciation of it. This stirred him to further efforts and he started a new preparation called *shir mal*[487] which is the pride of Lucknow to this day. Many kinds of bread were known and eaten in various towns. Muslims ate leavened bread in Persia and then started to bake it in underground ovens. In India their bread was plain and there was no ghee in it. Seeing the Hindus frying their puris, Muslims put some ghee into their griddle-baked bread and invented parathas. The first improvement on these parathas was the *baqar khani*, which was an extravagant form of bread for a rich man's table. In Lucknow, Mahumdu made great improvements on the baqar khani by producing the shir mal which in taste, scent, lightness and delicacy was very much better than the baqar khani and other luxurious breads. Even today the shir mal is not baked anywhere but in Lucknow: when efforts are made to bake it anywhere else, it is not the same. In a very short time the shir mal gained such popularity in Lucknow that any celebration at which it was not served could not be considered perfect.

Shir mal so increased the esteem in which Mahumdu was held that on the occasion of royal majlises and celebrations he sometimes received orders for a hundred thousand shir mals. His organization was able to cope with orders of any size. Mahumdu's successor was Ali Husain, who died only a few months ago. Shir mals of the same excellent quality can still be obtained from his shop today.

Nan jalebis is an improved variety of shir mal which has to be cooked with great care. It needs a cordon bleu chef to turn it out properly and the cooks of Lucknow claim that no one else can cook them as well as they. As regards parathas, Lucknow is up to the same standard as other cities and there has been no evident improvement in this line. It is said that Delhi bakers produce really excellent parathas and mix a whole seer of ghee with one seer of flour. But when I was living in Delhi I often had parathas cooked for me by well-known bakers. They certainly contained a large quantity of ghee but as it had not been thoroughly mixed with the flour the parathas could only be eaten fresh. When they were cold they were like leather.

Pieces of bread mixed with ghee and sugar are an everyday sweet dish generally partaken of on occasion of the ceremonies of Fatiha[495] and Niyaz.[496] From this developed the preparation of *malida*, a sweet dish with semolina, which was so light that it turned to sherbet in one's mouth and there was no need to chew it. Some rulers were very fond of it. Later, further innovations were made: only milk boiled several times was used, with its skin, in the preparation of bread and certain dishes, without the addition of flour. This led to the development of *panj giri*, a dish of semolina, dried fruits and milk, which was light, delicious and nourishing, and much appreciated in high circles.

The main Muslim dishes were pulau and qaurma, and more care was taken in their preparation than with any other dishes. I have written a lot about pulaus, yet there are other points still to be mentioned. For rich epicures chickens used to be fattened with musk and saffron pills until their flesh was scented with these two substances. Then a broth was made from them and rice was added to simmer with it.

Moti, the pearl pulau, was made to look as if the rice contained shining pearls. The method of making these pearls was to take about two hundred grains in weight of silver foil[497] and twenty grains of gold foil and beat them into the yolk of an egg; this mixture was then stuffed into the gullet of a chicken and tied around with fine thread. The chicken was heated slightly and the skin cut with a penknife. Well-formed, shining pearls appeared, which were cooked with the meat of the pulau. Some chefs used to make these pearls with cheese and cover them with silver foil. There were many more such variations which no one had thought of before. A number of chefs used to fashion small birds from the meat of the pulau and cook them with such care that their shape was not damaged. They were put on plates, the rice was made to look like grain and it appeared as if the birds were sitting on each guest's plate pecking at grain.

Another amazing variation was a large pie which contained some small birds; when opened the birds were released and flew away. This dish used to be prepared in Hyderabad Deccan, probably by the chef Pir Ali who had come from Lucknow, and used to delight distinguished Englishmen and their wives at Government dinners. The dish was first seen on Nasir ud Din Haidar's dastar khwan. But the bird pulau was a superior achievement.

One chef used to fashion large eggs, boiled and fried, which weighed as much as two pounds each and in which the whites and yolks were exactly the normal shape and proportions. Some cooks made almond curries which looked like broad beans, but were much lighter and more delicious. The Vazir Raushan ud Daula's cook used to cut continuous spirals out of whole tender cobs which were then mixed with yoghurt and spices to make a *saita*. He then made a sauce from them which was highly regarded.

My calligraphist, Munshi Shakir Ali, showed incomparable skill in writing the whole passage of 'Qul Huwallah' from the Quran on a grain of rice. But a chef here at the time of the monarchy did still better with poppy seeds. He cut each grain in such a way that it had spikes all around it.

Pir Ali, a famous chef of Lucknow, was employed in the kitchens of the Nizam. He used to cook a very expensive and delicious pulse which was formerly cooked in the kitchens of the Lucknow rulers, called Sultan's Dal pulse.

Some chefs used to cook *karela*, a bitter vegetable, with such care and delicacy that to look at it one would not think that steam had touched it. It remained just as green and as fresh as before. But if one cut into it and ate it, it was most delicious. An incident reminiscent of this happened to my good friend Saiyyid Ali Ausat recently. He related, 'Navab Ali Khan, a Lucknow aristocrat, said to me one day, "Wait for your evening meal, I will send you something." At dinner time his servant came round with a covered tray. With great eagerness I sent for the tray and had it opened up. There was only one plate on it with what seemed to be raw pumpkin. I was so disappointed that I said to the maidservant, "Take it away and cook it tomorrow." The servant laughed and said, "Please eat it as it is, there is no necessity to cook it." When I ate it I found it to be as delicious and tasty as anything I had ever eaten.' The chefs have reached perfection at these arts. Pir Ali used to fashion sweets like pomegranates in which the outer skin, the seeds and the inner tissues all looked like the real fruit: the kernels of the seeds were made of almonds, the seeds themselves of pear juice and the tissues between the seeds as well as the outer skin were of sugar.

Chefs also made marabbas, achars and various kinds of sweets, into which they skilfully introduced hundreds of innovations. Everyone knows mango marabba. But in Lucknow the chefs used to make marabba of whole unripe small mangoes in such a way that the green outer skin retained its original appearance. It looked as if small, unripe mangoes had just been plucked from the trees and made into syrup.

30

More Delicacies and Confectionery

The collective name for foods selected for feasts at home or sent out was *tora*. It consisted of *pulau*; *muzafar*, a sweet, rich rice dish with saffron; *mutanjan*, meat, sugar and rice with spices; *shir mal*; *safaida*, a simple, sweet rice dish; fried aubergine; *shir baranj*, a rich, sweet rice dish boiled in milk; *qaurma*; *arvi*, a fried vegetable with meat; *shami kababs*, croquettes of meat and lentils, along with *murabba, achar,* pickles, and chutney.

In most places the tora contained most of these foods but in Lucknow all of these dishes were eaten at home or sent out to guests.[498] Other varieties of food were scarcely ever served. These foods were put on the dastar khwan in front of each guest. If the dishes had to be sent out they were carefully carried away on large octagonal wooden trays.

It is a British custom to decorate a table with flowers and other embellishments. Wealthy people, nobles and princes in Lucknow followed the practice in so far as they had paper flowers placed on the food trays, but ordinary and middle-class people thought the custom superfluous and did not follow it.

The varieties of food typical of distinguished households were related to their rank and class and the dishes of the tora were made up accordingly. In the royal palace the king's tora consisted of one hundred and one trays, the cost of which was about five hundred rupees. Of the rulers of Avadh, Wajid Ali Shah's father Amjad Ali Shah was extremely conscientious, pious, temperate and abstemious. He avoided all sinful acts and adhered strictly to Muslim religious law. In the fervour of his piety he believed that the spending of the country's money on himself was unethical. He therefore asked all his relatives to send him money instead of food when they wanted to entertain him. The result was that people would send him five hundred rupees and at the same time made a point of sending a tora as well, but a much less elaborate one.

The most popular *khwan*[480] [tray] was made of wood with a coloured, dome-shaped lid, which was tied with a brace of white cloth. It was the custom in the royal kitchen, and also in upper-class homes, for the brace to be sealed so that no one could tamper with the tray. On top of the brace there was an extremely ornate, coloured covering usually made of silk. In important households these coverings were made of satin, silk or brocade, sometimes embroidered and sometimes of gold or silver lace.

It is possible that this custom was prevalent at the Mughal court and came from there to Lucknow, but I have never seen ceremonial observances in Delhi to equal those in Lucknow. Here, in the most minor matters of eating and drinking, etiquette was imperative and had become second nature. When water was served even for the most ordinary person, a servant used to place the glass on a small tray, put a cover over it and hand it to the recipient with the utmost courtesy and respect.

In the course of a hundred years this refinement and display produced excellent chefs in Lucknow who became famous throughout India. Wherever I have been, at Muslim courts or in Muslim States in India, I have found Lucknow chefs who had made a great impression on the wealthy and the rulers and who were greatly valued. It cannot be denied that today there are very expert cooks in Hyderabad Deccan, Bhopal and Rampur—but if you go into their background, find out about their families and personal history you will probably find that they came from Lucknow. If not they belong to a family of professional cooks who originally came from Lucknow, or are their pupils.

There now remains confectionery to discuss. The preparation of sweets familiar to the public is the work of the Hindu *halvai* [confectioner], but the standard of the Muslim chefs is much higher. These chefs cannot meet the needs of the masses and this is the business of the Hindu confectioner. The chefs prepare confectionery only for the few who are interested in refined delicacies. Their products are incomparable and most delicious. Confectionery in Lucknow is of two kinds, that of the Muslims and that of the Hindus. If you buy a sweet in an ordinary Muslim shop it will be no better than that made by the Hindus, but if you give an order in advance for any speciality, it is infinitely better. As a general rule *jalebis*, sweets formed in a spiral, glazed with syrup, *imertis*, thick sweets with syrup, and *balu shahis*, moist, round syrupy sweets, are all very well made in Lucknow.

It is difficult to determine which confections were Hindu in origin and which came to India with the Muslims. Taking the names and taste into consideration, it would appear that *halva* is of Arab origin and came to India via Persia, retaining its original name. But one cannot state this definitely and there are differences of opinion about it. *Tar halva*, a sweet made with clarified butter, which is usually obtainable from all the confectioners and eaten with puris, is purely Hindu. It is also called *mohan bhog*. But the four kinds of *halva sohan*, namely *papri*, hard and dry, *jauzi*, soft and crumbly, *habshi*, soft, crumbly and black, and *dudhia*, like a thick milk jelly, appear to be essentially Muslim.

Most sweets made by contemporary Hindu confectioners appear to have been devised since the time the Muslims arrived in India. For instance the name of the sweet *barfi*, dry, white and soft, shows that it originated in Persia (*baraf* is Persian for 'snow'). *Balu shahi*, *khurme*, hard folded pancakes; *nuktiyan*, tiny yellow beads of sweets; *gulab jaman*, soft, syrupy croquettes, and *dar behisht*, were all developed during the Muslim era.

Jalebis are called *zalabia* in Arabic, and it is clear that the word *zalabia* has become corrupted into *jalebi*; these sweets therefore should be included among those coming from Arabia and Persia. *Payras*, ball-shaped sweets, are definitely Hindu, as are *imertis*. I have been told that imertis were actually invented in Lucknow, but Lucknow has no particular distinction as regards imertis. An extraordinary thing is that Agra and Panjab confectionery are the most famed in Lucknow. I have seen in other towns that the confectionery of Lucknow and its neighbourhood is the most popular.

Taking all things into consideration, Hindu confectioners are on the whole much better and more popular than Muslim, and the people who really appreciate sweets are the Hindus. Possibly because Muslims are meat-eaters, they prefer food containing salt. Hindus on the other hand prefer a sweet taste. They will fill their stomachs with sweets, which is not the case with a Muslim. Because of this predilection of Hindus, Mathura, Benares and Ajodhya, their religious centres, are superior to other cities in the production of various kinds of tasty sweets.

Many people, in addition to Muslim chefs, are famous for the preparation of halva sohan. Recently the celebrated calligraphist, Munshi Hadi Ali, became particularly noted for his preparation of *papri halva sohan*. He used to add twenty-five or thirty seers of ghee to each seer of wheat germ and adorned each sweet with exquisite tughra writing, so that in addition to the production of halva sohan, examples of his penmanship and design were also displayed.

In Matiya Burj I often saw the Vazir, who came from a noble Lucknow family, adding about two and a half seers of ghee to two ounces of the other ingredients. His papri halva sohan, instead of being the usual yellow, was white and shining like a newly washed cloth.

31

Food Refinements and Water Cooling

In most Asian countries, in addition to delicacy of taste, great importance is placed on the presentation of food. It is made to look attractive through colour, and appetizing through smell. Special attention is paid to this in Lucknow. Interest in good food is usually confined to a few wealthy people and gourmets, but in Lucknow this interest is shared by nearly everyone. As a result not only have a large number of good cooks materialized, but ladies of noble families have also acquired the art. There is not a distinguished family in which the honoured ladies do not display great skill in delicate and delicious cooking.

Milk and yoghurt are universal. In Lucknow great attention has been given to preparations from them, like *balai*, clotted cream, which contains the most savoury constituents. In English it is called 'cream' and is much indulged in in Europe. But there they let the milk stand for a little until the thick, white and succulent portion comes to the top: this they skim off and call cream. In Lucknow the succulent portion is removed by warming the milk (in very shallow trays) over a slow fire. The many layers are then removed and carefully put together, one on top of the other, until the thick *balai* is formed.

In early Urdu this dish was called *malai*. Asaf ud Daula was so fond of it that it used to be very carefully prepared for him. Instead of *malai*, he called it *balai*, because it came from the top of the milk (*bala* means 'above' in Persian). The people of Lucknow liked this idea and the word *balai*, except for villagers and some illiterate people, became standard usage and the word *malai* was dropped in refined circles.

The late Maulvi Muhammad Husain Azad objected to this in his *Ab-e Hayat*,[247] saying that the word *malai* was more trenchant and eloquent. To my mind there is no point in saying that a word lacks eloquence merely because one does not like it. Every community has a preference for words that it has adopted and that have become current and popular in its idiom. To those people who use *malai* the word *balai* is doubtless tiresome, but where *balai* is used and has become part of the idiom, the word has greater eloquence. To them *malai* is used by the ignorant and villagers.

Eloquence and delicacy in a language cannot be determined by reason or logic but only by the preferences of the people who speak it. Today Delhi and Lucknow are considered the established schools of Urdu. Therefore the language of both is accepted as standard, even if a word used in one place should be unfamiliar in the other. Both *malai* and *balai* are correct—*malai* in the opinion of the people of Delhi and *balai* according to those who live in Lucknow.

To return to the subject of food, discrimination in the setting out and decorating of meals is as necessary as the actual cooking. At present in Europe tables are pleasantly decorated with flowers. In some countries on ceremonial occasions grains of coloured rice are put out on the table in the forms of letters or designs. Immaculately clean vessels and utensils, generally of silver, are used, but British cooks and butlers do not pay much attention to the decoration of the food itself, except for wedding cakes which are beautifully made and placed with great ceremony on the tables.

Unlike the practice in England, little attention is paid in Lucknow to the decoration of a dastar khwan, but the food itself is set out with much delicacy. Silver and gold foil is placed upon the food and designs and floral patterns are made with pistachio nuts, almonds and shredded coconut. Chefs take great pride in this art and their main task is in fact to make the food look as lovely as possible.

In Lucknow this ostentation originated with professional cooks and chefs and then passed on to upper-class families, where it became a special accomplishment of the ladies. In Europe it is said that women are better suited to delicate work and decoration than men. A proof of this can be seen in Lucknow where women show great natural skill in the embellishment of food.

Indian wedding cakes, which are usually placed before the bride and bridegroom at marriages, are made with boiled rice. The ladies of most households decorate them so daintily and with such finesse that one is quite happy merely to sit and look at them.

It will not be without interest to mention the improvements made in *abdar khana*, the name given to the methods of preparing liquid refreshments. In former days ice was unobtainable and in the hot season it was extremely difficult to obtain cold water. Thus special arrangements had to be made. Water was poured into *surahi*[499] [earthenware pitchers], and for drinking purposes, elegant *abkhoras*[500] [earthenware drinking vessels] were used. Red cloth, which was kept damp, was tied round the pitcher or drinking vessel in order to cool it by the wind. The hotter the wind, the colder it made the cloth, which in turn reduced the temperature of the water inside the receptacles. Often cloth was tied on the mouths of goblets, pitchers and even jars, which were then hung upside down from the branches of trees. As they were completely sealed the water did not spill out and they became beautifully cold. In the rainy season, earthenware jars were hung inside a hall.

An elaborate practice was to immerse small metal pitchers in a large earthenware vessel filled with brackish water and then spin them round and round. In a short time the water in the pitchers became as cold as ice. This practice was called *jhalna*, pitcher-cooling.

In later days a plan was developed to produce ice. In the depths of winter, hot water was poured into earthenware receptacles and put out in fields and open spaces at night. By morning the water had frozen. The ice was immediately buried in deep pits which had been especially prepared for this purpose. As long as the ice remained in the pits, it did not melt. In this way sufficient ice was stored in the pits to last the whole year. But it was not clean enough to add to drinking water, so the earlier methods had to be maintained at the same time. In any case the art of ice-making was confined to the wealthy.

I do not know whether the arrangements for the cooling of water were exactly the same in Delhi. It is probable that they were but I have not seen them practised in Delhi so well or so extensively. No doubt Lucknow is superior to most places in having evolved the efficient and better-shaped earthenware vessels. Additionally, the quality of the clay in Lucknow gives the water a special fragrance. The metal pitchers in Delhi may be good but not as delicate and practical as the earthenware pitchers of Lucknow. I shall describe these fully in a later chapter on pottery.

Traditionally, wherever kings went their kitchens and water-cooling equipment accompanied them, but in Lucknow water-cooling arrangements were so advanced that even wealthy people never went anywhere without them. For instance Mirza Haidar took it upon himself to provide such arrangements for weddings and entertainments to which he had been invited. His presence at these festivities was always a great blessing.

32

The Evolution of Men's Dress

The history of Indian clothing is shrouded in darkness. From the study of ancient sculpture and murals of Ellora[501] and Ajanta it is evident that in the pre-Muslim period it was not the custom in India to wear stitched clothes. Women and men covered their bodies with unsewn sheets, saris and dhotis. Arab travellers who came to India before the Muslim conquerors found the people in the coastal regions from Sindh to Bengal dressed in this manner.

Although the first Arab Muslims who came here wore *kurtas*, loose collarless shirts, and *tahmat*, unsewn cotton cloth worn from the waist to the ankles, and *qabas*, capes, their dress and appearance were not greatly superior to those of the local inhabitants. Dress started to make advances when the Abbaside court of Baghdad adopted Sassanide culture and evolved trousers, tunics, cloaks and well-fashioned turbans for the élite Arabs. These were largely copied from those worn by the nobles and dignitaries of the Sassanide court. In a short time they were worn by Muslims everywhere, and they brought the style with them to India. Paintings of the early Muslim crowned heads in India show them wearing practically the same clothes as the Persian and Abbaside nobles and rulers. The only difference was that the Indian sultans, following the example of Hindu rajas, covered themselves with jewels.

The latest fashion at the Mughal court in Delhi, as far as can be ascertained, was a turban, a short coat, tight ankle-length trousers, high-heeled shoes and a girdle round the waist. This was the outfit of the upper classes in Delhi and it remained unchanged until the time of Muhammad Shah Rangeley, or if there were any changes, they were scarcely appreciable.

This outfit included a short-sleeved undergarment with a sort of bodice up to the elbows and fixed to the chest with tapes. Over this was a coat which was an improvement on the Persian cape. It had a collar but the lapels on both sides, which were known as *parda*,[208] curtains, folded over each other and covered the chest. The upper portion of the chest below the throat was bare, as with an English coat or sports-shirt. The left-hand lapel was worn below and fixed to the right-hand lapel with bindings and this lapel in turn was attached to that of the left. From the waist a sort of skirt, very wide in circumference, hung down to the ankles. The trousers were tight at the bottom and those of wealthy men were made of silk. Over the coat a sash was tied round the waist.

This was the clothing of our ancestors two or three hundred years ago, and it was worn by all the nobles and wealthy men of India. It was the dress of the court, worn by Navab Burhan ul Mulk and Shuja ud Daula when they came from Delhi to Avadh. The cloth of the *jama*, a collarless shirt, was usually fine muslin, made in various towns in India, of a very delicate and light texture, and renowned throughout the world. The muslin and embroidered cloth of Dacca was particular to nobles and royalty.

Later the *balabar*, a copy of the Persian cape, was invented, the rounded collar of which was completely open because the short coat worn beneath it sufficiently covered the chest. This coat was in no way fastened, and to prevent it flying open a triangular piece of material was inserted on the right-hand side. This gusset was the first example of those used with *shervanis*, knee-length tunics, now fixed on the left-hand side.

As an improvement on the balabar the *angarkha* was invented in Delhi, which was a combination of the jama and balabar and created a new fashion. The bodice over the chest was copied from the qaba, but instead of leaving the throat uncovered a low-cut, semi-circular jabot was superimposed: over this and below the throat a crescent-shaped necklet was sewn and attached to a button-hole on the left side of the neck. The bodice was beneath this and the lapels fixed to each other across the chest. A little of the chest above the bodice was exposed. Although the bottom of the garment was like that of a qaba, it was pleated on both sides like that of a jama.

This was the old angarkha which was worn in Delhi and passed from there to the whole of India. When it came to Lucknow, it was made more close-fitting. The bodice was also tightened, the pleats at the sides disappeared entirely and the bottoms were edged with lace. After this princes and men of fashion changed the bodice so that instead of one, three fronts were superimposed over each other with pleats and ruffles.

After the angarkha had been evolved in Delhi, the bodice was discarded and the exposure of the left side of the chest was not considered incorrect but attractive. In Lucknow a *shaluka*, a waistcoat up to the neck, was worn in place of the bodice, with buttons in front. Buttons had just been introduced to India from Europe. Special styles were displayed in these waistcoats. People of taste wore tight waistcoats of muslin with embroidered patterns. Some people wore coloured waistcoats and the embroidery brought out the fine delicacy of the cloth.

The second improvement on the balabar after it had come to Lucknow was the development of the *chapkan*, a fitted cape. This had the same semi-circular jabot and lapels as the angarkha. The lapels were bow-shaped and sewn with buttons and there was an attractive bow-shaped ring of buttons near the neck. Like the balabar, it had a broad gusset fixed to the left side by buttons. This chapkan was made of wool or other thick cloth and was more suitable for winter wear; it was popular in the court. The British liked it very much and for some time dressed their servants in it.

Finally, in recent times the *achkan* was evolved on the lines of the chapkan and angarkha. Like the angarkha and chapkan it had a coat collar which was open in the centre and kept in position by the border hem. The coat was open from top to bottom and was fastened with buttons. The gusset which was inserted high up in the balabar was now fixed lower down to prevent the bottom of the garment from opening, thus overcoming the main fault of the balabar. The lower part of the achkan was exactly like that of the chapkan and angarkha and those who were fashion-minded had it edged with lace and embroidered.

The achkan was extremely popular and the style started to find its way from the towns to the villages. In a very short time it was worn throughout India. In Hyderabad, it developed with a few alterations into the *shervani*. Its sleeves were made like those of an English coat, the adornments over the chest were discarded and for the lower part the shape of an English overcoat was adopted. It became so popular everywhere, including Lucknow, that it is now the national dress of all Hindus and Muslims in India.

The shaluka, worn under the angarkha, was at first changed for a loose and shorter tunic. Because of Western influence this too was discarded after a short time and replaced by the English shirt with collar and cuffs. The adoption of the shirt with collar made the shervani even more attractive, as it became fashionable for the white collar to be shown over the collar of the coat. The length of the sleeves allowed a little of the cuffs to show. Although the present dress of the educated and middle-class in Lucknow is the shervani, this style is in no way particular to Lucknow.[502] Lucknow's last and final creation was the achkan, which is by now quite obsolete.

33

Forms of Headwear

I shall now turn my attention to headwear. Since the head in India is the most honoured and respected part of the body, its covering has an appropriately exalted status.[503] From ancient times it has been the custom here to wear *pagris*, turbans. The Arabs and Persians came to India wearing *ammamas*, large turbans, and because of their influence many changes were made. However, the turban was already an established form of headwear in India when they came.

The ammamas of the early Muslim rulers were very large. Probably because of this the pagris of the nobles and élite were also large. They wore beneath them the pointed conical cap of the old Turkish style, the fez, which is still worn in Afghanistan and has been made part of the uniform of the British Indian army.

During the course of the Mughal dynasty, turbans grew smaller and smaller. This was probably due to climate: in cold countries heavy and thick clothing is worn to keep warm, whereas in hot countries one dresses lightly. Although one hears about the thick and heavy clothing of the early Muslim conquerors, one can see how the clothing of the British and their wives is becoming lighter and more scanty day by day.

Accordingly, turbans in India continued to grow smaller and lighter and this affected the court fashions. By the end of the era of the Mughal court, the pagris of the nobles and other officials had become extremely light. This led to the making of hundreds of styles and most nobles and rich men created special types of tiny pagris for themselves.

Because of the reduction in size of turbans, the Turkish caps had to be abandoned. Some wore no caps at all under their turbans and others wore extremely small ones of light material which could be blown away by a puff of wind. I am not certain what these caps were like but they probably resembled those worn by present Muslim patriarchs and religious mendicants, a strip of cloth about seven inches wide going round the head and sewn at the top.

The pagri was removed in the house or in informal gatherings and because being bare-headed was an impropriety, a *kamrukhi* cap, which looked like a crown, was created in Delhi. It had a band round the head and was made with four sides; it is still worn by some nobles and princes in Delhi. The original name of this cap was *chau goshia*, four-cornered. This was improved upon and a dome-shaped cap was produced in Delhi. This had four or five sections and looked like an elongated dome on the head. People wearing this head-dress came to Lucknow and it influenced the styles of the court. The first improvement made here was that long conical sections were joined together and attractive crescent-shaped patterns were sewn on at the rim. These crescents were made of cotton and were stitched on the inside of the fine muslin panels. They showed through the panels and gave the head-dress an elegant but simple appearance. This cap was so popular in Lucknow that it could be seen on the heads of all and most people gave up wearing pagris. Further innovations were made as this cap became more and more popular. It became less elongated and more rounded, and wooden and copper moulds were invented to keep the shape properly rounded.

At the time of Nasir ud Din Haidar the Shia religion was in the ascendancy in Lucknow and there were corresponding reforms in religion, politics, culture and social etiquette. Opposition to the idea of the four Caliphs and love for the Panjtan, the five members of the Prophet's family, caused the number four to be out of favour and the number five to be loved in Lucknow court circles. The effect of this on headgear was that, at the instigation of the King himself, a panel was added to the four-cornered hat and it became five-cornered. The old cap disappeared completely and no one ever remembered that it once had four panels. However the name 'four-cornered' has lingered on. Though some people call it 'five-cornered', the majority call it 'four-cornered' to this day.

Nasir ud Din Haidar had invented this cap especially for himself and during his lifetime it was not possible for anyone else to wear it. However, the style was so favoured that after his death high and low started to wear it and it became popular throughout Lucknow.

A little later, a very attractive embroidered cap of the same type was created for the winter. The five panels were covered in thin muslin upon which gold and silver crescents and designs were stitched in different colours. In winter one saw no other covering on the heads of men of fashion. Later, when *chikan*[504] [embroidery on muslin] became popular, it was used for this purpose. A delicate chikan cap took up to a year to make and even the most ordinary ones cost anything from ten to twelve rupees.

About this time a Delhi prince came to Lucknow who was received with great honour by the court and in society. He wore a *dopalri* cap, which was made of two pieces of cloth to fit the head with a seam across the top. This cap was pleasing to most people for it was relatively simple and easy to produce. Many people adopted it. The prince came to be known as 'the prince of the dopalri cap'. At the end of the monarchy a very small and narrow cap was developed from it which was pointed in front and behind. This was called the *nukka dar* cap. When embroidered in heavy gold and silver thread it was worn by princes, nobles, wealthy men, court favourites and sons of Navabs.

Up to the time of the Mutiny, the people of Lucknow used to wear two types of cap. The first was the *chau goshia*, worn by religious leaders and traditionalists, and the second was the dopalri, worn, with minor exceptions, by everyone else from princes down to the humblest. It is still by far the most popular form of headwear.

Probably either at the time of Ghazi ud Din Haidar or Nasir ud Din Haidar, a round cap known as *mandel* became popular with some people. Its shape was that of a tambourine and it was usually embroidered with gold or silver thread. Rich men and the sons of Navabs adopted it and it acquired the distinction that no one was allowed to appear in the presence of the King or of princes without wearing either a turban or an embroidered mandel. In short, the mandel gained access to the court. From it evolved a cap known as the 'General's topi', which was slightly rounded at the forehead and back and usually made of black velvet and embroidered with gold and silver. This cap belonged to the British army and certainly had the allure of a uniform. However the princes and men of noble family liked it so much that they adopted it for themselves. This was probably the first instance of a British fashion becoming popular in India.

The last King of Avadh, Wajid Ali Shah, invented a new and strange form of court hat for those honoured with titles. It had a cardboard foundation covered with plain or embroidered satin which rose high over the forehead. A large pocket of muslin or veil was fixed to the top and hung down to the nape of the neck, covering the back of the head. The King called this court hat 'Alam Pasand', 'World-Pleasing', but most people called it 'the Swing'. The fashion was so unpopular that even during Wajid Ali Shah's lifetime it was not seen outside the court. Later it disappeared so completely that few people of today have ever seen it.

After the Mutiny habits in headwear changed considerably. For some time the only head-dress worn was the chau goshia, the dopalri, the mandel or the pagri. Then suddenly the four-cornered cap started to go out of fashion, so much so that it is now rarely seen. Most people who discarded it started wearing the dopalri, but some sought innovations by adopting first the embroidered mandel caps from Meerut (U.P.) and then British hats. A large variety of thin, light, velvet and satin caps then came into being, which gradually became similar to the dopalri caps. With the advent of the British era, their fashions became the vogue, and people started to follow them blindly. Some now wear British hats with their Indian costume.

When the late Syed Ahmad Khan adopted the Turkish cap and wore it in combination with British coat and trousers it eventually became popular with Muslim gentlemen. At first it was looked down upon and ridiculed: jokes were even made about it in the newspapers. But Sir Syed's persistence finally made it fashionable and in his lifetime thousands of people began to wear it and the style spread to Lucknow. Eventually educated and well-bred Muslims adopted it throughout India.

Shias in Lucknow are mainly distinguished, well-educated and well-bred. They maintain a separateness in their habits and customs. In addition, just as the Sunnis are culturally close to the Ottoman Empire, the Shias are faithful to the culture of Persia. Therefore when the Turkish head-dress started to become popular in Lucknow, stylish Shias felt it necessary to adopt for themselves the *kulah*, cap of the Persian court. As a result, any Muslim, on discarding his old head-dress, turned to a Turkish cap if he were a Sunni and to a Persian cap if he were a Shia. There are some broad-minded people of both faiths who do not approve of these distinctions, but they are a minority.

Educated Hindus have started to wear round felt caps like mandels which are also worn by some Muslims. The British call these 'babu caps'. However most people today, whether Hindu or Muslim, Shia or Sunni, wear the dopalri caps.

The period since the Mutiny has been one of great upheaval in Lucknow traditions. In addition to changes in social life, manners and customs, fashion and dress have also been affected. Among those who have had a modern education one no longer sees pyjamas, angarkhas, Indian shoes, Indian caps or turbans. They think they have crossed the seven seas and arrived in England and their clothing is now British coats, trousers, boots and hats. The majority would have liked to retain their traditional fashions, but change took place nevertheless. Instead of angarkhas, shervanis became the national dress. No general agreement, however, has been reached on headwear.

There have been scores of fashions for caps in Lucknow, either of local design or from outside, which have had varying durations of life. As the natural preference of the people of Lucknow is for daintiness and delicacy, they could not take to the Turkish, Persian or British hats. These did not conform to Lucknow tastes, however popular they might be elsewhere. The problem of headwear, therefore, still remains to be solved.[505]

34

More Headwear

Although at present in India and particularly in Lucknow the fashionable head-dress is a *topi*, the desire for elegance did not make the pagri obsolete. Pagris, the traditional head-dress of the court, especially the splendid *dastar*, a turban of fine muslin worn by the Delhi nobles, were replaced by topis in Lucknow. For court purposes, however, the pagri was essential until the end of the régime and even at present the pagri is maintained as part of the uniform of servants.

The old dastar remained the head-dress of the rulers up to the time of Navab Sadat Ali Khan. Navab Burhan ul Mulk, Navab Shuja ud Daula and Navab Asaf ud Daula used to wear white dastars similar to those worn by the officials of the Delhi court. On special occasions these dastars were adorned with clusters of jewels, aigrettes and bejewelled gold ornaments; but the dastars themselves remained plain white. However a new style of pagri was worn by Navab Sadat Ali Khan which the people of Lucknow called the *shimla*. The shimla was made with a circlet of wide fine cloth which fitted the head and was open at the crown. Long twisted folds of fine silk or brocade were wound round and sewn on to the circlet at the top and bottom. A broad band of silk or brocade above the circlet maintained the folds in position and prevented them from slipping down. But it did not cover the whole crown of the head and therefore an ordinary four-cornered or dopalri cap was worn underneath. This was Lucknow's shimla as worn by Navab Sadat Ali Khan. It was probably copied from the pagris worn at the Hindu and Muslim courts of central India. These pagris were of fine material in different colours, many yards long and twisted in various styles by special techniques. Navab Sadat Ali Khan wore this shimla himself and also conferred it on distinguished members of the court and ministers.

When Ghazi ud Din Haidar was crowned king by the British, his crown was not traditionally Indian or Oriental but European in style. From that time onwards, the Lucknow rulers discarded the shimla and dastar, and with them all the princes, nobles and dignitaries bade farewell to their pagris. The princes wore crowns on special occasions, but in everyday life they wore *nukka dar* caps which were heavily embroidered in gold, and distinguished men of the city followed their example. However, it remained customary from the time of Ghazi ud Din Haidar until that of Amjad Ali Shah for officials, ministers and others to wear shimlas at court.

After Wajid Ali Shah designed his Alam Pasand topi, it was conferred upon those honoured with the title 'Daula', and they, as well as those others closely connected with the court, had to wear it in his presence. Courtiers of lesser standing, in charge of sections or departments and having the title of Darugha,[389] Superintendent, were granted the shimla. The rest were required to appear in court wearing some form of pagri. Those who did not were obliged[503] to remove their topis. The shimla was probably also worn at the Murshidabad court and because of its influence lawyers of the Calcutta High Court wore a similar head-dress fifty years ago. When I saw them they were scantier than those worn at the court of Avadh.

Thus, except for officials, all other distinguished people of the city completely gave up the pagri. Even so it remained a symbol of honour at the court and with the people. Even today all bridegrooms invariably wear a pagri, and among Lucknow nobility they wear a brocaded shimla.

The court also allotted different forms of pagris to the various grades of employees, which could be worn with the same ease as a cap and did not have to be wound each time they put them on. A white muslin pagri similar in appearance to the shimla was for clerks. Court messengers wore red pagris. Attendants had white pagris on to which a tassel in gold and silver thread was attached in front on the right-hand side. The pagris of the palanquin-bearers were like those of the messengers but had three silver fish stitched to the right-hand side, and were worn with their loose red coats of broadcloth. In addition, the servants of distinguished individuals and army officers wore distinctive pagris by which they could be recognized.

The ammamas of the religious leaders were most elegant and dignified. The style of dress of the Sunnis differs from that of the Shias. The dress of the Sunnis has evolved from Arab style, while that of the Shias follows the fashions of the Persian priesthood.

In the days of the Prophet, the headwear of the Arabs consisted of a small piece of cloth, without any shape or cut, which was wrapped around their heads. At the time of the Abbaside Caliphs, when the Caliphate was established in Iraq, the Arab leaders adopted Persian and Sassanid fashions. Their large elegant ammamas and cloaks date from this time, but one could scarcely call them Arab dress. The Sunni religious leaders in India in the early days adapted this clothing to the fashions of the Delhi court. They still wear this form of dress even though all other Muslims of India have given it up.

The religious leaders of the Firangi Mahal wear a simple ammama which they tie without any effort to form an arch over the forehead. They cover their bodies with an old-fashioned jama, which is now obsolete everywhere else, and their legs with wide trousers reaching slightly above the ankles. They also wear a thin muslin scarf round the neck. In this dress they come to lead Friday prayers. But at home they wear ordinary, simple dopalri or chau goshia caps, long kurtas which fasten in the centre, angarkhas, and wide-legged trousers. However, they are now beginning to adopt the styles of the prelates of Syria and Egypt. This style has also been favoured by Maulana Shibli Numani[506] for formal dress. These distinguished men used to wear traditional shoes, but now they wear the popular curled-toe shoe of Lucknow or Delhi.

The styles of the Shia religious leaders are entirely different. They wear a dopalri cap on their heads which differs from what is worn by the general public in that it is stitched from one side to the other instead of from back to front. Over this they wear a large ammama tied in the Persian fashion and long kurtas, which fasten near the left shoulder instead of the centre. In the old days the fastening was on both shoulders, but this style has now been discarded. Prelates who have been to Persia and Kerbala put a cape over their kurta which is called *aba* in Lucknow. They wear wide-legged trousers and usually the *kafsh* type of shoe, which I shall describe in a later chapter.

35

Forms of Trousers (Pyjamas)

On the lower part of the body the Arabs wore nothing but the *tahmat*. The Arab tahmat and the Hindu dhoti are both unstitched, thin pieces of material like sheets. They differ only in the way they are fastened. The tahmat is wound round and tied at the waist. The dhoti is worn in different ways by various groups of people in India: one end is always tucked in 'at the back, but some people wind the other end round the stomach and others tuck it in near the navel and let it hang down in front in folds. Later on an improvement was made in the Arab tahmat and the two ends were sewn together and fastened at the waist, enabling the legs to be passed through.

At the dawn of Islam and for some time before that, this had been the lower garment of all Arabs. The upper-class Arabs showed their pride and arrogance by wearing their tahmats very long and covering their feet so that the ends trailed on the ground as they walked. This practice was forbidden by Islam because those who followed this fashion considered others to be beneath them. Religious leaders decreed that no form of legwear should come below the ankles. Pyjamas did not exist in those days, but they were later included under

19 Ghazi ud Din Haidar entertaining Lord and Lady Moira to a banquet. Gouache by a Lucknow artist, 1814

20 Nasir ud Din Haidar at table with a British officer and lady. Gouache by a Lucknow artist, 1831

21 Wajid Ali Shah in exile at Matiya Burj, Calcutta. Oil
painting by a Bengali artist

22 Maulana Abdul Halim Sharar.
Oil painting

23 Mir Anis. A recent family
portrait by L.Calaora, based on
earlier portraits

24 Centre: a name of Allah in Tughra style. Border: verses from the Quran in Naskh script by the Lucknow calligrapher S. Najmul Hasan, 1974

25 *Bismillah* written in Tughra in the shape of a falcon. Calligrapher and place of origin unknown

26 Part of a prayer relating to Ali in Qata style; Nastaliq script by the above Lucknow calligrapher, 1974

this ruling. In any case long leg-coverings were never related in India to such upper-class arrogance.

Pyjamas were introduced from other countries at the time of the Prophet. Later they became the dress of the Baghdad court. Arabs who left Arabia and settled in other countries took the style with them. In India, before the Muslims, the dhoti was the only form of leg-covering. Muslim conquerors introduced pyjamas, although there were also some devout religious leaders who came to India wearing tahmats. The tahmat appealed to orthodox taste, and became the special garb of devout Muslims and students of religion. Pyjamas, however, became the standard dress of Muslims and Hindus.

The original Muslim pyjamas were probably short and narrow at the bottom like the present *sharai* pyjamas worn by pious Sunni Muslims. They were worn in Baghdad, then became known in Persia and Turkey, and constituted the leg covering of the Muslims when they came to India. Later in India these pyjamas became tighter at the calves but the width at the hip remained much the same. Still later on, though they became longer, they did not reach beyond the ankles. This fashion prevailed in Delhi and the rest of India at the time of the Mughals. Although ordinary Muslims used to wear dhotis because of Hindu influence, upper-class Hindus wore pyjamas in society even if they dressed in dhotis at home.

In those days there were two completely different styles of pyjamas in Kabul and Qandhar. The people of Kabul wore them tight around the legs and so loose round the hips that the lower part of the body seemed to be enclosed in a large balloon. It took one or even two rolls of material to make up a pair of these pyjamas. This style still exists in Afghanistan. In contrast, the hips of the Qandhar pyjamas were not very loose but the bottom hems on each leg were so wide that if the wearer did not tuck them up or hold them with his hands he found it difficult to walk.

Many Qandharis came to the Delhi court and enlisted in the army. Because these people were considered very brave, Indian soldiers started to adopt their dress and manners and the dandies of Delhi began to wear pyjamas with very wide legs. This style also became popular with youths of upper-class families. Among those who came to Lucknow were many who adhered to their conventional style, but there were also many who preferred this fashionable dress.

In Lucknow these pyjamas became even wider. One cannot trace them at the time of Shuja ud Daula, Asaf ud Daula and Sadat Ali Khan, but it appears that in the days of Ghazi ud Din Haidar and his son Nasir ud Din Haidar, with other changes in dress and social customs, a new pyjama form was evolved from this dandy style which was neither very wide at the hips nor so tight at the bottom. This new fashion was light and practical and eminently suitable for the Indian climate. As a result, except for the few dandies, it became widely popular.

At that time in Lucknow there were only these two types of pyjamas. Nasir ud Din Haidar adopted the dandy's type, but he was also fond of British clothes, which he wore as well. He saw in the wide Indian pyjamas, which are called *gharara*[507] pyjamas in the Panjab, a resemblance to a British lady's evening gown, and liked them so much that he made the Begams of the palace wear them. The fashion spread throughout the city.

Under Navabi rule the army of Avadh fought along with the British against the Sikhs during their conquest of the Panjab. The Sikhs wore tight pyjamas which were cut slant-wise and called *ghutannas*. Many people who went to the Panjab liked this style and had ghutannas made for themselves when they came home. The legs were very tight and straight and ended with many folds at the ankles. Later they came to be known as *churidar* pyjamas.

These three types of pyjamas were current in Lucknow at the beginning of the British era. But among men, with the decline of the dandies and others who carried arms, the very loose, baggy style disappeared. Thanks to Nasir ud Din Haidar women adopted this style and still wear them. The remaining two types were the wide kind and the ghutanna, though a few devout Sunnis continued to wear the sharai pyjamas. During the British era, though the shape and style of pyjamas remained the same, people totally discarded satin and the ornately embroidered or coloured cotton material. Later a fashion became current in the Aligarh College for pyjamas modelled on English trousers. They are neither too tight nor too loose and are particularly popular with those who have had a British education. However, those who have become completely Anglicized have given up this kind of dress altogether in favour of British coats and trousers.

36

Footwear and Female Fashion

In the cold weather it was the fashion to wear over angarkha and chapkan the *doshala*, a shawl, such as used to be presented by the royal court as the khilat. Woollen scarves were also frequently worn. Both these garments came to Lucknow from Delhi, but the scarves were more often seen in Lucknow. In the hot weather embroidered muslin scarves were worn, and these were part of the dress of all elegant people. They covered their heads with chau goshia topis of chikan work, their bodies with angarkhas, their legs with wide pyjamas, and over their shoulders they draped scarves of light muslin or tulle. This was the accepted fashion of the upper classes and elegant people in Lucknow.

Before the Muslims, shoes were never worn in India because leather was repugnant to Hindus for religious reasons.[508] Wooden sandals were worn by all, including rajas. They are still worn by religious mendicants, devout rishis and some others. Along with all their other apparel, Muslims brought leather shoes to India.

Among the Arabs, the first Muslim shoe was merely a leather sole fastened by straps or laces. Then came the leather socks of the Persians and styles that dated back to the Romans. Later, when the Arab court was established in Syria and Iraq, the wearing of leather shoes commenced. These shoes were just simple footwear with soles, and it was this which the Muslims wore when they first came to India.

It can be seen from paintings that the nobles and kings of Delhi in ancient times used to wear shoes similar to *kafsh*, the Persian-type high-heeled shoes. Later in Delhi the *charhvan* shoe was designed. In this model the foot was covered from toe to heel, leaving the top exposed. There was a curling tongue fixed at the toe. This became known as the Delhi shoe and was much worn until about fifty years ago. After this the *salim shahi* shoe was designed, probably at the time of Jahangir (also known as Salim). It had a toe-cap which curled up at the end and was later decorated with genuine gold and silver thread. This decorative work was common to both the Delhi shoe and the salim shahi, but the latter became more popular and eventually replaced the Delhi shoe. This shoe is still popular at a time when British fashions have turned people from our traditional taste in dress.

During the rule of the Navabs in Lucknow, a new type of shoe known as *khurd nau* with a short toe-cap was designed which became a favourite of the people. The curled-up ends of the Delhi shoe and the salim shahi were sewn on to it so that only a small prominence remained. These shoes were made of very fine red kid and because of the general taste for daintiness some shoe-makers would produce them exceptionally light in weight. However, the same shoe when made for the masses and villagers weighed up to two or three pounds and became even heavier with the application of mustard oil.[509]

Attention was then paid to the appearance of khurd nau shoes. For the dry season they were made of brocaded velvet and for the rainy season of shagreen. There is no doubt that brocaded shoes are extremely dainty and pleasing. Shagreen is bluish green in colour and is made from the hide of a horse or a donkey. Little nodules are made to project from it. It has the quality of never changing its colour or appearance however wet it may get in the rain. The art of making shagreen did not originate in Lucknow, but here many workshops were set up and skills and techniques were greatly improved.

Still more efforts were made to beautify shoes. They were adorned with patterns in gold and silver thread and decorated with brocade tassels. Later, when these shoes became popular, embroidery made with expensive materials was used and shoes were produced at a low price and still had a very colourful appearance.

Along with this the *ghatela* shoe, on the lines of the Persian-style kafsh, was common in Lucknow and was worn by prominent noblemen and the élite. It was in fact the old Indian shoe and the Hyderabad *chappals* and other local shoes are copied from it. It is the shoe that was seen on the feet of courtiers and leading men of the country in bygone days. In Lucknow, the toe of the ghatela shoe, instead of being short, became long and was shaped like an elephant's trunk, curving over the feet in a large spiral. But after the *chaharvan*, or Delhi shoe, became fashionable, the ghatela shoe was worn only by women. The kafsh still exists in its original form and is worn by the devout Shia religious leaders.

The ghatelas and kafshs, with their embroidery, led to two specialized trades which many Lucknow Muslims depended on for their livelihood. The fraternity of Muslim shoemakers would make only ghatelas and considered the production of any other form of shoe beneath their dignity. They were a large, prosperous community of good Muslims who wore white clothes and were in a better position than others of their class. However, when fashions changed, women, following the example of men, completely discarded the ghatela and now this shoe can rarely be found. In the bazaars one will be lucky to find one or two pairs of poor quality, dusty and neglected. As a result most of these shoemakers have gone out of business. Those who survive, though frustrated and reduced to poverty, will not agree to produce modern slippers and shoes to improve their situation.

The second group of artisans connected with shoe-making were those who made *aughi*, embroidery in gold, silver and sometimes coloured threads. The aughi work of Lucknow was so delicate and beautifully done that it could not be equalled elsewhere. There was much demand for it and a large section of the community earned their living from it.

When ghatela shoes were abandoned, both of these groups suffered. Elite women had previously adopted *tat bani* (brocaded) shoes in place of ghatelas. Then they wore leather shoes without laces which could be pulled on and off. Now 'pump' shoes are the fashion and in households which have become completely Westernized women have started to wear all kinds of European shoes.

It appears appropriate that at this point I should describe the clothes worn by women and then conclude my dissertation on dress.

In India the ancient apparel of women was simply a long unstitched sheet which was tied at the waist and worn over the shoulders or the head. With it a garment was worn from early Hindu days which in north India was called *ungia* and in the south was known as *choli*. This garment is said to have existed in the days of Sri Krishna. Later the ungia and the choli became differentiated. In the choli of the south a wide band of cloth was passed from the back to the front and knotted between the breasts so that whilst covered, they were scarcely prominent. The ungia of the north had two receptacles fitting the breasts, which were sewn together with a hem of two or three inches and fastened at the back. It was attached to two half-length sleeves and the garment was put on by passing the arms through the sleeves. Unlike the choli, the ungia gave prominence to the breasts.

This was the old Hindu dress and I do not know what changes and improvements were made in it with the passage of time. At first sight the ungia appears to be the more recent development.

Beyond this there seem to have been no changes in women's dress in the Hindu era. Muslims introduced stitched clothing, kurtas and pyjamas. When they came to India, Muslim women wore wide, loose Persian pyjamas which were gathered and fastened round the ankles. Later the hems became narrow and the legs tight at the extremities but the body remained loose. Gradually it became the fashion to have them so tight that the extremities had to be sewn round the legs after the pyjamas had been put on and unstitched before they could be taken off.

The early dress of Muslim ladies in Lucknow was pyjamas which were very tight at the hems, tight-fitting ungia over the breasts with half sleeves and a kurta covering the lower front and the back. This had no sleeves, did not cover the breasts and was cut low in front below the ungia. The front and back were kept in place by two long straps hanging from the shoulders. Over this was a *duppata*, a light mantle three yards long, which was at first draped over the head but later only hung across the shoulders.

The Indian climate and the desire for elegance led to all these clothes becoming gradually lighter and shorter. Ungias of fine silk and mantles of crêpe became the fashion for élite women. At the time of Nasir ud Din Haidar ghutannas went out of fashion and in their stead women wore loose, wide pyjamas tied at the waist and attractively draped in front below the navel in such a manner that the pyjama hems should not be soiled by touching the ground. Towards the end of the Navabi rule a *shaluka*, a short-sleeved, tight blouse, was worn. This was first worn over the ungia in place of the kurta and eventually did away with the necessity for the ungia. But this dress proved inadequate as it was made of a very fine material and especially as the arms were left bare: it was eventually replaced by a loose kurta. However, all these garments have one by one been superseded by British-style jackets and blouses.

At present, because of the influence of other regions in India, some Muslim women have begun to think saris the most attractive form of dress, and a large number have discarded their old fashions and taken to saris. It is generally said that this is the most simple form of garment. Although I am not against women trying out various forms of new clothing to make themselves attractive to their husbands, I am extremely averse to their completely abandoning their traditional fashions and thus giving up their social identity. The sari is an untailored garment and a relic of primitive times. No doubt simplicity is attractive, but it must adhere to certain patterns and embellishments in order to serve any purpose, otherwise the simplest thing would be to remain nude. Human nature evolves fashion for its diversion and I fail to understand the special beauty of a sari.[510]

Just as a man may become bored by a most beautiful wife and be attracted by other young women, so young men seem to become tired of the fashions of their own women and develop a strong fancy for the fashions of others. But they should realize that just as they have developed this fancy, young men of other races find grace and attraction in the dress of their women. It is because of sexual impulse that they find the clothing of other women more attractive, and this is at the root of the controversy as to what is suitable apparel for Indian Muslim women.

This would concern me if it were connected with improvements in social conditions for women. Actually it has arisen from the same mentality as that which led our young men to adopt Western coats and trousers and decorate their heads with hats and in general to copy Western ways blindly. Similarly they would like their women to adopt British clothing. It seems quite useless to say anything about it. Until British skirts and bonnets are worn our social reformers and so-called leaders of fashion will have no peace.

37

Winter Clothing, New Fashions and Jewelry

Continuous improvements were made in Lucknow in the design and fashioning of different types of clothing. As India is a hot country, poor people wear only sufficient clothing to cover what is essential and leave the rest of their bodies uncovered. This is not only because of their poverty and lack of interest, but because of the climate. For the same reason in the Delhi court light and airy garments were preferred to thick, heavy clothing. In Lucknow especially, because there was little military activity or even thought of war, men entered upon lives of luxury and spent so much time in the society of women that they became affected by women's fashions. They introduced into their style and clothing a type of finery and frippery that was essentially feminine.

This was particularly so from the time when the local rulers gave up the title of Navab and assumed that of King. Members of the Nishapur families, as well as that of Salar Jang, who received considerable vasiqa, became completely stay-at-home and had no other society than that of women. The inevitable result was that not only did their style and clothing acquire a female element, but they even adopted feminine mannerisms. As they were considered leaders of fashion in the city, most other people followed their example. Unlike the élite in other regions, it became the fashion for them to part their hair in the centre, wear topis embroided with gold and silver, dress their hair in waves over their foreheads, have betel leaf in their mouths and lac dye on their lips. They wore tight angarkhas with three jabots and below these tight silken pyjamas. They covered their hands with henna[511] and wore embroidered shoes. In the cold weather, in place of angarkhas they wore colourful coats of brocade or velvet padded with cotton.

In the winter some of the élite usually wore qabas made of shawl cloth:[512] shawls and embroidered, woollen square scarves were universally popular. The kind of *doshala*[513] [brocaded shawl] that can still be seen in Lucknow cannot be found even in Kashmir nowadays, let alone in any other region. The enthusiasm for shawls reached such a pitch that many shawl-makers and thousands of darners and shawl-washers left their homes in Kashmir and became domiciled in Lucknow, although there is little trace of them now after fifty years.

The Muharram is a very important occasion in Lucknow. Special clothing and jewelry appropriate to express grief and mourning were created for it. Black and blue are the colours of affliction—also green, because in the days of the Abbaside court the Fatimide colour was green rather than black. Even today in Persia and India, some Fatimides display the old Saiyyid style with their green ammamas. Therefore women's dress for Muharram was made up in green, blue and black, as well as yellow, which for some reason was also included: red was prohibited. Jewelry was not worn. Even bangles were discarded and in their place black or green silk bracelets adorned the wrists. Black or green pendant earrings of silk were designed, which were made with more delicacy than gold and silver jewelry.

Apart from Muharram, innovations were continually being made in women's clothing in Lucknow at every season and period. Fifty years ago it was generally agreed that Lucknow was the Paris of the East. Today many people who love simplicity and reject the world of fashion object to this show and display, but they do not realize that at any court or in any city where culture is on the advance, practices of this kind always evolve and though nonsensical and superfluous from a philosophical point of view, they are considered of the utmost importance in cultured circles.

If the influence of women's styles on men's clothing had been confined to grace and colour it would have been all right, but in Lucknow the only difference between the padded coats, wraps and pyjamas of husband and wife was the woman's gold embroidered edging, lace and jewelry. Men wore gay, coloured silk clothing without any edging or lace. After the Mutiny, owing to the influence of the British, the taste for dress of this sort decreased and is rarely seen nowadays.

Just as there were special styles of dress for the various classes of male servants, each class of female servants had their special dress. The butlers, coachmen and grooms of the British are dressed in different uniforms, but these uniforms cannot be said to be their normal clothing which they wear at home. However, the special clothing assigned to male and female servants in Lucknow society and to indoor and outdoor employees became their everyday apparel. The watchmen at the gates, the caretakers, the messengers, all had special and distinctive clothing and so had superintendents, seamstresses and water-drawers in the women's quarters. This was so specific that one could see at a distance that a woman was a superintendent, a seamstress or a palanquin-bearer, and the strange thing was that their dress had nothing of the appearance of a uniform. The personal servants, valets and ladies' maids wore the same kind of clothing as their masters and mistresses because they would wear their employers' cast-off clothes.

After dress, the most important thing for a woman is jewelry, which she considers to be her wealth and inheritance. In most provinces in India, clumsy, heavy jewelry is more commonly worn as being more valuable, and this desire for heavy jewelry is increasing in the rural parts of Avadh as well as in most towns in India. When noble ladies came from Delhi to Lucknow they wore the jewelry that was common throughout India. However, in accordance with the new tastes that developed in Lucknow in all walks of life, the fashion for jewelry was for delicacy and finesse. Jewelry started to become lighter, elegant and exquisite. In recent times it became the fashion for élite ladies to wear simple dresses without decoration and to content themselves with one or two pieces of jewelry which were light and delicate but valuable. If they wore several pieces on their necks, noses and ears, they were very small. This jewelry made in Lucknow was more exquisite and delicate than could be found in any other place.

The *nath* [gold ring habitually worn in Lucknow on the left nostril], set with precious stones, has since Hindu times been considered an important adornment and a symbol of marriage. The idea was adopted by Muslims and village women today wear heavy rings weighing up to four or five tolas. In consequence the nostrils often split but the women have them re-pierced so that the nose should not lack a ring. Lucknow women discarded naths and replaced them by *kils*, jewel-studded gold pins worn on the side of the nostril, a very delicate and attractive piece of jewelry. Because of the desire for daintiness the goldsmiths of Lucknow fashioned these pins in such a manner that no other jewellers could imitate them.

For the last twenty-five or thirty years the fashion for wearing the *bulaq*, a tiny gold pendant set with precious stones, also worn between the nostrils, has greatly increased. Although this is not a particularly pleasing piece of jewelry, its small size has made it very popular.

At present, because of easy contact between cities, the craft of making jewelry has improved everywhere and different places have become noted for making particular types of ornaments. Before the advent of the railway (about 1843) had effected this facility of communication, one could not find better goldsmiths or jewellers than existed in Lucknow. Now however many cities are superior. Delhi in particular excels all cities in India in making beautiful ornaments of beaten silver work. Even so, refined people from many regions prefer the jewelry and silver utensils produced in Lucknow.

38

The Building of Houses

I shall now take stock of matters relating to Indian society and social etiquette, and consider how certain styles and habits were adapted and given special colour by Lucknow society.

In every society social intercourse generates a distinctive culture—associated with appearances, style of living, ethics, customs, etiquette, conversation, humour, houses, furniture and other elements that follow from these—that makes that society what it is. Every group and class of people and every town and city develops in its own way, and if one looks around the world one will see that every society has its own specialities and peculiarities. But in places where an esteemed court has been established and learning and literature are progressing, that culture holds sway over a larger part of the country and its towns and cities, and becomes a source and model for social mannerisms and etiquette.

In India the real centre of culture, refinement and polite society was certainly Delhi and the whole of India was subservient to it. For centuries the city had been India's seat of government and learning and the governors of Provinces were chosen from the ranks of the élite. In comparison to it, Lucknow has no special claim to distinction, but if Lucknow can be mentioned in this respect it is because in the last century, owing to the course of events, the mass of Delhi society transferred itself here. Nobles, scholars, poets, devout and pious men, all came to Lucknow. A strange thing is that the Delhi social community that became established in Avadh was confined to people of Delhi alone. There were no outsiders and there was no place in it even for the most honoured of old Lucknow residents.

Therefore Lucknow society of the last century is in reality Delhi society and constitutes its final phase. There developed two forms of Delhi culture at this time, one consisting of those who remained in Delhi, and the other of those who came to Lucknow. However, in the century prior to the end of Delhi's sultanate, those who remained in Delhi, owing to the decay of the Mughal court and the lack of patronage, had little chance of achieving any progress. The culture of Lucknow was on the advance whereas that of Delhi remained stationary.

In Delhi cultured life gradually disappeared owing to the ascendancy of uneducated and commercially-minded people and the departure of noble families to other parts of the country. Those who stayed on lived quietly at home in a state of isolation. The situation was just as it has been in recent times in Lucknow, when because of the influx of people from outside the area and the ruin of established élite families, the culture that developed here has been rapidly disappearing. But I am not concerned with the vulgarities adopted by the community, nor with the deterioration of cultural life that has taken place in Lucknow since the end of Navabi rule and that is on the increase. The things I should like to discuss are houses, furniture, social behaviour, etiquette, social gatherings and forms of greeting, everyday speech, wit, festive celebrations and mourning, and forms of religious assembly. I shall thereafter describe some objects essential for social intercourse.

Houses

In Delhi and Lucknow it was traditional to restrict outward pomp and ostentation to royal palaces and government buildings. The residences of wealthy men and merchants, however grand and spacious inside, had the outward appearance of ordinary houses. This was sound policy, for a house that was outwardly magnificent sometimes found favour with the King and its builder rarely got the chance to live in it. In addition, for a subject to build such a house was to show regal aspirations which were ascribed to insolence and rebellion and made it difficult for him to live in safety.

For this reason, except for tombs, you will see no elegant buildings of ancient times in Delhi that were built by nobles or rich merchants. It was the same in Lucknow, although in the days of Asaf ud Daula and Sadat Ali Khan a wealthy French merchant, Monsieur Martin, constructed some magnificent edifices. However, the reason for their construction was that they should find favour with the ruler and be sold to him. Of these buildings, one is La Martinière

College, which because of Sadat Ali Khan's sagacity, the State did not acquire. After Monsieur Martin, one of the local ministers, Raushan ud Daula, had a fine house built as his personal residence. It was confiscated by order of the monarchy. Because of this it fell into the hands of the British and was not handed over to Raushan ud Daula's heirs. But today it is still known as Raushan ud Daula's *kothi*[139] [residence].

The style of house in India is quite different from that of European houses. There is no necessity for courtyards in Europe because women are not confined to their homes and go out as men do. In contrast it is necessary for houses in India to have courtyards so that women may be able to enjoy fresh air within the perimeter of their own homes. A house is therefore normally constructed with a courtyard in the centre and the buildings around it. The main portion of the house takes up one side of this square and is approached through at least three and sometimes more arches constructed on pillars of brick and mortar. These are generally on the model of the architecture of Shahjahan, that is to say, large archways formed of small curves, beautifully joined together. These arches usually surround two or three contiguous halls, with one at the rear forming a large room with a door. The floor of this room is raised waist-high and called *shahnashin*, the royal seat, and serves as the principal reception room. On both sides of these large halls are rooms, the ceilings of which are so lofty that two rooms, one on top of the other, could be constructed within them.

On each side of the courtyard are corridors and large and small rooms, which include kitchens, toilets, storerooms, stairs, wells and maids' quarters. Opposite to the main hall, if it is considered necessary and if funds permit, other wide, covered passages are erected like those of the main building. Doors are usually on the sides connecting with kitchens and with servants' quarters. These doors are concealed by walls a little higher than a man's height so that the inside of the house remains unexposed.

In the houses of poor and middle-class people, instead of an approach by brick or concrete archways, there are wooden doors which enclose the main section of the house, opposite which there are sometimes other halls or double halls. In the better class of these houses there are rooms and halls on all four sides, each of which has a doorway leading to storerooms. One door leads to the outside.

This was the usual plan for houses. Some houses and their basements[514] were so skilfully planned that one is surprised at how much could be accommodated in such a small space.

If one looks into the history of architecture one will find that buildings and homes were at first built low. It was much later that lofty and strong houses were built, but the design remained simple. Then the idea arose of adding beauty by carving patterns and designs on walls and archways. Later, mosaic was introduced with its wonderful colouring. But the outer walls containing the large halls and reception rooms always remained thick.

The real accomplishment of Indian architecture was to create the maximum amount of accommodation in a limited space, like a tailor who makes the most of his material when cutting out clothes. This skill was first developed in Delhi, from where it spread to other regions. In Lucknow it reached a higher degree of perfection than anywhere else.

Nowadays there are some expert architects who have produced many fine buildings. They will create the most beautiful and elegant edifices which are magnificent to look at, but they cannot rival the old experts in their skill in building on a very small plot a fine house which contained so many halls, rooms, inside rooms and storerooms, and had inner walls so thin and light and at the same time so strong that they appeared to be wooden screens rather than brick and mortar.

This speciality of Lucknow architecture originated at the time of the former courts. But now in the British era, as this skill is not appreciated, it is dying out. The old experts have disappeared and even if one or two still remain they are not highly esteemed.

From early times there has always been a distinct difference between Hindu and Muslim houses and this exists to this day. In Hindu houses the courtyards are small and the building is constructed without regard to whether or not air and light will get in. In contrast to this, Muslims like bright, open houses and their buildings are so designed that there is no impediment to the passage of light and air.

Expert builders of earlier days also used to make delicate and colourful designs in relief on doors and arches and on the walls of rooms and halls. At present the art of painting is making advances but the craft of making designs in relief is disappearing because of the contemporary taste for simplicity. The few remaining craftsmen-builders, along with their own trade in general, have taken to painting murals, for which they show praiseworthy aptitude.

Skill in craftsmanship was by no means confined to builders. Take carpenters, for instance. Although they may not have been able to make particularly good tables, chairs, cupboards or railway carriages, they could carve dainty and intricate designs on pillars, arches and door frames, which would be difficult to reproduce in these days.

39

Domestic Furnishings

Our next concern is furniture, which comprises all the articles in a home, either for use or for decoration. In early times there were no tables and chairs in India. There were *takhats*,[515] low wooden platforms, and *palangris*,[516] low beds, which were placed on the takhats. The beds of the poor and middle-class were made of *ban*, rope of woven rush-grass, and those of the rich of woven *nivar*, broad bands of canvas tape.

Orderly homes were well-swept, their walls whitewashed, and their ceilings covered with white ceiling-cloth with tucked fringes on all four sides. In a room or hall or in the courtyard a few takhats, usually four, were put together, with *daris*,[517] cotton mats, over them. They were covered with a snow-white sheet, so carefully spread and stretched that there was never the sign of a crease. At all four corners of the takhat, dome-shaped marble weights were placed to prevent the sheets from being blown about in the wind or creasing. In later days there was a *farshi pankha*,[518] a large fan, but before this became popular there were hand fans of many types and designs according to the status of the household.

On the takhat one section was designed as the seat of honour. An elegant, beautiful bed was placed near it. The bed was made in this way: nivar was stretched across the frame, which was covered with a dari in the hot weather and a quilt in the cold weather, and this was in turn covered by a bright-coloured sheet. In royal or élite households a tucked fringe was stitched to the edges of the sheet, which hung nearly to the ground on all sides, giving the bed a very impressive appearance. The bedding was tied to the four legs of the bed with an elegantly tied strip of coloured silk to prevent the bed-clothes being disturbed while the occupant slept.

Covering the whole width of the head of the bed were four slender and very soft oblong pillows. These pillows were generally made of red tulle and had very fine muslin pillow-cases through which the bright red colour of the pillows could be seen. The pillows were placed one on top of the other in layers. Then on top of them were two tiny 'flower pillows' made of the same material which supported the cheeks on either side: these 'flower' pillows were no larger than the palm of one's hand. Lower down on each side of the bed were two small round cushions which supported the thighs. Depending on the season, there was a *dulai*, thin, embroidered cotton sheet, a *razai*, light quilt, or a *lihaf*, heavy quilt, over the bed, and in the day-time when no one was sleeping on it a bedspread was placed over it.

On the takhat in front of the bed a carpet was spread to mark the seat of honour. On this carpet and touching the bed was a *gau*, large barrel-shaped cushion, which for everyday use had a white cover but on important occasions was encased in costly silken and sometimes gold- and silver-embroidered covers. If there was no bed on the takhat a seat of honour was marked by a carpet with a gau upon it.

Although there were some paintings or prints on the walls, they were much less in evidence than they are today. In their place beautifully decorated qatat were framed and hung. In those days noblemen were so eager to obtain these qatat that calligraphists would earn their livings by making them.

In addition to takhats, stools of rush-grass and cane were used in the court-yards, the antechambers and outdoors. One can see these even today, but at that time no upper-class household was without them. They were made of thin bamboo sticks and rush-grass rope and in some houses the seats were covered with dried goatskins with the hair still on.

Except for the rich who had separate houses for women and men, most middle-class people and all the others had only one house. Nowadays efforts are made for each house to have an outer room by the door for the entertainment of male guests, but in those days stools were placed on the porch for this purpose. If there was no room on the porch, they were placed outside the door and no one saw any harm in it.

Paper posies were usually placed in niches in the walls of rooms and halls for decorative purposes. Curtains of cloth were generally thought necessary for the arches in corridors. Now bamboo, rush-grass or jute curtains are preferred, but at one time they were looked down upon. The tulle or linen curtains lined with cotton which were used were drawn only when necessary. Similar curtains were hung over the outer doors of the women's apartments and a maidservant or palanquin-bearer could usually be seen standing close by.

I have already discussed dress, but I should like to add here that the better class of people did not consider complete dress essential at all times. Inside or in the precincts of their houses they saw no harm in being practically naked and wearing only a *gharqi*, a long loin-cloth. This gharqi, like a pair of shorts, left the legs bare. At present people think it necessary to wear a vest, shirt and trousers in their houses, but in the past it was apparently unfashionable to wear so many clothes. They put on only angarkhas and pyjamas when they left their houses and for this reason one wash lasted for months and the clothes always looked as if they had recently been laundered. It was the custom that when angarkhas were delivered by the washermen, their edgings, tailpieces and sleeves were specially crimped and the marks of this crimping remained for a long time.

The amount of clothes worn by women was the same whether in their own houses or when they went to visit friends. The only difference was that they wore their finest clothes when going out and simple garments at home. Both men and women wore their most elegant clothes only at social gatherings, so that these were always bright and sparkling.

40

Hair Fashions, Etiquette and Courtesans

From ancient times it has been the practice of Muslim men not to cut their hair short, to clip their moustaches, and to keep their beards trim and rounded. Pious men and religious leaders, in accordance with the Prophet's ordinance, used to let their beards grow and exaggerated the clipping of their moustaches to the extent that hardly anything remained of them. But the style for noblemen and upper-class people was to provide a frame for the beard by shaving the lower throat and the cheek-bones and to keep the beard rounded and trimmed. Emperor Akbar was the first to relinquish his beard, and Jahangir followed his example. Even though some of Akbar's and Jahangir's courtiers may have been influenced by them, Muslim nobles as a rule adhered to the traditional style.

After the court was established in Lucknow, beards began to get shorter and shorter and eventually they disappeared from most men's cheeks. This was probably brought about by the influence of Persians at the court. In Persia from the time of the Safavi dynasty, kings and nobles attached less importance to beards than had been known since the advent of Islam. Although in Muslim tradition it was a punishment or an act of humiliation for someone's beard and moustache to be cut off, in Persia not to wear a beard was considered a sign of authority and power. The first member of the Nishapur family in Lucknow, Navab Burhan ul Mulk, wore a short, trimmed beard. Shuja ud Daula had no beard at all and following him all the nobles and kings of Lucknow had their beards shaved off. The inevitable result was that most Shias abandoned the custom of wearing beards. Later on, many Sunnis also had their beards clipped or shaved off. After the shaving of beards had become popular many new styles came into being. Some wore long thick sideburns below the ears and some grew thick hair on the cheeks. Inhabitants of towns in the neighbourhood of Lucknow and some Sunnis in the city itself adopted the fashion of wearing beards like Rajputs and Hindu warriors, that is, they were parted at the chin with hair carried up on either side of the ears. To keep their beards in position they would tie them up with a cloth for hours on end. They would also comb up their moustaches to match the beard and these in their turn had to be tied in place. This was considered throughout India to be a military style and a sign of bravery.

At the time of the Prophet, the hair was usually worn long and shaved or cut off at times of Haj.[381] Shortly after the birth of Islam, the usual fashion among Arabs was to have their hair shaved off and this custom seems to have prevailed with the Persians as well. When Muslims first came to India, they followed this practice and wore ammamas on their heads. However, Hindus would grow their hair and this appealed to the Muslims. Consequently, except for religious leaders, devout men, patriarchs and Sufis, the practice for upper-class and fashionable people in Delhi was to let their hair grow down over their ears. Of course there were also dandies who were always trying out new hair styles.

Nobles from Delhi came to Lucknow with this hair style, but here they developed more elaborate taste. They started to comb their hair with great care and like women wore it in waves over their foreheads. Such styles were evolved that adolescent youths looked as attractive as women. Then shortly afterwards when women copied the British fashion of combing their hair back and leaving the forehead bare, some men followed this example. Now that British fashions and styles have begun to be adopted, people in Lucknow, as in the whole of India, have their hair cut like the British and beards are no longer worn.

Women's styles in dressing their hair were probably the same in Lucknow as in Delhi. But here at the time of the monarchy, brides and women who took pride in their appearance used to plait their hair at the back from the top to the waist round thick swathes of coloured fabric, generally red. On ceremonial occasions they used silver brocade, which gave the impression that the whole plait was made of silver. The hair was waved on both sides of the forehead, and below the parting the forehead was decorated with various patterns made with gold and silver powder.

Henna was used on the hands and feet of women and some dissolute men started to use it as well. Seeing this, people from other places began to consider the men of Lucknow effeminate.

I shall now turn to another constituent of social life, etiquette. In this connection the citizens of Lucknow achieved particular distinction and this deserves special attention. Oriental culture reached its zenith in Lucknow, and nowhere else were the rules of polite society so strictly adhered to.

To be cultured is to follow certain formalities considered by human beings as evidence of refinement. Nowadays we often hear it said that the formalities of society are pointless affectation. But this is wrong. If it were the case, dress and all patterns of everyday life would also be useless affectation and all matters concerned with living in a community could be regarded as hypocrisy. It is all a matter of training, and those who know nothing of culture fail to appreciate it. They say that they do not understand all the display shown by city dwellers and persons of refinement, but when one gives the matter thought, humanity is all display. To dress well, to have nice things, to eat well and to accomplish anything with competence, is all display.

The primary consideration in etiquette is to give preference to others over one's own gains and satisfactions and put oneself in the second place. To stand up in order to show respect for someone, to give him the seat of honour, to sit with him respectfully, listen to him attentively and answer him with humility are all actions by which one tends to treat another as a superior. In the days of the monarchy in Lucknow, the extent to which these actions were practised by refined, well-bred people was unequalled anywhere else.

When social etiquette of this sort becomes second nature it engenders self-denial in a human being, so that in addition to being very gracious with his friends he is always ready to help them in any way he can. At the time of the monarchy in Lucknow there was such perfection in this that people quietly took responsibility for the maintenance of friends who had no means of support. Because of the unostentatious way the help was given, the latter were able to wear white clothes and move with the élite as equals, without any feeling of inferiority. There were scores of people in this situation in Lucknow who had suddenly lost their means of support at the collapse of the monarchy.

This altruism of the rich, in the way they showed regard for others and lavished generosity on them without a thought that they were conferring a favour, displayed their nobility and became the model for social etiquette. Wealthy merchants and other rich people all over the world give much money to deserving people, but their actions indicate that their charity is not selfless. In contrast to this, the manner in which help was given to friends and support to distressed gentlemen and their families in Lucknow was such that no one saw any difference between those who gave and those who received.

With the collapse of the monarchy very rich men became penniless and the class which had been secretly maintained by them faced starvation. But the formerly wealthy retained their unselfish character, which had become part of their nature, and many continued to hold out hopes of hospitality. However, on becoming their guests, distressed people found that these hopes could not be met. Many people called this hypocrisy. The sad thing was that it was not hypocrisy but an attempt somehow to maintain former values.

However, it cannot be denied that in the days of prosperity when most citizens were either of the nobility or supported by them, ideas of effort, toil and the value of time had no meaning in Lucknow society. The frivolous occupations they pursued led them further and further from the path of progress. Free from the worries of earning a livelihood, they did nothing except amuse themselves and turned to pigeon-flying, quail-fighting, dice-throwing, card games and chess, on which they spent most of their time and money. There were few noblemen who were not addicted to these idle pursuits and none who was not interested in them. No one thought of the future.

No town in the world is free from libertinism, but may God not allow the promiscuous and indiscriminate licentiousness of Europe to reach our towns. In Lucknow, association with courtesans started during the reign of Shuja ud Daula. It became fashionable for noblemen to associate with some bazaar beauty, either for pleasure or for social distinction. A cultivated man like Hakim Mahdi, who later became Vazir, owed his initial success to a courtesan named Piyaro, who had advanced her own money to enable him to make an offering to the ruler on his first appointment as Governor of a Province of Avadh. These absurdities went so far that it was said that until a person had association with courtesans he was not a polished man. This led the way to a deterioration of morals in Lucknow. At the present time there are still some courtesans with whom it is not considered reprehensible to associate, and whose houses one can enter openly and unabashed. Although these practices may have had a deteriorating effect on morals, at the same time manners and social finesse improved.[519]

Now we come to morality among women. I maintain, as a general rule, that the women of men who are addicted to adultery cannot themselves remain chaste. Even so, the morals of Lucknow women did not deteriorate as much as those of their men.

At one time the *charkha*[520] [spinning wheel] was the noble pursuit of élite women. With the advent of machinery, this pursuit became valueless. However, Lucknow women had given it up long before this, because they had considered it beneath their dignity. Instead they took to sewing, embroidery, the running and decorating of the house and supervising the maidservants. Ladies, because of household duties, did not have enough leisure to indulge in the pastimes and frivolities that occupied the time of their men. In fact, in those days men spent their time in amusements and merry-making. The running of the house and matters connected with it fell on the shoulders of the women. In wealthy households there were various types of maidservants to do all the work and the ladies were amused by domnis. In households where these were not regularly employed, a troupe would come with instruments and give a performance. Hundreds of such troupes materialized in the city. As far as I know their taste was coarse and association with them could not have had a good effect on genteel women, and like courtesans in the case of men, they were a bad influence. However, the most refined families did not associate with them and their ladies escaped this mischief and remained fine examples of good manners and morality.

The tradition of Lucknow women is to sacrifice everything for their husband. They consider their existence to be incorporated in his and do not hesitate for a moment to spend their own money on him if necessary. They may not be so

27 Lady seated against a cushion. Drawing by Miskin
Muhammad, Lucknow, 1770–80

28 Woman spinning cotton on a
charkha. Water-colour by a
Lucknow artist, about 1830

29 Courtesan Bi Haidar Jan.
Photograph

30   Lucknow miniature, 1760: ladies listening to the raga Madhu
     Madhvi, which excites the listeners and produces a storm

accomplished as some women elsewhere and may not be able to compare with them at housekeeping. They may be extravagant, wasteful and even self-indulgent, but they are unequalled in helping their husband and giving up their lives for him.[521]

41

More on Etiquette

In every civilized community there are special rules and principles of social behaviour which serve to indicate the refinement of that culture. Whether in centres of Christian culture like Paris, London and Berlin, or in refined Muslim centres such as Constantinople, Teheran and Shiraz, one can see how strict the upper classes are in their respective forms of social etiquette. In towns in India like Hyderabad, Bhopal or Rampur, where a court exists, or in other such places where it once existed, social etiquette is observed by all, both high and low. On the other hand in large industrial towns the rich and respected people show no trace of social graces and one will find no respect for conventions or consideration for people.

In the old days in Delhi, these social graces were certainly more pronounced than anywhere else because the court there was the largest and had been established for centuries. The patterns of social behaviour are laid down by those in authority, who prescribe how the lesser should behave towards the greater and the greater towards the lesser and how one should meet with an equal. But industrialization is an enemy to expressions of authority and observances of such etiquette. Preoccupation with business and the promotion of self-interest leave no place for self-denial, that is, giving one's time, money or skill to someone else for no particular gain, which is considered stupidity. Thus the culture of the gentry and élite cannot survive in a business society. The elegance of the former glorious Delhi courts was lost in this way, so that nothing remains of their old grandeur. The nobles of Delhi took refuge in Lucknow, and living here in congenial surroundings they continued their habitual rules of etiquette so that in a short time Lucknow became the main centre of culture and good manners in the whole of India. All refined men from other regions now follow the ways of the citizens of Lucknow. To give an example: when receiving people of different stations in life, whether one should go to the door to welcome them, whether one should stand up when they come in or half rise, or simply say, while remaining seated, 'Please come in', are all matters for personal decision, but the subtleties involved were better understood in Lucknow than anywhere else.

With an equal, you will show respect by standing up. You will vacate the seat of honour for him and until he seats himself you will remain standing.

You will then sit discreetly and respectfully next to him. You will look cheerful so that he doesn't feel ill at ease. If he gives you anything, you will accept it politely and pay your *taslim*[522] [respects]. You will take great care that you do not offend him in any way. If you should have to attend to some important matter, you will ask to be excused before doing so. If you have to get up and go somewhere, you will first ask his permission. If you go anywhere with him, you will keep behind and let him go before you. In accordance with correct etiquette, he will also insist that you should go first, and it may be said over and over again, 'Sir, you first'. If your companion refuses to agree and you precede him, thank him with taslim before going ahead, but be careful not to turn your back on him.

Many people laugh at these ceremonious manners and there is a proverbial joke in which two Lucknow citizens kept saying, 'After you'—'No, after you', and the train departed, leaving them standing on the platform. One cannot deny that to carry matters to such extremes can be harmful. But at the same time it shows that the good manners of Lucknow citizens were such that it never entered their heads that they were doing themselves any harm. A refined and well-bred individual will regard these practices as gems of deportment rather than as faults.

Nowadays in Lucknow as in all other towns tables, chairs and British furniture are used, but in former times people sat on the *farsh*[523] [carpet], which was costly and ornate according to the status of the householder. If an equal with whom you are not well acquainted, or an elderly or venerable person, came to the house, he was given the seat of honour with the *gau* behind him. Everyone else joined a large or small circle round him, according to the numbers present, and sat with him respectfully. Anyone to whom he spoke would join his hands together and answer with complete humility. It was considered a social misdemeanour to talk too much or to raise one's voice to a higher level than his.

If all present were equals and friends with similar tastes, there was a lack of ceremony, but even so they treated each other with respect. They would never think of turning their backs or doing anything to demean each other and would never forget to uphold the other's dignity. Servants could not sit on the carpet or in close proximity to it. In order to carry out orders they stood respectfully at some distance or waited away from view in some place within earshot. It was considered bad manners for them to stand too near or to talk unnecessarily.

When the servants brought in the *khas dan*[524] [betel box] or the *huqqa* [hookah], the host placed them in front of his friends with his own hands and they stood up and thanked him with taslim before accepting them. It was considered unsuitable for the young to be brought to informal gatherings of their elders. If for any reason they came, they bowed deferentially to those present and paid their respects with taslim. When the young came in, the conversation ceased to be free and easy and became more formal. As the young showed respect for their elders, so the elders gave consideration to the young and abandoned their informality.

It was not the custom in Lucknow with people who met frequently to go in for *musafiha*[525] [touching of hands]. One kissed the hand of a religious leader, and *muaneqa*[526] [embracing] was confined to those friends who had returned from a journey or those whom one had not seen for a long time.

When men entered women's apartments they always treated the women with respect. They were never in any way familiar with them or prolonged their visits to excess. Man and wife could be at ease with each other, but in the presence of older women of the household they had to drop this ease and behave formally. Well-bred brides in villages remained veiled in the presence of their husbands when in the company of other women until they had several children. It was not possible for a couple to approach each other in the presence of others. This was not the case in towns. Husband and wife would eat at the same dastar khwan but it was wrong for them not to behave formally even in the presence of maidservants.

Female gatherings, except in very wealthy households, had comparatively little ceremony. A certain amount of formality was observed with guests, but this was always accompanied by friendliness and warmth.

42

Social Gatherings and Forms of Greeting

It has not been the custom in India, as in Europe, Arabia and Persia, to form clubs and societies. In Europe there are clubs and societies, and Arabs, Persians and Turks have tea shops and coffee houses where people meet and exchange ideas. Wherever there are British people they will form a club to which they can go in their leisure time, read the papers and meet their friends. In the same way in any town where there is a sufficient number of Persians and Arabs, they will open up a tea shop or a coffee house where there will always be a group of them drinking tea, smoking huqqas, eating their food, chatting and joking.

It was not customary to have clubs or tea shops in India and it is not so today.[527] The British Government tried to arouse an interest in this and opened up tea shops in various towns at great expense but they had no success. About thirty-five years ago the late Mir Muhammad Husain, former Director of Agriculture and Commerce, before going to Hyderabad, opened a tea shop in the Chauk quarter of Lucknow with Government assistance. It was well furnished and provided every sort of liquid refreshment except liquors which are prohibited by religion. However, no one took any interest in it and eventually the Mir Sahib, having suffered financial loss, had to close it down.

The established custom here is that in every quarter or community some prosperous man makes arrangements for people to visit his house. At his personal expense he provides huqqas, betel leaf and other social facilities. His friends and those with similar tastes visit regularly and stay on for hours. Witticisms and pleasantries are exchanged and the guests are entertained with huqqas and betel leaf. The nature of these gatherings varies with the taste of its members. If they are interested in literature and language, the conversation is devoted to such things. If the members are scholars and men of erudition, they engage in learned discussions on abstruse subjects. If the company is composed of nobles the conversation turns to fashions, clothes, appurtenances of luxury, food and drink, and how they should be enjoyed with social grace and discretion. If the concourse consists of libertines, bazaar beauties will be in the company and one will witness dalliance and coquetry. One should remember that well-bred and chaste women are not able to take part in men's gatherings as they do in Europe,[528] so if you see any woman among a group of males you may be certain that she is a courtesan. Because well-bred and virtuous women associate with men in Europe, the standing and rank of prostitutes there has fallen so low in society that the door of no respectable household is open to them, neither can they set foot in clubs or societies of repute. In contrast, throughout India including Lucknow, some courtesans have achieved such status that they participate more or less as equals in the gatherings of refined and polished people. This state of affairs has progressed to the extent that some respected courtesans hold social gatherings, as described earlier, in their own houses, which well-bred people are not ashamed to attend. The houses of Chaudhrayan[427] Haidar Jan and some other courtesans of high status were the 'clubs' of genteel people. British influence has changed matters so that, although various new forms of social misdemeanour have come into being, people have begun to think it wrong to visit the houses of courtesans openly and enjoy their society.

Anyway, such houses and those of wealthy men were the Lucknow 'clubs'. It was and still is considered quite wrong to share expenses, or for the members of a circle to make contributions towards the cost of betel leaf, food or liquid refreshment. Dinners for which everyone contributed their share were considered by all to be a disgrace and contrary to decorum. All invitations whether for festive occasions or just for a friendly gathering emanated from one person. If anyone else was sufficiently well-off he could issue similar invitations, but he could not ask others to contribute a few rupees in order to join in.

People in Delhi who are connected with commerce collect subscriptions in order to arrange a party or an entertainment with dancing and singing. I am certain that this practice has evolved since the collapse of the sultanate, as a result of the commercial outlook.

The next important matter appertaining to social courtesy is salutation and greeting. The ancient, religious and simple form of Islamic salutation is *As Salam Alaik*, 'Peace be upon thee', or *As Salam Alaikum*, 'Peace be upon you', to several people. After making this salutation, in the morning, the Arabs say, *Subhakum Allah Bilkhair*, 'May God make the morning favourable to you.' If the meeting takes place in the evening, they say *Masakum Allah Bilkhair*, 'May God make the evening favourable to you.' These forms of greeting spread with the Arabs as far west as Andalusia and as far east as India. The Europeans learnt these salutations from them, as did the Iranians, Turks and Indians in the East. In Europe the essential Islamic salutation has been lost, and there remains only the benediction that followed it, like 'Good morning' and 'Good evening' in English and 'Bon matin', 'Bonjour' and 'Bonsoir' in

French. There is no doubt that these salutations were learnt from the Arab conquerors of Andalusia. In India and Persia, where it was the custom to show great respect for one's seniors and superiors, the simple words *As Salam Alaikum*, which signify equality, appeared improper and lacking in respect to the arrogant rich. Especially in the Mughal court, the crowned heads did away with many Islamic practices that interfered with the deference and subservience shown to them. They gave orders to their courtiers to stand before them with hands clasped and to bow in humility, just as a worshipper of God will stand before his maker. Following the example of the royal court, most nobles and wealthy men replaced *As Salam Alaikum* in their own ways and words like *taslim*, obeisance, *kornish*, adoration, *bandagi*, servitude, and *adab*, respect, came into use. Thanks to these self-glorious and God-forgetting Muslim nobles all these words are at present currently employed. In Arab countries no gesture except a smile accompanied the words 'As Salam Alaikum'. After the salutation there was a musafiha and as the hand was offered the words *Subhakum Allah Bilkhair* or *Masakum Allah Bilkhair* were uttered. When this Arab form of salutation was adopted in Europe, the head came to be slightly inclined while the words 'Good morning' were spoken and hands were shaken. On the other hand in India when uttering one of these greetings one places a hand on the forehead and bows almost as low as one would do in prayer. This bowing and putting the hand to the forehead are entirely due to Hindu influence. Both actions are tantamount to saying 'I bow to you and kiss the ground you stand on.'

As well as this, the court ordered the number of salutations that were to be made. Sometimes there were seven and sometimes three. When meeting older people or friends in the ordinary way one was sufficient. In Lucknow, the salutation of young people to their elders, or of persons of lesser rank to their superiors, was to use one of the above phrases and at the same time to raise the hand to the chest or bring it up to the face and slightly move it up and down several times. In this popular form of salutation the moving of the hand several times signifies many salutations, just as people sometimes use the plurals *taslimat* and *kornishat*, implying several salutations.

In Arabic the meaning of *taslim* is 'to offer a salam', and this was considered in Lucknow society to be more deferential than *As Salam Alaikum*. *Kornish* is a Turkish word introduced here by the Turkish conquerors. Its meaning is 'to bow whilst greeting', and therefore it carries the idea of bowing and kissing the ground or the feet. *Adab* is the plural of the word meaning 'respect'. Used as a greeting it conveys the sense of 'I am showing complete respect and deference.' *Bandagi* is the most debased and pagan of the words of greeting. The meaning of *bandagi* is worship. When used as a salutation, it can have no other sense than 'I offer you my worship', and this according to the Muslim faith can be said only to God.

In contrast to these Indian greetings, the simple translation of the words *As Salam Alaikum* used by the Arabs is 'May peace be with you', or in plain Urdu, 'May you be tranquil and safe', so that when you greet a person you are praying for his safety. In the Islamic faith the word *salam*, peace, is part of God's message to the Prophet, which he passed on to all Muslims and which they in their turn must pass on to all other Muslims till the Day of Judgment.

The word preceding *Salam* in *As Salam Alaikum* is the Arabic definite article and indicates that *Salam* refers to that message given by the Prophet.

The original Islamic *Salam* gives the idea of equality and is intended to engender love and brotherhood among all Muslims wherever they may be. But alas, they have discarded it and now our vain conceit makes us think that if an ordinary Muslim says *Salam Alaikum*, he is insulting us. Shia-Sunni differences have brought about a state of affairs where instead of uniting into one fraternity they prefer to remain separate. This applies not only to ordinary people: in recent times even the religious leaders of both factions encourage it. As a result, whereas in Arabia and Persia the greeting of both Shias and Sunnis was *As Salam Alaikum*, in India and especially in Lucknow the Shias have left *As Salam Alaikum* to the Sunnis and have appropriated for themselves the words *Salamun Alaikum*, although in prayers they still use the phrase *As Salam Alaik*.

Nevertheless the Arabic *Salam* is still used by devout people whether Sunni or Shia as having religious significance. In élite society *Adab*[529] and *Taslim* are the customary greetings. *Bandagi* is often heard also, but it is more commonly used by women.

In Lucknow society younger people will greet their seniors and the poor greet the rich by bowing respectfully and saying either *Taslim* or *Adab*. In answer the older person will say to the younger, 'Long be your life', 'May you grow strong', or 'May you be fortunate.' The rich just raise their hands to the poor without bowing and as they raise their hands will repeat the word *Taslim* or *Adab* or say *Bandagi*. Equals will both bow to each other and when in a gathering, stand up. After the salutation one usually says to the other *Mijaz sharif*, 'How is your health', or words to that effect. The other will clasp his hands and reply, 'I pray for the best.' This is the usual form of salutation for cultured people throughout India, but in Lucknow and in other places of former courts these matters are taken very seriously.

In recent times in Lucknow, since the collapse of the court and the disappearance of its social etiquette, ordinary people are coming back to the greeting *As Salam Alaikum*.[529] Would that the upper classes followed this example and such overt distinctions between high and low ceased to exist!

43

Everyday Speech in Urdu

Important aspects of social courtesy are conversation and style of speech. A person's manner of speech is the first sign of his good breeding and manners, and every developed civilization all over the world improves and reforms its language.

Culture and good manners demand that conversation should be free of obscene words. Words and opinions that might be displeasing to others should be left unsaid and unexpressed. If sometimes it becomes necessary to bring up an unpleasant subject it should be couched in such terms that the feelings of the person addressed are not hurt, and worded as gently and pleasantly as possible. The educated people of Lucknow attained perfection in this art. Although British cultural influence and the diffusion of present-day education have raised the general level of conversation everywhere, a polite and polished manner of speech is the distinction of the citizens of Lucknow.

People from other places are so awed by this skill that they become inhibited when talking to the people of Lucknow. Among themselves they may say, 'We like simple and straightforward speech: this Lucknow palaver is beyond us', but this is merely an excuse. I have seen Persian-speaking Indians remaining dumb before Persians. In England I have seen people who knew French who were too shy to say a word of French in front of Frenchmen. Because of Arab eloquence, foreigners sometimes became tongue-tied in their presence, and the Arabs thought, 'We are the only ones to whom God has given speech, and the rest of the world is dumb.' For that reason Arabs called the people from the outside world *ajam*, which simply means dumb. In the same way the inhabitants of Lucknow thought that they so excelled all others in eloquence and witty speech in Urdu that no one could open his mouth in their presence.

In polite conversation the choice of pronoun with which one addresses another person is of primary importance. There are two pronouns in most languages for the person addressed, one singular and the other plural. For an esteemed person, respect is shown by employing the plural. In Persian the singular pronoun is *tu* and the plural *shuma*. In Arabic the singular is *ak* or *enta* and the plural *kum* or *entum*. However, in Urdu there is one singular pronoun *tu*, but two plural pronouns *tum* and *ap*. One will say *tu* to a humble person and *tum* to one of slightly higher status, or familiarly to a relative and a junior. *Ap* is used for an equal and all respected persons. Sometimes upper-class people address one another familiarly as *tum* but with people with whom one is not well acquainted the use of *tum* is very improper, especially in Lucknow.

There are a large number of words in the Urdu language to express the standing of honoured and noble persons, which are employed particularly in Lucknow: *Janab*, 'Sir', *Janab-e-Vala*, 'Honourable Sir', *Janab-e-Ali*, 'Exalted Sir', *Hazrat*, 'Dignified Sir', *Hazrat-e-Vala*, 'Honourable and Dignified Sir', *Huzur*, 'Your Highness', *Huzur-e-Vala*, 'High Sir', *Huzur-e-Ali*, 'Exalted Highness', *Sarkar*, 'Master', *Qibla*, 'Exalted Sir', and *Qibla-o-Kaba*, 'Your Holiness'.[132] These, as well as some other terms, are employed to address a distinguished person, according to his rank. The exact nuances of these terms are better understood by the citizens of Lucknow than anywhere else.

I claim that no other language in the world has so many honorific words of address. Urdu is no longer looked upon as the model of a refined language in India and other literatures, free from Urdu influence, have started to assume predominance. Bengali, Panjabi, Gujrati, Sindhi, Marathi, Cantari, Telgu, all claim their own literary merit and eloquence, but I challenge not only these languages but celebrated languages, like Persian, Arabic, English and French, to produce as many forms of address as exist in Urdu. In spite of its short existence and the small area in which it is spoken, Urdu has achieved greater perfection as a language of courtesy, delicacy and social elegance than any other language in the world. Urdu is not the language of any particular province, group of people or religion. It developed at the royal court and became throughout India the language of refined people as well as nobility, scholars and literary men. It is rooted in culture, courtesy and refinement and grew up to meet the needs of polished society in India. Unfortunately in the British era Western culture and literature began to take predecence. At the same time old prejudices among Indians led Muslims to take pride in the fact that Urdu was their language while Hindus, thinking that they would not be able to compete with them in this field, left it to them and gave it up almost completely. This was harmful to the development of Urdu. Still, it cannot be denied that the eloquence and literary merit it possesses cannot be equalled by the newly developing language of Hindi,[530] or by any other Indian language.

Englishmen, Arabs, Afghans or Persians, when speaking Urdu, always address the other person as *tum*, because their own languages do not contain any pronoun that is more polite than *tum*.

In English there are special words of address, like 'Your Honour', 'Your Excellency', 'Your Highness' and 'Your Majesty', but these are used only for kings and aristocrats and are never used for anyone else. Similar words exist in Urdu as well, like *Jahan Panah*, 'Protector of the World', *Sahib-e-Alam*, 'Ruler of the World', *Murshid Zada*,[158] 'Son of a Religious Leader', *Navab Sahib*, 'My Lord', *Navab Zada*, 'Son of a Navab', *Sahib Zada*, 'Son of a Dignitary', and words like *Janab* and *Huzur* are added to them. Such forms of address probably exist in every language, but the variety of honorific words that are used for many different illustrious personages in Urdu is not to be found in any other language.

In other languages everyday words are used when inquiring after a person's welfare, but in Urdu special phrases are employed to show deference and respect, as for example, *Mizaj-e-Ali*, 'How is your Exalted Health?', *Mizaj-e-Mubarak*, 'How is your Blessed Health?', *Mizaj-e-Aqdas*, 'How is your Sacred Health?', *Mizaj-e-Mualla*, 'How is your Eminent Health?' In Lucknow educated people are particular about the correct pronunciation of *sh* and *a*, and, as far as possible, the proper articulation of Arabic words. In Persian constructions, attention is paid to the relative and the genitive. Among scholars, Persian and Arabic words are freely used and correctly pronounced and hakims employ Arabic medical terms. However, Arabic words are avoided when speaking to uneducated people. In the company of women, idioms and proverbs according to feminine taste are used.

A younger person speaking to a senior, a humble person to a superior, an ordinary man to a scholar, must all show respect and deference in every word and sentence, and keep their voices suitably low. At the same time when an older person talks to a younger one, a superior to someone below him, a scholar to an uneducated person, they should show kindness and affection in manner and words.

By paying attention to these matters, the people of Lucknow have developed a very polished and refined language. The masses and uneducated people speak better Urdu than many poets and men of letters of other places, and they show great delicacy and discretion in their choice of words. But alas, Lucknow courtesy is fading. The newly-arrived outsiders from different regions are displaying lamentably bad manners, while the local élite are living in seclusion and are out of currency. Along with this, the attainment of Civil Rights has made the ignorant and the common people so brazen and overbearing that all these forms of courtesy are rapidly disappearing and may cease to exist in a short time.

44

Wit and Female Celebrations

There is an old Arab saying, originating from a hadis of the Prophet, that 'Humour is to speech what salt is to food.' It is true that without wit and humour speech is insipid and the company dull. But if wit is expressed thoughtlessly it may cause grief and misunderstanding. It has often led to the drawing of swords and lifelong friends have in a moment become enemies. If one considers the matter, it is not wit itself that is to be blamed but the manner in which it is employed and the lack of moderation in its use.

The more advanced a language, the greater its ability to express wit and humour, though it is difficult to pin down this development. There are a variety of means which an eloquent man can adopt to this end, and to describe all these in detail could be the subject of a book. I will only say here that humour is as a rule based upon words with more than one meaning, any one of which can be utilized to make insinuations. Another variety is when such words are not employed, but comparisons are simply made between those persons or objects which, though unrelated, have something in common. This similarity is expressed in such a manner that it ceases to be a comparison and becomes a metaphor. One exalts or demeans oneself or someone else to such a degree as to be very far from the actual truth. All this requires great discretion.

A skilful person will make the most unpalatable insinuations and unpleasant comparisons without hurting anyone's feelings and without giving cause for disapproval, but a tactless person will annoy others and they will turn against him. Even the ordinary people of Lucknow possess a high degree of this kind of tact.

Dr Aghor Nath, a learned Bengali, a PhD in literature and an expert in Urdu, once said to me, 'What merit is there in a language like Urdu when I once said, "We all drink milk nowadays" and everyone burst out laughing?' My reply was, 'This is precisely the beauty of Urdu. Why do you blame the language instead of yourself?' In every language there are some words with more than one meaning. Those who are well versed in the language use these words in such a manner that there is no ambiguity. The meaning of 'conceive' in

English is 'to think' and also 'to become pregnant'. A well-known peer said in Parliament 'I conceive' three times and then fell silent in profound thought. Someone called out, 'My Lord has conceived three times and nothing has happened', and everyone roared with laughter. Similarly thousands of words in Urdu have more than one meaning, and when used incorrectly the speaker will always invite ridicule.

As regards Dr Nath's remark, the drinking of milk is the action of infants and to say in Urdu that an adult drinks milk is to imply that he is still a child. The people of Lucknow will use other expressions such as 'I make use of milk', 'my food is milk' and 'I eat rice and milk.' From such phrases an erudite linguist and poet from Agra got the impression that in Lucknow people 'eat' milk rather than drink it. He had a discussion on this subject with someone in Lucknow and I was more or less ordered to give my opinion. I said, 'Milk is a liquid, how can anyone eat it? However, in order to avoid comparison with an infant, Lucknow adults will never say "I drink milk" in regard to themselves.'

The people of Lucknow introduce witticisms and humour into their conversation in many ways. The greater a person's wit, the more he will be appreciated in literary and social circles. With the spread of the Urdu language in different parts of India, excellent humorists are now found everywhere and so promote the better understanding of the language. But the discretion with which the citizens of Lucknow couch their wit and humour in refined language is truly a pleasure.

In Lucknow the former wealth of the Muslims and their status as rulers has given their womenfolk the opportunity to gratify their wishes to a much greater extent than in most places. From birth till wedlock every joyous occasion in a child's life is celebrated. To begin with there is Chhati, on the sixth day after birth, then Chilla, on the culmination of the forty-day period after childbirth, the many Nashans, on the bathing of mothers, Aqiqa, on shaving the baby's head soon after birth, on weaning, on the first taste of sweetness, Bismillah,[531] the first lesson, the circumcision and most important of all Aqd, the marriage contract. All are occasions for celebration. In some families, children's birthdays are also celebrated. In addition, there are festivities on occasions such as bathing after return to health or the fulfilment of some special wish.

Female relatives and acquaintances and women of the neighbourhood all take part in these celebrations. They are organized in the following manner: the company is seated on takhats, or if there are too many guests a farsh is prepared on the floor. In rich households rugs, sometimes three of them, are placed in the centre of the farsh as the seat of honour. *Kanvals*, candles encased in coloured glass, and other decorative lamps are lit. A troupe of domnis sit in the centre and perform. The domni who dances wears bells on her ankles and gesticulates. In the course of the performance the domnis from time to time perform mimicry and there is a tumult of gaiety. Although the free nature of the domnis' performance creates a general atmosphere of laxity, good etiquette on the part of the assembly is preserved throughout. A large number of specific customs have to be followed for a given celebration, whose guardians and enforcers are elderly ladies of standing. The domnis are also well-versed in these customs and receive handsome recompense for their services.

At most of these celebrations the participants stay awake all night. Indian Muslim women believe that this all-night vigil is a form of worship to thank the Almighty, and the domnis' hymns help to keep everyone awake. In practice, however, the time is spent in singing, fun and frolic instead of worship. But at dawn they go to the mosque to make offerings of special sweets prepared for the occasion. In villages these celebrations are conducted on similar lines, but they lack dignity.

45

Festive Celebrations

I shall now give detailed descriptions of these festive occasions. Chhati[169] is the name of that ceremony when mother and child are bathed for the first time after birth. To bathe the mother in very hot water is beneficial to health, but it has been given the importance of a festive occasion. It is called Chhati, sixth, as it takes place on the sixth day after childbirth. After the mother and the child, all the women guests one after the other take a bath. New clothes are presented to the mother and child, according to the status of the household, while the women guests put on fresh clothes. The numerous details in the customs connected with this ceremony are probably similar everywhere with slight variations in different cities, and in fact in every family.

A complete set of new clothes for the mother and child, a tiny *tauq*, the semi-circular, flat necklace, *hansli*, a heavy, round necklace, rattles and other toys, are sent from the mother's family or from other relatives in procession, with much display and the beating of drums, together with food and other things. Arrangements are made for singing and dancing in the women's apartments, and if funds will not permit of professional entertainers, the women of the house themselves take the dhol in their hands and play and sing.

On the twentieth and fortieth days when bathing takes place there are similar celebrations. If within means, sumptuous festivities are held on both occasions, otherwise some importance is given to the fortieth-day celebration.

Aqiqa, the shaving of the child's head, is a Muslim religious ceremony taken from the Israelites and dating from the time of Abraham. Jews used to take a child on the eighth day after birth to a temple, have its head shaved and perform sacrifices while the priest blessed it. Muslims continue this practice to this day. At the present time, the rule of the eighth-day limit for Aqiqa is not strictly adhered to, but the ceremony must be performed within a year. The child is bathed, dressed in new clothes and a barber shaves its head in the presence of relatives and friends. As he places the razor on the child's head, two goats are sacrificed in the case of a boy and one in the case of a girl. After the shaving, sandalwood ointment is rubbed on the head and presents are given to the child. The meat of the sacrificed goat is distributed among the poor, as well as friends and relatives.

Khir Chatai, the taste of sweetness, is the ceremony when the child is given some food in addition to its mother's milk. This usually takes place when the child is about five months old. Usually this first food is an elaborately prepared rice pudding, which is simply put to the child's lips in the presence of female relations. The child is dressed in new clothes and the ladies, blessing it, put some money into its hand. The usual festivities then commence.

Dudh Barhai, weaning, takes place when the child ceases to be given its mother's milk. Sweets are prepared and if the child insists on milk, they are put into its hands. Usually sufficient sweets are prepared for distribution among friends and relations. The method of weaning is to dissolve aloes in water and dampen the mother's or wet nurse's breasts with this or some other bitter solution, so that the child will be put off by the bitterness and refuse the milk. If the child is still set upon it, this practice is repeated until it becomes disgusted with the bitter taste. The Dudh Barhai ceremony usually takes place when the child reaches the age of two. With the Hanafites, an orthodox sect of Sunnis, the period of nursing can go on up to two and a half years, but cannot be prolonged any further. However, the usual custom among all Muslims is to stop earlier. Those women who go on nursing their children till they are three or four years of age are regarded with disfavour as acting against religious law. This celebration is also accompanied by singing, dancing and much merry-making.

Bismillah takes place when a boy is given his first reading lesson. This is arranged according to custom on the day when he attains the age of four years, four months and four days. The number four has such significance in the ceremony, that along with four years, months and days, four hours and four minutes are also taken into account. The child is bathed and dressed in new clothes like a bridegroom for this ceremony, and, at the appointed hour, a maulvi or an elder member of the family starts him on his lesson. A book with the alphabet is placed before him and after reciting the phrase *Bismillah*, 'In the name of Allah',[531] another Arabic sentence is read out which means, 'O God, make this easy. Do not make it difficult and let it finish well.' Then a few letters of the alphabet are read out and sweets are distributed. The boy is given presents, and this day marks the commencement of his education.

Khutna, circumcision, was also an ordinance of Abraham and an ancient rite. In India the practice is confined to Muslims and it is thought that a boy becomes a Muslim only after its performance: the popular name for the ceremony therefore is Musalmani. During this rite the skin at the end of the boy's penis is severed. The operation is performed by our *jarrahs*, expert barber-surgeons, and is beneficial from a medical point of view. On this occasion relatives and friends are invited to the men's section of the house where it takes place, while the ladies congregate in their own quarters. Sweets are handed round after the circumcision and people who can afford it give dinners later on. When the wound heals and the boy has been bathed, many families who love and cherish their son dress him up like a bridegroom, seat him on a horse and take him in a procession to some shrine, where he lays a wreath of flowers and makes an offering of sweets. On arrival home, there are celebrations. Some people have a boy circumcised on the sixth or fortieth day after birth, but the general practice is to wait until he is six or seven years old.

Another ceremony is Roza Koshai,[60] breaking the fast. This takes place when boys and girls reach the age of nine or ten and are obliged to fast for the first time. The custom is to invite people who have observed the fast to break it with the boy by partaking of a large feast: a girl breaks her fast with women. As this is a religious occasion, singing and music are not permitted, but some irresponsible people make this occasion an excuse for such pleasures.

The most important of all celebrations, however, is on the occasion of *aqd-e-nikah*, the marriage contract. It is a momentous celebration, the extravagance of which causes hundreds of families to become financially ruined. Because of the exuberance of their joy and their desire to do the best they can, people pay no heed to the limits of their circumstances and give no thought to the future. They borrow money from friends, relations and money lenders, or raise it by selling property or other valuables. By the time the wedding is over, many families are almost reduced to a state of destitution.

Betrothals are usually arranged by *mashatas*, match-makers. In all large towns in India, especially those with an ancient culture, match-making has become a profession for certain women. The literal meaning of the word *mashata* is a woman who combs the hair of some great lady, dresses her and adorns her with jewellery. However, in popular use the word has come to apply to those women who suggest possible eligible marriage partners to the families and initiate arrangements leading to betrothals and weddings. Probably this profession started with those women who acted as ladies' maids, as the word seems to indicate. These women are very artful. When they describe a boy, they extol his wealth, education, prosperity, good manners and looks to such an extent that he appears like the Prince Charming Benazir in Mir Hasan's masnavi.[260] In the same way, when they describe a girl to the boy's family, they make so much of her beauty, charm, allure and fascination, that she becomes a fairy of the Caucasus mountains, or the Princess Badr-e-Munir of the Urdu masnavis.

After the mashata has interested the parents the men of the households look into the matter and make their own inquiries. However, it is the women of both families who become most involved. If they are satisfied, they get their husbands' approval and the betrothal is arranged. Sometimes, when children are born in two families of friends or relatives, solicitous mothers arrange for their betrothal at birth. In this case there is no need for a match-maker and the future bridegroom gets his bride without any trouble.

After preliminary approval, the boy is usually invited to the girl's home so that he may be displayed to view. He goes accompanied by his best friends and is seated in a place where the women of the household can also have a good look at him by peeping through the curtains. The men meet and talk with him. The boy's mother and sisters likewise go on an appointed day to the house of the intended bride and, by offering her sweets or by some similar excuse, manage to get a glimpse of her face, which is hidden from view by a veil. In some upper-class families it is not the custom to invite the boy to the house: the men of the family manage to get a look at him without his knowledge and to find out about him discreetly. In the same way particulars about the girl are quietly ascertained.

By these methods, if there is mutual approval after due consideration is given to appearance, manners, economic and social status and family lineage, which is of great importance, the betrothal is finally arranged. The boy's family sends delicacies, various ornaments made of flowers and a gold ring, which is often put on the girl's hand by the boy's close female relations.

From that time on, until the wedding, both families, on festive and ceremonial occasions, exchange offerings of food and sweets. The portions intended for the boy or the girl are particularly elaborate and well garnished. If the Muharram happens to occur during this period, each family ceremoniously sends the other some dry preparations of cardamoms, dali, betel nuts and similar things, along with a finely embroidered silken *batva*, pouch, to hold them.[532]

A few days before the Barat, the procession to the bride's house for the marriage ceremony, the bride, dressed in her festive yellow dress, is obliged to sit in *manjha*, seclusion, in a special room. *Butna*[533] cosmetics are applied to her body and, except for special purposes, she never comes out of her room. On the first day of her seclusion the butna and henna that she has discarded, together with jars of crystallized sugar and a large number of *pindi*,[534] are sent in a procession with a band to the bridegroom's house. The pindis which are specially intended for the bridegroom are decorated and placed on separate trays. Also in the procession is the bridegroom's fine yellow costume for his own manjha, a low carved or silver-decorated stool, a *lota*,[535] jug, and *katora*, bowl for drinking water. The lota and katora are tied tightly to the stool with string and are at the head of the procession after the band. They are followed first by trays intended for the bridegroom containing his things, usually placed on earthenware dishes, and then by the long line of trays of pindis. The bride's younger sisters and the domnis go with the procession in palanquins. On arrival at the bridegroom's house they divide up a pindi and crystallized sugar into seven portions, all of which the bridegroom is obliged to eat. This particular custom is probably of Hindu origin and is not connected with Arabian or other Muslim traditions, because the ceremony of manjha and the cotton wristlet worn on this occasion cannot be traced anywhere except in ancient India.

About twelve days after the manjha, the Sanchaq procession goes with the same pomp and ceremony from the bridegroom's house to that of the bride. *Sanchaq* is a Turkish word and a Turkish custom, and was probably brought to India by the Turks and Mughals. On this occasion, the bridegroom's parents send the bride an elaborate and very heavily embroidered dress. With it there is, for the bride, a chaplet with long, hanging gold and silver threads and another one of flowers, a plain silver ring, a gold-bejewelled ring and different floral ornaments. Also in the procession are different kinds of sweets and dried fruits. Earthenware pitchers are specially decorated for the occasion, four of which are joined together with bamboo and coloured paper to form a unit. The richer the family, the more units there are, sometimes up to one or two hundred of them. The pitchers contain a few sweet cakes and some sugar. Their tops are covered with red cloth tied around the rim. Preceding these in the procession is a small silver pitcher filled with yoghurt, also covered with red cloth and with one or two fish tied to it for good luck. When the procession arrives at the bride's house the sweets and dried fruits are offered to friends and relations.

46

The Wedding Ceremony

The evening after the Sanchaq procession the brightly illuminated Mehndi, henna, procession leaves the bride's house. This is probably an Arab custom, and its main purpose is to send the bridegroom the suit of clothes which he will wear at the wedding. This costume resembles the khilat of the Mughal courtiers, and is sent along with a *sehra*,[536] golden chaplet, *shimla*, a gold and brocade-ornamented turban, a plain turban and a bejewelled aigrette. If within means, a pearl necklace is also sent. In addition there are silken pyjamas, a gold ring and clothes for everyday use. Along with this there are several trays, which are beautifully illuminated with green and red candles, and contain henna for the bridegroom. Towards the end of the procession there are a large number of trays of *malida*, sweet semolina with dried fruits.

The day after the Mehndi procession, the Barat procession sets out from the bridegroom's house. In former times the hour for this was fixed at about three a.m., but this time is no longer observed and instead the procession starts at about nine a.m. or ten a.m. This new timing was established in the reign of Wajid Ali Shah when by chance his own marriage procession was delayed until after daybreak. Since then people have adopted the later time as it is more convenient and saves in illumination. Now the marriage procession usually starts early in the day and the Aqd, the marriage contract, is concluded at midday.

The wedding procession is as elaborate as possible. The usual three procession bands, that is, the dhol tasha with cymbals, the raushan chauki and the Scottish bagpipes are always included. In addition there are sometimes bands with kettle drums mounted on horseback, people carrying flags, spearmen, elephants, camels and horses. The wealthier the family, the greater the variety of bands. The bridegroom, wearing the costume sent to him with the Mehndi procession, is mounted on a horse, or, if he is of high status, on an elephant, and rides slowly with great pomp and dignity at the rear of the procession. The bridegroom is called *nau shah*, 'new king', and for one day he is really considered a king. One may wonder why, if he is considered a king, he should wear a shimla and not a crown. The answer is that Muslim rulers in India did not wear crowns but plumed shimlas with a bejewelled aigrette. Ghazi ud Din Haidar and his descendants had a crown bestowed upon them by the British, but the crown was not accepted by the people, who continued to dress their nau shahs in the style of the rulers of former times. Behind the bridegroom are the palanquins of his mother, sisters, female relations and the domnis. There are many customs and minor ceremonies before the departure of the procession from the house.

The procession arrives at the bride's house after she has finished being bathed. Her bath water, which has been kept, is brought out and poured on the ground at the feet of the bridegroom's horse or elephant. The water for the bride's bath is kept for seven days before being used. This stale and cold water is called *kilas*, jar-water. For the poor bride to bathe in this in the cold weather must be a terrible ordeal. Betel leaves are spread out on the small wooden stool on which she is bathed, and some of these leaves are included in the twenty-one prepared betel leaves which are the first things offered to the bridegroom on his arrival.

On arrival the bridegroom goes into the women's apartment. To cross the threshold he has to jump over a slightly elevated rope, after which scores of customs follow which are slightly different in every circle and family.

Meanwhile the bride, although her bath is finished, has not yet been dressed. She is wrapped in a sheet and some crystallized sugar is put into her hand. The bridegroom is brought in and made to taste this sweetness. At this point the bride's sisters, merry-minded women and domnis interrupt and make things as difficult as possible for him.

When he has surmounted this first marriage hurdle, the bridegroom goes into the men's quarters to join the merry-making. Here relations and friends dressed in ceremonial clothes are sitting on a farsh while being entertained by a troupe of male and female singers and dancers. The seat of honour, made of velvet with gold- and silver-brocaded embroidery, is in the centre, and the bridegroom is placed upon it. A small gau is arranged at his back and his friends are seated close to him so that he can converse with them. Everyone else sits a little further off on either side.

The bridegroom is obliged to evince bashfulness in his every gesture and action. He must not behave freely and must speak so quietly that his voice is only just audible. The sehra, which is tied to his forehead and covered by a second one made of flowers, makes it very difficult for anyone to see his face. His features become visible only after the marriage contract is signed, when the sehra is removed from his face and placed over the shimla. Even then he has to hold a handkerchief to his face as a sign of modesty.

Shortly after the bridegroom appears, steps are taken to expedite the completion of the Aqd. All the complicated preliminaries are simply a prelude to this. Among Shia families two mujtahids arrive at this time, one of whom is the attorney for the boy and the other for the girl. The girl's attorney either goes to the women's quarters to obtain his power of attorney from the bride personally, or obtains it from her through a reliable witness of his choice, in order to meet the religious ruling that this is not against her will. Then both attorneys sit before the bridegroom and read, on behalf of their respective parties, passages in Arabic stating the traditional conditions of the marriage contract and receive the couple's acceptance. If it is a marriage between Sunnis the passages are read by a maulvi. In villages a *qazi*[93] [Muslim magistrate], selected by the families, performs the ceremony in the following manner. One of the girl's relatives acts as her legal agent. He produces two witnesses to the effect that the girl has appointed him her attorney for this purpose. If the qazi is satisfied, he asks the attorney the amount of *maher*, promise of money to the bride. Then the bridegroom recites in Arabic the Kalimah, the Muslim confession of faith, and affirms his faith in the basic tenets of the religion. After this the qazi says to him three times, 'I have contracted your marriage with this girl in exchange for this amount of maher.' When the bridegroom has confirmed his agreement, the qazi recites a benediction and gives his felicitations. Congratulations are showered from all directions and dry sweet cakes and dates are lavishly offered to the guests.

On the arrival of the mujtahids or the maulvis, the singing and dancing cease, but as soon as they are gone festivities start again. The bridegroom is taken again to the women's apartment where the ladies fully exercise their privilege in the performance of innumerable customs. They make the bridegroom the target of all kinds of jokes and ridicule, and tease him in every way they can. His tormentors are the bride's sisters and domnis. All the things they do to him are completely unknown to a young bachelor until the moment arrives.

The bride, who has not yet been dressed in her going-away clothes, is wrapped up in a sheet like an inert bundle. She is brought in and those who carry her make her touch the bridegroom with her feet as if she were kicking him, and marriage songs commence. The bridegroom is made to promise total subordination to his wife and to undertake to perform every conceivable kind of service for her. Then the *arsi mushaf*, the mirror-look rite, is performed. For this the Quran is placed on a stand between the bridegroom and bride and a mirror is held above it in such a manner that the bridegroom gets his first glimpse of the bride in the mirror. But before seeing her face he must recite 'Surah-e-Akhlas', a passage from the Quran. The bride has kept her eyes closed all this time. The women who are present then cause the bridegroom to beg the bride to open her eyes, and make him promise her every sort of obedience and servitude. After much cajolery the bride opens her eyes, gives one glance into the mirror and shuts them again. With this the ceremony ends: the bridegroom is led out and he joins the men.

The bride is now dressed and adorned with jewelry in preparation for her departure to the house of her parents-in-law. At this moment the domnis commence the *babul*,[537] the heart-rending song of departure, and the joyous household becomes a place of mourning. Relations, friends and all present come to say good-bye with tears in their eyes and give the bride presents of money and jewelry.

47

The Wedding Procession

During the preparation for departure the articles of the dowry are brought out and an inventory is given to the members of the bridegroom's family. The dowry consists of jewelry, clothing, utensils, furniture and many other articles. Now the bride is quite ready to depart. She wears a simple crimson *kurta*, collarless shirt, and muslin or plain silken *gharara*.[507] The simplicity goes so far that there is no hemming and her gharara is tied with tape. As she leaves, her relations and friends say good-bye with impassioned words of sorrow and she herself weeps copiously. Her decorated palanquin is brought to the door and the bridegroom is sent for. He lifts her in his arms and seats her in the palanquin.

When the bridegroom says farewell he too is given presents, usually of money. In the men's quarters, jugs and glasses are brought to offer sherbet to the guests before leaving. In the general excitement, however, the sherbet is rarely drunk, but everyone puts some money on the tray for the bridegroom.

The marriage procession now returns to the bridegroom's house with the same pomp, but now there is the bride's palanquin in front of the bridegroom's horse. An elaborately embroidered shawl covers the top of the palanquin and the four corners are held by female bearers. All round the palanquin there is a crowd of the bridegroom's servants and special friends, followed by the bridegroom himself on horseback and then by the palanquins of the women.

In the procession the articles of the dowry are displayed behind the bands and in front of the bride's palanquin. Big utensils are placed on a basket while china and glass utensils, carried separately, are set out on trays. After them come boxes containing the bride's clothes, followed by the bed, complete with silken quilts, pillows and sheets. The bedding is tied to the four legs by silken cords, from each end of which hang tiny decorative silver cushions. The girl is provided with necessary things for her personal use: a mirror, comb, oil, perfume and other cosmetics, and, among the well-to-do a *pan dan*, betel box, *khas dan*, small betel case, *lota*, jug, *katora*, bowl, and similar things all made in silver. At the rear of the procession there are large containers with food, offered by the bride's family.

The procession is greeted at the bridegroom's house by festive music. The domnis, who arrive beforehand, sing wedding songs. In some families the bride is lifted out of the palanquin in the bridegroom's arms, in others his mother and sisters lift her out. She is seated inside the house and the bridegroom says a prayer of thanksgiving, using a corner of her veil as a prayer mat. The bride's feet are washed and the water is poured in every corner of the house. The veil is removed from her face so that all may see her and women and close male relatives present her with money and jewelry.

The bride spends the first night in her new home in utmost modesty and complete formality. She must not talk or look at anyone. The only people to whom she can say anything are the women who have accompanied her from her parental home. To relieve her of this misery, as soon as day breaks her brother or some other relation comes to take her back for the Chauthi ceremony. On this occasion, although she leaves with ceremony, there is no procession and no band. The bridegroom accompanies her and seven varieties of vegetable and seven kinds of sweet are sent with them.

In the evening the Chauthi ceremony takes place at the bride's home. She is now made up and clothed in her presentation dress, which is the most elaborate, heavily embroidered and ceremonious of all her dresses. All her jewelry is also put on. The bridegroom's sisters and female relations now arrive for the festivity and the groom and bride pretend to throw sweets at each other. The womenfolk of the groom and the bride actually pelt each other with vegetables and go through the motions of fighting with flower-covered sticks. They tear sweets, vegetables and flowers from each other's hands and throw them back at each other. Sometimes the frolic gets out of hand and some of the women get slightly hurt.

A day or two later the bride goes to the bridegroom's house, after which the ceremony known as the Four Chaleys takes place. The word *chaley* is derived from the word *chalna*, to walk or to move. The ceremony is so called because the bride is called away from her father-in-law's house to the homes of her fond relatives, but not to her parental home. Paternal and maternal aunts take it in turns to invite her, together with the bridegroom, to come and stay with them. The couple stay for only one day and night, during which time much hospitality is lavished upon them. When they leave, the bride is presented with jewelry and the bridegroom with a set of new clothes, in accordance with the means of their hosts.

In villages the ceremonies are different in many respects, but the procedure for the marriage contract itself is the same. The manjha is observed, but the bridegroom's yellow costume is provided by his sisters and female relations, so the procession from the bride's house is eliminated. Neither does the sanchaq come from the bridegroom's house, nor the mehndi from the bride's house. These functions are served in a slightly different manner on the day of the Barat itself. When the wedding procession approaches the bride's house, it stops a short distance away and, in place of the sanchaq, a presentation dress for the bride along with many other dresses and various things to bring good fortune, like sugar and parched rice-grains, are carried on trays to her home in a procession. Friends and relations of the bridegroom offer them to the bride's family and after being refreshed with sherbet, they take their leave.

A little later a procession from the bride's home brings the bridegroom's costume, and this take the place of the Mehndi procession in the towns. His costume consists of a short collarless shirt, a long garment to go over it, a turban and a pair of shoes. There is also a *sehra*, chaplet of flowers. When the bridegroom has been dressed in these clothes, the Barat procession starts again towards the bride's house or some other place which has been chosen for the wedding ceremony. Festivities with dancing and singing go on all night, except for the time when the qazi performs the marriage ceremony. The ceremony itself is much the same as it is in the towns. After the marriage contract has been concluded, the entire wedding procession is treated to an elaborate dinner by the bride's family. In towns except for the food sent by the bride's family to the bridegroom's house after the marriage ceremony, it is not necessary to invite the members of the procession for dinner. Usually the bridegroom's family makes such arrangements before they leave. However, in the villages it is most important for the bride's family to offer a sumptuous meal to all the members of the procession. The slightest shortcoming in their hospitality is considered a disgrace in the eyes of the whole village.

The meal consists of the complete dishes of a tora, which is offered to all, high and low, without distinction. The most important items of the meal are pulau, zarda, qaurma, shir mal and unleavened breads. When helping themselves to food, members of the bridegroom's procession help themselves to their heart's content. They also demand ample grain and fodder for their horses and bullocks. The girl's family must comply with these wishes graciously, or be forever dishonoured.

The ceremonies connected with the bride's departure from her home and her return to it are much the same as in the towns, but with one difference. Women do not accompany the bridal procession and the bride is not on the whole subjected to so many restrictions. But like the bride in towns she must remain in one place in her father-in-law's house until she returns to her home for the Chauthi. Similarly she must not eat, drink, go to the toilet, speak to anyone, move her hand from her face or open her eyes. All of these actions are considered immodest. To save her from the embarrassment of being obliged to go to the toilet, no food or drink is given to her for two days before her going away. Her hardship is further increased if she is a village bride marrying someone in another village, as is often the case, for she is then often obliged to travel a considerable distance in this state.

The reason the Sanchaq and Mehndi processions were discontinued in the villages, with the consequent importance placed upon the dinner for the bridegroom's procession, is probably as follows. The Barat often has to travel long distances from one village to another and it is difficult for the processions to be exchanged within the three days of the marriage ceremony. This also explains why, although the bridegroom's family arranges a dinner for members of the procession at the start, by the time the procession reaches the bride's house they are all famished and consider it proper to behave as if they have not eaten for days.

48

Funeral Services

Throughout India funeral services are the same among Muslims and I cannot think of anything in particular in this respect which is confined to Lucknow. When a death occurs, relatives and friends are informed immediately and all endeavour to come to the bereaved house. When women come, they themselves pay the palanquin-bearers.[538] On joyous occasions and other visits it is customary for the hostess to pay for the conveyance of a female guest, but this is not the case in a house of sorrow.

The first stage in funeral proceedings is for the corpse to be washed. Among Shias this is done at a special place reserved for the purpose by stony-hearted persons whose profession is to wash the corpse and swathe it in a shroud. With Sunnis the corpse is washed at home by relatives or friends. Men and women who have had experience in this are called in and usually a maulvi or some elder gives instructions as to the correct procedure.

The corpse is then dressed in burial clothes consisting of simple pyjamas and shirt, and wrapped in two sheets. Strips of cloth torn from the sheets are tied round near the head, waist and feet to prevent the sheets from opening.

Shias then place the corpse in a coffin, which is covered with a *doshala*, a brocaded shawl. Accompanied by someone reciting in a deep voice 'Surah-e-Rahman', from the Quran, the coffin is carried to the grave under the shade of a canopy. The people who carry the coffin and the canopy are of low class who over a long period have made this their profession. But because of their un-dignified behaviour Shias have begun to realize that it is better to carry the coffins on their own shoulders. Several committees have now been set up in the city whose energetic and devout members ensure that all arrangements are made under their supervision according to correct religious procedures.

Sunnis lay a corpse on a light bamboo bed and cover it with a sheet. If the corpse is that of a woman they fix several arches of bamboo to the bed and spread a sheet over it. The idea is that a woman should always be veiled, even in death. Relatives and friends carry the corpse slowly on their shoulders while reciting the Kalima, the confession of faith, in a low voice. On arriving at the graveyard they offer Namaz, special burial prayers.

The grave is generally rectangular in shape and about five feet deep. At the bottom another narrow cavity about three feet deep is dug, leaving a ledge on either side. When the grave has been carefully cleared of stones, the corpse is gently lowered into it. The head of the grave points north and the face is turned in the direction of Mecca and held in that position by clods of earth. The strips of cloth over the head are then untied so that the relatives can get a last glimpse of the face of the deceased. Among Shias, 'Talqin', a passage of instruction, is then read in Arabic by some devout person, who climbs down into the grave and touches the shoulder of the corpse while he addresses it. He states the answers it should give to the angels of death when they come to interrogate and repeats the confessions of the faith. After this the lower cavity is covered with planks and if there are any cracks between them they are filled with clods of earth so that nothing can fall through. The shroud inside the grave smells of camphor and scent and some people also sprinkle rose-water. The upper cavity is then filled in with earth thrown by those present and the raised grave is formed.

When the earth is being shovelled into the top part of the grave, everyone present takes a handful of earth three times and throws it into the grave while reciting three verses from the Quran, 'We created thee from this [earth]', 'We have brought thee back to this' and 'At a future time [the Day of Judgment], we shall take thee out and make thee stand again.' This throwing of earth into the grave is considered extremely important.

After the burial the grave is covered with the sheet in which the corpse was wrapped, or with a covering made of flowers for the whole grave. Fatiha, the opening surah of the Quran, is recited, and the people return to their homes.

On the day of death, the stove is not lit in the house. After the funeral procession has left, some relatives send in a cooked meal which the mourners, together with those who happen to be present, eat when they return. Food is provided in this way for three days. This practice started in the early days of Islam when the Prophet himself, on hearing of the death of his uncle, had food sent to the bereaved family. But in Lucknow nonsensical superstitions have grown around this noble custom. As soon as anyone dies all the food in the house is thrown away and all the jars and pitchers are emptied of water. Women tell children that the reason is that the angel of death washes and wipes the knife with which he takes life in food and drink.

On the third day after death, or occasionally on the fourth day, the Suyum ceremony is observed. On this day people come to offer their condolences to the family of the bereaved. These visitors read passages from the holy Quran and the religious merit obtained is dedicated to the soul of the deceased. In this ceremony mourning has gradually become secondary and all that now seems to matter is the size of the assembly and how many times the complete Quran is read and dedicated to the soul of the deceased. Towards the end people read some special passages from the Quran followed by Fatiha, the prayer for the dead. To this an absurd procedure has been added in which some oil in a sandalwood bowl and some flowers are passed round on a tray. Each person picks up a flower and puts it into the oil, which is then taken out and placed on the grave of the departed.

On the evening of the third day, when Fatiha prayers are offered, food is cooked in the house for the first time. Although under present circumstances the number of such sympathizers who can afford to send food to the house of the deceased for three days is much reduced, and poor households are forced to cook food within this period, even so the custom is still prevalent.

The Fatiha ceremonies on the third and fortieth days after death are especially important. Their original function was to distribute food among the impoverished and destitute in order to acquire religious merit for the deceased. However, in India, influenced by the Hindu ceremonies of the thirteenth day after death and the 'death anniversary', Muslims began to observe 'the third', 'the tenth', 'the twentieth', 'the fortieth', and 'the anniversary' rites. On all these occasions Fatiha prayers are offered, but food is distributed so lavishly and with such ostentation, that it would seem to be the occasion of a celebration. In addition, common people have come to believe that whatever food is given away to the poor on these occasions, by God's command, reaches the deceased. This belief makes the deceased a guest and great care is taken to provide his favourite dishes. In fact it should be the other way round. According to the principles of charity, the poor should be the guests and consideration should be given to their likes and dislikes.

Not only this, but nowadays at the time of Fatiha, four or five complete meals along with some water are laid out in a pleasantly prepared spot. New clothes, as expensive as the family can afford, bedding, a prayer-mat, newly-polished copper plates, a jug, drinking-bowls and cooking pots, are placed near the food for the deceased. A mulla then comes to offer the Fatiha prayer, after which all these items are sent to destitute individuals or devout Muslims for distribution to the poor.

The idea that the deceased is able to enjoy these things is so deeply rooted in the minds of some people that certain very simple women of the lower classes adorn themselves and sit near these articles, thinking that if a departed husband can get pleasure out of food and clothing, why should he be deprived of their grace and beauty?

An enormous amount of food is prepared for the Fatihas and besides its distribution to the poor, much is given to relatives and friends. Family servants, washermen, barbers, sweepers and others who attend this ceremony also get a share.

Besides these Fatiha ceremonies that I have described, there is also a Fatiha prayer every Thursday for the family's ancestors. In Shia households, every Fatiha is followed by a Majlis.

49

Forms of Religious Assembly

I shall now discuss two important religious gatherings: Majlis, the mourning assembly, and Maulud Sharif, the commemoration of the birth of the Prophet. Although Majlises are more common to the Shias and Maulud Sharifs to the Sunnis, they are observed by both sects. However, in Lucknow Majlises are more important and have had a great effect on local society, whereas the Maulud Sharif celebrations are not different from those anywhere else in India, although the élite sometimes invest them with the distinction and refinement of the Majlises.

So many Majlises take place in Lucknow that should anyone so desire, he could, simply by attending them, get enough food to live on the generosity of devout Shias. These assemblies have given rise to many types of orators who describe in their own styles the calamities suffered by Imam Husain and his family and reduce their audience to tears. To begin with, there are mujtahids and then *hadis khwans*, reciters of the hadis, who recount the virtues of the Prophet's family and the tribulations of some of its members in Kerbala in such a moving manner that their audience cannot restrain their tears. Then there are *vaqia khwans*, narrators of anecdotes, who recount these misfortunes in such eloquent language that people want to go on listening and weeping. The eloquence of these narrators has in fact made ordinary story-telling appear insipid. *Marsia khwans*, reciters of elegies, recite in simple but poetic manner and by gesticulation and facial expressions draw such a vivid picture of events in Kerbala that the audience is filled with appreciation and deeply moved. Mir Anis and Mirza Dabir attained the greatest heights in this form of poetry. It used to be said that 'a fallen poet becomes a chanter of elegies', but this art attained such perfection in Lucknow that the whole country came to recognize its excellence. A large number of marsiya khwans have emerged here, who are sought after all over India to recite marsiya.

Soz khwans,[443] who are accomplished musicians, sing dirges and elegies according to classical principles. They sing in a group of three: two of them, known as the accompanists, are responsible for maintaining the melody, while the third, sitting between them, sings the dirge. In Lucknow there are many soz khwans who are better than professional singers. They have attained the same status in the field of music as the marsiya khwans in poetry.

These arts all came into being in Lucknow and developed as a result of the Majlises. They greatly enriched Urdu literature and invested it with the power to arouse human emotions through appropriate words and expressions. This art was originally developed by the Greeks to make their oratory effective by choosing the right words and gestures for the occasion. They discovered which sounds and which intonations aroused joy, sorrow, pity or anger. Since then, no attention seems to have been paid to this art anywhere and only recently have attempts been made by orators in Europe to revive it. However in Lucknow, great strides were made as a result of the reciting of elegies.

At the end of these assemblies, it is customary to offer sherbet, sweets or food to everyone present. The élite have now adopted the practice of sending a portion of these sweets or food along with the invitations, since to emerge from an assembly with one's hands full of edibles does not seem very elegant, although ordinary people see no harm in this. After a Majlis the upper-class people hand over their portions to the servants to carry home, and if there are none around they give them to someone else.

Majlises are addressed from a wooden pulpit with seven or eight steps that is placed on one side of a hall or room, with the audience sitting all around on an immaculate farsh. If there is a large attendance, all the space is filled. When sufficient people have arrived, the orator mounts the pulpit, raises his hand and says, 'Fatiha', upon which everyone raises his hand and quietly repeats a part of the opening verse of the Quran. After that the orator, if he is a hadis khwan or a vaqia khwan, opens his book and begins to speak. If he is a reciter of marsiyas he begins with the pages of his compositions. People listen to the prelates and narrators of the hadis in respectful silence and weep copiously at the mournful passages. But on listening to the recital of marsiyas, all present loudly express their appreciation of the poetry, except when the sorrowful verses cause them to shed tears. The soz khwans do not mount the pulpit but sit with other members of the assembly and chant their dirges and elegies. They too receive loud appreciation from the audience.

As a general rule one orator follows another of a differing type. The narrating of the hadis is followed by the recital of marsiya and by soz khwani. Because the latter is music it is very popular, not only in Lucknow, but throughout India. Still, soz khwani is avoided in the assemblies of Shia prelates or of very religious elders, since music is prohibited by religion.

In Lucknow, the Majlis held on the ninth day of Muharram in the Ghuframab Imam Bara is very impressive and people come from great distances to attend it. On this occasion, after the orations, camels are brought before the audience to represent the ruined caravan of Husain's family. Their saddles and panniers are draped with the black cloth of mourning. This sorrowful spectacle affects some people so much that they faint.

Many innovations resulted from the dramatic aspect of the Majlis. Some people carried these to such extremes that they made the assemblies look like dramas.[539] For instance, the late Maulvi Mahdi Husain had curtains, painted with scenes of the Kerbala, lowered from time to time to induce lamentations during Majlis. Assemblies held by the ladies of the late Maulvi's household went even further: instead of orators narrating the calamity, the scenes were acted by people.

As far as I know, mujtahids and Shia prelates do not approve of such innovations, but popular interest in them is increasing day by day.

The Majlises have had a very marked influence on Lucknow society and because of them culture and etiquette became a part of life for a large number of people. The taste for marsiyas and soz gave new life to poetry and music and the love for these two arts spread not only among men but reached as far as noble ladies in purdah[208] as well. In Europe dancing and singing are part of a well-bred girl's education, but in my view, a taste for musical accomplishment could not have been developed anywhere in Asia as it has in Lucknow.

Another gathering held by Shias is known as Suhbat, which starts on the period beginning on the ninth day of the third month of the Muslim calendar and goes on for a few days. The Majlises are mourning assemblies, whereas the purpose of Suhbats is to scoff at and humiliate the enemies of the Prophet's family. Since Shias consider both Ayesha, a wife of Muhammad, and Omar Faruq, his second successor, to be enemies of Fatima, Ali and their children, they are the main targets of derision and paper effigies made of their persons are burnt. Naturally these gatherings are never attended by Sunnis. One hears of such bad behaviour on these occasions that no refined Shia could help feeling disgusted.[540] It is largely because of these gatherings that quarrels between Shias and Sunnis break out from time to time.

The Maulud Sharif assemblies of the Sunnis, which commemorate the nativity of the Prophet, are conducted in much the same way as the Shia assemblies. One difference is that Sunnis have no pulpit and instead the maulvi or reciter sits on a small takhat covered with a farsh in some prominent place. Traditionally a maulvi recounts the circumstances of the nativity and when he reaches the moment of the Prophet's birth all those present stand up in respect. The narrator also recites a poem to express joy at the event and rose-water is sprinkled all around the audience. If no maulvi is available, a well-respected man reads out from the pages of *Maulud-e-Sharif*, 'The Exalted Birth', by Maulvi Ghulam Imam Shaheed. But the public seems to be no longer satisfied with this form of recital and has replaced it by a new type which imitates soz khwani. As in soz khwani, the reciter is accompanied by two persons who maintain the melody. He sits between them chanting the circumstances of the nativity and at intervals, when he comes to verses and qasidas in honour of the Prophet, they join in. But whereas the soz khwans have given vitality to music, these people who sing about the nativity remain amateurs.

Lucknow can claim no special distinction for these gatherings as they are the same in Sunni circles throughout India. This applies also to the Sufis' Hal-o-Qal[425] meetings in which a state of ecstasy is reached: they are the same throughout India. Although Sufi meetings started in India at the time the Muslims first came here, except for producing a group of qavvals,[417] they did not improve the character of these gatherings in any way. Even the qavvals failed to attain a high status as musicians. But soz khwani has within one century acquired fully-fledged status as a musical form.

50

Betel Leaf, its Appurtenances and Tobacco

I shall now describe some articles that are used in everyday life whenever people meet. Such articles are numerous, but at the moment I shall deal only with the most important, which are the *huqqa* [hookah], *khas dan*, *lota*, and the spittoon. These articles are so widely used that the servants of the élite carry them wherever they go. Until recently, these servants carried a huqqa as well, but this is no longer the case. The huqqa is actually a Delhi invention, and various types were designed for the royal smoking rooms. In Lucknow improvements were first made in the size and shape of these huqqas, and then *pichvans*, huqqas with long spiral stems, were designed as well as *chilams*, tobacco bowls to hold the fire, and *chambars*, covers for the chilams. The Delhi huqqas were clumsy and ugly but in Lucknow they were well-shaped and pleasing to the eye. In addition to those made of copper, brass and pewter, very attractive earthenware huqqas were produced which proved extremely popular because of the delicacy of the design. The cool and sweet-smelling smoke of the earthenware huqqas made them preferable to the grand and costly ones.

After improvements had been made in huqqas, the tobacco was refined and enriched. The process of pounding up tobacco with crude sugar or syrup, which probably originated in Delhi, made the tobacco smoked in India superior to that of any other country. Tobacco is smoked everywhere, but though efforts were made in Europe to improve and refine the tobacco used for cigars, cigarettes and pipes, it never occurred to anyone that the addition of sugar or syrup would remove the bitterness and the acridity. In Lucknow further improvements were made by the addition of a syrup specially prepared with spices and perfumes. This not only removed a bad odour or unpleasant taste but made the tobacco so pleasant that if a huqqa bowl was filled with it, it gave out such a sweet smell that even a non-smoker would be tempted to try a few puffs. Excellent tobacco is grown in some parts of India and is known by the name of the town of its origin, but this is a gift of nature not connected with human achievement. However, the excellent Khamira tobacco blended in Lucknow is the result of skill and many experiments and is unequalled. Many people in other towns do not like this mixture and suspect that the syrup might induce catarrh. However, this is merely because they are not used to it, just as the British do not like *qaurma*, spiced curry, and are unable to digest it.

Appurtenances of the huqqa were also improved. The chilams have been made more delicate and beautiful. The chambars are decorated in various ways and have triple silver chains on them. Various kinds of dainty and attractive mouthpieces have been designed, and lately the huqqa has been decorated with flowers. In fact, Lucknow society has embellished and beautified the huqqa to look like a bride.

Of even greater importance in Lucknow society is the *khas dan*, betel box, which is so frequently used that the servants carry it with them when their masters go out. In it are placed *gilauris*,[541] folded betel leaves, carefully prepared for chewing. Chewing betel leaf is an ancient Indian custom which dates from early Hindu times. If a raja or a king had to entrust an important task to someone, he would place before his courtiers a prepared betel leaf and say, 'Who will take it up?' meaning, 'Who will conduct this affair or who will take on this responsibility?' Whoever among those present picked up the betel leaf gave, as it were, his promise to accomplish the work. This custom no longer exists but we still say, 'A certain person has picked up the betel leaf for this affair', meaning that he has assumed responsibility for it.

In ancient times when favours and rewards were bestowed at court, it was the custom to give betel leaf with them. Ibn-e-Batuta[542] mentions this in his book of travels. As the betel leaf played such an important part in the social life of India it would seem natural that its appurtenances should have been improved upon in the course of time. But this was not the case. For the entire period of its use in Delhi no improvement was made and the ingredients remained unchanged since ancient times. The ingredients used in the preparation of betel leaf in the past were *kathha*, a vegetable extract, lime, *dali*, the betel nut, and cardamoms: later on, before it came to Lucknow, tobacco was also added. But it is impossible to ascertain whether any special changes were made during the hundreds of years in which it was in use in the numerous royal courts. In Lucknow, prepared betel leaf became much more popular than in Delhi. Special appurtenances were designed for its use and everything connected with it was improved, including the natural leaf. Excellent betel leaf grows naturally in towns like Mahuba, but although quite a lot of betel leaf grows in the vicinity of Lucknow, it is not of good quality. However, because of the interest taken by the élite here, the dealers started to make improvements in the plant itself with the use of chemicals and soon it came to excel the betel leaf grown elsewhere. The leaves are buried in the ground for months until all traces of rawness and unpleasant smell disappear. The fibres become delicate and soft, the colour becomes yellow and the leaf, so to speak, matures. This delicious leaf has no comparison for taste and savouriness. It is called *begami*, and is sent to many distant places where it is received with much appreciation.

After betel leaf, the next important ingredient is lime. In all other towns, ordinary lime is used, often not properly slaked. Lime is a sharp and corrosive substance and when new and fresh a slight excess of it would cut one's lips. To avoid this unpleasantness, the lime here is well filtered and slaked, and a little cream and fresh whey are added.

Another ingredient is *kathha*, which is extremely astringent, bitter and unpleasant in taste. It is added to counteract some of the unfavourable qualities of the lime and to give a good colour to the betel leaf. One may in time get used to its unpleasantness, but it cannot be denied that it has a nasty taste. Its preparation, which is the same everywhere, is as follows. The herb is cut into small pieces and boiled in water until it becomes red like sherbet. It is then strained through a cloth and placed in a bowl in water to coagulate. In Lucknow, a tray is filled with ashes, covered with a cloth, and the coagulated kathha put on top of it and sprinkled with water from time to time. The moisture, together with the red colour which contains the astringency, is absorbed by the ashes. What remains looks fresh and white and is free from astringency. Then rose-water is added, or the flowers themselves. This practice is now followed in some other places as well, but it originated in Lucknow and the same standard is not attained elsewhere. This kind of kathha is very popular and is now sold in Lucknow shops, some of which are especially renowned for it. But the preparation made in the houses of some meticulous rich men is of such high quality that the very best, bazaar-made kathha cannot compete with it. In Poona and the towns of Hyderabad, a new kind of kathha is sold which is put into betel leaf in a dry state without being made into paste. People there like it, but I fail to appreciate its quality.

The next ingredient is *dali*, the betel nut, which is cut up into small fragments with special scissors and put into the leaf. To cut them up was a very ordinary operation, but in Lucknow it was made into an art by the ladies, who cut the pieces as small as a millet seed with each one exactly alike. Care is taken also to use the whole nut and not to lose the kernel.

Cardamoms are used in their natural state and no improvements have been considered necessary. However, etiquette demands that on festive and special occasions they should be wrapped in special edible silver foil. When they are put into a betel box or on a dish they shine like pieces of silver.

Tobacco is smoked throughout the world and its popularity for chewing is also on the increase. I have seen many Englishmen in England who rub up dried tobacco leaves and put them into their mouths. In India it has been the custom for a long time to chew dry tobacco leaves. In Delhi because of the golden colour of the leaf they call it *zarda*, yellow. In earlier times raw tobacco leaves used to be chewed with betel leaf. But even then, in many households the stalks would be boiled with the leaves and some moderating sweet-smelling spices added to the juice in order to control the bitterness of the tobacco according to personal taste. This produced a refined tobacco with a pleasant flavour and an agreeable smell. However, this practice was confined to particular families and households. The common man used raw tobacco leaves and women kept them in their betel boxes.

About twenty years ago, Munshi Saiyyid Ahmed Husain[543] made a special preparation of tobacco which looks like coarse powder. It became so popular that within a few years it almost completely replaced raw tobacco leaves.

51

Preparing and Serving Betel Leaf

The preparation I have just described for making chewing tobacco was preceded by another one known as *qivan*. In this the tobacco leaves and stalks were boiled thoroughly until the juice became thick like paste, and then musk, rose-water and other perfumes were added for fragrance. The tiniest morsel added to the betel leaf would impart the taste of this sweet tobacco and the fragrance would remain in one's mouth all day. After that, minute pills were made of this paste, each one sufficient for a portion. When wrapped in silver or gold edible foil they looked like pearls. A certain lady of Mufti Ganj quarter used to prepare such excellent qivan paste and pills that connoisseurs of Lucknow would buy them only from her and nowhere else. About the same time, the firm of Asghar Ali and Muhammad Ali[544] started to manufacture both of these articles on a commercial basis and sold them throughout India. After the death of this lady, Asghar Ali's firm became the sole manufacturer of the qivan paste and goli pills. Since then many people and firms have begun to manufacture them, but the quality of their products could not match that of the late Asghar Ali's firm. There was however in these preparations one defect, namely that the pungent taste of the tobacco was lost as soon as the juice was spat out, although the fragrance remained for some time. To remedy this, Munshi Saiyyid Ahmed Husain started to manufacture *pati*, scented tobacco leaf, in which the taste of both bitterness and fragrance remains in the mouth as long as the betel leaf lasts. Everyone adopted it and it has become so popular that the paste and pills seem to be disappearing.

Several new ideas also developed in Lucknow. Cardamoms were processed in such a way that one's lips became redder from eating one than from chewing betel leaf itself. But although in preparation some of the ingredients of betel leaf are filled into the cardamoms and they produce a better colour, they cannot be regarded as a substitute for betel leaf. Another method is to fill cardamoms with *missi*,[545] a cosmetic tooth powder, so that when the cardamom is placed in the betel leaf and chewed, the powder adheres to the teeth and a firm dark tinge appears in the interstices. But the red cardamoms cannot properly replace betel leaf and the black ones do not have the pleasant smell of properly scented missi. For these reasons cardamoms are mainly used for decorative purposes and have never become widely popular.

I shall now say something about *chikni dali*, betel nuts boiled in milk. Although this is not an indispensable ingredient of betel leaf, it certainly adds to its refinement. Some people use it in the preparation of betel leaf in place of ordinary betel nuts and many chew it along with cardamoms, as its taste is very pleasant. Hindu friends cannot chew betel leaf prepared by Muslims, and so they are offered only chikni dali and cardamoms, and these two things have thus become necessary adjuncts to social intercourse.[546]

Chikni dali is the same betel nut used in betel leaf, but after special processing. This is not done in Lucknow, Delhi or Hyderabad, but comes already prepared from the places where it is grown. It is said that the nuts are boiled in milk. Whatever the method of preparation, the result is that they become juicy and lose all dryness. Sometimes if one eats too much natural betel nut, one's throat becomes dry, but this never happens with chikni dali. When further processed it also becomes very delicate and tasty.

As far as I know chikni dali is used to a much greater extent in Hyderabad, Delhi and some other towns than in Lucknow. One might have thought that enthusiasts in those places would have improved upon it, but strangely enough it was left to the people of Lucknow to do this. The kernel of dali is delicate and fine in taste, but the portion near the rind is a little astringent and the bottom is insipid in flavour. In order to avoid the bad taste of these parts, special ways were devised in Lucknow of cutting the nuts. One way of doing this is called *do rukhi*. In this a good deal of the top and bottom and a little of the sides of the nut are cut, leaving a bowl-shaped residue which contains the soft and delicate kernel. Another way which is called *ek rukhi*, rounding, is to scrape the nut all round but leaving the bits of the defective portions either at the top or bottom. A third variety takes the form of octagonal lumps cut entirely from the kernel. The scrapings left after the kernel is cut are sold separately and constitute another quality. All the scrapings are divided into various categories according to quality, the scrapings from the kernel being at the top, followed by those resulting from *do rukhi* and *ek rukhi*. They all differ very much in delicacy and taste and there is a corresponding difference in cost.

Now I shall turn my attention to the appurtenances used with betel leaf. The most important among them is *pan dan*, the betel box, which transforms the raw leaf into a thing of glory. In former days in Delhi, these were little boxes of all shapes—round, square or octagonal. Probably when these boxes arrived in Hyderabad from Delhi, copies were made in metal. To this day, on the occasions of weddings in Hyderabad, they are liberally filled with the usual ingredients and placed before the ladies. The same were brought to Lucknow from Delhi about two centuries ago by the honoured ladies, and modifications were made here shortly after.

In the first place, the shape became round and they were made only of silver-plated copper. Then their lids were raised and rounded until they looked like a white dome, as they do at present. An elongated ring was fixed at the top to hold them, which lies on its side when not in use. In the boxes are two metal cups to contain kathha and lime, and three smaller, equal-sized receptacles for cut nuts of various kinds. All of these are arranged in a circle, in the middle of which is another small container to hold cardamoms or cloves. The lids of the small receptacles are firmly fixed, in fact they are difficult to open, but the cups are simply covered. There are tiny spoons for the kathha and lime, sometimes with a peacock crest and sometimes plain. Placed over all these containers is a large tray the same size as the betel box in which raw betel leaves are placed, wrapped in a damp cloth. In former times raw betel leaves were placed in a separate covered receptacle, called *nagardan*, but since this was kept shut the air could not reach the leaves and they went bad. For this reason the nagardan, although still seen in some old-fashioned houses, has gone out of fashion and will soon be quite forgotten.

In the course of time the handy betel box also came to serve as treasure-house and cash box for women. The size began to increase until it came to weigh as much as twenty to forty pounds. At the same time it became necessary for ladies to take it with them wherever they went. Just as 'the larger the turban, the greater the learning', so the larger the betel box, the greater was the status and grandeur of the lady. Eventually the betel box took up all the space in the palanquin and there was no room for the lady.

Then suddenly the taste for daintiness showed itself in this direction and a new, small, narrow-domed betel box with a decorative protrusion in the top centre was designed. At first this was called *aram dan*, but it is now known as *husn dan*. It was attractive in appearance and convenient to handle, but the internal arrangements remained the same. In Lucknow they were first adopted by those not given to show and display, but they soon became generally popular here and in other regions as well. Although old-fashioned betel boxes have not disappeared, the husn dan is at present more generally in use.

In addition to husn dan there is *khas dan*, the betel case, in which the prepared betel leaf is served in formal gatherings as well as everyday life. In Delhi betel leaves were served on trays, on which chopped up betel nuts and betel leaves with lime and kathha in them were placed. They are still served in this manner to this day. Probably it was the same in Lucknow, but here they started to use two betel leaves and fold them into triangular shapes to make a *gilauri*. The present shape of a gilauri is conical, and the leaves are kept in place by a tiny peg. At first cloves were used for pegs, but later small chains were attached to a tiny silver weight and the betel leaves were fixed to the pegs attached to the chains, and then placed in the khas dan. This was however an elaborate system and in everyday life it became the custom to hold the prepared betel leaf in shape with a small nail. A better method which is becoming popular is to make a conical container out of raw betel leaf and place the prepared betel leaf inside it.

It was not considered proper to serve gilauris in an open tray and so a dome-shaped lid was designed to cover them. This made the khas dan look like a small husn dan.

52

Utensils for Everyday Use

In spite of all improvements, the silver-plated copper khas dans became over-heated in the hot weather and the carefully prepared betel leaf became so hot and dry that there was no pleasure in chewing it and the mouth became even more parched. Therefore in the hot weather the leaves were kept in bowls made of unbaked earthenware which kept them fresh and cool, and increased their fragrance. These delicate bowls were wafer-thin and beautifully designed. When sprinkled with water to cool them they looked so refreshing that one felt that one could leave the betel leaf till later. Simply looking at them was cooling.

To keep these bowls continuously wet was a problem, and so the practice began of wrapping cloth soaked in water around them. This kept the moisture for a longer time. White cloth gets dirty quickly and stains easily from the betel leaf. Red tulle was therefore used for this purpose. This red cover was decorated with silver threads and made to look very beautiful.

Similarly khas dans, pan dans and husn dans were covered with elaborately decorated material. In the same way *surahi*, pitchers, were also wrapped around with decorated tulle to keep the water inside them fresh and cool.

When one chews betel leaf one usually wants to spit out the liquid. This can be annoying as one has to keep getting up, and in rooms with fine farsh it is difficult to find a place to spit without going some distance. To solve this problem an implement was devised. This is known as an *ugal dan*, spittoon. They were probably first made in Delhi, and in the original design the base was circular with an elongated rim opening up at the top. This type of spittoon, made in copper, brass and pewter, was common throughout India. In Bidar,[547] it was decorated with silver work. In Lucknow, designs were engraved on the copper, and later they were made on a larger scale in Muradabad, with their own local delicate engraving. In Lucknow the same type of spittoon was also made in earthenware.

The bottom of this spittoon was too light, however, and the upper portion wide and long, with the result that it was top-heavy and spilled easily. For this reason another form of spittoon was made in Jaipur, Hyderabad and later in Muradabad, which was probably also designed in Delhi. It looks rather like one side of a small inverted tambourine. In Lucknow it was readily adopted, although the old-fashioned spittoon has not quite disappeared and is in fact still being made. Although spittoons are more in use in Lucknow than anywhere else, no improvements have been made here.

Nowadays a new style of flat, broad spittoon made of china or enamel is

31 Lucknow miniature, late eighteenth century: Krishna with gopis

32   Lucknow miniature, 1770: prince and princess watching a dancer
with candles

imported from England, but these would seem to be designed to spit out bits of tobacco leaves when smoking cheroots and are not at all suitable for use after chewing betel leaf.

In addition to khas dan, *lota*, a water jug, accompanies well-to-do people when they go out. It is carried by a servant and is usually of medium size and made of copper decorated with engravings. Those men of means whom wealth has apparently freed from the restrictions of religious law use lotas made of silver.[548]

The lota dates from Hindu times when it was a rounded vessel without a spout, with a narrow neck and a broad body. As water used to be drawn from wells, every traveller always carried a lota and cord with him on his journeys. Hindu and some Muslim villagers still use this kind of early vessel, but Muslims generally speaking use one with a spout to facilitate the pouring of water. I do not know what kind of lota was used in Delhi, but Lucknow was influential in fashioning its present style and making it attractive.

In the hot weather servants also carried *farshi pankha*, a cloth fan with fringes, and lately umbrellas have become popular. They are held over their master's head by servants to protect him from the sun.

Inside the house *salafchi*, a basin and *aftaba*, ewer, have been in use for a long time in wealthy Indian households for purposes of washing. They were brought to Lucknow from Delhi and have remained very much the same. Here another kind of basin, *tasla*, slightly bigger and deeper, became more popular, but it was not nearly as good. The salafchi has a wide round base and its rim is slightly narrower than the body. A net cover is inserted over the top, through which the water falls into the basin. In this way the unpleasant and dirty water is out of the sight of fastidious people. This net can be taken out and cleaned. Some grass is placed over the net to prevent the water from splashing. In Lucknow, a lota has come into use in place of an aftaba, and was developed from it. The aftaba was a cylindrical brass utensil in which the circumference of the body and the mouth was much the same, except that it gradually narrowed toward the neck and the rim was curved, with a spout added. They are still seen in Hyderabad today. Their shape is reminiscent of the earthenware ewers of ancient Egypt and Asia Minor or the present china jugs on the wash-stands in England. This leads one to believe that they were probably brought by the Muslims from Arabia and Persia. With the influence of Hindu culture, the body of the vessel became more rounded, and a distinct neck was formed. But it remained elongated, and the body was oval rather than spherical. This is the shape of the aftaba which is mentioned in old Urdu masnavis and tales. Gradually in Lucknow its body changed from oval to spherical. Its height and width were made in proportion to each other and it is perfectly symmetrical. The necks were widened, fine rims were attached to them and the spout curved downwards and narrowed attractively at the end. This is the present-day Lucknow lota, which is sought after by those of good taste throughout the country.

The receptacle for containing *besan*[549] is a tiny copper vessel without a spout shaped like a lota. Besan is rubbed on the hands to remove grease before rinsing them with water. A few people put *butna* or *khali*, cakes of mustard seed, into this receptacle instead of besan, as they think that besan, being

H 225

edible, is wasted when used for washing, as well as not being in accordance with the principles of religion. But butna is prepared mainly for marriage and other ceremonies and the strong smell of khali makes it unpleasant, so that they are rarely used in everyday life.

53

Conveyances and Dress for Outings

My next topic is outings and excursions. As in all other Indian towns, everything in Lucknow has now become so Anglicized that traditional ways have almost completely disappeared. I shall therefore describe some things which have vanished or are about to vanish. The picture I shall draw for my readers takes us back sixty to seventy years and cannot be seen today.

In those days there were no motor cars, large phaetons or landaus and there was no need for broad and open streets. There were narrow alley-ways in which elephants, horses, camels, *hava dars, bochas, finases, miyanas, dolis,*[550] *sukhpals, raths* and *bahails,* all used to push through the human throng with shouts of 'Out of the way'. Whether it happened to be a bazaar or a popular place for outings, it was the same everywhere.

Apart from camels which were used by the army and for carrying despatches and loads, the rest of the conveyances were used by the different levels of the aristocracy. Princes, navabs and the highest dignitaries used to ride in bochas or hava dars. *Hava dar,* the tandem (popularly known as *tamtam* in India), was a carriage with a leather hood which could be opened or shut by means of metal springs. When there was no sun and the hood was lowered, it was open on all sides. Horizontal poles were attached to the front and back, which were carried on the shoulders of four bearers. The owner sitting inside would pass through the bazaars with much dignity, leisurely looking all around and exchanging greetings. The form of the hava dar shows that it was made by the British, according to their taste, after they had arrived in India. Its attractive design made it very popular with the Indian nobility. By now it has gone out of fashion though it can still be seen in the households of a few nobles and occasionally in marriage processions of wealthy Hindus.

The *bocha* was a more stately and dignified conveyance. Its style was much the same as that of the present-day brougham, but with legs instead of wheels. It had horizontal poles at the front and back and was carried by at least eight and generally sixteen palanquin-bearers, as it was the heaviest of all such vehicles. It was probably used by the nobility, although I have seen only Wajid Ali Shah using it. He used to go out in it when visiting his different parks, palaces and residences. The vehicle was surrounded on all sides by a large number of palanquin-bearers and honoured ministers as well as by favourite courtiers, who went on foot. Probably this vehicle was also copied from British carriages of that period, adapted to be borne by bearers.

The *sukhpal* was a highly esteemed vehicle for women in those days. It was entirely Indian and a perfect example of Indian ceremonial taste. It had a red dome with gold and silver decorations and the seat was the size of a large bed. Curtains hung from all four sides. It was carried by a large number of bearers, with one and sometimes two horizontal poles attached at the back and front. This conveyance was used only by ladies of the highest nobility and members of the royal household.

The *rath* was a wheeled vehicle similar in design but drawn by bullocks. It is still used in the country by taluqdars and zamindars[211] but is gradually dying out. There used to be thousands of these in Lucknow for the use of the royal ladies. Bahu Begam, who ruled as queen in Faizabad, had in her household alone eight to nine hundred raths. Long before that, when the emperors of Delhi used to undertake long journeys, their ladies would accompany them riding in raths.

The *bahail* was an ordinary cart drawn by bullocks. Its seat was large, about the size of a bed, and it had two wheels. There were four vertical poles covered with an awning from which curtains were hung. It was used as a conveyance by men as well as women, as in former days it was the only means of transport for middle-class villagers and city-dwellers alike. They are still very much in use in the villages, but the need for them is diminishing day by day and they will soon be a thing of the past. Except for the bocha and hava dar, all these vehicles came from Delhi and were not in any way peculiar to Lucknow. There were other conveyances besides those I have described, but as they are still in use, there seems to be no need for me to give a description of them.

The majority rode in *finases*, sedan chairs. Religious leaders, hakims, nobles and the well-to-do employed four palanquin-bearers who worked as indoor servants as well. People with a taste for sports and the military arts, which is so common here, rode on horseback in style. The horse was decorated with a silver necklace and other jewellery, and the trappings were of gold- and silver-decorated velvet. Distinguished persons went about on elephants which, in spite of their bulk, managed to get through the lanes and alleys without trouble. The elephants had brocaded cloth or gold- and silver-embroidered velvet hanging down on both sides. On top was placed an open or covered howdah.

Sukhpals, finases and other vehicles used by ladies were ostentatiously decorated. The finases were covered by red, richly embroidered shawls, which were sometimes stitched with gold and silver lace. The bearers wore knee-length, red broadcloth jackets, and on their heads were red turbans with silver fish sewn on to the edges. In India the fish is considered to be a good omen. Before a journey, or when someone is about to undertake an important task, women say ritualistically, 'Come back with fish and yoghurt.' This is probably connected with astrology and it would seem that the silver fish were sewn on to the front of the bearers' turbans to precede the palanquin and remain visible at all times.

A female bearer used to run with the ladies' finases holding on to the corner of the shawl. Their style of dress was peculiar to them and was characterized by the wide borders of their ankle-length skirts. These were in fact more border than skirt. Of all these conveyances, only the finas remains in the city, although noblemen are sometimes seen riding on horses or elephants.

How did these people dress when going out? I have already described the dress that came to Lucknow from Delhi, but in course of time improvements were made and it became different. In this connection I mentioned that it was not considered wrong to discard kurta or shirt when sitting at home and that people simply wore a *gharqi*, a knee-length loin-cloth, when in their own houses. The Lucknow court was Shia and everything here was cast in the Shia mould. From the point of view of Shia jurisprudence there is nothing objectionable in exposing part of the thighs. For the Hanifites, orthodox Sunnis, on the other hand, the entire body from the navel down to the knees must be covered. Therefore in Delhi it was the practice to wear a loin-cloth in the nature of a tahmat, which came below the knee.

In Lucknow, although everyone realized that he must go out properly dressed, at home it was not considered wrong to entertain a friend in this state of semi-dress. However, it was very different when a gentleman went out. He then dressed in *chau goshia*, a four-cornered cap, fresh from the mould, an immaculately clean angarkha, which looked as though it had just come from the laundry and the hems and sleeves of which had just been crimped, wide linen or muslin pyjamas, a triangular scarf over the shoulders, a handkerchief and cane in hand, and Lucknow-made *khurd nau*, light, short-toed velvet shoes, on the feet.

Many people took such care when going out that their clothes always looked freshly laundered, although they may not actually have been washed for months. The practice was to go out in the evenings and stroll through the fashionable area of the Chauk market, taking great care not to let anything touch the clothes, even shying at one's own shadow. At night on returning home the first thing that was done was to put the chau goshia on its mould and cover it with a cloth, then the angarkha, pyjamas and handkerchief were carefully folded with the scarf wrapped round them and put away. Then one put on the gharqi and some old shoes or slippers and got comfortable. In this way expensive clothes, especially those made of shawl material, lasted four or five generations. Because of the care bestowed on them, they did not become dirty, torn or moth-eaten and always looked new. People used to attend weddings and celebrations so gorgeously dressed that those who knew their circumstances often wondered how they managed to look as they did.

Although noble and wealthy people, especially princes, religious leaders and hakims, used to go out in conveyances, it was not considered out of place, as it is nowadays, for persons of rank to go about on foot. All sorts of individuals used to walk the streets and rub shoulders with the most exalted nobles and men of distinction and no harm was seen in it.

54

Pottery

I should like to conclude with a description of the arts and crafts that developed in Lucknow. Man has made earthenware pottery from the earliest times. Potsherds of antiquity have been dug up in all corners of the globe, demonstrating the skill of prehistoric man at making pottery by baking clay in kilns. Clay vessels from the period of the Pharaohs have been unearthed in Egypt, and clay eating- and drinking-vessels, together with well-baked bricks, have been discovered in Babylon and Ninevah. The mummies of Egyptian nobles of the time of the Pharaohs were encased in coffins made of clay, and for a long period the ancient world used earthenware tablets in place of paper for the purpose of writing.

People of India also acquired this art in the remote past and it appears from the antique utensils that have come to light that the progress made in Lucknow was on a par with that of any other region. In particular the carving of images laid the foundation for the sculpting of figures among Hindus, and later grew into an art. In the course of time the potters became a caste whose family profession was to make and bake earthenware utensils and toys.

During the Mughal era there arose a new class of craftsmen, known as *kasgars*, who also worked in clay. They were Muslims and their main profession was to make utensils, but to improve their trade they made toys as well, even though the making of images is prohibited by Muslim religious law. These kasgars came to Lucknow with the Delhi nobles. Here their craft developed further and, in the course of time, the work of both the Hindu potters and the Muslim kasgars achieved the level of creative art.

The clay of Lucknow is of the right quality for fine pottery, and this gave impetus to the craft, with the result that the utensils and toys made here are so fine, light and attractive that they cannot be rivalled. In Amroha (U.P.) too, the clay is very suitable and the craft is developing. But it is different in style.

Among articles in everyday use, the *ghara*, water pitcher, and *badhni*, a vessel with a spout, are light and very delicately proportioned. The gharas are perfectly rounded and the badhnis look just like copper lotas. Earthenware dishes are especially attractive. However, as the custom of eating from this kind of plate has died out, potters are no longer interested in making them. Instead they have turned to making *abkhoras*, *jhajris*, huqqas and pots for serving rice-pudding, and in this show great skill.

Abkhoras are vessels for drinking water. Although light and attractive glass, enamel and copper drinking vessels are frequently used these days water is not palatable in the hot weather unless earthenware vessels are used. Only these can keep the water cool and fresh. Additionally the water acquires a most refreshing smell of clay in these vessels. The smell of the clay is so fragrant that in Lucknow people even started to make perfume from it. For this reason, the abkhora survived and was continually improved upon. Such excellent abkhoras are made that they are even finer than glass. They are decorated with designs and a coating of sand is applied to the outer surface to keep the water cool for a longer period. Special trays have been made on which to serve them. These drinking vessels have become so exquisite that one has to admit that the skill of these craftsmen is in no way inferior to the skill of those who work in metal and glass.

Among the receptacles for containing water are *surahis*, pitchers in the shape of vases. They date from ancient times and were used in Persia and Egypt. But in Lucknow the surahi became so well-shaped and the curvature of its spout so well-proportioned, that it cannot be equalled anywhere. Then there is the *jhajri*, pitcher, which is much the same as the surahi, but in place of a long neck it has a broad rim at the top. Its workmanship is no less skilled than that of the surahi.

It is essential that the smoke of a huqqa should be cool and for this purpose thin clay huqqas were made here, which were also very light and well-designed. These Lucknow huqqas were such that they could not be copied elsewhere. Their smoke was so satisfying that during the monarchy some aristocrats would not smoke any other type of huqqa. Azim Ullah improved them still further and designed the huqqa named after him, which remains the best earthenware huqqa to this day. I heard in London that the Poet Laureate, Lord Tennyson, liked to smoke clay pipes and always kept a basket filled with them handy. He could only smoke one for a few minutes, then he would have to throw it away. He would sit in this way all day, filling, smoking and breaking up pipes. I feel that if Lord Tennyson had been lucky enough to have an Azim Ullah Khani huqqa from Lucknow, he would have forgotten all about clay pipes.

Earthenware cooking pots and dishes to serve *khir*, rice-pudding, are made everywhere, but those in Lucknow are distinctive in quality in that they serve the same function as those made of copper. Dishes to serve khir on formal occasions are as delicate and pleasing as the surahis and abkhoras. Lately some people have started to keep their prepared betel leaf in them in the hot weather.

The potters display even greater skill in making toys and models. The art of carving images is as old as idol worship. Egyptians, Babylonians, Persians, Greeks and Romans, have all evinced great skill in this art, which can be seen even today in the museums of Europe. The Greeks in particular showed such skill in sculpting out of stone and giving the human body its correct proportions that they are still considered the masters in the art. But the uneducated potters of Lucknow display great skill in proportioning their models and figures and in making them very life-like. They can make an accurate model of someone by observation only, and their small figures, of differing types and descriptions, are a tribute to their skills. At the time of the Diwali festival, Hindus buy a great number of toys and the work of the potters is greatly in demand.

The various groups of figures that these potters have produced are worth seeing: British bands, troupes of courtesans and bhands, social gatherings of navabs and nobles, assemblies of different groups of tradespeople. A local potter made a model of a complete Indian village, which was displayed in an exhibition, in which there were shops, houses and alleys, with all manner of people in them. Bullocks and bullock carts were in the fields and there were peasants ploughing. Water was flowing into the fields and one could see tiny ripples and visualize the flow. This was not all: the bullocks drawing the ploughs were emaciated and their ribs were evident. I have also seen a model of Lucknow in the days of the monarchy, complete with people, streets and bridges. It is most regrettable that such wonderful work can be seen only for a few days before disappearing from public view. There is no place where they can be preserved. In London there is a waxwork museum called 'Madame Tussaud's', in which life-size reproductions of famous persons are exhibited. Some of these waxworks are so life-like that it is impossible to distinguish them from a living person. If a museum were opened here for the local earthenware figures, I think it would be of value. It would give encouragement to the craft and would also be lucrative. There could be an admission fee and probably foreign visitors would not leave without seeing the museum. But the trouble is that no one has sufficient interest or enthusiasm, and we all look to the Government for such enterprises.[551] If some wealthy man, instead of pursuing a life of luxury, were to take an interest in the matter, he would do great service to his country and his efforts would be much appreciated by all. As things are, there are only a few museums in India which exhibit some of these works, in a small section. But their standard is so high that they deserve a museum for themselves in Lucknow.

Notes

Chapter 1: *Faizabad and the Early History of Avadh*

1. The name of Avadh (Oudh), a Province from the end of the sixteenth century, was derived from the popular version of the ancient town of Ajodhya, which was the capital of the mythological kingdom of Raja Dasratha (5) in prehistoric times. Sravasti, also of this region, and where Gautama Buddha spent many years, features in the Buddhist literature of the centuries immediately before the Christian era. Later on in the fourth century AD it was part of the Gupta Empire, after which it seems to have become a wilderness which was deserted by the seventh century.

In the following century it is supposed that the Tharus tribe, from the foot of the Himalayan mountains, descended upon this area. By the ninth century the whole area had become part of the Kingdom of Qanauj. Two centuries later, in 1194, Qutub ud Din finally defeated the ruler of Qanauj and broke up the last great Hindu kingdom of this region. Subsequently the Bhars who rose into importance in Bundelkhand spread into parts of Avadh, but were crushed in 1247. From 1394 until 1478 almost this whole region was part of the Sharqi Kingdom (429) whose capital was Jaunpur in U.P. The region then changed hands many times between different adversaries who were trying to establish themselves on the throne in Delhi. In 1555 the Mughal King Humayun emerged as the final victor and this area thus became part of the Mughal Empire. His successor, Akbar, created the Suba (Province) of Avadh as one of the units of his Empire, the Governor of which was called a Subedar (12), and the official name of the town of Ajodhya also became Avadh. (*Imperial Gazetteer* vol. 1, pp. 225–28)

At that time Avadh was 'bounded by the mountains [the Himalayas] in the north, Bihar in the east, Manikpur Sarkar [a Sarkar is equivalent to a present-day Division, an administrative unit of several districts] in the Allahabad Suba in the south and the Qanauj Sarkar in the west . . . and divided into five *havelis*, districts: Avadh [Faizabad], Gorakhpur, Bahraich, Lucknow and Khairabad.' These boundaries seem to have remained unchanged until the reign of the Mughal Emperor Muhammad Shah, two centuries later. (Srivastava [A], pp. 31–32)

Emperor Muhammad Shah appointed Sadat Khan the Subedar of Avadh in 1722. This may be regarded as the foundation date of the dynasty of the Navabs of Avadh, which ruled until 1856. With the disintegration of the Mughal Empire the office of Subedar became hereditary and this Province, like most others, achieved de facto independence, with no formal break from the Mughal court of Delhi. The first three rulers of Avadh, Sadat Khan, Safdar Jang and Shuja ud Daula, in addition to this office, held important offices in the Mughal court. Safdar Jang was Vazir (135) from 1748 until 1753 (Srivastava [A], p. 127) and Shuja ud Daula held the office of Vizarat in 1762 (Srivastava [B], p. 141).

Sadat Khan extended the boundaries of his Province considerably by leasing the Suba of Murtaza Khan in 1728. His eastern frontier then came to include the Sarkars of Benares, Jaunpur, Ghazipur, Chunargarh, Azamgarh, Ballia and the eastern portion of Mirzapur. The western frontier came close to the city of Qanauj, after his capture of the fort of Chachendi from Hindu Singh in 1729. Later, in 1735, with Sadat Khan's appointment by the Mughal Emperor as Faujdar (military commander) of Kora Jahanabad in Allahabad Suba, this region also became part of his dominion (Srivastava [A], pp. 44–49). His successor, Safdar Jang, annexed the territory of the Navab of Farrukhabad (Chapter 3) but could not retain it; thus the boundaries of his Province remained the same during his reign.

During the rule of Shuja ud Daula the territory of Avadh was diminished after he was obliged to give away certain areas of his dominion to the East India Company by the Treaty of Allahabad (Chapter 4). However, in 1773 he bought back some of these areas from the British. In 1774 he annexed, except for a small area, the entire territory of the Khans of Ruhelkhand (23) which formed his northern frontier and some territory near Farrukhabad from the Bangash Navab (Chapter 4). Thus his dominion lay from the districts of Allahabad, Benares, Ghazipur on the east to Fatehpur, Kanpur, Etawah and Mainpuri on the west. (Ahad Ali, p. 16)

Shuja ud Daula's successors continued to lose parts of their Province to the British in exchange for various treaties. As soon as he came to power in 1775, Asaf ud Daula ceded Benares to the Company, and after him Sadat Ali Khan did likewise with half of his dominion. From then on the dynasty continued to rule under the protection of the British.

In 1856 Avadh was annexed into the British Raj and became a Chief Commissioner-ship with a separate administration. In 1877 the two Provinces of Agra and Avadh (Oudh) were brought together under the Lieutenant Governor of the North-Western Provinces who was also the Chief Commissioner of Avadh. In 1902 the name was changed to the United Provinces of Agra and Oudh and the title of Chief Commissioner was abolished. The unit had forty-eight Districts, thirty-six in Agra and twelve in Avadh, among which were Lucknow, Unao, Rae Bareilly, Sitapur, Hardoi, Faizabad (Fyzabad), Sultanpur, Partabgarh and Bara Banki (*Gazetteer* vol. 1, pp. 1–5, 100). The name was once again changed to United Provinces on 1 April 1937. The capital of the Province had already been shifted to Lucknow in 1936, when the remaining Govern-mental offices were transferred from Allahabad.

In August 1947 the Province became one of the States of the Republic of India, and on 24 January 1950 it was given the name of Uttar Pradesh, Northern Region, but retained its abbreviation of U.P. At present it has fifty-one Districts and ten Divisions. The area of Avadh is included in the Division of Lucknow, which includes the Dis-tricts of Lucknow, Unao, Rae Bareilly, Sitapur, Hardoi, Khari and the Division of Faizabad, which includes the Districts of Gonda, Bahraich, Sultanpur, Partabgarh and Bara Banki.

2. The reference is mainly to the Muslim Princely States of Hyderabad (42). Bhopal and Rampur (124) which were flourishing in India during the author's lifetime and lasted until 1947.

3. *Hindustan Men Mashriqi Tamaddun ka Akhri Namuna* (literally, 'The Last Example of Oriental Culture in India'), the original title under which the articles comprising the present work were first published between 1913 and the early 1920s, in the author's journal *Dil Gudaz*. See the Note on the Present Edition, page 25.

4. Sanskrit *rajya*: a kingdom, principality. Raja was originally the title of a Hindu king or prince in ancient India. Maharaja: Great Raja, Emperor. In later times these titles were bestowed by the Mughal Emperors and then by the British Government of India on Hindus of rank. The Republic of India in 1947 abolished the creation of new Rajas and Maharajas, but recognized the existing ones for their lifetime.

5. In Hindu mythology Rama, Ramchandra, or simply Ram, was the eldest son of Raja Dasratha, who fought and destroyed the evil Ravana, with the help of his half-

brother Lakshman. He is regarded as the seventh incarnation of the God Vishnu. His adventures are the theme of the Sanskrit epic *Ramayana* (*Ramayan*), attributed to Valmiki, the ancient Sanskrit poet. The present popular version of the *Ramayan* as known in U.P. is the work of Tulsi Das, who composed this poem in Avadh's local dialect, Avadhi, in the latter half of the sixteenth century. The capital of Raja Dasratha's legendary kingdom was Ajodhya (Sanskrit, Ayodhya), situated on the banks of the River Ghagra, about three miles from the present town of Faizabad and an important place of pilgrimage for the Hindus. The worship of Rama holds its ground particularly in Avadh and Bihar where he has numerous worshippers. A common form of salutation among Hindus is 'Ram-Ram'. The *Ramayana* along with the *Mahabharata* remain to this day the two sacred epics of India.

6. A dramatic presentation of the heroic deeds of Rama in his struggle against evil, usually performed by amateurs as a popular celebration in village squares or other open-air places.

7. Persian *abad*: populated, an ending for the name of a town, added to the name of the founder or an adjective. Thus Faizabad, The Settlement of Liberality; Daulatabad, Town of Wealth; Tarababad, Town of Entertainment.

8. Arabic *Navab*, plural of *Naib*: Deputy, but used honorifically as a title. Under the Mughal Government the title of Navab was prefixed to the name of a high official and the Viceroy or Governor of a Province. At the time of the disintegration of the Mughal Empire, some of the Navabs became independent rulers, hence the word came to be a common title for a Muslim sovereign in India. The title was retained by the British Government of India, who would confer it upon a Muslim of high rank or a dignitary without any office being attached to it. In 1947, the Republic of India abolished the creation of new Navabs, but recognized the existing ones for their lifetime. The Navabs of Avadh had the title prefixed to the names of all the members of the family including the women. This practice continued among the Muslim aristocracy in Lucknow even after the demise of the ruling dynasty.

9. Arabic *ul*, the, and *Mulk*, land or country. Added to a noun or adjective and given as a title by the Mughal Emperors: Burhan ul Mulk, Credit to the Country.

10. Khan, Afghan and Pathan are common appellations of men coming from the warrior tribes of Afghanistan and the north-west frontier of the sub-continent. Khan is used as a surname. Sometimes the name of the tribe is also added, as in Ahmad Khan Bangash, Ahmad the Khan from the Bangash tribe. This tribe was originally domiciled partly in the Kohat area and partly in the Khurram valley in the north-west region of the sub-continent.

11. Of Nishapur, a town in the north of Persia. Following the Muslim practice, some families in India appended to their names the name of the town or tribe from which their families originated: Bilgrami, from the town of Bilgram in U.P.; Tabrizi, from the town of Tabriz; Shirazi, from Shiraz, in Persia; Dehlavi, from Delhi; Lakhnavi, from Lucknow. Urdu poets as a rule added the place of their origin after their name.

12. Arabic *subah*, province, and Persian *dar*, holder. The title of the Governor of a Province under Mughal administration.

13. Arabic *shaikh*, elder, head of a Muslim tribe or village, a scholar, and *zada*, born of. Originally a designation of those Muslims who profess to be descended from the first or second Caliph or from the Prophet's uncle.

14. *Tarikh-e-Farah Baksh*, 'The Delightful History', is in two parts: 'Memoirs of Delhi', Part I, and 'Memoirs of Faizabad', Part II. The manuscript is in Persian, a copy of which (265 pages, dated 1832) is in the British Museum, London. Its preface is dated 1233 AH (1818 AD), Faizabad. The work was translated from the author's original manuscript into English by William Hoey in 1887 in two volumes and printed by the Government Press, North-Western Province of Agra and Oudh, in 1888 and 1889. A copy of this translation is in the India Institute Library, Oxford.

The author, Muhammad Faiz Baksh, came in his early boyhood from Kakori near Lucknow to Faizabad in 1768, the fifth year after the city's rise to fame. He writes: 'I saw six years of the rule of Shuja ud Daula and remained after his death for twenty-seven years under Jawahar Ali Khan [Chapter 27]. After his death the office of Nazarat [Superintendent] was filled by Darab Ali Khan and during his time up to the present [1818] a space of some twenty years more, I have witnessed events all of which I have faithfully committed to writing. Hereafter, if it pleases God to spare me, I shall record whatever comes to pass provided I be above fear of want and my faculties remain unimpaired.'

15. Hindi *bangla*: a thatched house, a summer house made after the fashion of those made in Bengal. The word would seem to have been adopted into English as 'bungalow'.

16. Persian *jang*: war. Added to nouns or adjectives and bestowed by the Mughal kings as a title, implying brave and chivalrous: Safdar Jang, Warlike Conqueror; Sher Jang, Martial Lion; Bahadur Jang, Brave in War; Salar Jang, Martial Commander.

17. Turkish *Mughal*: Mongol-Turks. The Mughals originally came to India from Central Asia and Turkestan (Land of the Turks). They belonged to the Chaghtai tribe. See also Introduction.

18. Persian *divan*: a royal court, a minister, the title of the Finance Minister in the Mughal Empire. Later the word came to signify a high-level administrator in the court of an Indian ruler.

19. Arabic *risala*, a troop of horses, cavalry, and Persian *dar*, holder. The commander of a force of cavalry.

20. Persian *khwaja-sara*: eunuch. The eunuchs had a special role in royal and wealthy households. Being sexually impotent they had free access to the ladies' quarters and acted as the messengers between men's and ladies' apartments. Usually they performed the duties of a male servant, but during the days of the later Mughal Emperors and early Avadh Navabs some eunuchs occupied a high position and rank in the Government administration.

21. Arabic *ud*, the, and Persian *daula*, court. A title of the Mughal Court, usually added to an adjective or noun: Shuja ud Daula, Brave of the Court; Muzaffar ud Daula, Victorious of the Court; Raushan ud Daula, Light of the Court.

22. The joint army of the Mughal Emperor Shah Alam, Mir Qasim of Bengal and Shuja ud Daula was defeated at Baksar (Buxar) by Major Hector Munro on 16 August 1765. The Treaty of Allahabad was then signed, according to which Shuja ud Daula was given back his dominion on payment of a war indemnity of fifty lakhs (85) of rupees to the East India Company. The areas now known as Kanpur, Fatehpur and Allahabad were however taken from him and given to Shah Alam who had now gone over to the British (Srivastava [C], pp. 11–16). Before the treaty Shuja ud Daula with some help from the Ruhelas and Marathas faced the British for a second time in 1765 but was again defeated in Jajmau near Kanpur District. (*Gazetteer* vol. I, pp. 228–30)

23. The name given to the region of Katehr by the Afghans who had come originally from the mountainous area of Afghanistan (in the Pashtu language *roh* or *rohu* means a mountain). In the early eighteenth century Ali Muhammad Ruhela was rewarded for his services to the Mughal Emperor by a grant of land and the title of Navab. By 1748 he had finally established himself as a ruler and extended his dominion considerably. It lay on the north-west frontier of Avadh in the regions now known as Bareilly Division, Rampur and some areas in Naini Tal District (*Gazetteer* vol. I, pp. 244–46). Following Ali Muhammad's rule, there was a Confederacy of twelve Ruhela Chiefs, of which Hafiz Rahmat Khan was the head, with headquarters at Bareilly (Najmul Ghani, vol. II, p. 38). The latter's son Muhammad Mustajab Khan wrote in 1792 the history of the Ruhelas up to the time of his father. The manuscript, *Gulistan-e-Rahmat*, is in the British Museum.

24. The son of Muhammad Khan, the Navab of Farrukhabad in Ruhelkhand. At the

time of his death in 1743, Muhammad Khan held most of the present Districts of Farrukhabad, Mainpuri and Etah with parts of Aligarh, Etawah, Badaun, Shahjahanpur and Kanpur. The entire dominion was annexed by Safdar Jang in 1749 but was recovered from him by Ahmad Khan in the following year. (*Gazetteer* vol. I, pp. 419–22)

25. Town founded in 1639 in the region of present-day Delhi by the Mughal Emperor Shahjahan (99) which became the capital of the Mughal Empire. The city of Delhi is composed of at least eight different towns, Shahjahanabad being one of them.

26. Hindi *tri*, three, and *pulya*, a foot-bridge. The name of a small area in Ajodhya near the River Ghagra where there were three foot-bridges.

27. Hindi *chauk*: a square or open space inside a city, around which was situated a shopping centre. The name still applies to the main market in small towns and villages.

28. Mosques are sometimes known after those who had them constructed.

29. Hindi *ghat*: quay, where sometimes Hindu temples are built and Hindu mendicants (68, 69) live in huts and pursue a life of meditation.

30. Sanskrit *nila*, dark blue, and *gau*, a cow or a bull. A large short-horned deer. The males are of slate-blue colour and the females rusty red.

31. Persian *bagh*: a park or garden. Parks and gardens are usually named by adding a noun or adjective before the word Bagh: Anguri Bagh, Garden of Grapes; Moti Bagh, Pearl Garden; Lal Bagh, Red Garden; Aish Bagh, Park of Pleasure; Qaisar Bagh, Garden of Qaisar (216).

32. Persian *shah*, king, and *alam*, the world. The title of the Mughal Emperor who ascended the throne in 1759, was blinded in 1788 and died in 1806 (22).

33. 'Breech loader' was the name of the muskets used at this time, which were loaded from the back. Perhaps because of his position in the army, the popular name for these muskets—*bareech*—was added to Navab Murtaza Khan's name.

34. *Brahmanas* were originally the texts which dealt with instructions and correct procedures in making sacrifices in Aryan times. Later the scholars of these texts came to be known as Brahmans and served the function of priests (Gokhale, pp. 25, 188). They are the first of the Hindu castes; *Pandit* (Sanskrit, scholar) is an honorific title used before their names.

35. An Arab tribe among the Shaikhs, descended from Abdulla bin Zubair; hence they are also known as Zubairis. In U.P. they had settled in Bareilly and Etawah.

36. A Hindu race, or member of it, originally from South India who later settled in the present region of Maharashtra (41).

37. Arabic *mir*: a chief, headman, Saiyyid, used as a prefix to the name. A Saiyyid is a descendant of the Prophet through his daughter Fatima.

38. There were four grades of Bakhshis in the Mughal court, the highest being Mir Bakhshi, Paymaster General. In Shuja ud Daula's court, however, there was only one office of the Bakhshi who served as the Paymaster General, hence Tahawar Jang the Bakhshi. In later times the word has sometimes been added before or after the names of the descendants of those who held such offices.

39. Hindi *singh*: lion. A title borne as a suffix by men of royal or military caste of Rajput and Sikh soldiers. Later borne by all Rajputs, Jats and Sikhs. Raghu Nath and Prashad belonged to the Rajput caste of U.P.

40. Persian *vala*, eminent, dignitary, and Bansi, a town in the District of Bansi, U.P.; also a bamboo fence. Thus Saiyyid Ahmad either originated from the town of Bansi or was so called because of bamboo fencing that was probably extensively used around his house.

41. The Marathas (36) were a dominant power in eighteenth-century India, with Poona as their capital. They attacked the territory of the Khans of Ruhelkhand in 1773 (Srivastava [C], p. 215). Their leader Mahaji Sindhia attacked Delhi at the time of Shah Alam II, and the latter became his virtual puppet from 1789 until 1803, when the British deported them and replaced them as councillors of the Emperor. Their rule

came to an end in 1818 when Baji Rao II, the Peshwa, surrendered to the British. Peshwa was the title of the hereditary Chief Minister, who was the most powerful member of the Maratha Confederacy. (Majumdar, pp. 698–709)

42. Originally, Nizam ul Mulk Mir Qamar ud Din was appointed Governor of the Deccan Suba (later Hyderabad) by the Mughal Emperor Farrukhsiyar in 1713. In 1724, when the Mughal Empire began to weaken, he established himself as independent ruler and assumed the title of Asaf Jah. Nizam Ali was his third son who ruled from 1762 to 1803. There have been nine ruling Nizams in the dynasty (Majumdar, p. 982). The Hyderabad State became part of the Indian Republic in 1948 and has since been added to the State of Andhra Pradesh. Its last ruler, Mir Osman Ali Khan, died in 1966.

43. Zabita Khan was the ruler of the northern part of Ruhelkhand north of the present Divisions of Bareilly and Meerut, with Najibabad, Bijnor (U.P.) as his headquarters. The house was founded in 1755 by his father Najib ud Daula Najib Khan who in 1757 rose to the position of Royal Bakhshi in the Mughal court. He later became Vazir of the Empire, after which he established his own rule in this territory (*Gazetteer* vol. I, pp. 244–48). In 1774 Zabita Khan yielded to Shuja ud Daula. (Srivastava [C], p. 265)

44. Zulfiqar ud Daula, Najaf Khan administered Kora and Allahabad on behalf of the Mughal Emperor Shah Alam, after the Treaty of Allahabad (Srivastava [C], p. 11). In 1774 he conquered Agra from the Marathas on behalf of the Emperor and lived there as an important official of the court until his death in 1779. (*Gazetteer* vol. 1, p. 405)

45. Sabit Khan tribesmen who originally came from Afghanistan.

46. A Rajput caste settled in the Bundelkhand area, which used to be approximately south of U.P. Chandela: a tribe of Bhangis, sweepers, from Bundelkhand, known for their fighting qualities.

47. A Rajput caste of Meos who were converted to Islam from the area of Mewar (Panjab). (*Gazetteer* vol. I, p. 223)

48. Colonel J. B. J. Gentil lived in Faizabad from 1763 to 1775. He arrived as a military man but later became French Resident. He saw himself 'uniquement occupé de la politique, du gouvernement et de la littérature' and completed in Faizabad his *Abrégé historique des Souverains de l'Indoustan ou Empire Mogol* (1772–75), *Divinités des Indoustan* (1774), *Histoire des Pièces de Monnoyes qui ont été Frappées dans L'Indoustan* (1773) and *Histoire des Rajah de l'Indoustan depuis Barh jusqu'à Petaurah* (1774). His *Mémoires sur l'Indoustan ou Empire Mogol* was published in Paris in 1822. In addition to these literary activities, he was also a collector of objets d'art. Most of his collection, including the above manuscripts and albums of miniatures, is in the Bibliothèque Nationale, Paris. Two portraits of Shuja ud Daula, one by T. Kettle and another, a copy of Kettle's portrait of Shuja ud Daula with his ten sons, by Nevasi Lal, were presented by Gentil to the King of France in 1778. The first is in the Palace of Versailles and the second in the Musée Guimet, Paris. (Archer, pp. 53, 118)

Colonel Polier was a Swiss French, employed by Shuja ud Daula from 1774 until 1775, when the ruler was required by the British to dispense with his services. However, he was allowed by Governor General Hastings to stay in Lucknow in order to complete his research on Indian literature and write his memoirs. He was also a collector of paintings and manuscripts. After his murder in Avignon in 1794 his collection was dispersed, and parts of it were obtained by the British Museum, the Bibliothèque Nationale, Paris, and the Bibliothèque Cantonale, Lausanne. The part of his collection acquired by E. Pote in 1788 in India was given to King's College, Cambridge and Eton. (Archer, pp. 53, 118)

Claude Martin (137) was also present in Faizabad at this time. (Archer, p. 54)

49. Arabic *munshi*: a clerk, secretary, a regular post in élite households. During the British Raj Europeans used this term to denote a teacher of Arabic, Persian and Urdu. Munshi ul Sultan: Private Secretary to the King, Chief Clerk.

50. Sanskrit *nagar*: a city, town; also used to denote a quarter. Mumtaz Nagar, Distinguished Quarter; Ram Nagar, Ram District.

51. A cold, sweet drink with wheat-paste as a base.

52. Arabic *hakim*: a practitioner of the Yunani, Greek, medicinal system in India. (Chapter 14)

53. The principal denomination of Indian currency. It was introduced as a silver coin in the first instance by Sher Shah (1540–45) and has survived to this day with changes in its silver content. (236)

54. In particular, Madrasas, Muslim religious seminaries where religious and philosophic instruction was given and which were usually located in or around mosques. Students joining these seminaries were looked after and provided with food and clothing by the believers, through the teacher. The students in return performed certain religious duties for the spiritual benefit of the community. In all fields of activity, they showed complete obedience to their teacher, whose authority was never questioned.

55. Sharar here means courtesans. (Chapters 25, 40, 42)

56. Arabic *hafiz*: guardian, protector, used as a prefix to the name of one who knows the Quran by heart, that is, guards it in his heart. According to believers, this is the surest way of preserving the words of God.

57. The Marathas (41) were at this time encamped at Ramghat and ravaged the northern portion of Ruhelkhand.

58. Persian *do*, two, and *ab*, water: the waters of the two rivers in U.P., the Ganges and the Jamna. The Doab refers to the land lying between these two rivers.

59. In 1773 another agreement was made between Shuja ud Daula and Warren Hastings in Benares according to which the Allahabad territory was returned to Shuja ud Daula on payment of five million rupees. He also agreed to pay two and a half million rupees a year, besides the cost of a brigade of British troops to be stationed in his territory. A permanent British Resident was also appointed at his court for the first time. This marked the beginning of the East India Company's control over Avadh (*Gazetteer* vol. I, pp. 228–30). Shuja ud Daula obtained special permission from the British to use their troops in this campaign. At the time Shuja ud Daula's revenues came to twenty-seven million rupees from which he paid eight million three hundred thousand rupees to the British. (Ahad Ali, p. 16)

60. Arabic *Ramadhan*: the ninth month of the Muslim calendar, during which the faithful are required to observe a fast every day from dawn to dusk, a principal obligation for the followers of Islam.

61. Hindi *bahu*, daughter-in-law, and Turkish *begam* (begum), lady of the house, the lady daughter-in-law. Bahu Begam was the title by which she was generally known though her given name was Ummat-uz-Zahra. She died in 1815 at the age of eighty-six. Begam came to be used as a title of a king's (and later high dignitary's) wife or wives, and subsequently was used simply as the ending of female names in élite Muslim households in India, mainly in Avadh. Begams were addressed as 'Begam Sahiba'. The term is now used both in Lucknow and elsewhere to signify a Muslim noblewoman and is added to the name of the husband: Begam Agha Khan, Lady Agha Khan.

Chapter 2: *The Origins and Early History of Lucknow*

62. Families of repute usually kept a record of lineage and important events connected with family life. Sometimes these records also provide information about social and political affairs.

63. Sanskrit *pur*: fortified town. A common ending for the name of a town.

64. Sanskrit *Shesha Naga*: in Hindu mythology, the king of the serpent race, a

serpent with a thousand heads forming the couch of the God Vishnu when he sleeps during the intervals of creation.

65. During worship Hindus sprinkle drops of water at the deity and make an offering of flowers by placing them at its feet.

66. Sanskrit *Yudhishthira*: the son of Dharma, the God of Justice in Hindu mythology. He was the nephew of Raja Dasratha who appointed him his heir to part of his kingdom of Hastina Pura in preference to his own son.

67. Hindi *ji*: life, soul, self. Also used to mean 'Sir' and added to the name as a form of respect.

68. Sanskrit *rishi*: a savant, religious author and teacher. In common usage the term is applied to a Hindu ascetic of superior holiness, whose entire life is devoted to the study, writing and teaching of religion and the practice of Yoga.

69. Sanskrit *muni*: a Hindu holy man, an inspired sage, who has attained a more or less divine nature through self-mortification and withdrawal from the world.

70. Persian *salar*: commander. Masud, a religious saint, was also a general in the army of Mahmud of Ghazni. He attacked Bahraich in U.P. in 1033 and made many converts to Islam, thus acquiring from the believers the title of Ghazi, Conqueror in the Name of Islam. His tomb in Bahraich was built in the thirteenth century and is still an important Muslim shrine. (*Gazetteer* vol. I, pp. 21, 233)

71. A general in the army of the Delhi King Qutub ud Din Aibak (died 1210). He attacked Hansi and Meerut in U.P. (Ali Azhar, p. 75)

72. A Hindu caste or a member of it, born of a Kshatriya (warrior caste) father, and Vaisya (trader caste) mother. Their occupation has traditionally been that of clerk or accountant.

73. The son of the second Mughal Emperor Humayun. He reigned from 1556 to 1605 and firmly established the Mughal Empire. An enlightened ruler who was a patron of scholars and artists.

74. Persian *shah*: king. The title is sometimes also used as a prefix or suffix to the names of ascetic and inspired Muslim religious leaders. Shah Pir Muhammad was popularly known as Shah Mina.

75. On Thursday evenings, the eve of the Muslim sabbath, some Sunni and all Sufis (207) go to the tombs of religious leaders and saints. Here they recite a prayer and sing *qavvali* (417), hymns and songs of a religious nature. This practice has continued to the present time at Shah Mina's tomb.

76. The Mughal Emperor who ruled from 1658 to 1707, well known for his religious fervour.

77. Arabic *mahal*: palace. Nadan Mahal: Palace of the Ignorant. Firangi Mahal: European Palace. Moti Mahal: Pearl Palace.

78. Persian *mahi*, fish, and Arabic *maratib*, dignity, honour. The Honour of the Fish. A title conferred by the Mughal Kings as a mark of distinction on individuals of the highest order. The ceremony consisted of the presentation of a fish, or part of one, of metal gilt, borne upon a pole with two circular gilt balls similarly elevated.

79. Hindi *machchi*, fish, and *bhavan*, palace. Palace of the Fishes. It was destroyed by the British at the time of the Mutiny. Earlier during the Mutiny the British made this their fortress but abandoned it a few days later in favour of the Residency (84). As they could not transfer overnight the ammunition they had stored there, the palace was blown up and razed to the ground. (*The Lucknow Album*, p. 48)

80. Sanskrit *Abhir*: a caste of Hindus or its members who were originally cultivators and followed the occupation of a cowherd.

81. A town in the present District of Bareilly in U.P.

82. Hindi *gol*, round, and Persian *darvaza*, door, gate. A huge gate, so called because of the arched ceiling under the roof. The Gol Darvaza is still in existence.

83. A town in Bara Banki District, U.P.

84. The residence of the Envoy of the East India Company to the Court of Avadh, officially described as Vakil, literally a lawyer but actually an envoy. The British envoy was known as the Resident, for whom this house was constructed by Sadat Ali Khan (Ahad Ali, p. 27). During the Mutiny of 1857 the entire British population in the area took refuge in it and it was attacked by the mutineers. The ruins of this building are still in existence.

85. Sanskrit *laksha*: one hundred thousand.

86. A subcaste of the Qanauj Brahmans. Traditionally, offerings made to religious leaders are used for religious purposes.

87. Caste whose members were engaged in manual work.

88. Caste whose members were formerly nomadic freebooters but who later settled down to agriculture.

89. Hindi *banjara*: a trader. A caste of traders who travelled over the countryside.

90. Hindi *tola*: a quarter, district, or part of a town inhabited by people of the same caste or occupation. Bajpai Tola: Quarter of the Bajpais.

91. Arabic *mir*, chief, king, and Persian *zadah*, born of a prince. Originally a prefix to the names of princes, as in Mirza Salim. Later the term came to signify a Mughal Turk of high rank, or noble birth, as in Mirza Fazil, and subsequently became a common prefix to the names of Mughal Turks.

92. The son of Akbar who ruled under the title of Jahangir from 1605 to 1627. He is remembered for his patronage of the fine arts.

93. Arabic *qazi*: one who fulfils; title of a district judge or magistrate under the Mughal administration. Mahmud, the Qazi, from Bilgram (Hardoi District, U.P.). Later used as prefix to the name of the male descendants of those who had held this office.

94. Persian *ganj*: a store, treasure. Hindi, a food market, a populated place. Shah Ganj, Shah Market; Hazrat Ganj, Market of His Highness; Alam Ganj, World-wide Market.

95. Arabic *mulla, maulvi* or *maulana*: a Muslim doctor of law, a man learned in religion. These titles are also prefixed to the name of a religious leader or a person in charge of a mosque.

96. Mulla Nizam ud Din Sehalvi was a renowned Muslim scholar and religious leader from Sehali (hence Sehalvi) in Bara Banki District in U.P. He was the founder of the house of Firangi Mahal scholars, which in succeeding generations produced many important religious scholars, popularly known as the Firangi Mahal school. The tradition still flourishes in the family, though many members now follow secular professions. The original houses in the enclosure survive to this day and are occupied by members of this family.

97. Arabic *silsila*: a chain, a series. *Nizamia*: of Nizam. This curriculum has been formalized and used by the Madrasa Nizamia, a school opened by Maulana Abdul Bari of this family in 1923 (351). The institution survives to this day on a modest scale, but since the late forties has emphasized secular rather than religious instruction.

98. The reference is to the many Islamic religious seminaries, *madrasas*, in Afghanistan, Persia, Turkey and Central Asia.

99. Jahangir's son, who ascended to the throne in 1628 and was deposed in 1658. He founded Shahjahanabad (25) and is well known for his architecture. He built the Taj Mahal in Agra, and the Red Fort and Jumma Mosque in Delhi.

100. Persian *nau*, new, and Hindi *basti*, settlement. New Settlement.

101. Hindi *garh*: a small fort. Now refers to the area in which the fort is situated. The quarter around the Pir Khan Fort.

102. Muhammad Shah ruled from 1719 to 1748. He was called 'Rangeley', colourful, because of his voluptuous nature.

103. Arabic *khilat*: a robe of honour, bestowed as a mark of distinction by kings upon

dignitaries. At times accompanied by jewels, arms, a horse or an elephant, the *khilat* was usually considered an insignia of office.

104. Hindi *katra*: a market-place. Rani Katra: market-place founded by Rani. Saiyyid Husain Katra: market-place founded by Saiyyid Husain. Later the word came to be applied to residential quarters which grew up around the market, as in Katra Bizan Beg: the quarter founded by Bizan Beg.

Chapter 3: *Burhan ul Mulk, Safdar Jang and the Foundation of the Avadh Dynasty*

105. Mughal Emperor who ruled from 1707 until 1712.

106. Arabic *imam*: spiritual and religious chief. The Shia sect of the Muslims believes in a succession of twelve Imams from the family of Ali, Muhammad's cousin and son-in-law, who is himself regarded as the first Imam, followed by his two sons Hasan and Husain. Musa Kazim is the seventh in this line. The last of the twelve Imams is supposed to be alive and will remain so until the Day of Judgement; he is called the Present Imam.

107. Akbarabad (7) was founded by Akbar (73) about 1566 as his capital. It was situated on the right bank of the River Jamna; to the left was Agra. The present town of Agra includes both these towns.

108. The two Saiyyid brothers from Baraha in Muzaffarnagar (U.P.), Abdullah and Husain Ali, were regarded at this time (c. 1707) as the 'king-makers'. Within a short period of time they had put several Mughal Emperors on the throne, only to depose each in turn (Majumdar, p. 529). Muhammad Amin was among those who had conspired to murder Husain Ali and played a leading part in calming the resultant situation. (Srivastava [A], pp. 12–21)

109. The levy imposed by the Marathas (41) on such dominions as had come under their influence but retained their independence by paying them one quarter of the Government revenue. (Majumdar, p. 519)

110. The battle took place in 1737 near Agra. Burhan ul Mulk then offered to expel the Marathas from the whole of north India, but his opponents at the imperial court advised the Emperor to the contrary as they thought that Burhan ul Mulk would thus become too powerful. (Srivastava [A], pp. 54–58)

111. Persian *naubat*, drum, and *khana*, house. It was the custom in the Imperial household to have a guard-house near the main entrance where drums were beaten on special occasions and to announce the time of day and night. (Chapter 27)

112. Nadir Shah was a Persian adventurer who became the King of Persia in 1732. He entered Delhi in 1739, where the Mughal Emperor was at his mercy, and he carried away with him all the crown jewels and immense wealth estimated at about twenty *karor* of rupees, including the Koh-i-Nur diamond and the Peacock Throne of Shahjahan with 27,000 gems set in it (Majumdar, pp. 531–34). The Koh-i-Nur diamond later found its way back to India and eventually to Queen Victoria, and is at present among the crown jewels of the English monarchy. The Peacock Throne is in the possession of the present Shah of Iran and was used for his coronation in 1967.

113. Sher Jang was the son of Burhan ul Mulk's brother. Safdar Jang was his sister's son.

114. Burhan ul Mulk's *vakil* (84) and representative to the Mughal Court. (Srivastava [A], p. 81)

115. Burhan ul Mulk left behind him five daughters, but had no male heir to succeed him in office (Srivastava [A], p. 83). Under Mughal administration the assets and property of nobles theoretically became Crown property at their death, but in practice part was restored to the heirs as a favour from the Emperor, and sons were often granted an official position. (Moreland and Chatterjee, p. 211)

116. Hindi *karor*: ten million, equalling one hundred *lakhs* (85).

117. Under Mughal administration, the title of a Chief of Police, who also acted as a city magistrate and additionally had many duties of a civil administrator. The post was continued under the Avadh administration (Srivastava [C], p. 319)

118. In common belief green was the colour of the banner of Ali which was carried with him in battle.

119. Persian *gulab*, rose, and Hindi *bari*, enclosure. A garden in which a high pavilion was built by Shuja ud Daula. He and his wife, Bahu Begam, were later buried in it. It is still in existence and is popularly known as the Tomb of Bahu Begam.

120. Shuja ud Daula spent three lakhs of rupees on this construction (Srivastava [A], p. 250). This tomb is still in Delhi, although in a state of decay.

Chapter 4: *Shuja ud Daula and Asaf ud Daula*

121. Ahmad Shah belonged to an Afghan tribe called Abdali. On succession to the throne he assumed the title of Durr-i-Dauran, Pearl of the Age, after which his clan came to be known as Durrani. (Majumdar, p. 534)

122. Ahmad Shah Durrani succeeded Nadir Shah in 1747 and invaded India five times between 1748 and 1759, finally leaving the country in 1762. (Majumdar, pp. 534–36)

123. As soon as Asaf ud Daula came to power, he was required to sign a new agreement with the British. Under its terms he ceded to the East India Company the areas of Benares, Jaunpur and Ghazipur, the income from which was twenty-three lakhs of rupees, and the cost of keeping the British brigade in his dominion was raised from two lakhs and ten thousand rupees to two lakhs and sixty thousand rupees. He was also required to pay the costs of an additional army, which came to twelve lakhs of rupees, and to pay the salary of the British Resident to his Court, along with that of an additional agent, which came to two lakhs and twenty thousand rupees. The latter post was soon abolished by the Company. By 1779 his payments to the Company were one karor of rupees. In return, the British promised to look after his territory in case of invasion (Ahad Ali, pp. 17–18)

124. When Asaf ud Daula came to power, his half-brother Sadat Ali Khan was the Governor of most of Ruhelkhand, having been so appointed by Shuja ud Daula. At Asaf ud Daula's request he was removed from this position under threat by the British army and the area was added to his dominion (Ali Azhar, p. 168). However, this did not affect the part of Ruhelkhand which was still in the hands of the Pathans and which ever since Shuja ud Daula's occupation (Chapter 2) had remained in the hands of a Ruhela Chief, Faizullah Khan, who, under British guarantee, was allowed to retain his estate in the Rampur area, under the control of Avadh (Najmul Ghani, vol. II, pp. 262–65). The State of Rampur, consisting of six towns and 1,120 villages (*Gazetteer* vol. I, p. 486), survived until 1947, when princely States all over India merged with the new Republic. There have been seven ruling Navabs of this house; the last Navab, Muhammad Raza Ali Khan, died in 1967.

125. After receiving two payments from his mother, Asaf ud Daula signed an agreement with her in 1775 renouncing any further claims on her property (Najmul Ghani, vol. II, pp. 187–88). However, in 1782 he asked for the help of British troops in seizing the personal treasuries of his mother and grandmother (Safdar Jang's wife). They succeeded in obtaining for him one karor and twenty lakhs of rupees (Najmul Ghani, vol. II, pp. 225–28). Warren Hastings's responsibility in this affair by lending the British troops featured as one of the major counts against him in his trial by the British House of Commons between 1788 and 1795, in which he was acquitted.

126. The second and last ruler of Mysore, 1783–99.

127 Persian *daulat*, wealth, and *khana*, house. The Exquisite House. The expression is currently used for the residence of an élite person. Sultan Khana: House of the King.

128. Persian *darvaza*, gate, and *Rumi*, Asia Minor and Turkey. The Gate of Asia Minor. The Rumi Darvaza is a huge gate about fifty yards high, said to be modelled after a gate of Constantinople (*Gazetteer* vol. II, p. 309). It exists to this day.

129. Arabic *imam*, spiritual and religious chief (106), and Hindi *bara*, a house, an enclosure. The House of the Imams. The premises where *tazias*, or paper models of Imam Husain's mausoleum situated in Kerbala, Iraq, are kept throughout the year. This building is used only for mourning assemblies known as *majlis*, to commemorate the deaths of Ali, Hasan and Husain and the members of this family. On the 10th of Muharram (first month of the Muslim year), when Husain and his family were killed, these models are taken to the local Kerbala of the town and buried there. This is known as the Muharram or Tazia Procession. The main period of mourning is from the 1st to 10th of Muharram, which is called the Observance of Muharram. Well-to-do Shias around Lucknow try to build an Imam Bara of their own. The poor reserve a section of their house, ranging from a shelf to a hall for these purposes, and call it an Imam Bara.

130. Asaf ud Daula insisted that this architecture should be original in conception and not a copy of any Mughal building (*The Lucknow Album*, p. 50). He spent ten lakhs of rupees on chandeliers and other glassware to decorate the Imam Bara. (Ahad Ali, p. 71)

131. To build a roof of this size, flat on the top surface and slightly arched within, without the help of a single iron or wooden beam, is an architectural achievement. It was done by using the bricks in a special way, *kara dena*, that is, breaking them in different sizes at different angles and joining them together at these points to interlock them. Concrete is then used as a covering. The Imam Bara is covered with concrete several feet thick.

132. Arabic *mujtahid*: one who shows the right path, a religious leader or doctor of law. The title of the leading Shia priest. He is addressed as *Qibla-o-Kaba*, the one who shows the way to Kaba, 'Your Holiness'.

133. The building is now (1975) one hundred and ninety-one years old, but these remarks are still applicable.

134. Arabic *nakhas*: horse or slave market, originally a cattle market around which a residential quarter later developed.

135. Arabic *wazara*: to bear a burden. *Vazir* has been the traditional title of the 'Councillor of State' or chief administrator of a Muslim ruler at various times and in various countries. He appears to have been a ruler's companion too. Under the Mughals, from the time of Akbar, administration at the highest level was divided into four sections. General business was brought before the Emperor by the *Vazir ul Mumalik*, the rough equivalent of a present-day Chief Minister; revenue affairs were in the charge of the *Vazir-e-Maliat*; the head of the military administration was the *Bakhshi*, the Paymaster (38); the *Subedars*, Governors of the Provinces (12), received direct orders from the Emperor. The Navabs of Avadh followed the same administrative system.

136. Arabic *mahalla*: population. The section of town inhabited by people of the same caste or profession. Rastogi Mahalla: Quarter of the Rastogis. Kashmiri Mahalla: Quarter of the People from Kashmir.

137. Claude Martin joined the army of the East India Company as a common soldier at the end of the seventeenth century. He rose to be a General in the army of the Navab of Avadh where his services were later transferred (Ghani Najmul, vol. III, p. 206). About 1774 he served as military and political adviser to Shuja ud Daula in Faizabad, where he lived in grand style with four concubines and a large staff of eunuchs and servants. He was a collector of miniatures and other works of art and employed local

artists to execute works for him. Some water-colours of plants made for him are now at Kew Gardens, London. He had a large library of four thousand books including some in Persian and Sanskrit (Archer, p. 54). These belongings were auctioned among the British after his death in Lucknow, where he had moved with the shift of the capital.

He had amassed a large fortune by trade and by winning bets on cock-fights with Sadat Ali Khan and left properties worth three lakhs of rupees to be spent equally for founding three schools for orphan children in his home town, Lyons, in Calcutta and in Lucknow. He had willed that all three schools were to be called 'La Martinière'. These schools were opened accordingly after his death. The Lucknow school opened in 1833 (Najmul Ghani, vol. III, p. 206). His magnificent house Constantia, named after his deceased lady-love in France, was willed to be a hostel, or caravanserai; thus it became a hostel for Europeans in and around Lucknow (Ahad Ali, pp. 71, 73). Some time later his school was transferred to these premises where it exists to this day as an expensive place of learning on the model of an English public school. Students no longer receive financial assistance from this institution. When this school opened its admission was restricted to European and Eurasian children only, but the situation has changed and since the beginning of the century, soon after Sharar wrote this essay, Indian children were also admitted to this school.

138. Arabic *sahib*: friend, master, sir. Added to the name or title as a sign of respect. *Sahiba* is the form for ladies. *Markin* is a popular version of Martin, hence Markin Sahib.

139. Hindi *kothi*: originally a mansion of the élite; now a European-style house.

140. Persian *darbar*: a court, the court of a king or chief, held on important political and religious occasions and to announce proclamations. Holding court has a long tradition among Indian rulers and chiefs.

141. The East India Company's Resident in Benares State at the time.

142. Other sources state that Wazir Ali was imprisoned and died in Fort William (Calcutta). (Majumdar, p. 720)

143. While thirty lakhs of rupees were spent on his wedding, his funeral expenses came to a modest figure of about seventy rupees (Ahad Ali, pp. 23). This remark has been repeated in Lucknow over successive generations to exemplify the changes of fortune in a man's life. Wazir Ali was probably the legitimate son of Asaf ud Daula but he was unacceptable to the Resident as his successor because of his anti-British leanings. (Irwin, p. 102)

Chapter 5: *Sadat Ali Khan and Ghazi ud Din Haidar*

144. Before coming to power in 1798 Sadat Ali Khan entered into an agreement with the British Governor General to increase the payments from fifty-six lakhs to seventy-six lakhs of rupees (Ahad Ali, p. 24). In 1801 another agreement abolished these payments and in their place he was required to cede the following areas: Kora, Kara, Etawah, Kanpur, Farrukhabad, Kheragarh, Gorakhpur, Batul, Allahabad, Ruhelkhand, Navabganj, Khali and Mahal, the revenue of which was one karor and thirty-five lakhs of rupees. His own revenue, after this, amounted to about one karor per annum. (Najmul Ghani, vol. III, pp. 3, 22–28)

145. In order to plead for this transfer Sadat Ali Khan sent an envoy to the Board of Directors of the East India Company in London. They demanded a payment of eighteen karor of rupees before the hearing and for this purpose the Navab had saved up to seventeen karor when he died.

146. Sadat Ali Khan died in 1814 at the age of sixty-three (Najmul Ghani, vol. III, p. 58). It is possible that the British Resident Sir John Baillie (1807–14), who had a

series of disagreements with the Navab because of Baillie's interference in the internal administration of Avadh, was involved in the plot to poison him. Sadat Ali Khan had made a request to the Governor General for the transfer of Baillie but this was not granted. (Kamul ud Din Haidar, vol. I, p. 199)

147. A Persian hemistich. In Persian and Urdu prose it used to be common for a couplet or hemistich to be included in the text. This is no longer so today.

148. After the agreement of 1798 and before the second treaty of 1801, Sadat Ali Khan was required to reduce his own army while the British army in his dominion was increased to twelve thousand soldiers at his expense. He resisted this at first, but yielded when the British troops moved to encircle Avadh. (Ahad Ali, p. 25)

149. Farhat Baksh was a vast complex of buildings only part of which, near the river, was built by General Martin. It remained the chief royal residence until Wajid Ali Shah built Qaisar Bagh. Soon after the British occupation the remaining part of Farhat Baksh, near the river, was joined to the Chattar Manzil, built by Ghazi ud Din Haidar (*Gazetteer* vol. II, p. 310). The area was the scene of bitter fighting during 1857 and the complex was almost destroyed (Kamul ud Din Haidar, vol. II, p. 267). Chattar Manzil became a British club during the period of the Raj; since 1947 it has been the seat of the Central Drug Research Institute.

150. Hindi *barah*, twelve, and Persian *dar*, door, portal, archway. A building of twelve archways used as a reception hall. Hindi *lal*, red. The building was so called because of the coloured stone or the thick red plaster of which it was built. This part of the massive Farhat Baksh complex known as Qasr-ul-Khaqan, King's Palace, served as throne-room, coronation hall and hall of assembly for Avadh rulers from the time of Sadat Ali Khan (*The Lucknow Album*, p. 32). This building and the adjoining Gulistan-e-Iram now house the Provincial Museum (*Gazetteer* vol. II, p. 310). Sadat Ali Khan also built a canal between Farhat Baksh and Lal Barah Dari, which no longer exists. (Ahad Ali, p. 32)

151. The Dil Kusha became the residence of the British General of the Commanding Division in 1857. Subsequently, as a result of damage during the Mutiny, it was reduced to ruins, so that at present only part of the massive walls and staircases remain (*The Lucknow Album*, p. 10). The modest premises in this compound now house a club for the local élite.

152. The Commissioner in Lucknow who succeeded to the British Civil Command in July 1857. He was shot by the mutineers on 20 July. (*Gazetteer* vol. II, p. 304)

153. In the British administration, Deputy Commissioner was the title of a civil administrator in charge of a District, who also exercised some judicial functions. The Commissioner above him was in charge of an administrative unit of several Districts called a Division. The Deputy Commissioner of some important towns, less than half a dozen in the whole of India, was called a Chief Commissioner. This post was created in Lucknow in the early days of British supremacy but merged with that of Lucknow Division soon after 1857. These posts have been retained under the present Indian administration.

154. Arabic *manzil*: destination, lodging, a storey of a house, a house. The word is generally used as an ending for the name of an impressive residence: Khurshid Manzil, The Sun House; Mubarak Manzil, The Welcome Residence; Shah Manzil, King's Residence; Asad Manzil, The House of the Lion.

155. A Hindu sub-caste of Vaisya. Traders, in Lucknow they are also known as Mahajan, and their profession is to lend money.

156. After annexation, the Moti Mahal (77) came into the possession of the British and was used at first as a commissariat. Later it was sold to the Maharaja of Bulrampur, who made alterations to the buildings and the 'Pearl Dome', which was a unique architectural achievement, disappeared (*The Lucknow Album*, p. 19). About 1950 the Maharaja's successors sold the palaces.

157. Sadat Ali Khan had told the British Governor General that he would like to abdicate in favour of his son and go to live in Mecca or Kerbala—provided he were allowed to take his treasury with him. As this condition was not agreed upon he did not pursue the matter. (Najmul Ghani, vol. III, p. 39)

158. Arabic *murshid*: religious preceptor. Persian *zadi*: female, born of. The daughter of a religious leader.

159. Ghazi ud Din Haidar had in fact received between seventeen and eighteen karor. (Ahad Ali, p. 29)

160. Both of these houses (154) have since been destroyed. Ghazi ud Din Haidar also built two palaces called Chattar Manzil for his wives. *Chattar*: umbrella, dome (*Gazetteer* vol. II, p. 303). They were referred to as the 'large' and the 'small' palaces. One of them was destroyed during the Mutiny; the surviving building was added to what remained of Farhat Baksh (149).

161. A contemporary of Sharar and like him a scholar of Islamic theology and history, and the Arabic, Persian and Urdu languages.

162. Arabic *qadam*: footprint, and *Rasul*: Messenger (of God). An impression on a black stone of the supposed footprint of Muhammad, and according to popular belief brought from Mecca by some distinguished pilgrim. Hence a Muslim shrine. The building was heavily damaged in the 1857 war and has since fallen into decay. However, a stone bearing a footprint believed to be a copy of the original is still standing on a high pedestal near the Sikandar Bagh.

163. The British Governor General had suggested to Ghazi ud Din Haidar that he could declare himself King if he wanted to. This he did on 9 October 1819 by issuing new coins in his name and removing the name of the nominal Mughal ruler Shah Alam, and by spending one karor of rupees on the crown, throne and other regalia. (Ahad Ali, pp. 28–30)

164. Ghazi ud Din Haidar had given loans to the East India Company on the following occasions: in 1814, the sum of one karor, eight lakhs and fifty thousand rupees at six per cent interest per annum. In 1816, one karor at six per cent per annum interest, which was cancelled when he was given the areas of Khera Garh and the land lying between Ghagra and Gorakhpur. In 1825, one karor (the provision for the maintenance of Shah Najaf was made from the interest on this loan). Lastly, in 1826, half a karor at five per cent per annum interest for a period of two years. In 1827 the Navab wanted to convert this last sum also into a perpetual loan, but the Company did not agree. (Najmul Ghani, vol. III, pp. 77, 78, 118, 120)

165. The Safavi Dynasty ruled from 1500 to 1736 and declared the Shia faith the State religion in Persia.

166. Arabic *shia*: follower. The followers of Ali who believe him to be the rightful successor of Muhammad. Those who follow the Twelve Imams are also known as Asna Ashari. (106)

167. The Sunnis recognize the four Caliphs as the successors of Muhammad; Abu Bakar, Omar and Usman were the first three, while Ali was the fourth. (Chapter 10)

168. Also known as the Mujtahid family, the family of Shia priests descended from the family of Maulvi Dildar Ali Guframab who was prominent during the reign of Asaf ud Daula (Najmul Ghani, vol. II, p. 230). His descendants have continued the tradition up to the present and among other things lead Friday prayers at Asaf ud Daula's mosque.

169. Hindi *chhati*: sixth. A Hindu celebration on the sixth day after the birth of a child (Chapters 44, 45). For a further account of this queen see Maulvi Muhammad Faiq, *Waqa-e-Dilpazir*, written in 1849 at the request of J. D. Shakespeare, second secretary to Col. J. Lowe in Lucknow. The manuscript is in the British Museum.

170. Hindi *janam*, birth, and *ashtmi*, eighth. A festival held on the anniversary of the god Krishna's birthday.

171. Najaf in Iraq is the presumed burial place of Ali (106) where his mausoleum is to be found; hence The Tomb of Ali. Like Kerbala it is an important place of pilgrimage for Shias.

172. The British Government had undertaken to distribute the interest of the perpetual loans (164) and later some others for the upkeep of the respective Imam Baras of Asaf ud Daula, Shah Najaf and Husainabad. This was known as *vasiqa* (394), an endowment arrangement. After the commencement of British rule in Avadh in 1886, *vasiqa* legislation was passed in the Governor General's council to regularize the arrangements (*Gazetteer* vol. I, p. 102). As a result a trust with a board of trustees, which continues to this day, was instituted to manage the funds. The chairman was the Commissioner of Lucknow Division, while the members were Shias descended from the royal family. At the end of the British Raj in 1947 these obligations, as well as certain others, were transferred to the Republic of India and the *vasiqas* continue to the present time. (394)

Chapter 6: *Nasir ud Din Haidar and Muhammad Ali Shah*

173. Passages from the Quran are read by Muslims and dedicated to the souls of departed friends and relatives. The Shah Najaf Trust employs people to do this for the benefit of Ghazi ud Din Haidar's soul.

174. Burial place of Imam Husain in Iraq. A copy of this mausoleum known as the local Kerbala is the place of final mourning on the 10th of Muharram, when paper models of the shrine are taken from the Imam Baras (129) and buried in the grounds surrounding the local mausoleum.

175. The building is now in a dilapidated state and serves as the headquarters of a bank.

176. Under British administration detailed local information was collected by the officials of the Districts through the Indian staff and published in a Government publication called the *Gazette*, which dealt mainly with administrative problems. From the *Gazette*, information was compiled covering the whole Province under the title of *The Gazetteer*. This was done for the benefit of the newly arrived British civil servants. The one referred to here is *The Imperial Gazetteer of India Provincial Series, United Provinces of Agra and Oudh*, vols I and II, Superintendent of Government Printing Press, Calcutta, 1908.

177. Nasir ud Din Haidar's frivolous activities have been described in detail by one of his British courtiers, William Knighton, in his book *The Private Life of an Eastern King*, London, 1855. For details about the British reaction and the warnings they issued see Sleeman, vol. I, ch. 6, and vol. II, chs. 3 and 4.

178. In 1832 Nasir ud Din Haidar had posters put up in the town stating that Munna Jan was not his son but the son of a palace employee. He also informed the Resident of this (Najmul Ghani, vol. III, pp. 151–54). This was in all likelihood done to annoy his mother. Munna Jan was probably his son (Irwin, ch. 4). For further details of this affair see Sleeman, vol. II, ch. 4.

179. The Fort of Chunar is situated on the banks of the Ganges about seven miles from Benares. In the first instance it was given to Shuja ud Daula by the East India Company in exchange for the Allahabad Fort but subsequently it was ceded to the Company by Sadat Ali Khan in 1801 (144). (*Gazetteer* vol. I, p. 11)

180. The treaty was signed in 1837, the year Muhammad Ali Shah ascended the throne and the same year that he laid the foundations of his Imam Bara. (Najmul Ghani, vol. IV, p. 5)

181. In 1839 Muhammad Ali Shah deposited twelve lakhs of rupees and later an additional sum of 2,400,000 rupees with the East India Company, at an interest of four

per cent per annum. This income was to be used for the upkeep of his Imam Bara (Najmul Ghani, vol. IV, pp. 5–6) and the surplus income to be devoted to charity. (*Gazetteer* vol. II, p. 309)

182. Arabic *jami*: collector; *juma*: Friday, Muslim sabbath. The main mosque of a town in which prayers are held, especially on Fridays. The Jamey Masjid mosque of Delhi was built by Shahjahan in Shahjahanabad (25), with two minarets 130 feet high and three marble domes. It is considered to be one of the largest and most beautiful mosques in existence.

183. Built between 1880 and 1887, the clock-tower, with its chiming bells, is still standing. It was built after Moorish design and is 221 feet high and 20 feet square at the base. (*Gazetteer* vol. II, p. 304)

184. The ruins of this building are still standing.

Chapter 7: *Amjad Ali Shah, Wajid Ali Shah and the End of the Dynasty's Rule*
        —Urdu Drama

185. One of the basic obligations of Islam, according to which one is required to give one-fortieth of one's annual income to charity.

186. A poet in the court of Ghazi ud Din Haidar and later in that of Wajid Ali Shah, who adopted the pen-name Akhtar. He died in 1858.

187. It was the custom for Urdu poets to adopt a part of their own or some other name as a pseudonym, which was invariably added to their name, and by which they were generally known. Sometimes their town of origin was also added to it: Asghar Ali Khan, Nasim Dehlavi, pen-name Nasim, of Delhi. This practice is no longer regularly adhered to.

188. The residential and office quarters of the British civil servants in Indian towns during the early years of British supremacy. In time the Civil Lines became the residential quarters of the Indian élite as well.

189. A Hindu shrine dedicated to the god Shiva: sometimes an abode for rishis and munis.

190. Sibtain is the joint name for Hasan and Husain, the two sons of Ali and grandchildren of Muhammad. Sibtainabad: The House of Sibtain. (7)

191. During the ten days of Muharram, all the Imam Baras are illuminated. The Imam Baras of Asaf ud Daula, Shah Najaf and Husainabad are famous for their decorations, with lights and oil-lamps all around the building. People flock to see this every year.

192. Followers of Guru Nanak (1469–1539). Sanskrit *guru*: religious saint, teacher. The Sikhs ruled north-west India in the late eighteenth century. After two wars their empire was annexed to British India in 1849.

193. Persian *nazim*: administrator. This post was originally created by the Mughal Emperor in 1705 as his Divan in Bengal. By 1740 the dynasty became practically independent. However, after the Battle of Baksar (22) they became Deputy Divans to the East India Company, which abolished the post in 1772.

194. Wajid Ali Shah arranged to meet the courtesan Waziran several times in the house of Azim ud Daula, who lived near her in the Gola Ganj quarter. He first met Ali Naqi Khan on one of these occasions. (Najmul Ghani, vol. IV, p. 23)

195. The *ghazal* is composed of two-lined verses, the second line of which must end in a rhyme. Amorous in character but at times containing matters of a mystical nature, it is the most popular form of Persian and Urdu poetry. It is Arabic in origin. For a selection in English translation of some Urdu gahzals see D. Matthews and C. Shackle, *An Anthology of Urdu Love Lyrics*, Oxford University Press, 1972, and Ahmed Ali, *The Golden Tradition*, Columbia University Press, 1973.

196. A long laudatory poem in praise of some earthly or religious lord written in a forceful and fanciful style.

197. Muhammad Taqi Mir: born Akbarabad 1722. Came from Delhi to Lucknow in 1782 at the invitation of Asaf ud Daula, where he died in 1810. He is regarded as one of the most celebrated masters of ghazals, which are characterized by their melancholic tone.

198. Muhammad Rafi Sauda: born Delhi 1703/7. Went to Faizabad at the court of Asaf ud Daula and came with him to Lucknow where he died in 1781. He wrote poetry in most forms and is acknowledged as a master of *qasidas* and *hajv*, satires. For essays in English on Mir, Sauda and Mir Hasan, see R. Russell and K. Islam, *Three Mughal Poets*, Allen & Unwin, London, 1969.

199. Shaikh Imam Baksh Nasikh. Probably born in Faizabad, he was employed in the courts of various lords including Agha Mir, the Vazir. He died in 1839. As a ghazal writer he paid special attention to the use of language and along with Atish is considered to be a founder of the Lucknow school of Urdu poetry.

200. Khwaja Haidar Ali Atish: born Faizabad 1806. He became a courtier to a local lord and came to Lucknow with the transfer of the court, where he died in 1846. He is famous for the melancholic tone of his ghazals.

201. Persian *rind*: a rake, libertine. A style of ghazal in which amorous feelings and religious scepticism are expressed rather freely in a mystical interpretation of life, love and religion.

202. Navab Syed Muhammad Khan Rind: 1797–1857. A nephew of Burhan ul Mulk, he wrote sensuous ghazals in an elegant style.

203. Mir Wazir Ali Saba: 1794–1854. Employed in the court of Wajid Ali Shah. His sensuous ghazals are written in a highly decorative language.

204. Originally an Arabic form. A long narrative poem with flexible subject-matter and style.

205. Navab Mirza Tasaduq Husain Shauq: died 1871. He was a hakim in the court of Wajid Ali Shah and wrote sensuous poetry in an elaborate language.

206. Arabic *khalifah*: a successor. The term refers, in the main, to the four religious and political successors of Muhammad between 632 and 661. Later, some Islamic dynasties also ruled under the title of Caliph.

207. Arabic *suf*: wool. A sect of Muslim mystics originally from Persia in the tenth century who wore coarse woollen garments and lived very simply in silent protest against the luxuries of the world. Some Sufis rank among the most important poets and writers in Persian and Urdu literature.

208. Muslim women are required by religion and custom to live in purdah (behind curtains), that is, inside the house. Only immodest and loose women did not follow this custom. Hence the expression 'veiled women' meant modest and chaste women whom no male outside the family had seen, 'not even the sun' as the expression goes. This custom is dying out.

209. This vast complex was built between 1848 and 1850 at the cost of eighty lakhs of rupees. Only the rear portion remains. (*Gazetteer* vol. II, p. 304) Part of it was destroyed in the fighting of 1857 and part demolished later as the result of redevelopment plans for the city.

210. See Chapter 8.

211. Arabic *taluqa*, estate, and Persian *dar*, holder. Holder of an Estate. Persian *zamin*: land. *Zamindar*: landowner. According to Mughal practice, reorganized and defined under British administration, state revenue was collected from the peasants through persons known as *zamindars* and *taluqdars*, who kept some of the income for themselves and had a proprietary right over the land. A *zamindar* was a land-holder and lesser proprietor while a taluqdar had double proprietary rights and exercised authority over a considerable area. A taluqdar usually carried in U.P. the title of Raja or Navab and had some civil power to dislodge peasants who could not pay their dues.

In the last days of the rule of the Navabs, taluqdars held two-thirds of the villages. (*Gazetteer* vol. I, pp. 109–111) The *zamindari* and *taluqdari* system was abolished in U.P. in 1952. Zamindars and taluqdars were given bonds by the Government equal to their income for a period ranging between eight to twenty years depending on the size of their holdings, redeemable over a period of forty years.

212. The requirement to maintain the houses applies to this day.

213. After the British occupation in 1856 this Barah Dari became the headquarters of the Avadh Taluqdar Association, which became defunct in 1947. Once used for their lavish receptions it is still used for important civic functions, and thus serves a different function from town halls in Europe. The offices of the Municipality founded in 1862 are housed separately.

214. Mahal (77) was also a title Wajid Ali Shah gave to his better placed wives, who were given their own palaces. The titles began with Navab, were followed by an adjective and ended with Mahal. Navab Khas Mahal: Arabic *khas*, principal wife. Navab Hazrat Mahal (*Hazrat*, Highness) was his second wife. Others included Navab Akhtar Mahal (*akhtar*, star) and Navab Mashuq Mahal (*mashuq*, beloved).

215. Sanskrit *yogi*: a Hindu hermit who has renounced the world in order to seek self-realization through the union of his soul with the universe by means of Raja Yoga, meditation, and Hatha Yoga, control of his body. The eighty-four postures of Hatha Yoga are an aid in the achievement of Raja Yoga. (Raghavan, pp. 141–49) A yogi usually wears red-ochre robes, covers part of his body with ashes and sits in meditation in lotus posture under a tree.

216. Qaisar was the pet name of Wajid Ali Shah. His pen-name was Akhtar, under which he wrote over forty works, mainly poetic compositions in various forms, and prose of a scholarly nature. His *thumris* (440) were composed under the name of Kadar Piya. (Saxena, p. 118)

217. In mythology, a circular dance performed by Krishna with a flute in his hand, his love Radha in the centre and *gopis* (219) worshipping around them. The term now refers to a dance representation on this theme.

218. Sanskrit *Sri*: Lord, Sir; a title of respect, Lord Krishna. The word has now come to be used in India as a simple prefix, like Mr.

219. *Krishna* is regarded as the eighth incarnation of Vishnu, the second aspect of the Hindu trinity. He features in the pages of the *Mahabharata*. The *Bhagavadgita*, Krishna's teachings to Arjuna, is part of this epic. His image represents him as a handsome youth playing the flute in Mathura (U.P.) where he grew up. A mass of love-legends and fables has gathered round him, the main theme being how he sported in his youth with *gopis* (cowherd damsels) and wives. Their love symbolizes human yearning for union with God.

220. On 4 February 1856 General Outram, the Resident, who was also Chief Commissioner of Lucknow, gave Wajid Ali Shah a document of abdication from the British Governor General. He asked him to sign it and abdicate within three days, but Wajid Ali Shah refused. On 7 February the Resident announced the annexation of Avadh to the British Indian territory by affixing notices in police stations. He called various important officials to the Residency and issued orders to them directly. (Najmul Ghani, vol. IV, pp. 105–17) Wajid Ali Shah died in exile in Matiya Burj in 1887.

The indictment against the rulers of Avadh was formulated for the benefit of the directors of the East India Company by the Governor General, the Marquis of Dalhousie, under the title *Oude Blue Book*. Major R. W. Bird who was the Assistant Resident in Lucknow replied to these charges after his term of office in his book *Dacoitee in Excelsis, or the Spoliation of Oude Faithfully Recounted*, London 1857.

For accounts of the rulers of this dynasty see Munshi Inam Ali, *Asaf ul Asif*, written about 1850, covering the period from the beginning of the dynasty's rule to 1783; Ghulam Ali, *Emad us Sadat*, a history to about 1801 written in the nineteenth century;

Fakhr ud Daula Ratan Singh, *Sultan ut Tawarikh,* a history up to the death of Muhammad Ali Shah (1844), written about 1850; Kamal ud Din Haidar, *Savaneh Hayat Salatin-e-Avadh,* covering the period up to 1849 when the work was completed, published in Lucknow in 1879. These manuscripts are in the British Museum.

Chapter 8: *Wajid Ali Shah in Matiya Burj—The Mutiny*

221. The immediate cause of the Mutiny on 6 May 1857 was the introduction of the Enfield rifle in the British army. The cartridges for this rifle were greased with animal fat. The Hindu sepoys thought that the grease was made of the fat of cows, a sacred animal for them, and the Muslims thought it was of pigs, detestable to them. It was thus an abomination to the followers of both religions. The deeper cause was the dissatisfaction of these soldiers with the expansion of British rule. (Sir Henry Lawrence, quoted by Ali Azhar, p. 231) Ali Azhar argues that the annexation of Avadh was an important issue in this respect as the Bengal army, which was the main British army of Indian soldiers, was three-fourths composed of men from Avadh. For details see Ali Azhar, essays 11–13.

222. On 10 May the mutineers galloped from Meerut, U.P., to Delhi, occupied the palace and proclaimed the aged and nominal Mughal King Bahadur Shah II as Emperor of Hindustan. He was popularly known as Zafar Shah, Zafar being his pen-name as he wrote poetry in Urdu. Delhi was recaptured by the British between 14 and 20 September 1857. This event marks the formal end of the Mughal Sultanate in India. From then until his death Zafar Shah remained a prisoner of the British in Rangoon, Burma, where he eventually died. His poetry at that time is filled with lamentations.

223. Popular name for the British Resident's headquarters (84) in Lucknow, officially known as the Residency. With Sir John Baillie (146) the British army came to be stationed in Lucknow for the first time, and the number of guards at the Residency was increased. This led the local population to refer to this building as the Baillie Guard.

224. Lucknow was finally captured on 21 March 1858 by Sir Hugh Rose with the largest British army in Indian history to that date, after two earlier attempts had failed on 25 September and 17 November 1857. For details of fighting in Lucknow from the local point of view see Kamul ud Din Haidar vol. II and Ali Azhar, chs 11, 12 and 15. For the British account see *Gazetteer* vol. I, p. 232; L. F. Ruutz Rees, *Siege of Lucknow,* Longman Brown, London 1858; and a recent work, M. Edwardes, *Season in Hell, The Defence of Lucknow Residency,* Hamish Hamilton, London 1973.

225. Shaikh Sa'di: 1189–1291 (both dates approximate). A classical Persian poet from Shiraz, author of *Gulistan,* a book of tales and anecdotes each with a moral, which has been translated into many European languages, and *Bostan,* a poem of similar content.

226. His Excellency Sir Harcourt Butler was the Governor of U.P. from about 1921 to 1925. He was a popular figure as he did much for the social welfare of the people, such as establishing in Lucknow the King George Medical College (now known as Mahatma Gandhi Medical College, Teaching Hospital of the University), and the Avadh Chief Court. He also developed Canning College which was founded in 1864 and later became Lucknow University, and shifted the Revenue Office of the Province from Allahabad to Lucknow, thus making Lucknow the de facto capital of the Province. He used to go to the gatherings of wealthy people where he spoke Urdu, sometimes wearing Indian dress. Butler Palace, now used as a Government office, for which he laid the foundation stone himself in 1921, was a private palace built and named after him by Maharaja Sir Ali Muhammad Khan of Mahmudabad.

227. In 1700 British factories in Bengal were established in a new fortified settlement near Calcutta named Fort William. Subsequently it became the headquarters of the East India Company.

228. Persian *jahan*, world, and *panah*, protection. Protector of the World. A form of address for a king or a way of making reference to him.

229. Arabic *Huzur*, Your Lordship, Your Highness, a mode of addressing a dignitary.

230. The Embassy of the Ottoman Empire before World War I. The graves were transferred to a cemetery in the suburbs of Paris.

231. Arabic *mutah*, enjoyment; marriages contracted for a limited period, usually in exchange for some monetary consideration on the part of the woman. It was frequently practised in the past among wealthy Shias.

232. Music as well as other forms of intoxication are important prohibitions of Islam.

233. Persian *ab*, water, and *khana*, house. *Abdar khana* refers to the system of cooling water for drinking purposes (Chapter 31). Persian *khas*, fragrant grass. Curtains made of this were hung on the doors and windows and kept damp in order to keep the rooms cool and to provide a fresh smell.

234. *Marsiya* is an elegy about Ali, Hasan, Husain and the calamities that befell their family in Kerbala. *Nauha* is a short poem on the same theme. (Chapters 26 and 49)

235. Persian *bahadur*: brave, hero; added as a suffix to the name of the members of a royal family and as a title to that of high dignitaries, meaning 'Honourable'.

Chapter 9: *Mirza Birjis Qadar—Urdu Poetry*

236. Hindi *kauri*: a small shell; also the smallest denomination of Indian currency, which became obsolete in the 1920s. At that time four cowries were equivalent to one paisa, four paisas one anna and sixteen annas a rupee. In the late 1960s India adopted the decimal system in currency and one rupee is now equal to a hundred new paisas.

237. Arabic *shair*: poet. A literary gathering in which poets recited their verses and the audience showed their appreciation: hence it became a sort of contest among poets as to who could win the greatest acclamation. Traditionally everyone sat on the floor in rows parallel to the walls, the poets in a rectangle in the centre of the hall and the audience between them and the walls. A candle was passed around inviting poets to recite in turn. This order was hierarchical, the novices first and the masters last. The session, which usually started after the evening meal and ended at dawn, was considered an important social occasion. The practice is today no longer common, and in its place one or several poets might be invited to someone's house to recite his poems before selected guests.

238. Opium was taken by a small section of the people in the form of tablets. This was done in a group where fantastic story-telling sessions took place amid general intoxication (232).

239. Written in flowery prose, often accompanied by a poem. Some of those written by Shaida Begam have survived, in which she describes the conditions in Lucknow during and after the Mutiny. A collection of Wajid Ali Shah's own letters from Matiya Burj to Navab Aklail Mahal in Lucknow have been published in Lahore recently under the title *Tarikh-e-Mumtaz*, ed. Muhammad Baqar.

240. A favourite saying of Jahangir (92) was that he had exchanged with his Queen, Nur Jahan Begam, his empire for a cup of wine. She was of Persian origin.

241. The ruler of the Carnatic region in the south of India, the capital of which was Arcat.

242. Hindi *thag*, cheat, and *daku*, armed robber. Organized bands of armed highway robbers active in central India who killed their victims and then robbed them. They were finally crushed by the British in 1801. (*Gazetteer* vol. I, p. 452)

243. Arabic *Hadith*: a body of Islamic religious knowledge based on accounts of acts

attributed to Muhammad and, in a wider sense, to his companions. It is a compilation of records which cover matters of religious doctrine, ritual, and rules of conduct for almost any conceivable action in everyday life.

244. Muhammad Wali: probable dates 1668–1744 (Saxena, p. 12). Born and brought up either in Gujrat or the Deccan, he came to Delhi in 1700 and wrote his poetry in Rekhta, the early form of Urdu. Until then poetry in Delhi was written in Persian.

245. An up-to-date account of Urdu literature can be found in Muhammad Sadiq, *History of Urdu Literature*, Oxford University Press, 1964.

246. Siraj ud Din Ali Khan Khan-e-Arzu: born Delhi 1689, died Lucknow 1756. A Persian scholar and poet of Delhi who wrote poetry in Rekhta and thus helped further to establish the language. He came to Lucknow in 1739, to the court of Salar Jang. (Saxena, pp. 47–48)

247. Maulana Muhammad Husain Azad: 1832–1910, of Delhi (Saxena, p. 219). Arabic and Persian, a prose stylist and an Urdu poet. The reference here is to his *Ab-e-Hayat*, a history of Urdu language and literature.

248. Mirza Mazhar Jan-e-Janan: 1698–1780. A religious preceptor and scholar of Delhi who wrote ghazals in an easy, flowing and sensitive style, in a language closer to present-day Urdu. (Saxena, p. 49)

249. 1720–84, of Delhi. A scholar, poet in Persian and Urdu, musician and religious preceptor. He renounced the world at the age of twenty-eight and later succeeded his father as spiritual chief of the sect of Chistis. (Saxena, pp. 55–57) His ghazals offer the best examples of Sufi (207) poetry in Urdu.

250. Persian *shagird*: one who studies under a master. A novice, scholar or poet, a writer or musician, and also craftsmen in other fields, spent a period of apprenticeship under an *ustad* in Islamic tradition, or guru in Hindu tradition, to whom he showed sometimes total obedience and always great respect. The relationship signified a spiritual bond between them in their personal lives and lasted a lifetime even when the period of learning was over.

251. Died 1772. He was attached to the court of Ahmad Shah in Delhi (Saxena, p. 52) and ranks among those poets who brought the Urdu language nearer to its present form.

252. Hindi *koka*. When a wet-nurse gave her milk to the infant of an employer, her own son became a *koka* brother to the child.

253. Born Delhi 1720, died Lucknow 1798. He came to Lucknow in the reign of Asaf ud Daula who became his shagird in poetry. (Saxena, p. 59) His ghazals show a youthful spirit.

254. Born Delhi about 1737, died Lucknow about 1792. A pharmacist by profession, he became courtier to various lords on arrival in Faizabad during the reign of Shuja ud Daula; he later moved to Lucknow. (Saxena, p. 98) His introspective ghazals are on love themes.

255. Born Delhi, died Lucknow 1797. He spent most of his life in Lucknow during the reign of Asaf ud Daula. (Askari, p. 349)

256. This name probably refers to Hasan Dehlavi (260). The Editor has been unable to trace any other person to whom this name could refer.

257. A scholar and poet who wrote in Persian, attached to the court of Shuja ud Daula. (Saxena, p. 62)

258. He came from Delhi to the court of Shuja ud Daula in 1765 with his young son Mir Hasan. He wrote marsiyas. (Askari, p. 349)

259. Shaikh Baqa ullah Khan Baqa: born Delhi, died Lucknow 1832. Wrote mainly satires in a language that borrows expressions from Hindi. (Askari, p. 217)

260. Mir Ghulam Hasan Hasan Dehlavi: born Delhi about 1741, died Lucknow 1786. He came to Faizabad with his father in 1766, later joined the court of Salar Jang and then went to Lucknow when the capital was shifted. He is the author

of the famous masnavi *Sehr ul Bayan* which was completed in 1785. (Saxena, p. 67)

261. Went to Faizabad and then to Lucknow in the reign of Asaf ud Daula.

262. Came from Delhi to Faizabad and then to Lucknow; later went to Patna (Azimabad) where he died. He was a contemporary of Sauda and wrote in a difficult style. (Askari, p. 216)

263. Shaikh Muhammad Qaim ud Din Qaim: born 1722, died 1793. Went to Delhi at an early age whence he came to Lucknow about 1776, later moving to the court of Rampur about 1778. He was a very prolific writer who wrote masnavis, qasidas and ghazals. (Saxena, p. 97)

264. Arabic *sajdah*: prostration, the touching of the ground with the forehead in Muslim prayer. *Sajjada*: prayer mat, and Persian *nashin*: sitting. The successor to the prayer mat, the spiritual leader of a religious order.

265. Shaikh Qalandar Baksh, Yahya Khan Jurat: died 1810. Born Delhi, spent his early childhood in Faizabad and went to Lucknow in 1800 when he became attached to the court of Mirza Suleman Shikoh (Saxena, p. 88). He composed amatory ghazals with an easy flow of language.

266. Saiyyid Insha Allah Khan: 1756–1818. He became a courtier to Sadat Ali Khan but was later dismissed. A soldier, hakim, scholar and poet who wrote frivolous and sensuous ghazals, he is the author of *Darya-e-Latafat*, the first grammar of the Urdu language to be written by an Indian. (Saxena, pp. 82–86) The conversation quoted in the text between the courtesan and the nobleman is from this book.

267. Shaikh Ghulam Hamdani Mushafi: born 1750 Amroha, U.P., died Lucknow 1824. Came to Lucknow in 1783/4 during the reign of Asaf ud Daula and saw the rule of three other Navabs in his lifetime. A very prolific writer whose ghazals are full of pathos. (Saxena, pp. 90–92)

268. Mirza Muhammad Hasan Qatil: died 1824. He was a Hindu convert to Islam from Faridabad, Delhi, who came to Lucknow and was attached to the court of Mirza Suleman Shikoh and probably later to the court of Ghazi ud Din Haidar: a Persian scholar who wrote some Urdu prose as well.

269. Navab Sadat Yar Khan Rangin: born Delhi 1757, died Lucknow 1835. A wealthy lord, soldier and scholar who wrote ghazals in *rekhti*, feminine language of a frivolous and sensuous character (322). (Saxena, p. 93) Qatil, Insha and Rangin were personal friends: the last two gave Urdu poetry of the Lucknow School a carefree, youthful and merry tone.

270. The first day of the new month after Ramzan (60) which is the day of the Muslim festival called Eid ul Fitr. Hence people look for the sign of the new moon the evening before, which is called the Eid moon. The expression refers to some very welcome thing or person which is so rare as to show up only once a year.

271. Of the ten days of mourning in Muharram (129) the eighth is devoted to the memory of Abbas, the half-brother of Husain and the commander of his forces in Kerbala. A procession takes place in his honour.

272. The Delhi flower shows which herald the spring originated in Delhi under Akbar Shah II and continue to this day. The main feature is a procession of big fans made of flowers, followed in the evening by songs, dances and entertainments.

273. Arabic *shams*, sun, and *ulema*, plural of *alim*, scholar. One who shines among scholars. A title bestowed by the British Government of India on Muslim scholars and religious leaders. The Republic has discontinued this practice and instead gives State and Presidential Awards.

274. Khwaja Muhammad Wazir Wazir: died 1854 in Lucknow. He remained preoccupied with spiritual matters and twice refused the invitation of Wajid Ali Shah to join his court. (Saxena, p. 108) He composed in difficult rhymes and styles.

275. Navab Faqir Muhammad Goya: died 1850. A Risaldar in the Avadh army of the Navabs. (Saxena, p. 257) He was preoccupied with language and style.

276. Mir Ali Ausat Rashk: 1799–1867. Born in Faizabad, he was mainly concerned with the correct employment of phrases and expressions, and famous for his dictionary of Urdu. (Saxena, p. 108)

277. Navab Asghar Ali Khan Nasim Dehlavi: 1794–1864. Born in Delhi, he lived in poor circumstances in Lucknow employed by Newal Kishore Press as an Urdu translator. (Saxena, p. 152) He wrote with facility in a flowing style.

278. Saiyyid Muzaffar Ali Khan Asir: 1800–81. He was a scholar of the Firangi Mahal school who joined the court of Nasir ud Din Haidar and later Amjad Ali Shah and Wajid Ali Shah, after whose deposition he went to the court of Rampur. (Saxena, p. 120) He concentrated on language and technique.

279. Pandit Daya Shankar Kaul Nasim: 1811–43, from a family of Kashmiri Brahmans settled in Lucknow. He was a Munshi in the army of Amjad Ali Shah. In poetry he concentrated on language, expression and idiom. He was the author of the famous masnavi *Gulzar-e-Nasim*. (Saxena, p. 114)

280. Hakim Momin Khan Momin: 1800–51. A well-to-do noble of Delhi who also practised medicine and was a scholar of Persian and Arabic. (Saxena, p. 148) His ghazals are noted for their subtle thought. His masnavis are erotic in nature.

281. Shaikh Ibrahim Zauq: 1789–1854. Of humble origin, he found his way to the Mughal court and became the Ustad (250) of Bahadur Shah Zafar. (Saxena, p. 152) He wrote elegant ghazals and qasidas polished in language and technique.

282. Mirza Asad Ullah Khan Ghalib: born in Akbarabad and lived in Delhi; of noble birth but in reduced circumstances. (Saxena, p. 158) He was a Persian scholar who wrote poetry in Persian as well as in Urdu. His ghazals and qasidas in Urdu are philosophic in character. He is also a prose stylist in Urdu, which he practised in his private letters. His biography, under the title of *Ghalib's Life and Letters*, has been compiled and translated into English by R. Russell and K. Islam, Allen & Unwin, London 1969. He is perhaps the best known Urdu poet, representing, with Momin and Zauq, the Delhi school of Urdu poetry, characterized by a subtle quality of thought and craftsmanship. For a short selection in English translation of Ghalib's poems see S. Jafri and Q. Hyder (eds), *Ghalib and his Poetry*, Popular Prakashan, Bombay 1970. For a study of Ghalib see Sayyid Fayyaz Mahmud, *Ghalib: A Critical Introduction*, University of the Panjab, Lahore, 1969.

283. Munshi Mufti Amir Ahmad Amir Minai: 1828–1900, from the family of Shah Mina (74): a religious scholar, poet and magistrate. He was connected with the court of Wajid Ali Shah, after whose deposition he went to the court of Rampur. His delicate ghazals have a moral tone. He is also the author of the incomplete Urdu dictionary in two volumes, *Amir ul Lughat*. (Saxena, pp. 182–85)

284. Navab Mirza Dagh Dehlavi: 1831–1905, stepson of the heir apparent of Bahadur Shah Zafar. After the Mutiny he spent most of his life in the courts of the Navab of Rampur and the Nizam. His ghazals deal with the agonies of love in simple, tender and eloquent language. (Saxena, pp. 186–88)

285. Syed Ismael Husain Munir: 1819–1881, from Shikohabad, U.P. but lived in Lucknow until 1857. From 1860 until his death he was attached to the court of Rampur. (Saxena, p. 110) His poems, mainly masnavis, have a simple and elegant style.

286. Ahmad Husain Taslim (alias Amir Ullah): born 1820, died Rampur 1911. He was a scholar and calligraphist and a soldier in the army of Muhammad Ali Shah, later attached to the court of Wajid Ali Shah as a poet. (Saxena, p. 196) His masnavis and ghazals have a vigorous and easy style.

287. Mir Mahdi Majruh: died 1902. Left Delhi after the 1857 Mutiny and entered the courts of Alwar and Rampur.

288. Hakim Syed Zamin Ali Jalal: 1834–1909. A hakim and scholar of Arabic and Persian: he went from Lucknow to the court of Rampur in 1857 but later returned to

Lucknow. He is the author of several books in prose (Saxena, p. 192) His ghazals are written with careful craftsmanship.

289. Syed Hasan Latafat. Son of Amanat (319): he wrote ghazals in sensitive language, expressing simple sentiments. (Rizvi, p. 11)

290. Both sons of Asir and his shagirds. (Saxena, p. 120)

291. The tradition of Urdu poetry in Lucknow goes further than the account in this narrative takes it. Between the early 1920s, where Sharar's account ends, and the late 1940s, Urdu poetry continued to flourish in Lucknow. Some prominent poets of this period are Syed Anwar Husain Arzu (born 1873, died Karachi 1954), Hakim Mirza Fida Ahmad Danish (1858–1928), Maulvi Ali Mian Kamil (1835–1906), Naubat Rai Nazar (1866–1923) and Mirza Wajid Husain Yas Yagana (born Azimabad 1883, died Lucknow 1956). They all had their own style within the framework of the Lucknow school. However, Mir Madhi Husain Ahsan (1867–1935) was also well known as a playwright, Ali Naqi Safi (1862–1950) wrote some descriptive poems as well, Pandit Brij Narain Chakbast (born Faizabad 1882, died Lucknow 1926) wrote mainly on patriotic and nationalistic themes. Mirza Muhammad Hadi Aziz (1882–1935) was famous for his qasidas, Mirza Zakir Husain Saqib (1869–1954) and Mirza Kazim Husain Mahshar (died 1941) also wrote ghazals. Writers of comic verse were Maqbul Husain Zarif (1870–1937) and Rafi Ahmad Khan (1888–1944).

These were followed by a group of ghazal writers prominent among whom were Navab Jafar Ali Khan Asar (1885–1967), Shahen-shah Husain Iram (died Karachi about 1967), Muhammad Askari Khan Sarosh Tabatabai (1913–66), Qadir Ahmad Khan Qadir (1890–1969), Syed Siraj ul Hasan Siraj (1894–1968), Syed Muhammad Ahmad Bekhud Mohani (1883–1940), Syed Al-e-Raza (born 1897, now in Karachi) and Shabir Husain Khan Josh Malihabadi (born 1901, also now in Karachi), famous for his poems. At present Pandit Anand Narain Mulla (born 1901, a retired judge and M.P. for Lucknow), Syed Muhammad Hasan Salik (born 1910), Muhammad Umar Ansari (born 1912) and Maharaj Kumar Muhammad Amir Haidar Khan of Mahmudabad (born 1917) are living in Lucknow and represent the last phase of the Urdu poetry of this school.

Ali Jawad Zaidi (born Azamgarh 1916, a civil servant in Delhi), Israr ul Haq Majaz (1913–55) and Ali Sardar Jafri (born Agra 1913, at present in Bombay) are well known as politically conscious poets from Lucknow, the last two being 'progressive' (345) communist poets.

In 1947, with the partition of the sub-continent into the states of India and Pakistan, the position of Urdu poets and prose writers in Lucknow changed. Some of these poets migrated to Pakistan, while in U.P. Hindi was declared the state language, and since then the vogue for Urdu poetry seems to have been dying out. However, in 1971 the Government of U.P. established the Urdu Academy for the promotion of the language, the secretary of which is the poet Sabah ud Din Umar (born Lucknow 1913). For brief character-sketches of some literary personalities of Lucknow up to the late 1940s, see Shaukat Thanvi, *Sheesh Mahal*, Urdu Book Stall, Lahore 1950.

Chapter 10: *The Development of Urdu Poetry*—Masnavi, Marsiya *and Forms of Humorous Verse*

292. Abul Qasim Hasan Firdausi: died about 1020, from the region of Khurasan. His *Shah Nameh*, 'Book of Kings', which took twenty-five years to complete (Levy, p. 177), is the national epic of Iran.

293. Nizami Arudi: born in Samarqand; lived in the early twelfth century. A courtier and poet.

294. Maulvi Jalal ud Din Maulana Rum: 1207–73. One of the greatest Sufi poets.

295. Nasir-e-Khusrau: 1004–77. Traveller, sceptic and poet.
296. Nur ud Din Abdul Rahman Jami: 1414–1592. Born in Jam in Khurasan. A poet of religious and Sufi sentiments.
297. Maulana Abdullah Hatifi: died 1521. Of Khurasan, nephew of Jami. The poets mentioned in notes 292–97 are all masters of classical Persian poetry.
298. Khwaja Arshad Ali Khan, Aftab ud Daula Qalaq: one of the court poets of Wajid Ali Shah in Lucknow. His poetry is of sensuous character, couched in elegant language. (Saxena, p. 121)
299. The reference is to linguistic mistakes. In 1905 a literary controversy began in Lucknow in the columns of *Avadh Akhbar*, and later continued in the pages of *Avadh Punch* and *Dil Gudaz*, on the literary merits of the language employed by Nasim: Sharar was one of his chief critics. This controversy was published later in the form of a book, *Marka-e Chakbast-o-Sharar*, ed. Mirza Muhammad Shafi Shirazi, Newal Kishore Press, 1913.
300. Muhammad Husain Naziri: born Nishapur, died Ahmedabad (India) 1614. He came to India as a young man and joined the court of Akbar and then that of Jahangir.
301. Khwaja Saidi Muhammad Urfi: born in Shiraz, died 1591. He came to India and was attached to the court of Akbar.
302. Mirza Muhammad Ali Saeb: died 1669/70. Brought up in Isfahan, went to Delhi and other parts of India before 1629 but returned to Persia to the court of Shah Abbas II. (Browne, vol. IV, p. 163)
303. Shaikh Abul Fazal Faizi: born Agra 1547, died 1595. Poet, philosopher and scholar of Arabic and Persian; an important personality and poet at the court of Akbar, reputed to have written one hundred and one books. (*Tarikh Muslim Adabiyat* vol. IV, pp. 278–88)
304. Muhammad Ikram Ghanimat: died 1688, born Qunjah (Gujrat). A poet who was also a military commander of Sialkot. (*Tarikh Muslim Adabiyat* vol. IV, p. 426)
305. It is said that a religious leader, Mir Ali Haidar of Isfahan, referred to himself as *Tabatabai* instead of *Qaba Qabai* (Arabic *qaba*, the robe of a religious scholar, and *qabai*, one who wears it) because of a speech defect. Members of his family subsequently adopted the word as a suffix to their name.
306. The contrast between the Urdu idioms and expressions used in Delhi and in Lucknow has been a favourite issue among Urdu scholars.
307. Wali Muhammad Nazir: died 1830. Spent most of his life in his home town of Akbarabad earning his living as a private tutor. He declined the invitation of Sadat Ali Khan to join his court, renounced the world and became a Sufi towards the end of his life. His natural and simple poetry is expressed in commonplace words. *Banjara Nama* is a long poem about the toils of those engaged in menial occupations.
308. Arabic *rajaz*: verses read at the battlefield to arouse the martial spirit.
309. The Sassanide dynasty (of Zoroastrians) ruled Persia from 224 to 651 before the advent of Islam, when it was overrun by the Arabs. Under this rule Persia was a country of imperial splendour and many of its manners and institutions were adopted by the later Muslim Abbaside dynasty.
310. The Abbaside dynasty, whose members ruled in Baghdad from 750 to 1258 under the title of Caliphs, is known for its development of architecture and art and for the many men of letters, philosophers and scholars whom it attracted to the court.
311. Hindi *Mian*: Sir. A polite form of address for a young master, but sometimes added before a name as a title.
312. Mir Mustahsan Khaliq: 1774–1804, the son of Mir Hasan. Spent early years in Faizabad and then came to Lucknow. He began as a ghazal writer but abandoned this style in favour of marsiyas. (Saxena, p. 124)
313. Mir Muzaffar Husain Zamir brought about changes in the pattern of marsiya

writing of the time and evolved, together with Zamir, a new form which was later popularized by Anis and Dabir. (Saxena, p. 125)

314. Mirza Salamat Ali Dabir: born Delhi 1803, died Lucknow 1875. Came to Lucknow with his father at the age of seven and became famous as a writer of marsiyas.

315. Mir Babar Ali Anis: born Faizabad 1802, died Lucknow 1874. He is regarded as one of the greatest of Urdu poets. Anis and Dabir were both recognized as masters and were much sought after by the local lords. They recited before Wajid Ali Shah on special invitation only. Dabir also recited before Ghazi ud Din Haidar. (Saxena, pp. 126–33)

316. In 1835 Lord William Bentinck introduced a new plan of education for India inspired by the writings of Lord Macaulay. It was orientated on the British pattern of secular education and instituted the use of vernacular and English in place of Persian as the languages of instruction, thus marking the beginning of a new outlook among educated people. (*Gazetteer* vol. I, p. 130) The plan was finally approved by the directors of the East India Company in 1854. (Moore, p. 108)

317. Persian *khwani*: reading. This style may appear to be theatrical but in fact the use of mime or acting was strictly prohibited.

318. The families of Mir Anis and Mirza Dabir continued the tradition of composing and reciting marsiyas for three to four generations. The last in the line of the former was Syedi Zafar Husain, popularly known as Babu Sahib Faeq (d. 1943) and of the latter, Mirza Sarfaraz Husain Khabir (d. 1948). Saxena, pp. 135–39; Syed Safdar Husain, 'Marsiya Bad-e-Anis', PhD thesis in Urdu, Aligarh University, U.P. (about (1940). Through the later members of the family of Mir Anis who were attached to the court of Mahmudabad State, this art was passed on to the Rajas of Mahmudabad. The last exponent in this family was Raja M. Amir Ahmad Khan who died in 1973.

319. Syed Agha Hasan Amanat, popularly known as Mian Amanat, 1815–58. Began as a marsiya poet but abandoned this form to write ghazals. In 1853 he wrote *Indar Sabha*, 'The Court of Indra', a musical comedy with dialogue in verse that is generally supposed to be the first theatrical work in Urdu. He was asked to write this comedy by Wajid Ali Shah and his flowery and artificial language is regarded as typical of one aspect of the Lucknow school. (Saxena, pp. 121, 351) For details see Rizvi, *Urdu Drama and Stage*.

320. Persian *Parsi*: Persian. However, the name is applied in India to those Zoroastrian Persians, or Fire-Worshippers, who fled their homes in the eighth century with the advent of Islam and came to settle near Bombay. (Moreland and Chatterjee, p. 134) After the fall of Wajid Ali Shah, a Parsi named Pestonji Framji formed his 'Original Theatrical Company' to stage Urdu dramas, in which many actors were also Parsis. This was the starting-point of Urdu theatre, which is generally referred to as Parsi theatre. (Saxena, p. 353)

321. The vogue for Urdu drama died in its infancy in Lucknow. In the 1940s there existed in Bombay, for a short time, the Indian People's Theatre Association followed by the present Indian Theatre of Delhi which stages plays in different Indian languages, including Urdu.

322. Derived from *rekhta* (244). The feminine form of language; artificially adopted speech of uncultured women in poetry to arouse lustful sentiments. (Askari, p. 25)

323. Mir Jafar Zattali: 1659–1713. A contemporary of Wali in Delhi, and employed as a soldier in the army of the Mughal prince.

324. Little is known about this poet except that he was under the patronage of a local lord in Lucknow.

325. Mir Yar Ali Jan Sahib: born 1818 in Farrukhabad, U.P., he went to Lucknow and after 1857 to Rampur where he died. A scholar who took part in the literary controversies of his day, he would appear at mushairas wearing a woman's veil. (*Tarikh-e Adabiyat* vol. VII, p. 331)

326. The masculine gender is no longer employed by contemporary poetesses in Urdu.

327. Anvari is a woman's name.

Chapter 11: *The Development of Urdu Prose*

328. Persian *serai*: singing. Ghazals (195) were usually chanted by poets in mushairas (237) though sometimes by individuals in private company. This is distinct from ghazal singing (442), where a distinct style evolved.

329. The reference is to the middle classes in north India, mainly U.P., and to the élite in some other courts. In 1835 Persian was replaced by Urdu as the administrative language by the British.

330. In 1880 a college was added to Fort William to teach Indian languages to the newly arrived British administrators. Dr John Gilchrist, the head of the college, brought many Indian scholars into this institution who prepared text-books for the British officers and other publications of a literary nature, thus creating a standard Urdu prose. One of these scholars was Mir Amman Dehlavi who in 1801 translated into Urdu the famous story *Qissah-e-Chahar Darvesh*, 'The Four Dervishes', under the title of *Bagh-o-Bahar*.

331. Mirza Ali Lutf: from Delhi, where his father was attached to the imperial court. In 1801 he wrote *Gulshan-e-Hind*, 'Garden of India', at the suggestion of Dr Gilchrist. (Saxena, p. 252)

332. Maulvi Ismail was known as *Shahid*, martyr, as he was killed in the name of Islam. He came from Delhi and went to Kojistan to fight the infidels. (Saxena, p. 254)

333. Mulla Nur ud Din Muhammad Zahuri: 1537–1616. Born Qaen, Persia, he came to Ahmadabad in 1580, where he was attached to the court of Ibrahim Adil Shah of Bijapur as poet. (*Tarikh-e Adabiyat* vol. IV, pp. 313–16)

334. Hakim Mirza Muhammad Nemat Khan-e-Ali: 1640–1709. Hakim, poet and scholar, came to India from Shiraz at an early age and was attached to the Mughal court. (*Tarikh-e Adabiyat* vol. IV, pp. 414–18)

335. Shaikh Abul Fazal Faizi (303). Probably the best known literary figure of his time and the doyen of the intellectuals.

336. Tahir Wahid of Bukhara: died 1120. A poet who was also secretary to two vazirs of Persia, court historian, and later a government minister. (Browne, vol. IV, p. 264)

337. Born Lucknow 1786, died Benares 1867. Prose writer, calligraphist and musician, he was deported by Ghazi ud Din Haidar but later returned under the rule of his son. He was court poet to Wajid Ali Shah and wrote *A Tale of Marvels* in 1824, a romantic story in ornate style, with adventures, demons, charmed forests and witchcraft, on the model of popular Persian tales. (Saxena, pp. 257–62)

338. Died 1829. Originally from Delhi but later came to Lucknow. He was a contemporary of Mir and Sauda. (Qadri, p. 200)

339. From the District of Lucknow. A scholar, famous poet and hymn-writer in Urdu and Persian who earned his living as a clerk in the law courts in Allahabad. (Saxena, p. 300)

340. Sir Syed Ahmad Khan: 1817–98, born Delhi. A Muslim scholar, literary figure and social reformer. In 1870 he started a monthly journal in Urdu, *Tahzib-ul-Akhlaq*, 'The Social Reformer', to introduce Western ideas to Muslim readers. He is best remembered as founder of the Anglo-Oriental College at Aligarh, which developed into a university in his lifetime and is now known as the Muslim University of Aligarh, U.P. He is the author of *Asar ud Sanadid* on the architecture of Delhi. (Saxena, p. 269)

341. Started by Munshi Sajjad Husain in 1877 as a humorous journal, it became

famous for its witty prose style and literary merit. The journal ceased publication with his death in 1912. In 1930 it was re-started under the editorship of Hakim Mumtaz Husain Osmani, after whose death his son Zaheer Osmani took over. He died prematurely and for a short while the latter's sister continued to edit it from purdah (208); the magazine eventually ceased in the early 1940s. Some other famous contributors were Sharar himself, Sarshar, Vilayat Ali Mambuq Kidwai, Abbas Husain Hosh, Bishan Narain Dar, Jwala Parshad Barq and Akbar Allahabadi.

342. Pandit Ratan Nath Sarshar: born Lucknow 1846, died Hyderabad 1902. Editor, translator, poet and journalist, later attached to the court of Maharaja Krishna Prashad in Hyderabad. He is best known as a novelist, *Fasana-e-Azad* (1880) being one of the first modern novels in Urdu literature. (Saxena, pp. 325–34) For a detailed study see Feroz Husain, 'Life and works of Sarshar', Urdu PhD thesis, London University, 1964.

343. *Avadh Akhbar* (Arabic *Akhbar*: news, newspaper) was started in Lucknow by Munshi Newal Kishore (382) in 1859 and continued until the early 1940s. In its early days some pages of this newspaper were reserved for literary writing and many Urdu writers of Lucknow contributed to its columns. Sarshar was its editor from 1878 until probably 1894. Sharar was its assistant editor from 1880 until 1882. *Fasana-e-Azad* appeared in the columns of the newspaper between 1878 and 1879. (Saxena, p. 325)

344. Shams-ul-Ulema (273) Maulvi Nazir Ahmad: born 1836 in Bijnor, U.P., died 1912. He was employed in the Education Department, later as a civil administrator in U.P. and then in Hyderabad. About 1858 he was commissioned to translate the Penal Code, but is better known for his innovations in Urdu novel-writing. (Qadri, pp. 536–58)

345. This covers the period to about 1925. To complete the picture it should be added that a group of Urdu novelists emerged in Lucknow after this time. They were Muhammad Ali Tabib, Munney Agha Hosh (died about 1930), and Mirza Muhammad Hadi Ruswa (1857–1931), a poet and essayist but better known as a novelist, and Mirza Fida Ali Khanjar (died 1956).

A development of a different kind took place in Lucknow about 1936 when a group of communist/socialist writers and poets who called themselves 'progressive' writers became prominent in the field of short-story writing. They are Saiyyid Sajjad Zaheer (1905–73), Dr Rashid Jahan (died Moscow 1953) and Professor Ahmad Ali (at present in Karachi). Journalists of this group are Muhammad Raza Ansari (born 1917) and Saiyyid Sibte Hasan (now in Karachi). The younger short-story writers of this group are Pandit Brij Mohan Nath Kachar (born 1932) and Ram Lal (born 1923). Among the novelists and short-story writers of this period who do not belong to the 'progressive' group are Syed Abid Husain (born 1899), Hamid Ullah Afsar (born 1898), Ali Abbas Husaini (born Azamgarh 1899, died Lucknow 1971), Hayat ullah Ansari (born 1911, editor of *Qaumi Awaz*, Urdu daily in Lucknow), and the novelist Shaukat Siddiqi (now in Karachi) and Miss Qurratul Ain Haider (at present a journalist in Bombay).

Along with this writing Urdu literary criticism developed. Some of the critics are Professor Syed Masud Husain Rizvi (born 1893), Abdul Bari Asi (1893–1946), Professor Ehtisham Husain (born Azamgargh 1912, died 1973), Niyaz Muhammad Khan Niyaz Fatehpuri (born Fatehpur, died Karachi 1969), Professor Nurul Hasan Hashimi (born 1913, presently head of the Department of Urdu in the University of Lucknow), Dr Ibadat Barelvi (born Bareilly), Mumtaz Husain (born Azamgargh), and Dr Muhammed Ahsan Farrooqi, who is also a novelist and a short-story writer. These last three now live in Pakistan. A prominent writer of humour and satire was Muhammad Umar Shaukat Thanvi (born Lucknow 1905, died Lahore 1963).

Chapter 12: Dastan Goi—*the Art of Story-Telling*

346. *Dastan-e-Amir Hamza*, a fairy tale in Persian covering about 18,000 pages in many volumes, concerning the adventures of Amir Hamza. It contains magic, charms, fairies and devils and was written, probably in its present form, by Faizi, to entertain the Emperor Akbar. (Askari, p. 100)

347. Abul Hasan Amir Khusrau: 1255–1325. A Sufi, distinguished scholar, soldier, musician (422) and poet. He was an eminent person in the court of Muhammad Tughlaq. As a poet he wrote ghazals in rekhta and employed Hindi words freely in his Persian poetry. For a detailed study see Muhammad Waheed Mirza, *The Life and Works of Amir Khusrau*, Calcutta 1935.

348. The most well known are *Tilism-e-Hosh Ruba* in seven volumes which is part of *Dastan-e-Amir Hamza*. The first four volumes were translated from Persian into Urdu by Mir Muhammad Husain Jah and the last three by Ahmad Husain Qamar; another part entitled *Nausherwan-Nama* was translated by Shaikh Tassaduq Husain. Equally well known is *Bostan-e-Khayal* by Mir Taqi Khayal, the last two volumes of which were translated by Chotey Agha in Lucknow, who also revised the five earlier volumes translated by Khwaja Aman of Delhi. (Askari, p. 100) In style and content all these stories are based on the *Arabian Nights*.

349. In kite-flying, bamboo poles are used to hook in the kite after the string is cut. (Chapter 20)

350. Since most of the dastans referred to (348) were published by Newal Kishore Press in Lucknow, the book on Zila was probably also one of their publications.

Chapter 13: *Islamic Studies*

351. The pattern of Muslim education in India, as elsewhere, was confined within the religious framework, the subjects taught being the Quran, its commentary and exposition, Muslim jurisprudence, ethics, history and medicine. The Silsila-e-Nizamia (97) enlarged the scope by incorporating some social and physical sciences into the curriculum, which then became standard. The period about which Sharar writes seems to mark the end of this type of instruction, with the introduction of British education (316).

352. Arabic *mufti*: one who is authorized, in view of his scholarship, to issue a religious decree.

353. 1809–1891. The leading Shia *fiqh* (jurisprudence) scholar and Mujtahid (132) at the beginning of the present century.

354. i.e. in Arabic and Persian literatures.

355. Popularly known as Nadwa College, this institution was founded in 1894 from donations of the Muslim public, with the purpose of revising the course of instruction in Islamic (Sunni) theology, Arabic and Persian languages and literatures. At the suggestion of Maulana Shibli (506) in 1895, certain secular subjects and the English language were also included in the curriculum. Its present foundation was laid in 1909 when the British Government in U.P. gave it a substantial grant (Saxena, p. 290). The college exists to this day supported by the present Government of U.P. and is regarded as an important institute of Islamic studies in India.

Chapter 14: *The Development of Yunani Medicine*

356. The Iberian Peninsula was conquered in the first instance by the Muslims in 711. It was ruled by the Umayyad Amirs of Cordova from 756 until 961, by which time the court had become a seat of Islamic culture. (Hitti, p. 514)

357. Beyond the study of basic texts, there was no standard curriculum for the training of a hakim. A beginner studied under an old and experienced hakim who improvised the course as the studies progressed. In this process he usually reserved the finer points of professional skill for members of his own family or some special pupil. As a result, the profession at a higher level tended to run in families. Besides medicine, the same system of instruction applies to music and some other crafts to this day.

358. Hereditary title of the ruler of the Indian Princely State of Baroda, from 1721 until 1947.

359. They flourished until the 1920s, after which their school of medicine was superseded by Western medical science.

360. Arabic *haziq*, expert, and *ul Mulk*, of the Country: Expert of the Country. An honorific title for outstanding hakims.

361. The medical college exists to this day. Its curriculum includes Vedic and European medical systems along with the traditional Muslim curriculum.

362. Traditional Hindu medical knowledge derived from ancient Sanskrit texts. For the Hindus the source of all forms of human knowledge was revealed to human beings through the four *Vedas*, which go back to Aryan times. They are: 1) *Rig Veda*, a book of hymns; 2) *Yajus Veda*, sacrificial rituals; 3) *Saman Veda*, hymns set to music at the time of offering sacrifices; 4) *Atharva Veda*, magic, medical formulae, mysticism and philosophy. (V. Raghavan)

363. Takmil ut Tib College still survives today on a modest scale on the same lines. Hakim Abdul Aziz was succeeded by his two sons, both of whom were hakims. Members of the family still continue the tradition but medical practice is no longer their principal occupation. A student of this college, Hakim Dharam Paul, now practises in London.

364. This tradition continued in Lucknow until the 1940s and several famous hakims flourished until this period. Today however, they have been replaced by advocates of Western medicine and hospitals.

Chapter 15: *The Significance of the Persian Language*

365. Hindus, especially Brahmans, are prohibited from eating meat. Thus a Hindu convert to Islam would say jokingly that he changed his religion to be able to eat meat.

366. A member of a troupe of male performers who entertained by acting, dancing, jesting and mimicry.

367. A group of pandits (34) originally from Kashmir, some of whom became attached to the court in Delhi and later settled in parts of U.P. In Lucknow this community lived in a quarter named after it, Kashmiri Mohalla, which is still in existence.

368. Hindi *bhasha*: language. Sanskrit has always been a literary language and a language of intellectual discourse. The vernacular spoken in parts of Avadh was called Purbi, Eastern Bhasha.

369. In parts of north India under the British, Persian was replaced by Urdu as the administrative and court language in 1832. (Qadri, p. 202) It became the language of instruction in 1835 (316). This policy was extended to the remaining parts of U.P. after the annexation of Avadh and remained so until 1947 when Urdu was replaced by Hindi.

370. Author of *Bostan-e-Avadh*, a short history of Avadh in Urdu, published by Maktba Dabdaba-e-Ahmadi, 1892.

371. Muslims bow to the Quran, placing their foreheads upon it. Hence the expression 'to place the brow upon' means to show extreme respect.

Chapter 16: *Scripts—Calligraphy and the Urdu Press*

372. Naskh script is a cursive form of Arabic writing, where the letters are not necessarily vertical as in Kufic, but the foliation attached to them is derived from Kufic.

373. Developed in Hira, a medieval Arab town near the site of Babylon.

374. Kufic script, also known as Cufie, after the name of the town Al-Kufah south of Baghdad, where this form of writing developed, is one of the earliest forms of Arabic script writing. It is characterized by heavy, solid vertical lines which are used to form the letters. According to Grube, there are eight distinct styles within this group, the three main ones being: simple Kufic, with straight vertical strokes and angular forms of letters; foliated Kufic, in which the vertical strokes end in leaves and half-palmettes; and floriated Kufic, where the endings of the letters are enhanced by floral designs and half-palmettes and the round forms are rendered as rosettes. (Grube, pp. 11–13)

375. Tahir Ibn al Husain, a Persian general, was appointed Governor of the region east of Baghdad in 820 and later became its ruler. His successor remained in power until 872 and extended his dominion as far as the Indian frontier. (Hitti, p. 460)

376. Timur (Tamerlane) conquered Persia between 1370 and 1383. Mir Ali lived at that time. One of his works, a collection of poems in his handwriting dated 1396, is in the British Museum. The work is entitled 'Khamsah', five poems of the poet Khwadju Kirmani, who died in 746. For an account of Nastaliq writers, see *Ahwal-o-Asrar-e-Khushnawaisan*, Tehran University Press, 1970.

377. *Katba* is the stylized writing of a Quranic verse, excerpts from a hadis in Arabic, or one or two aphoristic lines or verses in Urdu or Persian.

378. Arabic *katib*: a scribe. Urdu publications are still printed lithographically. Katibs prepare the entire manuscript for printing, usually in Nastaliq style. This process of copying the manuscript is known as *kitabat*.

379. Turkish tughra: sign, symbol. A Quranic verse, a sentence from a prayer or Hadis, so written that the composition outlines an animal figure which is not considered unclean or of ill omen. Usually it is a dove or a tiger.

380. The printing-press was first introduced in India at Fort William College in 1814 by missionaries to translate the Bible into Urdu in five volumes. In Lucknow the letter-press method was established during the reign of Ghazi ud Din Haidar. The litho press however was introduced in 1837 by a certain Mr Archer who had first established one in Kanpur. (Qadri, pp. 96–97)

381. Arabic *hujja*: to bear witness. Haji is an honorific title of one who has made a pilgrimage to Mecca, one of the basic obligations in Islam.

382. Munshi Newal Kishore established his press in Lucknow in 1858 to publish classics and religious books in Arabic, Persian and Sanskrit. (Saxena, p. 318) Its main publications were, however, contemporary works in Urdu, and some in Hindi. It was regarded as one of the most important publishing houses in India in the field of Oriental scholarship, unequalled in its range of subjects and literary works. Since the 1940s the firm has severely reduced the number of Urdu, Arabic and Persian publications. It now operates under the name of Newal Kishore Book Depot and is still run by the same family.

383. Except for the Nastaliq style, which is used in Urdu litho printing, the art of calligraphy has now died out in Lucknow and other parts of the sub-continent. If it is continued at all it is in the occasional work of amateurs. The art of musleh sangi has disappeared completely.

Chapter 17: *The Arts of Combat and Self-Defence*

384. The remuneration was not intended for the personal use of the Saiyyids (37) but as charity for the poor, to be distributed by the Saiyyids.

385. To pinion in bānk is to render the opponent helpless by twisting his limbs in such a way that his body becomes a knot.

386. Arabic *sabha*: to praise. *Tasbih* is the Muslim rosary carried by believers, who say a short prayer on each bead whenever they have the opportunity. The number of beads corresponds to the ninety-nine attributes of Allah.

387. The sacred thread worn by male Hindus, especially Brahmans, over the left shoulder which hangs diagonally across the body to the right hip. The investiture of the sacred thread marks, according to the ancient Hindu tradition, the initiation of a boy into the first stage of manhood, or *brahmacharya*, the period of studentship: the other three stages in life following this are *grahastha*, domestic life, *vana prastha*, life in hermitage, and *sanniyasa*, complete renunciation.

388. Persian *kushti*: something between Japanese judo and Western wrestling. The game is won by the person who can throw his opponent in such a way that the backs of his shoulders touch the ground.

389. Persian *darugha*: supervisor, in charge of the whole or a section of the staff of a wealthy household.

390. Wedding processions went from the house of the bridegroom to that of the bride and were accompanied by bands of music, displays of acrobats and other forms of entertainment. (Chapter 47)

Chapter 18: *Animal Combats—Beasts of Prey and other Quadrupeds*

391. A spiked iron bar about one foot long with two circles in the centre into which the fingers are placed for a firm grip. For a detailed description of these animal combats, see Knighton, chapters 7, 10 and 11.

Chapter 19: *Bird-Fighting and Pigeon-Flying*

392. For details on the varieties of Indian birds, see Hugh Whistler, *Popular Handbook of Indian Birds*, Gurney and Jackson, London 1949, and Salim Ali, *The Common Birds of India*, Thacker and Co., Bombay 1945.

393. The custom of offering charity or alms for the poor as a form of sacrifice for the granting of a specific prayer, such as welfare of someone in distress or health for the ill. In this case the charity was for the man himself, from God, for the well-being of the Imams.

394. Persian *vasiqa*, endowment (172), and *dar*, holder. *Vasiqa dar* were usually the descendants either of the ruling house or of the leading employees of the court, hence the grant of a vasiqa signified nobility. At the present time the amount of the vasiqa pension has been greatly reduced owing to the increase in family numbers over the successive generations since they were originally instituted. When the amount of vasiqa for an individual reaches under five rupees per month, a lump sum equal to the total for twenty years is paid as a final settlement.

395. Persian *jamadar*: headman, a non-commissioned officer in the Indian section of the British army.

396. In fact there are many varieties of quail in India, but bush quail and button quail are the best known.

397. Arabic *itr*: essence, fragrance; a perfume extracted from flowers with sandal-oil as the base, without clarified spirit or alcohol. There are three varieties: those which have the freshness of clay, those which have the fragrance of summer flowers, and those which are especially prepared to have a warming effect in winter.

398. Girah baz are usually white and blue and the seven varieties are a mixture of

these two colours. They are flown early in the morning and fly high in the sky, coming back in the evening or after dark, sometimes somersaulting as they return. They fly vertically from the ground, so that if a bowl of water is placed at the point where they have taken off their reflections can be seen in it for some time.

Goley are found in three major varieties, and in many colours except white. They fly low in the sky covering long distances, usually in flocks. In competitions they return at the sound of their master's whistle, bringing with them some pigeons from his opponent's flock and so increasing their number and in this way winning.

399. Considered a better variety of goley, large in size. The head, beak, mouth and wings can be of different colours, although are usually red or green. The body and tail are white, with a beautiful, coloured, floral-like pattern on the breast. Originally the breed was brought from Shiraz (11).

400. Guli, like shirazi, have white breasts with the back and wings of different colours, but are quite small in size. They have coloured floral-like designs on the upper parts.

401. A variety of girah baz from Peshawar, now nearly extinct. Its breast is white and its back a mixture of white, black and grey.

402. Gulvey is usually white, but is found also in other colours. It is not flown but is reared for its beauty only, as the feathers on its neck are especially attractive.

403. Laqa is usually white with a small head and distinctive long neck, which it twists backwards to touch its fan-shaped tail, sometimes to such an extent that the bird somersaults. It is delicate and cannot tolerate being mixed with other varieties: when this happens the bird withdraws and loses its special characteristics.

404. Lotan has a white head, black wings and a small white crest. If held by the head and shaken it quivers for some time. There is one variety which, unless stopped, would continue to quiver until it dies. This bird is now almost extinct.

405. A variety of girah baz, now extinct. There were two kinds, *kapur chandan* and *choya chandan*, both grey in colour, small in size, with a white beak and a crescent at the throat. They were bred for their beauty.

406. A white variety of lotan, small in size, which keeps its tail tightly closed. It makes the sound resembling 'Yahu' when breathing.

Chapter 20: *Parrots and Kite-flying*

407. The idea of infidelity is expressed in Urdu with the phrase 'he has the eyes of a parrot'.

408. Hindi *akas*, sky, atmosphere; and *diya*, oil-lamp. According to Hindu mythology the abode of the Gods is on three spheres—sky, atmosphere and earth. In popular belief, stars are lamps lit in honour of the Gods of the first two regions.

409. The string used in kite-fighting is of two kinds. The front part, which is involved in the fight, is specially prepared with powdered glass so that it can cut sharply. The back part is untreated so that it can be handled safely.

Chapter 21: *The Origin and Growth of North Indian Music*

410. This and the following chapters on music apply in the main to the school of music known as Hindustani music: the other school is South Indian or Karnatic. For an account see Peggy Hoyle.

411. Hindi, song. The science of classical Indian music is composed of three elements: singing, instrumental music and dancing. In singing various combinations of *surs* (413) are interpreted in a definite and pleasing order. If this is done through meaningful words instead of vocalizing the names of the surs (*sa, re, ga* . . .) the composition is called a

git. (Mohtashim, p. 10) Originally a git was of devotional nature but later the term came to be applied to love songs as well.

412. Projection of a git through a musical instrument, which may be one of two types: those which accompany a singer but are unable to convey all the notes in the phrases of the git on their own, like *pakhavaj, tabla, dhol* and *duf*; and those that can express all the notes like *sarangi, sitar* and *esraj*, and hence can be played on their own. (Mohtashim, p. 10)

413. Sanskrit, *svara*. A sur is a tone of a definite pitch, a note of the scale. In ancient times they were called *surtis* or *shruti* and recognized as twenty-two in number, the pitch rising in an ascending order and with equal distance between each note. In the contemporary system they have been reduced to seven. They are popularly known as *sa, re, ga, ma, pa, dha, ni, sa.* (Mohtashim, p. 12)

414. Sanskrit *raga*. A raga is a melodic form made up of a series of surs within the octave distinguished by a 'particular sequence of notes, number of tones, ascending and descending orders, most prominent notes, notes of different lengths, characteristic phrases and a principal mood'. It is the melodic base of the Indian musical system on which the musician improvises in any style, for any duration and in any tempo, either as a solo or accompanied by tabla; it may have a composed bass song or instrumental gat. (Ravi Shankar, p. 29) Ragas have been classified according to emotional mood and time of day, usually early morning or evening. Although a large body of theory exists, musical knowledge in practice is learnt directly from a master and is never written.

415. Brahma, Vishnu and Mahesh are the supreme gods of the Hindu trinity. Brahma is the first aspect as the creator of the universe, Vishnu the second aspect as the preserver and sustainer of the universe. He had nine re-births, the seventh time as Rama (5), the eighth time as Krishna (219) and the ninth time as Buddha: one more incarnation is expected. Mahesh, also known as Mahadeo or Shiva, is the third aspect. He is the god of destruction who changes nature. It is believed that after the creation of the universe he danced with joy with his consort Parvati. Hence he is regarded as the creator of music, dance and drama. (Ravi Shankar, pp. 156–60)

416. Feminine word for raga, employed to express the lighter and technically less vigorous version of the raga.

417. Singers of a Muslim hymn or *qavvali*, a religious song sung in gatherings of the devout in a fast tempo. This style originated with Amir Khusrau (422) and is known as the qavvali style of singing.

418. An elongated stringed instrument with a gourd made of hide at one end and a narrow metal finger-board. The sarod is played with a plectrum and as well as the main strings for playing, there are sixteen sympathetic strings which resonate as in the sitar.

419. The *chang, barbat* and *rabab* were ancient stringed instruments, now obsolete. A variation of rabab known as *rudra bin* was invented by Tan Sen. (Ravi Shankar, p. 50).

420. The *shahnai* is a wind instrument made of a wooden stem with a metal funnel attached at the end, similar to an oboe. Traditionally the shahnai was played outside a house to announce celebrations, especially marriage, but during the last few decades it has become a solo concert instrument, sometimes accompanied by other instruments.

421. The *zangula* or *jangla* and *zaif* were adopted as proper ragas or raginis within the Indian musical system by Amir Khusrau. Tan Sen (430) composed *shahana* raga to display royal splendour and grandeur and also *darbari* raga, which consists of three ragas—*darbari kanrah, darbari kalyan* and *darbari asavari*. Originally Tan Sen composed the three ragas known as *tori, sarang* and *malhar*, which were quite different from the established ragas at the time. Akbar liked these new ragas and they were sung frequently at his court. Hence they came to be known as darbari ragas. (Bare Ahga, pp. 7, 8).

422. As a musician Amir Khusrau (347) invented the tabla as well as the sitar, and

composed a large number of ragas and raginis like *sanam, aymet basant, kankali, kafi* and *ghara*, which were a departure from the traditional ragas of that time. Moreover he initiated several new styles of singing which were gay, colourful and less demanding than the strict singing of the ragas. Prominent among these are qavvali, ghazal and trana styles of singing. (Bare Agha, p. 7)

423. Persian *seh*, seven, and *tar*, strings. The sitar is about four feet long with a hollow gourd at the base, on which lie the seven strings used for playing. In addition, it has about twenty other strings, the purpose of which is to amplify the sound, and twenty metal frets, some of which can be moved by the player. The strings are plucked with a plectrum. This instrument has become the most popular in India and is well known in the Western world.

424. A light, entertaining melody free from the rigid structure of a raga.

425. Arabic *hal*, ecstasy, and *qal*, condition: to be thrown into ecstasy. On Thursday evenings the Sufi prayer meetings are followed by qavvali singing, during which some people go into a trance and are said to attain cosmic unity.

426. Muhammad Tughlaq ruled from 1326 to 1351. Soon after coming to power he transferred his capital from Delhi to Deo Garh about 700 miles away and gave it the new name of Daulatabad (7). Later however the capital was removed to Delhi.

427. Hindi *chaudhri*, village headman. Feminine *chaudhrayan*. A title used for the chief of a group of people who live together or follow the same trade.

428. Arabic *tarawih*: prayers and reading of the Quran, offered by Muslims after the evening meal during the month of Ramzan (60).

429. Sultan Husain Sharqi (1719–48) was the third and last king of the Saiyyid dynasty which ruled from Jaunpur and was established in 1414. He was a patron of music and himself composed fifteen ragas, some of which, like *shyam kadar, shyam des, rama tori* and *jaunpuri*, became famous. (Bare Agha, p. 6) The *khyal* style of singing, the origins of which are attributed to Amir Khusrau (422), was promoted and made popular by Sharqi. (Ravi Shankar, p. 33)

430. Mian Tan Sen (Hindi *tan*, musical phrase; *sen* from *chaien*, peaceful; *mian* [311], one who brings peace through music) was the title Emperor Akbar gave to Ata Muhammad Khan who was born of a Brahmin family in Gwalior and given the name of Ramtanu. (Ravi Shankar, p. 49) He is the greatest name in North Indian music and is generally believed to be the most accomplished singer that has ever lived. Various legends have grown about the perfection of his art, one being that by singing the *dipak* raga he was able to light the oil-lamps and another that he could bring rain by singing the *megh malhar* raga.

431. Hindi *nau*, nine, and *ratan*, jewel. Emperor Akbar collected in his court the nine foremost men of letters, musicians and soldiers of his time. He called them the Nine Jewels: Tan Sen was the first.

432. The family of Tan Sen, descending through his son and daughter, have devoted themselves to music over a period of centuries. It was this family and their pupils who established the tradition of North Indian music as it is known today. The last great masters of the family were Wazir Khan at the court of Rampur (438) and Muhammad Ali Khan at Lucknow, the latter a vocalist who died at the turn of the century. Some members of the family continue as top-ranking musicians to this day, among them Vilayat Khan, a sitar player, Imrat Khan, a surbahar player and the Dagar brothers, singers of khyal.

433. The reference is probably to the numerous members of the Tan Sen family who dominated Indian music over centuries. But Hindu musicians have also been prominent all along.

434. Thick pancakes about six inches in diameter fried in clarified butter or oil; hence an expensive item.

435. Thick clotted cream, nearly semi-solid with the skin on the top.

436. Urdu *pichvan*: a type of huqqa which has a flexible extension of the stem some-times several yards long. A huqqa is an elaborate smoking-pipe with a water bowl attached at the bottom, through which the smoke is drawn.

437. In the old Indian system of weights, four *chitanks* were one *pao*, four *paos* a *ser* (roughly two pounds) and sixteen *sers* a *man*. The metric system has been recently adopted.

Chapter 22: *The Development of Light Classical and Instrumental Music*

438. Wazir Khan was Ustad (250) of the Navab and head of more than five hundred musicians at the court of Rampur (124), at least fifty of whom were among the most renowned instrumentalists and vocal artists in the whole country. (Ravi Shankar, p. 53) About this time, at the beginning of the century, the court of Rampur was the greatest single patron of musicians in India, a tradition which continued to flourish at this court.

439. Hindi *kadar*, mean, and *piya*, lover, husband: the mean lover, pen-name of Wajid Ali Shah as a writer of amorous songs.

440. Hindi *thumri*: a short love song expressing romantic longing; a style of both vocal and instrumental music where parts of different ragas are joined in a rhythmic pattern. It had been known already in Benares but was popularized by Wajid Ali Shah. Some other members of his court who followed his example and also composed thumris were Navab Wazir Mirza Qadar, Navab Kalbe Ali Khan, Binda Din Binda and Lallan, thus establishing the Lucknow style of thumri singing. (Mohtashim, p. 583)

441. Arabic *khyal*: imagination, fancy. A love song expressing feminine feelings about the imaginary meeting or separation from the lover. This is in accordance with the tradition of Hindi poetry of expressing sentiments in the feminine form of the language. As a style of vocal music it is a composition of colourful melodies which take prece-dence over the verses. It was originated by Amir Khusrau (422), improved upon by Sultan Husain Sharqi (429) and made popular by his court musician Shah Sadarang. In the first half of the eighteenth century, Mian Sadarang composed khyal songs in many different ragas. At present, it is the predominant vocal style of North Indian classical music. (Ravi Shankar, p. 33).

442. Initially, Amir Khusrau started the singing of Persian ghazals in light and attractive melodies. Over a period of time this style developed new techniques, using Urdu ghazals. It became very popular in Lucknow. Now known as light classical style, it is a common form of singing in parts of North India. The singing of a ghazal, usually accompanied by tabla and sarangi, starts from the middle stages of a raga, leaving out the earlier parts, and concentrates on the airs. Some favourite airs of ghazal-singing are *kaharva, pashtu* and *rupak*. Begam Akhtar (b. 1914) was an outstanding contemporary ghazal and thumri singer from Lucknow. She died in 1974.

443. Persian *soz*: lament; the recital of marsiya elegies in a majlis (129). Because of religious prohibition of music a special style was evolved in which the ragas and raginis remain in the background as a framework only, omitting the surs and stressing the rhythm. This style of singing must never be accompanied by any instrument.

444. For details of the development of music in Lucknow see Raja Muhammad Navab Ali, *Maaruf-ul-Naghmat*, 2 vols, Mumtaz ul Mutaba, Lucknow (probably 1920), and Hakim Muhammad Karam Imam Khan, *Maadan ul Mausiqi*, ed. Munshi Syed Wajid Ali, Hindustani Press, Lucknow 1925.

445. Originally a form of folk singing from the camel cart drivers in the Panjab. Tappa was later developed to a classical level by Minan Shori. The style consists of improvisations on a melody, usually in fast tempo.

446. Persian *tarana*, melody, song; a song in a raga composed of simple words,

usually Persian, sung in a colourful and gay melody in fast tempo. The style was initiated by Amir Khusrau as a result of a competition in the court of Sultan Husain Sharqi. Gopal Naek sang a raga and Amir Khusrau was challenged to reproduce it. He did so, but not being proficient in the Sanskrit language he replaced the Sanskrit words in the song with Persian and sang the raga. (Bare Agha, p. 7)

447. A set of two small spherical drums with skin stretched across the flattened top surface and a range of about an octave. The tabla is the most widely used accompanying instrument.

448. Small stringed instrument with a rounded body and wide neck played with a bow and held vertically. It has three main strings and many vibrating sympathetic strings.

449. Known as *vina* in South India: an ancient stringed instrument going back to Aryan times, in various sizes, often elaborately decorated. It is capable of much diversity and subtlety of tone quality.

450. A simple stringed instrument with a narrow neck and a gourd at the end; it has four to six strings. One or two are plucked in playing. Its function is to repeat the tonic at appropriate intervals throughout the performance of both vocal and instrumental music.

451. A cylindrical drum, formerly made of clay but now of wood. A skin is stretched over both ends, each of which is tuned to a different pitch.

452. Also a cylindrical drum with a skin stretched over each end, played on both sides.

453. Muhammad Ali Khan was an eminent vocalist, who returned to live in Lucknow towards the end of his life. He left a disciple, Khurshid Ali Khan, who furthered the development he had begun. His pupil, Raja Thakur Navab Ali Khan, author of *Maaruf-ul-Naghmat*, in turn became a very renowned musician in Lucknow, both as an artist and theoretician. With his death in the 1930s the torch was passed to his pupil Syed Shams ud Din Haidar, popularly known as Bare Agha: artist, author on music and Vice-Principal of the School of Music in Lucknow. In addition to these men, there have been many other prominent singers and instrumentalists in Lucknow. An important development took place when the Marris College of Hindustani Music was founded by the British in the 1920s under the leadership of the well-known musicologist V. N. Bhatkande. Since 1947 this institution has been called Bhatkande Sangeet Vidyapeeth.

Chapter 23: *Dance and the Development of the* Kathak *School*

454. Wandering minstrels who chanted *kathas*, Hindu mythological stories, while making appropriate bodily movements. This is the origin of *kathak* dancing. Later the kathak school of dancing changed its characteristic mood from devotional to erotic.

455. Instrumental compositions which do not allow for free improvisation. They can be played in any rhythm and with any number of rhythmic cycles from two to sixteen. They are accompanied by tabla.

456. A *tora* (plural *torey*) is a complete cycle of one rhythmic pattern. The dancer or player of an instrument, e.g. a sitar, tries to create a false impression to his accompanying instrumentalist, usually a tabla player, as to when and where he or she is going to complete the cycle, sometimes performing as though it were about to end and then continuing. The result is a kind of playful game to see whether the tabla can answer the question put by the dancer or the sitar.

457. This was the greatest school of kathak, sometimes referred to simply as the North Indian or Lucknow school of dancing. It is characterized by very quick alternations of rhythmic footwork. It is one of the four Indian schools, the others being

Kathakali and Bharat Natyam in South India and Mani Puri in Assam. For an account, see E. Bhavnani.

458. A short rhythmic composition, many of which make up a dance.

459. In Indian dance a collection of small bells is frequently worn on a band round the ankles by male and female dancers alike. In kathak dancing one of the finer points is the control with which the performer is able to jingle the bells with his leg movements.

460. Hindi *batana*: to tell. In dance terminology, to depict through bodily movements. In kathak dancing there is sometimes another person who gives a verbal commentary to clarify what the dancer is illustrating through movement.

461. Kalka Prashad had three sons who were dancers of repute and who maintained the family tradition. The son of one of them, Birju Maharaj, is the contemporary authority on this school. For some time he had a private school of dancing in Lucknow, but he is now in Delhi, attached to the Indian Academy of Fine Arts.

Chapter 24: *Light Entertainment*

462. Time-beat in a rhythmic cycle, the completion of which is emphasized by the clapping of hands.

463. Sanskrit Vikramaditiya, Sun of Power, the legendary King of Ujjain who established the Vikrama era starting in 58 BC. Its use became very popular in north India and is still referred to by many Hindus under its new name of Samvat. The name Vikramaditya was adopted by many kings of ancient India including the Gupta Emperor (375–413). The deeds of all the Vikramadityas seem to have become part of one series of legends and probably reflect the achievements of the Gupta period from about 320 till about 500. (Moreland and Chatterjee, pp. 70–578)

464. A male performer or a troupe of them who entertain by jesting, joking and mimicry. Feminine: *domni*. (Chapters 44, 47)

465. A *dhari* is a performer similar to a *dom* but who dances as well.

466. Hindi *babu*: clerk. The expression 'Babu English' came to signify the Indianized form of English used by clerks.

467. Hindi *divanji*: *divan* (18), *ji* (67). After the rule of the Navabs it became the title of an accountant or bookkeeper, usually Hindu, employed in a wealthy household.

468. Stalls were set up in Lucknow on the days when the Muharram processions took place for the benefit of the participants.

469. Female entertainers who specialized in singing popular tunes.

470. Hindi *jagna*: to be awake. A troupe of female entertainers whose main function was to keep the female household awake throughout the night during celebrations. (Chapter 44)

471. These forms of light entertainment have declined rapidly since the author's time and now they have disappeared entirely.

Chapter 25: *Courtesans and Theatre*

472. Hindi *sabha*: assembly. Following the great popularity of *Indar Sabha* (Chapter 10), hosts of theatrical societies, and later companies, sprang up in Lucknow, and all had 'Sabha' as part of their name.

473. Hindi *natak*: drama. Popular amateur theatre in India, the roots of which go back to the Sanskrit drama of ancient times.

474. The vogue of theatre in Lucknow died in its infancy and the Bombay Parsi theatre developed from it, employing writers from Lucknow. This theatre was taken over in the 1930s by the film industry, of which Bombay remains the centre to this day.

Chapter 26: Soz—*the Chanting of Dirges*

475. Mir Ali Hasan and Mir Bandey Hasan initiated and evolved the *pukka soz* style, in which dirges were sung rigidly according to a few raginis selected for the purpose, mainly from the *malkaus* group. The two other styles of soz are (1) the Mufti Ganj school, in which to make soz more acceptable to religious people, Shaikh Ata of the Mufti Ganj quarter evolved a style in which the raginis were not developed or elaborated but remained 'curtained' and hidden in the background; and (2) Rangeen soz, which developed in Lucknow in the 1930s with gay and colourful raginis like *pahari* and *pilu* as a base. Its main exponent was Navab Asghar Ali Khan from the family of Bahu Begam's (61) brother, Navab Salar Jang.

476. Manjhu Sahib was the popular name of Mir Muhammad Husain (1870–1944), a pensioner of Mahmudabad State and a very prominent exponent of soz khwani. He travelled frequently to Bihar and Hyderabad for his recitals. His contemporaries included: Mir Hamza Ali Kinturi; Fazal Husain, a pupil of Mir Bandey Ali; Navab Asghar Ali Khan and the courtesans Imam Bandi and Kajjan.

477. Women as well as some men from Shia families in Lucknow continue to chant dirges to this day in an amateur fashion as part of the mourning assemblies in Muharram. However, the remaining exponents of it as an art form are Maharaj Kumar Muhammad Amir Haidar Khan of Mahmudabad, Begam Akhtar and Muharram Ali. Prince Sultan Hasan Mirza, from Benares and at present in Karachi, is also one of the last remaining masters of soz khwani.

478. An oral account describes how the situation changed in the early 1920s in Lucknow, soon after Sharar wrote this essay: 'Mir Bandey Hasan and his brother Mir Ali Hasan went to Mujtahid Mir Muhammad Abbas [353] to seek his ruling on soz khwani. They were persistent, and hence were allowed to sing a soz as a specimen of their form of art. This touched the Mujtahid to such an extent that he became ecstatic and fainted. His judgment was in their favour but only for those soz where the raginis remain hidden in the background.'

Chapter 27: *Bands, Processions and the Telling of Time*

479. The dhol, tasha, raushan chauki and naubat have by now almost all disappeared from public sight, as have the turhai and the qurna. The bugle and the danka are still seen in the occasional wedding procession, but are more frequently present in political or religious processions, which sometimes also include bagpipes and other British band instruments. As a result of the gradual disappearance of wedding processions this type of music has lost much of its popularity.

Chapter 28: *Gastronomy*

480. Persian *dastar khwan*: tablecloth, usually square and yellow in colour with verses in Urdu or Persian printed by wood-cut around the edges in black. Food was served on this cloth, usually placed on the floor and later, in more Westernized homes, on tables. *Khwan*: a wooden octagonal tray for carrying food.

481. A rich rice and meat dish with a high proportion of meat, prepared in an elaborate manner and flavoured and coloured by saffron and other spices. In Lucknow the dish is prepared so that separate grains of rice are coloured yellow and white.

482. A thick, highly spiced conserve of vegetables, with an oil and vinegar base.

483. Braised meat curry in thick sauce, of dark gold colour. In Lucknow it is prepared without vegetables.

484. *Zarda*: a sweet rice dish with saffron and raisins, prepared for special occasions.

485. *Kabab* is prepared in Lucknow from finely ground meat, spiced and fried in the shape and size of hamburgers.

486. *Biryani* is a variety of pulau containing slightly different spices and with meat sauce employed in preparing the rice.

487. *Chapati, paratha, shir mal* and *rogni roti* are Indian breads. *Chapati* is a very thin, light unleavened bread made of whole-wheat flour and grilled on a hot plate. An everyday bread. *Paratha*, a pancake made with milk and fried in clarified butter, is thick, crispy, six to nine inches in diameter and used on special occasions. *Shir mal*, an unleavened bread, is about six inches in diameter, made with milk and butter with saffron on the top and baked in an underground oven. It is used on special occasions. *Roghni roti*, another variety of unleavened bread, is about eight inches in diameter, prepared with clarified butter and milk. It is used for breakfast in well-to-do households.

488. A preparation of fruits and vegetables cooked in spices to a thick paste and preserved in vinegar. In Lucknow some special chutneys are also prepared from fresh vegetables without cooking or vinegar.

489. Different vegetables, first cooked and marinated, pickled in oil, salt and spices.

490. A specially prepared clarified butter of high quality with a sweet taste.

491. A simple dish of boiled rice and lentils. This is a common everyday dish for the poor.

492. *Gulathi* is a sophisticated rice pudding made of milk, clarified butter and dried fruits.

Chapter 29: *Delicacies and Confectionery*

493. A hard sweet similar to toffee, prepared with clarified butter and dried fruits.

494. A breakfast curry prepared in Lucknow according to a special recipe, with spices and cuts of meat.

495. Fatiha is the opening surah of the Quran. It is also the name of the ceremony in which this surah is read with a prayer, usually over food, for the souls of religious saints but occasionally for relatives as well. The food is intended for distribution to the poor but can be eaten by the members of the household.

496. Persian *niyaz*: desire. This ceremony is similar to Fatiha, but the prayers are for the souls of relatives and friends. The food over which the prayers are said is usually not eaten in the house but given to the poor.

497. Edible, gossamer-thin wafers prepared with gold and silver foil and used for decorative purposes.

Chapter 30: *More Delicacies and Confectionery*

498. The custom of sending food to people's homes arose in order to include the women, since owing to purdah, their movements in visiting homes were restricted.

Chapter 31: *Food Refinements and Water-cooling*

499. A small, decorated earthenware pitcher with an elongated neck like an ancient Greek vase, made of a special clay found at the bottom of lakes. It is baked but only very slightly glazed in order to allow air to pass through and so keep the water cool.

500. An earthenware goblet for drinking-water, baked, but left totally unglazed. In

both surahis and abkhoras, the unglazed clay imparts a refreshing fragrance to the drinking-water.

Chapter 32: *The Evolution of Men's Dress*

501. At Ellora and Ajanta near Aurangabad are situated shrines and monasteries carved out of solid rock into rock temples or caves. The oldest go back to the pre-Christian era but the series ranges from the first to the sixth century, displaying in the three groups of temples the sculpture and frescoes inspired by Buddhism, Jainism and Hinduism. Their subject remains religious throughout the centuries, though the content changes according to the different religious point of view. The sculpture of Buddha with his attributes, sometimes more than life-size, is to be seen beside sculpture presenting other religious images. Frescoes, also painted over a period of centuries, have survived in six out of the twenty-nine caves of Ajanta. In the earliest period their subject-matter is the life and legends of Buddha, who is painted in heroic proportions. Religious images of later periods have court scenes, nature and animals around them. Hindu art emerges fully in the last phase. These works are the earliest known examples of Hindu sculpture and painting, and summits of Indian art.

502. The dress most popular today for everyday life in the cities is kurta and trousers. Black shervani and *churidar*, tight pyjamas (Chapter 35), and Gandhi cap (Chapter 33) have become the dress for formal and official occasions in Lucknow and Delhi. The angarkha survived in Lucknow as the dress for the law courts until the 1930s when it was replaced by English legal costume.

Chapter 33: *Forms of Headwear*

503. Since ancient times in India, male dress was not complete without head-dress, originally some form of pagri, later a cap, and it was considered an impropriety to go outdoors bare-headed. To remove someone else's headwear was considered a great insult.

504. Embroidery of floral designs on muslin, in which the thread is used in such a manner that it remains invisible and the design appears to be part of the fabric. The four kinds of *chikan* work in Lucknow are: *katao*, where minute patterns of different materials are sewn into the muslin; *murri*, where designs are embossed upon the muslin with the use of thread; *phanda*, a design made of thread in chain stitch; and *jali kholna*, in which individual threads are carefully removed from the material and re-used in the same place to form the design. Chikan work from Lucknow is still popular in the rest of India and can be seen on the kurtas worn by young people today. Because of its popularity this craft has now been taken under the wing of the Cottage Industries Plan of the Government of U.P.

505. In the 1930s the *taluqdari* cap, also known as the Lucknow cap, was finally evolved. This was usually made of black velvet and had two sides, between four to eight inches high, joined by a piece of cloth on the top centre. This cap, when made from white *khadi* (hand-spun and hand-woven cloth), became known as the Gandhi cap and is the most widely used head-dress in India at present.

Chapter 34: *More Headwear*

506. Born Azamgarh (U.P.) 1857, died 1914. A scholar of Islamic theology and Arabic, Persian and Urdu literatures who was for a short time professor at Aligarh,

associated with Nadwa College (355) and founder of Darul Musanifin (Azamgarh), an institute for Islamic research which survives to this day.

Chapter 35: *Forms of Trousers (Pyjamas)*

507. Similar to an ankle-length skirt and at present a popular form of ladies' dress in Lucknow.

Chapter 36: *Footwear and Female Fashion*

508. The cow from which the hide is obtained is of course a sacred animal for Hindus.
509. Mustard oil was applied to soften the leather and to prevent cracking.
510. The sari is at present worn throughout India, as well as in Lucknow.

Chapter 37: *Winter Clothing, New Fashions and Jewelry*

511. The paste prepared from the leaves of the henna tree. As part of their make-up, women applied henna paste as a dye to the palm of the hand and finger-tips in different patterns. After a few hours the dried paste was washed off and the patterns remained in fast red dye. In later days the fashion for men was to cover the top joint of the small finger of the right hand with henna dye.
512. A piece of woollen cloth roughly the size of a sheet, embroidered with colourful patterns in cotton and wool. This delicate and fine craft is special to Kashmir.
513. Just as the Mughal Emperors honoured a person by bestowing upon him a khilat, the later Navabs of Avadh bestowed a doshala, a brocaded shawl of rectangular shape hung over the shoulders.

Chapter 38: *The Building of Houses*

514. This part of the house was the coolest and served mainly as a rest room during the heat of the day.

Chapter 39: *Domestic Furnishings*

515. The *takhat* is a large rectangular or square plank of wood supported by four short legs.
516. The *palangri* is a low bed made of cane or jute with a wooden frame and four small legs.
517. The *dari* is a thickly woven cotton material in colourful designs used as a mattress.
518. Hindi *pankha*: fan. *Farshi pankha* was a large fan made of bamboo leaves or cloth and operated by the servants. The hand fan, small in size, was used by individuals. Another variety of fan not mentioned here was of rectangular cloth with a wooden frame on three sides, suspended from the ceiling and operated by a string.

Chapter 40: *Hair Fashions, Etiquette and Courtesans*

519. The salons of high-class courtesans were important centres of social etiquette as well as dancing and music. Sometimes young boys of good families were even sent there a few times with an older person to acquire social polish. Such courtesans were usually attached to a rich noble on a regular salary and did not practise the profession of a prostitute. For details about the life of a Lucknow courtesan, see Mirza Muhammad Hadi Ruswa, *Umrao Jan Ada*, translated into English by K. Singh and M. A. Husaini, Orient Longmans, Calcutta 1961; and *The Beauties of Lucknow—Twenty-four Portraits of the most celebrated and Popular Living, Historic Singers, Dancers and Actresses of the Oudh Court and of Lucknow*, Central Press Co. Ltd, Calcutta 1874.

520. A simple wooden spinning-wheel for cotton or silk thread, with which coarse cloth is traditionally made in India. In the 1920s under the leadership of Gandhi, spinning charkha became associated with nationalist sentiments, for men and women alike. It became a symbol of protest against machine-produced cotton cloth from Britain, which was prepared from Indian raw materials and considered economically exploitative.

521. For a detailed account of the life of women in India, especially Muslims, based upon their own observations, see Mrs F. Parks, *Wanderings of a Pilgrim in Search of the Picturesque*, London 1852, and Mrs Meer Hassan Ali, *Observations on the Musulmans of India*, Humphrey Milford, Oxford University Press, London 1917. While Mrs Parks was a traveller, Mrs Hassan Ali, an Englishwoman, stayed in Lucknow from 1816 to 1828 and her account provides a detailed description of life, manners, customs, ceremonies and religious practices of Lucknow at the time.

Chapter 41: *More on Etiquette*

522. Persian *taslim*: submission. A common form of greeting which is also used to express thanks. (Chapter 42)

523. Persian *farsh*, floor; this consisted of a *dari* of thickly woven cotton over which a clean white sheet was spread. In well-to-do houses a Persian carpet or velvet cloth embroidered with gold and silver threads was placed on top.

524. A small dome-shaped, silver receptacle, elaborately decorated with carvings, used for serving prepared betel leaves.

525. The placing of each hand alternately between each hand of the other person, while bowing slightly.

526. Consisting of three embraces on each shoulder without touching the other's face. *Musafiha* and *muaneqa* are Arab forms of greeting.

Chapter 42: *Social Gatherings and Forms of Greeting*

527. In large towns coffee houses have now become a meeting place mainly for intellectuals, artists and journalists.

528. This practice is no longer followed.

529. The expression *Adab arz*, 'I pay my respects', accompanied by an inclination of the head and a hand movement to the forehead, became the usual form of greeting for middle-class Muslims and many Hindus. Ordinary Muslims continue to say *As Salam Alaikum* among themselves while Hindus greet each other with a gesture in which the palms are pressed together and the hands held close to the face while saying the words *Ram Ram* (5) or *Namaskar*, in obeisance.

Chapter 43: *Everyday Speech in Urdu*

530. In its present literary form Hindi goes back to about the same time as that of Urdu prose, when translations and works were commissioned in Hindi, along with Urdu, at the Fort William College (330). Since 1947 Hindi has become the national language of India. (Qadri).

Chapter 44: *Wit and Female Celebrations*

531. 'Bismillah ir Rahman ur Rahim', 'In the name of Allah, who is kind and merciful', is the first phrase of the Quran, recited by Muslims before commencing any new activity. It is sometimes shortened to the first word only. In Lucknow, as well as with Muslims in other parts of India, it was also the name of the ceremony initiating the education of a young child, as described in Chapter 45. It is still often observed.

Chapter 45: *Festive Celebrations*

532. During the first ten days of Muharram, as a part of mourning, Shias are obliged to give up, among other pleasures, eating *pan*, prepared betel leaf. They simply use some of the dry ingredients, which have been specially prepared.
533. A paste prepared from barley flour, dry flower petals, oil, sandalwood and perfumes, and rubbed over the body before bathing, in order to impart a fragrance.
534. Large sweets shaped like balls, four to eight inches in diameter and decorated with silver foil, prepared from fine flour, clarified butter and dried fruits. They are specially prepared for wedding celebrations, as well as to celebrate childbirth.
535. A jug with a round body and rim and with a long pouring spout, used to hold water. (Chapter 52)

Chapter 46: *The Wedding Ceremony*

536. A head-band with heavy gold and silver threads hanging down to the waist with various embellishments.
537. 'Babul mora nahyar chuta jai . . .' is the opening line of a song, the theme of which is, 'When I crossed the threshold, I felt as if mountains had come between us.' Probably composed by Amir Khusrau, the song is still sung exclusively on this occasion in a melancholic tone in the thumri style (440) in which the morning raga (414) Bhairavin is prominent.

Chapter 48: *Funeral Services*

538. Those households that did not employ regular palanquin-bearers would hire them when needed.

Chapter 49: *Forms of Religious Assembly*

539. The popularity of this and other innovations was of short duration and they are no longer in practice.
540. In fact the custom is simply to burn the effigies and make derogatory remarks.

Chapter 50: *Betel Leaf, its Appurtenances and Tobacco*

541. A prepared betel leaf folded in a conical fashion and decorated with edible silver paper. (Chapter 51)

542. Ibn-e-Batuta (1304–77) was a Moroccan Arab who travelled extensively, as far as China in the east and the interior of Africa in the south. In the account of his travels we are told that he arrived in India during the reign of Muhammad Tughlaq (426), and spent a few years at his court.

543. The firm he founded exists to this day.

Chapter 51: *Preparing and Serving Betel Leaf*

544. This firm exists to this day and is renowned throughout the country for its products of tobacco and scent.

545. A black cosmetic tooth powder for women prepared from chemicals based on a copper salt. It was rubbed on the teeth with the finger and washed off, leaving the interstices black. The main function of this cosmetic was to clean stains left on the teeth, mainly from chewing betel leaf.

546. For religious reasons Hindus and Muslims did not eat food or accept liquid refreshments prepared by each other. Dried fruits and other dried edibles were exempt from this prohibition. By now this practice is very much on the wane.

Chapter 52: *Utensils for Everyday Use*

547. Hyderabad is famous for inlaid silver-work of floral design on black metal. Usually done on small objects for everyday use, this craft is known as Bidar work. After the beginning of this century, Lucknow and Murshidabad also became important centres of this craft.

548. In Islam it is prohibited to display one's wealth by using gold and silver utensils.

549. Hindi *besan*: flour of chick-pea, used for washing and bathing before the introduction of soap.

Chapter 53: *Conveyances and Dress for Outings*

550. *Finas* and *miyanas* were elaborate forms of palanquins used mainly by women and carried by palanquin-bearers. The *doli*, much smaller in size and made of bamboo, was the simplest and most common form of transport for ladies of the average household.

Chapter 54: *Pottery*

551. In the late 1920s the British Government did open a museum of local history, arts, crafts, costumes, weapons and other objets d'art in Lucknow. There is also a section for pottery and clay models (150).

Since then, the museum has developed considerably. At present it is well known for the collection of paintings in different styles done in Lucknow. The most important are the miniatures, done in two styles, both beginning at the outset of Shuja ud Daula's reign. These continue the Indian miniature tradition. The style generally known as 'Later Provincial Mughal School of Lucknow' depicts the full bloom of Lucknow's luxurious way of life, painted with intricate craftsmanship and great attention to minute details of setting as well as figures (see, for example, the illustration in the present edition 'A Prince and Princess watching a Dancer with Candles'). Occasionally, when the artist turns his attention to some other subject, such as a saint, a hermit or a Hindu deity, he treats it with the same air of affluence and abundance ('Krishna with Gopis'*). The other style of miniature, which also probably came from Delhi and became very popular, is known as *Raga mala*. Its subject is raga and its concern is with nature as well as human emotions. The scene, which is occasionally semi-erotic, is painted against a simple but elegant background ('Ladies Listening to the Raga Madhu Madhvi'). These remained the dominant styles up to the time of Asaf ud Daula, when European taste in painting began to be popular with the rulers.

The new taste began when Shuja ud Daula invited Tilly Kettle to Faizabad (1771–73). He completed six large paintings of the ruler. To the court of Asaf ud Daula came John Zoffany in 1784 and Ozias Humphry in 1786. About this time in Lucknow, T. Daniell worked independently. Robert Home was attached to the court of Ghazi ud Din Haidar and stayed in Lucknow until 1828. In addition, at least three other British artists lived and worked in Lucknow. One of them was Robert Smith. The work of the unknown British artist 'Panorama of Lucknow' probably belongs to this period. John Beechey went to Lucknow in 1828 and stayed there until his death in 1852. He painted for all the Navabs who ruled during his lifetime, including Wajid Ali Shah. The portrait of Wajid Ali Shah reproduced in the present edition shows his marked influence.

However, the direct influence of this new taste upon the work of the local artists seems to begin with Gentil, who around 1765–70 employed three local artists for ten years at Faizabad to illustrate his manuscripts on the Mughal Empire and Hindu deities (Bibliothèque Nationale, Paris). One of them was Nevasi Lal. Because of Gentil's instructions the work was slightly different in style and colour from the usual court style of the time. Polier also had an album of paintings prepared for him, part of which is in the British Museum. About the same time, Shuja ud Daula's portraits by Tilly Kettle began to be copied by the local artists, notably in 1775 by Mir Chand at Faizabad, who was well known in his time. This was followed by many others, an example of which is the portrait of Shuja ud Daula by an unknown artist of Lucknow, about 1800. Through these copies local artists discovered new techniques and mediums, including oils. These new skills were incorporated into their own styles. Asaf ud Daula's water-colour portrait of 1780 by an unknown Lucknow artist, though based on Kettle's portrait, does not seem to be a copy but an attempt to create a new style by a miniature painter. The European technique seems to be far more pronounced in the oil portrait of Sadat Ali Khan by a Lucknow artist. A typical example of the local traditional style in portrait painting is 'A Lady Seated against a Cushion' by Miskin Muhammad. A further development of this new style can be seen in the gouache painting of Ghazi ud Din Haidar's banquet. The details include the paintings on the wall, and the royal coat of arms on the door which opens on to the River Gomti. Another gouache of 1831 portrays Nasir ud Din Haidar seated at a table with a British officer and an English lady. Besides the principals, there are ministers in the background and dancing girls and musicians at the sides, along with chandeliers, fountain and flowers.

With the commencement of British rule, another new style emerged in Lucknow, which can roughly be described as the 'Company style'. Artists, here as well as in some other parts of the country, started to portray, for the British, themes connected with local life, customs, people and animals, to be kept as souvenirs or to be sent home. A significant artist of this period was Mummoo Jan, who was employed by the King

---

* Many of the works and artists mentioned in this note are reproduced in the present edition (see List of Illustrations).

of Avadh in the 1850s and probably worked with John Beechey. For further details see Archer, chapter 6.

In the late 1920s the British Government also started a School of Art and Crafts in Lucknow. It exists to this day and is run on the model of art schools in Britain.

Besides the collection in the Lucknow Museum, collections of works of Lucknow artists can be seen in the Victoria and Albert Museum, the British Museum and the India Office Library and Records in London (which also has a collection of works of British artists who worked in Lucknow), the Bibliothèque Nationale, Paris, and the Berlin Museum.

For comments on some Lucknow paintings see also *Company Drawings in the India Office Library Catalogue*, ed. M. Archer, London, H.M. Stationery Office, London 1972.

Bibliography

Agha, Bare, Preface to Motashim, *Indian Music* (Urdu).

Ali, Ahad, *Shabab-e-Lucknow* (Urdu), Parts I and II, Al Nazir Press, Lucknow 1912; Part II is a translation from William Knighton, *The Private Life of an Eastern King*, Hope and Co., London 1855.

Archer, M. and W.G., *Indian Painting for the British 1770–1880*, Oxford University Press, London and New York 1955.

Askari, Mirza Muhammad, *Tarikh Adab-e-Urdu* (Urdu translation of Saxena, *A History of Urdu Literature*), 3rd edition, Munshi Newal Kishore, Lucknow 1929.

Azhar, Mirza Ali, *Tarikhi Shahparay* (Urdu), All Pakistan Educational Conference, Karachi 1971.

Bhavnani, E., *The Dance in India*, Taraporevala and Sons, Bombay 1965.

Browne, E. G., *A Literary History of Persia* vols. I–IV, Cambridge University Press, London 1928; Macmillan, New York 1929.

Gokhale, B. G., *Ancient India, History and Culture*, Asia Publishing House, London 1959; Taplinger, New York 1959.

Grube, E. J., *The World of Islam*, Paul Hamlyn, London 1966; McGraw-Hill, New York 1967.

Haidar, Kamul ud Din, *Qaisar-ul-Tawarikh* (Urdu), vols. I and II, Munshi Newal Kishore, Lucknow 1907.

Hitti, P. K., *History of the Arabs*, Macmillan, London 1964; St Martin's Press, New York 1967.

Hoyle, Peggy, *Indian Music*, Allen and Unwin, London 1972.

Imperial Gazetteer of India vols. I and II, Provincial Series, United Provinces of Agra and Oudh, Superintendent of Government Printing, Calcutta 1908.

Irwin, H. C., *The Garden of India, or Chapters on Oudh History*, W. H. Allen, London 1880.

Levy, R., *An Introduction to Persian Literature*, Oxford University Press, London 1923; Columbia University Press, New York 1969.

Majumdar, R. C., ed., *An Advanced History of India*, Macmillan, London 1948; St Martin's Press, New York 1948.

Mohtashim, M. M., *Indian Music* (Urdu), with a Preface by Bare Agha, Nizami Press, Lucknow 1939.

Moore, R. J., *Sir Charles Wood's Indian Policy*, Manchester University Press, 1966.

Moreland, W. H. and Chatterjee, A. C., *A Short History of India*, Longmans, London 1956, New York 1953.

Najmul, Ghani Khan M., *Tarikh-e-Avadh* (Urdu), Vols. I–IV, Matla-e-Ulum, Muradabad 1909.

Qadri, Hamid Hasan, *Dastan Tarikh-e-Urdu* (Urdu), Urdu Academy, Sindh, Karachi 1966.

Raghavan, V., *The Indian Heritage*, The Indian Institute of World Culture, Bangalore 1958.

Rizvi, Masud Husain, *Urdu Drama and Stage* (Urdu), Kitab Nagar, Lucknow 1957.

Rouse, G. H., ed., *Lucknow Album*, Baptist Mission Press, Calcutta 1874.

Saxena, R. B., *A History of Urdu Literature*, Ram Narain Lal, Allahabad 1927.

Shankar, Ravi, *My Music, My Life*, Jonathan Cape, London 1969; Simon and Schuster, New York 1968.

Sleeman, Major-General Sir W. H., *A Journey Through the Kingdom of Oude*, Richard Bentley, London 1858.

Srivastava, A. L., *The First Two Navabs of Oude*, The Upper India Publishing House, Lucknow 1933 [A]
    Shuja ud Daula vol. I, The Midland Press, Calcutta 1939 [B]
    Shuja ud Daula vol. II, The Minerva Bookshop, Lahore 1945 [C]

Tarikh-e Adabiyat-e Musalmanar-e Pakistan o Hind (Urdu) vols. I–XVI, Panjab University, 1971.

Index

Notes are referenced by note numbers

aba (cape), 176
Abbaside dynasty, 12, 84, 96, 133, 140, 152
169, 175, 182; n 310
abdar khana (water-cooling), 74, 167–8;
n 233
Abdul Aziz, Hakim, 98; n 363
Abdul Aziz Muhaddis, Shah, 95
Abdul Baqi (calligraphist), 105
Abdul Hafiz, Hakim, 97
Abdul Hai, Munshi (calligraphist), 105, 106
Abdul Haq, Shaikh of Delhi, 17, 79, 94
Abdul Latif, Munshi (calligraphist), 105
Abdul Majid, Munshi (calligraphist), 104
Abdul Moid, Hakim, 97
Abdul Qasim Khan, Navab, 160
Abdul Shakur, Maulvi, 95
Abdullah Beg (calligraphist), 103
Abdullah Khan, of Hyderabad, 88
Abdullah, Saiyyid, of Baraha, 40; n 108
Abdullah Tabagh (calligraphist), 105
Abdur Rahim, Shaikh (Mahi Maratib), 37
Abdur Rashid, Agha (calligraphist), 103
Abdur Rashid, Hakim, 97
abkhoras (drinking-water vessels), 167,
229–30; n 500
Abu Bakar, Caliph, n 167
Abu Tarab Khan, Agha, 131
Abul Barkat Khan, of Kakori, 32, 33
achars (vegetable dish), 157; n 489
achkan (man's garment), 170
adab (respect), 197, 198; n 529
Afghanistan, 13, 171, 177; n 10, n 23, n 98
Afghans, 30, 35, 43–4; n 23, n 121
aftaba (ewer), 225
Afzal (son of Asir), 81; n 290
Agha Mir, Vazir, 54, 55; n 199
Agha Mir quarter and caravanserai, 54
Agra, 51, 100; n 1, n 44, n 107, n 110
Ahiri caste, 37, 38; n 80
Ahmad Ali, Munshi, 18
Ahmad Ali, Navab, 105
Ahmad Khan Bangash, 30–1, 35, 43,
44; n 1, n 10, n 24
Ahmad, Maulvi (Sharar's great-uncle), 107

Ahmad, Saiyyid, Bansi Wala, 33; n 40
Ahmad Shah Durrani, 44, 80; n 121, n 122,
n 251
Ahmad Ullah (Shah Sahib), 57, 66–7
Ahmed Husain, Munshi Saiyyid, firm of,
220, 221
Ahsan Kambohi, Shaikh, 32, 33; n 35
Aish Bagh, 48
Ajanta wall paintings, 10, 168; n 501
Ajodhya, 29–30, 33, 39, 42, 134, 141; n 1,
n 5; *see also* Avadh
Akbar the Great, Mughal Emperor, 9, 13,
36, 37, 38, 134, 189; n 1, n 73, n 92,
n 107, n 135, n 346, n 430, n 431
Akbar Shah II, 134
Akbarabad, 40, 41, 80; n 107
Akbari Gate, 38, 41, 42
Akhtar (Wajid Ali Shah's pen-name), n 216
Akhtar, Begam, n 442, n 477
Akhtar Mahal, Navab (Ali Naqi Khan's
daughter), 69
Akhtar, Qazi Muhammad Sadiq Khan, 60;
n 186
Alam Nagar, 52, 110
'Alam Pasand' topi (the 'Swing'), 173, 175
Alam, Shah, Mughal Emperor of Delhi,
32, 112, 130; n 22, n 32, n 41, n 44,
n 163
Alavi Khan, Hakim, 97
Ali Akbar (calligraphist), 105
Ali Ashghar (calligraphist), 105
Ali Ausat, Saiyyid, 163
Ali Baksh Khan, 107
Ali Hasan Khan, Navab Agha, 157
Ali Hasan, Mir (dirge-singer), 148, 149;
n 475, n 478
Ali Husain (cook), 162
Ali Husain, Munshi Saiyyid (stone
corrector), 108
Ali, Imam (Muhammad's cousin), 44, 55;
n 106, n 118, n 129, n 166, n 167, n 171
Ali Jan (entertainer), 145
Ali Kinturi, Mir Hamza (dirge-singer), n 476
ali mad combat, 110

Index

291